The Politics of Policy Making in Defense and Foreign Affairs

CONCEPTUAL MODELS AND BUREAUCRATIC POLITICS

third edition

Roger Hilsman

with Laura Gaughran and Patricia A. Weitsman

Columbia University

PRENTICE HALL
Englewood Cliffs, New Jersey 07632

Library of Congress Cataloging-in-Publication Data

Hilsman, Roger.
   The politics of policy making in defense and foreign affairs: conceptual
models and bureaucratic politics/ Roger Hilsman with Laura Gaughran
and Patricia A. Weitsman. – 3rd ed.
      p.   cm.
   Includes bibliographical references and index.
   ISBN 0-13-681651-7
   1. United States–Foreign relations. 2. United States–Politics and
government. 3. United States–Military policy. I. Gaughran, Laura.
II. Weitsman, Patricia A. III. Title.
JX1417.H54   1992
353.0089–dc20   92–27034
                                                                  CIP

Editorial/Production Supervision and Interior Design: **Benjamin D. Smith**
Cover Designer: **Joe DiDomenico**
Prepress Buyer: **Kelly Behr**
Manufacturing Buyer: **Mary Ann Gloriande**

©1993 by Roger Hilsman
Published by Prentice-Hall, Inc.
A Simon & Schuster Company
Englewood Cliffs, New Jersey 07632

Printed in the United States of America

10   9   8   7   6   5   4   3   2

ISBN   0-13-681651-7

Prentice-Hall International (UK) Limited, *London*
Prentice-Hall of Australia Pty. Limited, *Sydney*
Prentice-Hall Canada Inc., *Toronto*
Prentice-Hall Hispanoamericana, S.A., *Mexico*
Prentice-Hall of India Private Limited, *New Delhi*
Prentice-Hall of Japan, Inc., *Tokyo*
Simon & Schuster Asia Pte. Ltd., *Singapore*
Editora Prentice-Hall do Brasil, Ltda., *Rio de Janeiro*

Contents

The Institute of War and Peace Studies
School of International Affairs
Columbia University

This book was prepared under the sponsorship of
The Institute of War and Peace Studies
of Columbia University's School of International Affairs

In addition to *The Politics of Policy Making in Defense and Foreign Affairs,* the Institute of War and Peace Studies has sponsored four other books by Roger Hilsman: *To Move a Nation: The Politics of Foreign Policy in the Administration of John F. Kennedy* (1967), *The Crouching Future: International Politics and U.S. Foreign Policy, a Forecast* (1975), *The Politics of Governing America* (1985), and *George Bush vs. Saddam Hussein, Military Success! Political Failure?* (1992).

The Institute of War and Peace Studies sponsors the publication of works in international relations, international institutions, and American foreign and military policy. Among its studies of policy and the policy process by other authors are *The Common Defense* by Samuel P. Huntington; *Strategy, Politics, and Defense Budgets* by Warner R. Schilling, Paul Y. Hammond, and Glenn H. Snyder; *Planning, Prediction, and Policy-Making in Foreign Affairs* by Robert L. Rothstein; *The Illogic of American Nuclear Strategy* by Robert Jervis; *How Nations Behave* by Louis Henkin; and *Economic Statecraft* by David Baldwin.

PREFACE

In the early 1960s a handful of scholars, later called the "first wave" of theorists,[1] devoted themselves to studying the politics of policy making, mainly the politics of making foreign and defense policy. Richard E. Neustadt, Gabriel A. Almond, Charles E. Lindblom, Warner R. Schilling, Samuel P. Huntington, and Roger Hilsman, the present author, worked independently but were all very familiar with what the others were doing.

What got many of this group started on this line of research was dissatisfaction with the then-current set of assumptions about why states behave the way they do—which was really an unarticulated theory of state behavior. At the time this theory was generally accepted without question by most analysts to explain or predict the actions of states in international politics and by policy makers to devise policies to accomplish their nation's goals.

This traditional, strategic, essentially geopolitical theory dictated the following procedure. First, the analyst identified the power or strategic goals of the state in question. The next step was to examine the alternative means available to the state for achieving these goals. If the problem was explaining the past, the final step was to assume that the reason the state had chosen the alternative it did was because that alternative would realize the goal most efficiently and economically. Similarly, if the problem was predicting future action, the final step was

---

[1] By Robert J. Art in "Bureaucratic Politics and American Foreign Policy: A Critique," *Policy Sciences* (December 1974).

to assume that the state would choose the alternative that was likely to achieve the goal most efficiently and economically.

In a number of books and articles, these scholars developed what most of them thought of as a "political process" model of how policy is made. Somewhat later, Graham T. Allison applied this model to the Cuban missile crisis, but he called it the "bureaucratic-politics" model— and this was the name that stuck.[2]

In fact, however, Allison's description of the model developed by the first wave contained enough of his own elements to make him the first of a "second wave" of theorists who focused mainly on the role and power of the great bureaucracies in the making of policy. Others of this second wave include Morton H. Halperin, I. M. Destler, and Alexander L. George.[3]

By 1974, the difference in emphasis created by the focus on bureaucracy was sufficiently marked that many people regarded the work of the second wave as a separate theoretical model. In fact, Robert J. Art set out to compare the "political process" model of the first wave and the "bureaucratic-politics" model of the second wave.[4] The ensuing debate has been vigorous, and by 1987, when the first edition of this book was published, the time seemed to have come to hear once more from the first wave.

This third edition not only updates the second in terms of events and contributions to the literature but also has been both reorganized and revised. Part I is devoted to the various models that were intended to explain why states behave the way they do. The first chapter uses the "traditional," "strategic," "geopolitical," "classical," "rational-unitary-actor," or "black-box" model to try to explain why the states involved behaved the way they did in seven case studies: the Soviet deployment of nuclear missiles to Cuba in 1962; the U.S. decision to bomb North Vietnam and to intervene in South Vietnam with ground forces in 1965; Communist China's 1972 invitation to President Richard M. Nixon to visit and so begin the process of normalizing relations between the two countries; the Soviet invasion of Afghanistan in 1979 and later withdrawal; Iran's taking and holding of American hostages for 444 days; the Iran-Contra affair in the closing years of the Reagan administration; and the U.S. decision to go to war against Iraq in the Persian Gulf. The second chapter then turns things around and shows how the same "black-box

---

[2]Graham T. Allison, *Essence of Decision: Explaining the Cuban Missile Crisis* (Boston: Little, Brown, 1971).

[3]Morton H. Halperin, *Bureaucratic Politics and Foreign Policy* (Washington, D.C.: Brookings, 1974); I.M. Destler, *Presidents, Bureaucrats, and Foreign Policy* (Princeton University Press, 1972); and Alexander L. George, "The Case for Multiple Advocacy in Foreign Policy," *American Political Science Review* (September 1972).

[4]Art, "Bureaucratic Politics."

model can be used to come to exactly opposite conclusions in the same seven case studies. Chapter 3 attempts to do to this model what Einstein did to Newton's—to make its implied assumptions explicit.

Chapter 4—"Pink, Purple, Brown, and Blue Boxes"—looks at refinements of the "black-box" model. It describes the work of authors who have concentrated on how differences in the international system in different historical periods have affected state behavior—bipolar systems, multipolar systems, and so on. The chapter also describes the work of authors who have examined the effects on state behavior of ideology, culture, national character, the elements of national power, and geographical position.

Chapter 5—"Opening up the Boxes"—looks at the work of authors who have examined what goes on inside the nation-states in the making of policy. The conceptual models examined here include the "organizational" or "bureaucratic-SOP" (standard operating procedure) model and the "constitutional-law" model.

Chapter 6 examines the nature of politics and ends up outlining the "political process" model—that is, the chapter concludes that policy is made in a political process, that policy making is politics. Chapter 7 applies this political process model to the original seven case studies to see if it can resolve the puzzlements and inconsistencies left by the other models.

Part II explores the specific roles and powers of the inner ring of "power centers" (both individuals and institutions), those who are most directly involved in making defense and foreign policy. Chapter 8 analyzes how presidents are elected to determine if in the process they incur debts that affect their policies. Chapter 9 looks at the power that presidents wield; Chapter 10 deals with the role of the White House staff; and Chapter 11 examines the power of political appointees, the secretaries and assistant secretaries of the great departments and others who come in and out of government with each administration. Chapter 12 discusses the Congress, and Chapter 13 focuses on bureaucrats, especially those involved in national security; the foreign service of the Department of State, the CIA, and the military.

Part III looks at the second ring of policy makers, those individuals and organizations who are not an official part of government but whose principal reason for being is to influence foreign and defense policy. Chapter 14 deals with interest groups and Chapter 15 with the press and television.

Part IV examines the outer ring of power, with Chapter 16 concentrating on public opinion and Chapter 17 on the electorate.

Part V looks at the outputs of power—at foreign policies in Chapter 18 and at defense policies in Chapter 19.

Part VI asks, "Where next?" Specifically, Chapter 20 asks how well the policy-making process described in the preceding chapters will be able to cope with the foreign and defense problems that lie ahead.

The hope is that this book will not only set forth a more fully developed version of the "political process" approach but also provide students with a realistic description of how Washington actually works in making defense and foreign policy.

Roger Hilsman
Laura Gaughran
Patricia A. Weitsman

ACKNOWLEDGMENTS

I wish to thank Ben Smith at Prentice Hall for his dedicated labor in readying this third edition for production.

Thanks also go to the staff of Columbia University's Institute of War and Peace Studies for research help.

Laura Gaughran and Patricia A. Weitsman also wish to express thanks to Susan Varisco, J. Samuel Darkin, George E. Shambaugh, and Scott Adler for help and advice of several kinds.

All of us are particularly grateful to Eleanor H. Hilsman, who served not only as consulting editor but also as research assistant and indexer.

1

THE CASE STUDIES

Why do states behave the way they do? To the extent that analysts of international affairs are armed with concepts and theories that permit them to answer this question, they can do three things. First, they can explain why a particular state took the action it did in the past. Second, they can forecast how a particular state is likely to act in the future. Finally, they can devise policies for one state that will influence the way another state will act in the future. The question is, how good are these concepts and theories about why states behave the way they do?

This first chapter will use the classical, or traditional, mode of analysis to explain why the states involved took the actions they did in seven cases:

1. the Soviet deployment of nuclear missiles to Cuba in 1962
2. the U.S. decision to bomb North Vietnam and intervene with ground forces in South Vietnam in 1965
3. Communist China's invitation to President Richard M. Nixon to visit China in 1972 and so begin the process of normalizing relations between the two countries
4. the Soviet invasion of Afghanistan in 1979
5. the seizing of fifty-three American hostages in the U.S. embassy in Iran and holding them prisoner for 444 days in 1979–1981
6. the U.S. decision during the second Reagan administration to trade arms to Iran (while urging its allies not to do so) and then to use the

money to buy arms for the Contras fighting against the government of Nicaragua in violation of the ban on such aid by Congress

7. the U.S. decision to go to war against Iraq in the Persian Gulf

THE CASE STUDIES

The Cuban Missile Crisis

Why did the Soviets deploy nuclear missiles to Cuba in 1962? The answer accepted by the U.S. government at the time was the same as that yielded by the classical, or traditional, mode of analysis.[1]

The final Soviet decision to deploy medium-range ballistic missiles (MRBMs) and intermediate-range ballistic missiles (IRBMs) to Cuba was made in June 1962, just after the Soviets had obtained Fidel Castro's permission. The plan called for six battalions of the 1000-mile MRBMs and four battalions of the 2000-mile IRBMs to be located at four missile sites; it also included surface-to-air missiles (SAMs) to ring the island, Soviet forces to protect the nuclear missile sites, and vast quantities of equipment for the Cuban air and ground forces. A measure of the size of the deployment is the fact that a ship can carry several trainloads of material and that the plan required more than one hundred shiploads. The shipments began immediately.

By mid-August 1962, U.S. intelligence was aware that a huge arms shipment to Cuba was underway, but it had no information about missiles. Still, President Kennedy issued a series of very stern warnings to the Soviets against shipping "offensive weapons" of any kind to Cuba. As late as September 6, 1962, he said at a press conference that should Cuba "become an offensive military base for the Soviet Union, then this country will do whatever must be done to protect its own security." On October 14, an American U-2 spy plane took pictures of western and central Cuba, as had been routinely done since the middle of August. When these photographs were examined on Monday, October 15, they clearly showed

---

[1]What follows is drawn mainly from my private papers in the Kennedy Library in Boston (hereinafter cited as Hilsman Papers, Kennedy Library), which are largely described in Roger Hilsman, *To Move a Nation: The Politics of Foreign Policy in the Administration of John F. Kennedy* (Garden City, N.Y.: Doubleday, 1967). I have also drawn from Arthur M. Schlesinger, Jr., *A Thousand Days: John F. Kennedy in the White House* (Boston: Houghton Mifflin, 1965); Theodore C. Sorenson, *Kennedy* (New York: Harper & Row, 1965); Graham T. Allison, *Essence of Decision: Explaining the Cuban Missile Crisis* (Boston: Little, Brown, 1971); Raymond L. Garthoff, *Reflections on the Cuban Missile Crisis* (Washington, D.C.: Brookings, 1987); and McGeorge Bundy, *Danger and Survival: Choices About the Bomb in the First Fifty Years* (New York: Random House, 1988); and McGeorge Bundy, transcriber, "October 27, 1962: Transcripts of the Meetings of the ExComm," *International Security,* ed., James G. Blight (Winter 1987–1988).

both MRBMs and IRBMs being emplaced. Why did the Soviets so massively deploy nuclear missiles to Cuba, just 90 miles from the American coast?

A month earlier, on September 19, the U.S. Intelligence Board had addressed the question of whether the Soviets would send missiles to Cuba. The Intelligence Board, composed of the directors of the Central Intelligence Agency (CIA) and of the intelligence bureaus of the departments of State, Defense, Army, Navy, and Air Force, as well as representatives from the Federal Bureau of Investigation (FBI) and the National Security Agency (NSA), concluded that on balance the Soviets would not. The board reasoned as follows. First, the Soviets must have known that the United States was flying the U-2 and that the likelihood of discovery was therefore high. Second, the Soviets must have realized that the United States would probably react strongly if they sent missiles to Cuba. Third, although the problem of Soviet strategic inferiority would be eased by having missiles in Cuba, it would not be solved. Fourth, Castro was a self-proclaimed Communist, and the Soviets were not likely to regard him as trustworthy. Finally, the Soviets had never sent nuclear missiles outside their own borders, even to their Eastern European satellites. Thus, the judgment of the Intelligence Board was that the Soviets would *not* send missiles to Cuba. However, the National Intelligence Estimate (NIE) that the board approved did hedge by saying that the gains in deploying missiles were large enough to tempt the Soviets and therefore cautioned the intelligence community to maintain a high state of alert.

President Kennedy formed an Executive Committee of the National Security Council (NSC), which came to be known as the ExCom. When it met on Tuesday, October 16, the first question asked was, "Why?" Did the Soviets intend to use the nuclear missiles to launch a surprise attack along the lines of Pearl Harbor? Or had the Soviets misinterpreted some piece of intelligence and therefore come to believe that the United States was about to attack them? Or was the motive political, designed to blackmail the United States into, say, giving up Berlin?

Determining the Soviet motive was crucial. If the Soviets intended to use the missiles to launch a surprise attack, the United States had no choice but to use force to remove them immediately. On the other hand, if the Soviets intended to use the missiles for some sort of political blackmail, the United States might find a way to deal with the situation without resorting to force. Various members of the ExCom came up with a total of six possible explanations. Four were rejected, and two were accepted:

Defense of Cuba. The first explanation was that the missiles were intended for the defense of Cuba. Perhaps the Soviets and Castro feared that the United States would invade to make up for the failure of the Cuban brigade at the Bay of Pigs.

This explanation was rejected. Since President Kennedy had refused to use American troops to help the anti-Castro Cuban brigade at the Bay of Pigs, it was doubtful that the Soviets expected an American invasion, and even if they did, nuclear missiles were hardly necessary. A few Soviet troops would be a sufficient deterrent, just as one battalion each of American, British, and French forces had provided an adequate, "plate-glass-window" deterrent in Berlin for years.

A diverting trap. The second explanation was the notion of a diverting trap. Perhaps the Soviets thought that putting missiles in Cuba would provoke the giant United States into actually invading little Cuba, which would horrify its European allies and American domestic opinion. The Soviets could then take Berlin with impunity.

This explanation was also rejected. Not only would using such a massive deployment as a provocation be much too costly, but it would also be much too risky.

Berlin for Cuba. The third explanation was Secretary of State Dean Rusk's variation of the diverting trap. Perhaps, Rusk suggested, the Soviets intended to put the missiles in place secretly. Then, in a dramatic gesture at the United Nations (UN), the Soviets could pull back the curtain, reveal the missiles, and offer to trade Cuba for Berlin.

This explanation was rejected, again on the grounds that it was both too costly and risky. In addition, what would the rest of the Communist world think if Moscow sacrificed its Cuban ally so brutally and cynically?

Cuba missiles for Turkey missiles. The fourth explanation was the possibility that the Soviets wanted to exchange the missiles in Cuba for the American Jupiter missiles in Turkey.

This explanation was rejected. The Eisenhower administration had decided to send Jupiter missiles to Turkey at the request of the North Atlantic Treaty Organization (NATO) allies as a response to the Soviet deployment of MRBMs and IRBMs in the western Soviet Union aimed at Europe. The Jupiters were already obsolete when the decision was made. They had a long countdown and were very vulnerable to a sniper on a hill a mile away. Their deployment had been largely symbolic, and the Soviets knew all of this. They also knew that some months earlier Kennedy had ordered the State Department to negotiate with Turkey for their withdrawal.

The missile gap in reverse. The fifth explanation was the so-called missile gap in reverse. In the latter part of the Eisenhower administration and the first six months of the Kennedy administration, the United States intelligence community was convinced that the Soviets held an advantage in missiles that had created a "missile gap." However, in the summer of 1961 the first U.S. reconnaissance satellites revealed that in fact the United States was ahead in the arms race.

In the fall of 1961 the Soviets were threatening to seize Berlin, apparently taking advantage of the American belief in a missile gap in favor of the Soviets. To disabuse the Soviets of this notion and discourage them from following a risky policy on Berlin, the United States had arranged for the Soviets to find out that it knew the true situation. The first step was a speech spelling out that the United States had solid intelligence of this fact. If such a speech were made by the president, the secretary of state, or the secretary of defense, the Soviets might be alarmed. To avoid this possibility, the speech was delivered by Deputy Secretary of Defense Roswell Gilpatric, since his position was high enough to attract the Soviets' attention but not high enough to alarm them. The second step was to describe the true situation, corroborated by satellite photographs, to the NATO allies and especially those known to have been penetrated by the KGB, the Soviet intelligence service.

It is important to note that this decision was made in full appreciation of the very high probability that when the Soviets learned that the United States knew the true situation, they would take some form of countermeasure. At the time, it was assumed this would probably be a crash program to build intercontinental ballistic missiles (ICBMs). In the fall of 1962, a year later, it seemed logical to conclude that the Soviets were deploying their MRBMs and IRBMs, of which they had a vast oversupply, as a "quick fix."

This explanation was accepted. The Soviets certainly could not believe that the rather vulnerable MRBMs and IRBMs would be an effective substitute for ICBMs. But the MRBMs and IRBMs would be a useful stopgap until the Soviet ICBM program went into full production. However, some members of the ExCom found it puzzling that the Soviets thought they could deploy the missiles secretly when they must have known that the United States was flying U-2s over Cuba.

A cold war probe. The final explanation offered was that the Soviet deployment of missiles to Cuba was a cold war probe. Soviet premier Nikita Khrushchev had told the American poet Robert Frost, when he visited Moscow, that the West was "too liberal to fight." Kennedy was a new and inexperienced president with a very narrow electoral victory. The Soviets might have thought, "Why not test the will of the West and the new president?" They could always pull back if the United States reacted strongly, but if the United States weakened over the missiles in Cuba, the Soviets could push their advantage in Berlin and even more in Latin America. Ambassador Llewellyn Thompson, a lifetime specialist on the Soviet Union, pointed out that a favorite adage of Russian Communist leaders since Lenin has been that if an enemy left an opening, you should thrust hard with your bayonet. If you met only soft flesh, you should push even harder. But if you met solid bone, you should withdraw.

This explanation was also accepted. However, Kennedy himself expressed some puzzlement: "If they doubted our guts," he said, "why not just take Berlin? Why horse around with Cuba?"

So the classical, traditional mode of analysis—as used by the top leaders of the United States—yielded both strategic and geopolitical answers to the question of why the Soviets deployed nuclear missiles to Cuba. The U.S. government, to repeat, had reached two conclusions. First, the Soviets were seeking a "quick fix" to their inferiority in ICBMs. Second, they were trying to test the resolve of the United States and the new president in anticipation of further moves in both Berlin and Latin America.[2]

The Escalation in Vietnam

Why did the United States escalate the struggle in Vietnam by bombing North Vietnam and deploying half a million American ground forces to fight in South Vietnam, thereby turning a Vietnamese struggle against Communist guerrillas into an American war?

In the wake of World War II, European colonies in Asia and later in Africa began demanding independence. Because the French were deter-

---

[2]In his article "The Cuban Missile Crisis: Trading the Jupiters in Turkey?" *Political Science Quarterly* (Spring 1980), Barton J. Bernstein makes much of the fact that although the decision to deploy the Jupiter missiles to Turkey was made in the Eisenhower administration, they did not actually arrive in Turkey until the Kennedy administration had begun. He also suggests that Kennedy did not *order* the missiles out of Turkey, "but only implied a study of its feasibility." Presidents rarely order moves that reverse a previous president's promise to an ally, and they certainly never do so without consulting the ally. Kennedy made his desires very clear on at least three occasions at which I was present. But he understood that the timing of the withdrawal would depend on the attitude of the Turks.

Donald L. Hafner, in "Bureaucratic Politics and 'Those Frigging Missiles': JFK, Cuba and U.S. Missiles in Turkey," *Orbis* (Summer 1977), talks about the "myth" that Kennedy was "shocked and surprised" to find that his instructions about removing the Jupiters from Turkey had "not been executed by State Department bureaucrats," because this left the United States vulnerable to Soviet pressure to make a "deal" exchanging the U.S. missiles in Turkey for the Soviet missiles from Cuba. The evidence, however, is quite different. Kennedy was not "shocked and surprised," for he, as well as the others involved, knew that the U.S. missiles were still in Turkey. Kennedy was *angry* but not shocked and surprised. He was angry because the delay in getting the missiles out of Turkey left the United States vulnerable to pressure to do something that would shake the NATO alliance. However, as Dean Rusk later testified, Kennedy had already taken steps to make a trade of the missiles in Turkey for the missiles in Cuba less harmful politically if such a "deal" turned out to be necessary. He had asked Rusk to arrange with Andrew W. Cordier, then a UN undersecretary, to have the secretary general of the UN "request" both the United States and the Soviet Union to remove their missiles from Turkey and Cuba, respectively. Such a request would have made it politically much easier for the United States to agree to the "deal."

mined to maintain their colony in Indochina, the independence movement there, which came to be dominated by the Communists, turned to guerrilla warfare. The crisis in this First Indochina War came in early 1954, when Communist Viet Minh guerrilla forces surrounded the French at Dienbienphu in a mountain valley at the junction of roads from China, Laos, and Vietnam. It was in a press conference at this time that President Dwight D. Eisenhower enunciated the "falling domino theory." He warned that if Indochina fell to the Communists, the other states of Southeast Asia would also fall, like a row of dominoes.[3]

The French government proposed that American air power be used to destroy the Viet Minh forces surrounding the French. However, the Eisenhower administration decided against the idea. The French forces at Dienbienphu surrendered, and a settlement was negotiated at Geneva making Laos and Cambodia independent countries. The Geneva agreement also "temporarily" divided Vietnam into the North, dominated by the Communists, and the South, dominated by a French-educated, Catholic, Vietnamese elite led by Ngo Dinh Diem. The United States embarked on a program of sending military and economic aid to South Vietnam, including several hundred military advisers.

In Laos a struggle quickly developed among three factions: a right-wing faction, a Communist faction, and a neutralist faction. When Eisenhower turned the presidency over to Kennedy, he warned Kennedy that the hardest problem facing him was Laos and said that Kennedy might have to intervene with American troops. If so, Eisenhower said, he would come to Washington and stand in support beside Kennedy in front of the TV cameras. In the end, however, Kennedy decided on negotiations, and in the Geneva Accords of 1962 the great powers agreed that Laos should be neutralized.

Early in the Kennedy administration, the South Vietnamese government requested economic and military aid to counter renewed attacks by Communist Viet Cong guerrillas. Kennedy sent General Maxwell D. Taylor and White House adviser Walt W. Rostow to Vietnam to investigate and make recommendations. They suggested an increase in both aid and the number of advisers, which Kennedy approved. They also recommended that the United States send 10,000 combat forces to Vietnam, which Kennedy refused to do. During the remainder of his administration, the United States continued to support South Vietnam and increased the number of military advisers to 16,500.

In July 1962, Kennedy ordered his secretary of defense, Robert McNamara, to start planning for the phased withdrawal of American

---

[3]For a study of United States policy during the First Indochina War, see Melvin Gurtov, *The First Vietnam Crisis* (New York: Columbia University Press, 1967).

military personnel from Vietnam; it was not until May 1963, however, that the Pentagon produced a satisfactory plan.[4]

At about the same time, South Vietnam was wracked by internal struggles centering on President Ngo Dinh Diem's policies toward the Buddhists. Kennedy became convinced that the South Vietnamese were not able to organize themselves effectively enough to win the conflict, a view that was strengthened by a coup that removed Diem. Kennedy then began to implement the withdrawal plan by ordering one thousand of the advisers to return to the United States.

On November 22, 1963, President Kennedy was assassinated. Vice President Lyndon B. Johnson was sworn in as president, and during the first year of his administration, the situation in Vietnam steadily worsened. Johnson gradually increased the number of military advisers until, by the beginning of 1965, they numbered over twenty-five thousand.

Then, in February 1965, the United States decided to launch a program of bombing North Vietnam and the supply routes leading to South Vietnam. A few weeks later a limited number of American combat ground forces were sent to Vietnam to defend the airfields from which American planes were operating. In spite of the bombing of North Vietnam, the situation continued to deteriorate, and in July the United States introduced ground forces on a large scale, eventually reaching over half a million soldiers.

Again the question is, "Why?" If the classical, traditional mode of analysis is applied, the first answer it yields is that if the Communists came to control all of Vietnam, they would have a formidable base from which to penetrate and dominate first Laos and Cambodia, then Thailand, and finally all of Southeast Asia. Vietnam would also be an avenue for the Communist Chinese into Southeast Asia, and the Vietnamese Communists would find it extraordinarily difficult to maintain their independence of China.

The second answer is based on the domino theory's concern with internal, Communist-led guerrillas, and not with invasion by either Vietnam or China. The belief was that if Vietnam fell to a native Communist insurgency, then the Communist parties of all the other Southeast Asian states would be encouraged to rebel, the Soviet Union and China would be encouraged to aid them, and the regimes of the threatened countries

---

[4]U.S. Department of Defense, *The Pentagon Papers (Senator Gravel Edition)* (Boston: Beacon Press, 1971–1972), Vol. 2, pp. 670–671. For Kennedy's policy toward Vietnam, see also Schlesinger, *A Thousand Days;* idem, *Robert F. Kennedy and His Times* (Boston: Houghton Mifflin, 1978); Hilsman, *To Move a Nation;* and idem, "Vietnam: The Decisions to Intervene," in *The Superpowers and Revolution,* ed., Jonathan Adelman (New York: Praeger, 1986).

would be disheartened. Implicit in this theory was the assumption that Southeast Asia was strategically crucial if the United States was to maintain its position in Asia and hence protect its own security.

A variation on this theme was that the Soviet Union was bent on dominating the world and that Communist China was bent on dominating Asia. U.S. nuclear and missile superiority had so far successfully deterred the Communists from any aggression that risked a global, nuclear war. The U.S. willingness to fight in Korea in 1950 had successfully deterred a recurrence of large-scale, conventional aggression. In a guerrilla insurgency of the type being pursued in Vietnam, the argument continued, the Communist world had found what it believed to be a new, less risky, but still effective form of aggression. The United States accordingly must find a way to meet such aggression in order to deter both the Soviets and the Communist Chinese from instigating such insurgencies all over the world.

One of the most sophisticated arguments for the American intervention derived from the classical, traditional mode of analysis was offered by President Johnson himself. In a reflective mood at a meeting of the National Security Council, he said that the fabric of international peace and stability was made up of sets of the expectations held by all the nations of the world, whether enemies, allies, or neutrals, about how each of the others would behave in a crisis. If the United States let South Vietnam "go down the drain," then every nation would have to reexamine its assumptions about its security position. Japan would have to ask itself whether it was wise to place itself under the American nuclear umbrella. Germany would have to rethink its position about the North Atlantic Treaty Organization (NATO) alliance. In short, all of our friends and allies would have to think hard about their friendship with the United States. One thing was certain, Johnson went on to say, and that was if we let Vietnam "go down the drain," many, many more nations would decide that they had to build their own nuclear weapons. Nuclear proliferation would become rampant.[5]

Thus the answer yielded by the classical, traditional mode of analysis to the question of why the United States escalated the struggle in Vietnam into an American war is strategic and geopolitical. If Vietnam falls to the Communists, other Southeast Asian countries will also fall. Also, if the United States lets South Vietnam be conquered, the whole geopolitical fabric of international politics will be rent; both friend and foe will be forced to reexamine their expectations and policies, inevitably to the detriment of the interests of the United States.

---

[5]"Notes on NSC Meetings," Hilsman Papers, Kennedy Library.

China's Invitation to Nixon

Why did China invite President Richard M. Nixon to visit China and so begin the process of normalizing relations between China and the United States? If the classical, traditional mode is used, the analysis goes as follows.

Following the takeover of mainland China by the Chinese Communists, China and the Soviet Union found themselves increasingly at odds. Their dispute was first concerned with ideology: What was the true meaning of the sacred texts of the Communist world and the Communist vision of the future? It also was concerned with power: Who should have power, who should lead, and who should follow?

The Sino-Soviet dispute was also concerned with whether Russia's national interests should be synonymous with the interests of the whole of the Communist world or whether the national interests of the other Communist parties should also be considered in determining policy. This issue also extended to policy toward the "in-between world": Should the friendship of the Communist world be extended to "national bourgeois" regimes, as in India, or only to the radical nationalists and "national liberation movements"?

Finally, the Sino-Soviet dispute was concerned with grand strategy: How aggressive should the Communist world be in its dealings with the West, and how much risk of nuclear war should be run? This difference was symbolized by the exchange between Mao Zedong and Khrushchev at the time of the Cuban missile crisis, with Mao saying that the West was only a "paper tiger," and Khrushchev replying that this particular paper tiger had "nuclear teeth."

Both China and the Soviet Union had increased their military forces along the long border between them, and on a number of occasions heavy fighting broke out. Along the Ussuri River, the fighting at least once involved several divisions on each side.

At the same time, China was facing tension on other fronts. The bitterness and hostility created by Japan's invasion and occupation of China before and during World War II continued. Economic tension between the two was also high. By the late 1960s the Chinese had become convinced that Japanese militarism was on the rise again. (The Chinese later admitted that they had been wrong in this judgment, but they believed it at the time.)

China was also under tension with the United States. U.S. support of the Nationalist regime during the Chinese civil war was highly resented, and continued American support of the Nationalist government in Taiwan only exacerbated relations. The Korean War found China and the United States in a major conflict in which the Chinese casualties were particularly heavy. One of Mao's own sons was killed in Korea.

Then, in 1965 came the American intervention in Vietnam. Perhaps most threatening was the multibillion-dollar American military base at Cam Ranh Bay, a deep-water port suitable for a huge navy. The Chinese could not see that Vietnam had any strategic, political, or economic value for the United States, and so they concluded that the motive behind the American intervention had to be to provide a base from which the United States could dominate China. Many Chinese leaders thought that the United States actually intended an invasion. Lin Piao, then China's defense minister and Mao's designated successor, made a speech on September 5, 1965, that expressly addressed the question of what strategy China should follow when the U.S. invasion came.

Thus China found itself isolated and surrounded by hostile powers: the Soviet Union, Japan, and the United States. The classical solution to such a dilemma was to form a grand alliance such as the European powers had put together when faced with an aggressive Louis XIV, Napoleon, German kaiser, or Hitler. But with whom could China ally? India was too weak, the Southeast Asian countries too small. The only alternative was to lessen tension on one front or the other.

The historical example of a country lessening tension on one front to escape a war on two fronts was England at the turn of the century. In the late nineteenth century the war that everyone thought was inevitable was that between England and Russia. The tension was focused in the northwest frontier of India at the Khyber Pass. Both England and Russia were gearing up for war. But then Germany decided to build a fleet that would make it a first-class naval power. England saw this as an intolerable threat and thus decided to ease its tensions with Russia; it was only later that the relationship blossomed into an alliance.

In the case of China, the nearest and most dangerous enemy was the Soviet Union. The Chinese could have had little hope of forming an alliance with the United States, but if relations at least could be eased with the United States, they would automatically be eased with Japan, and what was essentially a potential three-front conflict would be reduced to a one-front conflict. Thus the answer to why the Chinese invited Nixon to visit yielded by the classical, traditional mode of analysis is also strategic and geopolitical. China found itself in strategic isolation, under tension on three fronts. Easing tensions with the United States reduced the fronts to one.

The Soviet Invasion of Afghanistan

Why did the Soviets invade Afghanistan? If the classical, traditional mode of analysis is used, the answer is as follows:

In 1953 Prince Muhammad Daoud became prime minister of Afghanistan, and for the next ten years he ran the country as a strongman representing the monarchy. In 1954 trouble developed with Pakistan over the Pushtun people who lived on both sides of the Afghanistan-Pakistan border. Prince Daoud approached the United States for military aid but was refused. He then turned to the Soviet Union, which agreed to supply equipment and to train and advise the Afghan army. Throughout his ten years as prime minister, Daoud followed a policy of close ties with the Soviet Union; rapid economic development; and dictatorial, oppressive domestic policies. The Soviets seemed well satisfied with the arrangement, a position that was probably influenced by the fact that the Afghan Communists were bitterly split between the Parcham faction and the Khalq faction.

In 1963 the king dismissed Daoud to permit an experiment in political freedom and wider participation in government. Greater freedom encouraged the development of a large number of highly emotional political factions, many of them agitating for radical policies that alarmed the more traditional elements of Afghan society. At the same time Afghanistan's economic troubles—resulting partly from the difficulty of digesting the rapid modernization—added to the political turmoil. In early 1978 Daoud seized the opportunity to return to power in an almost bloodless coup engineered by the Parcham faction of the Communist party. Since the Soviet Union had favored this faction over the Khalq faction, it immediately vastly increased its aid. Parcham party members became ministers in most of the key departments.

An election in which Daoud would have completed his return to full power was scheduled for November 1979, but the Khalq faction—by now somewhat anti-Soviet—launched a coup in April 1978 and seized control of the government. Over the next few months the Khalq faction, headed by Prime Minister Hafizullah Amin, maneuvered to shut out the Parcham faction entirely. Once this was accomplished, the Khalq faction announced a very radical program of land collectivization that shocked the traditional peasantry. Riots broke out in a number of towns and cities, and a guerrilla resistance movement began in the countryside.

The Soviets, who had counseled against the Khalq policies, were clearly becoming increasingly doubtful that the regime could survive. They conspired with the president of Afghanistan, Nur Muhammad Taraki, for still another coup. Amin defeated the attempt, and the rift between Amin and the Khalq faction on the one hand and the Soviet Union on the other was complete. However, the Soviets continued to exercise enormous influence through their network of advisers in the Afghan armed forces.

In the meantime, the guerrilla resistance movement had been growing stronger and bolder. In the government itself, Amin and other Khalq leaders had not only excluded the Parcham leaders but also alienated the officer corps of the army and lost the confidence of leaders in the bureaucracies. The Soviets became convinced not so much that the country would be conquered by the "resistance fighters," as they called themselves, but that the Amin government would be overthrown by non-Communist, pro-Western elements from within the government itself. The Soviets thus invaded Afghanistan on December 27, 1979, and at the same time either murdered Amin themselves or arranged for his murder. They then replaced the Khalq leaders with members of the Parcham faction.

In Washington, the explanation for the invasion offered by the administration of President Jimmy Carter followed the classical, traditional mode of analysis. First, according to this view, the Soviets were basically aggressive and expansionist, and the invasion represented still another move to extend their empire. Second, and more ominously, the Soviets' long-run intention was to secure Afghanistan as a base from which to "lunge" at the Middle East and its treasure of oil. The Carter administration announced to the Soviet Union that it considered the invasion a hostile act that threatened détente. The United States solicited other Western countries to join in a unified response and assured the countries bordering Afghanistan of U.S. protection from further Soviet aggression. It also began to lay the political groundwork for an increase in the defense budget. Carter asked the Senate to delay consideration of the Strategic Arms Limitation Treaty (SALT II) already negotiated. He embargoed the export of grain and high-technology goods to the Soviet Union, prohibited Soviet fishing in U.S. waters, put a moratorium on the opening of new U.S. and USSR consular offices, suspended cultural exchanges, and, some time later, announced a boycott of the Olympic games to be held in Moscow. Thus in this issue also the classical, traditional analysis put strategic and geopolitical factors central.

Iran and the American Hostages

An explanation of the seizure of the American hostages in Iran based on the classical, traditional analysis is as follows:

Shah Muhammad Reza Pahlevi had taken over dictatorial power in Iran in August 1953 as a result of a coup that was assisted by the CIA. For the next twenty years, Iran was an ally of the United States, which supplied it with large amounts of military aid and equipment. But the shah was tyrannical and arbitrary, alienating many segments of Iranian society. By 1978 his position was deteriorating badly. His chief opponent was Iran's top religious leader, the Ayatollah Ruhollah Khomeini, who was living in exile in Paris. Many U.S. diplomats, including the ambassador to Iran, advised the Carter administration that the shah was doomed and urged the United States to establish relations with the Ayatollah. But the Carter administration continued to support the shah.

The shah, however, continued to lose domestic support, and when it became clear in January 1979 that even the army was no longer loyal, he went into exile. The Ayatollah Khomeini arrived in Iran on February 1. Khomeini's choice for prime minister, Mehdi Bazargan, took over on February 11.

The shah, who was in Mexico, had become increasingly ill with cancer and asked for permission to come to the United States for medical treatment. The American embassy in Teheran opposed admitting the shah to the United States until steps could be taken to protect the embassy from terrorists. The embassy also warned that if the shah were granted entrance, the Iranians might take American hostages.

Nevertheless, the Carter administration allowed the shah to enter the United States for treatment on October 22, 1979. During a march in protest against this decision, a group of militants took control of the American embassy in Teheran. The militants demanded that the shah be returned to Iran to stand trial. The next day Khomeini condoned both the takeover and the militants' demand. Fifty-three American hostages were held for 444 days.

What made these events unique in modern history was the fact that the government of Iran sanctioned the holding of the hostages in violation of international law and almost five hundred years of diplomatic tradition and custom. Terrorists have taken American embassy personnel hostage a number of times in history, and most frequently in the decades since World War II. But in every other case the government of the country, even when it was extremely anti-American and sympathetic to the seizure, either negotiated the release of the hostages or rescued them by military force. Why was Iran behaving so differently?

The classical, traditional mode of analysis produces a threefold answer. First, the Soviet military buildup over the preceding fifteen years had made many Iranians wonder whether their alliance with the United States offered as much security as it once had. Iran, after all, was particularly exposed, situated as it was on the border of the Soviet Union and on the path to the oil of the Middle East. Showing direct hostility toward the United States by taking hostages would signal a concrete step toward a policy of independence.

Second, Iran was ambitious. It aspired to leadership in the Muslim world, and to establish that leadership Iran had to show its independence of the United States. Taking the hostages not only demonstrated Iran's independence but also showed that the United States was, in former

President Nixon's phrase, a "pitiful, helpless giant" in the face of the Ayatollah Khomeini.

Third, seizing the hostages carried an ideological appeal. By confronting and defying a superpower and getting away with it, the leaders of the Iranian revolution showed that they stood on the side of downtrodden peoples of the Third World.

In its public announcements and in its policies, the Carter administration seemed to be following this same mode of analysis with one additional point: In addition to the essentially strategic and geopolitical motives suggested by the classical, traditional mode of analysis, another motive attributed to Iran was revenge for U.S. support of the shah over the years and for the more recent decision to let him come to the United States for medical treatment.

The policies adopted by the Carter administration to deal with the hostage situation combined carrots and sticks. On the one hand, the administration tried to negotiate with Iran through various channels. On the other hand, the United States froze several billion dollars in Iranian assets held in American banks, boycotted Iranian oil, dispatched naval units to the Arabian Sea, ordered a reduction in the number of Iranian diplomats in the United States, ran an immigration check on the tens of thousands of Iranian students in America, and put pressure on our allies to join in economic sanctions. At several stages the U.S. government believed it had reached an agreement for the release of the hostages, but each time Iran failed to carry out its side of the bargain. On April 7, 1980, the United States broke off diplomatic relations.

On April 25, a military operation with helicopters was mounted in an attempt to rescue the hostages by force. The rescue force rendezvoused at an isolated spot in the desert some distance from Teheran, but an equipment failure caused the mission to be canceled. Eight American servicemen were killed when two of the rescue aircraft collided.

The Carter administration then renewed its attempts to negotiate the release of the hostages with the help of Algeria. The shah died in July. Many observers, especially those who thought that revenge was one of the Iranian motives, believed that with the shah dead, negotiations would be successful. But there was still no progress. It was not until after the American election in November that the negotiations conducted by the Algerians began to show results. An agreement was reached just forty-eight hours before the inauguration of the new president, and the hostages were released immediately afterward.

In hindsight, the argument that revenge was a motive seemed less persuasive than it had at the beginning of the crisis, principally because the death of the shah seemed to make no difference in the negotiations.

The strategic and geopolitical motives, on the other hand, seemed even more persuasive, since it was the various pressures, especially the economic, that seemed to bring Iran to an agreement.[6]

The Iran-Contra Affair

Why did the United States trade arms to Iran during the second Reagan administration while urging its allies not to do so, and then use the money from the deal to buy arms for the Contras fighting against the government of Nicaragua, an act that violated the ban on such aid by Congress?

If the classical, traditional mode of analysis is used, the answer goes as follows: The Middle East is of prime strategic importance. First, it has the treasure of oil, the most strategic of all commodities in today's world. Second, the Middle East is a vital crossroads of world communication routes. Finally, just as the North German plain was a possible avenue for the Soviets into Western Europe, so was Iran a possible avenue for the Soviets into the Middle East and Africa.

The Iran-Iraq war was at its height at the time and threatened the stability of the whole Middle East.

In spite of the instability the war created, the United States followed a policy of neutrality. Iran under the ayatollah had been actively hostile to the United States. After the fifty-three hostages were released, Iran sponsored terrorist attacks on individual American citizens and on U.S. installations. Iraq, for its part, had not been quite so hostile as Iran, but it had certainly not been friendly. The United States, however, not only maintained its neutrality but also actively lobbied its allies and others not to sell arms to either side, especially not to Iran. In addition, the United States sought to isolate Iran both economically and politically.

At the time of the Iran-Contra affair, three or four Americans were being held hostage in Middle Eastern countries by groups under the influence of Iran, if not under its actual control. On this problem the

---

[6]On the hostage crisis, see Pierre Salinger, *America Held Hostage: The Secret Negotiations* (Garden City, N.Y.: Doubleday, 1981); Paul B. Ryan, *The Iranian Rescue Mission: Why It Failed* (Annapolis, Md.; Naval Institute Press, 1985); Hamilton Jordan, *Crisis: The Last Year of the Carter Presidency* (New York: Putnam's Sons, 1982); and Amir Taheri, *Nest of Spies: America's Journey to Disaster in Iran* (London: Hutchinson, 1988).

For a chronology of events from January 1, 1978 to December 31, 1980, see the report prepared for the Committee on Foreign Affairs, U.S. House of Representatives by the Foreign Affairs and National Defense Division, Congressional Research Service, *Iran Hostage Crisis: A Chronology of Daily Developments* (Washington, D.C.: U.S. Government Printing Office, 1981).

United States had followed the policy set by Israel: Never negotiate with terrorists under any circumstances. If you make a deal with terrorists to release one hostage, they will only be encouraged to take more.

What seemed to worry the United States most about the continued Iran-Iraq war was the instability it created for the whole of the Middle East. The greatest fear was that this instability would provide an opportunity for the Soviets to increase their political influence in the region—or even an excuse for military intervention. When the United States announced that Kuwaiti oil tankers would be reflagged and escorted by U.S. naval vessels, it justified the move on the grounds that if the United States did not provide the protection needed, the Soviet Union would—and so enlarge its role and influence.

Then, an opportunity arose to negotiate with "moderate" elements in Iran about trading arms for hostages. The Reagan administration, according to its own account, saw in this opportunity a chance to kill two birds with one stone—strengthen the moderates in Iran and obtain the release of American hostages. So, the United States began in utmost secrecy to negotiate a trade of arms to Iran in exchange for American hostages, in spite of U.S. public and declaratory policy.

As for the Contra side of the Iran-Contra affair, when the arms deal generated surplus funds, Navy Admiral John Poindexter, Reagan's national security adviser, and Marine Corps Lieutenant Colonel Oliver North, a member of the National Security Council staff, thought it would be a "neat idea" to use the money to supply arms to the Contras in lieu of an appropriation by Congress, which was not available after the Boland amendment had specifically forbidden such aid to the Contras.

When the story of the Iran-Contra affair leaked, White House staff members tried to avoid embarrassment by telling the press that President Reagan had not been informed about these machinations. The historical parallel here apparently is Henry II and the murder of Thomas à Becket, archbishop of Canterbury. King Henry had not *ordered* the murder of Becket. Rather, annoyed to the point of exhaustion by the archbishop, the king had only said—rhetorically—"Is there not one who will rid me of this low-born priest?" Two Norman knights hastened to do just that and thus please the king.

The Reagan administration offered three reasons for its actions in the Iran-Contra affair—two geopolitical and strategic reasons and one humanitarian: The first geopolitical and strategic reason was that selling arms to Iran would encourage moderates in the Iranian government and thereby help end the Iran-Iraq war, which in turn would bring stability to the Middle East and block an avenue for Soviets to increase their political influence, if not their actual military presence in the region. The second geopolitical and strategic reason was that using the money generated by selling arms to Iran to aid the Contras would help them overthrow the Communist government of Nicaragua. The Reagan administration was convinced that continued Communist control of Nicaragua would provide both the Soviet Union and Cuba vital political opportunities in Central America, and eventually bring Soviet submarine and missile bases right on our doorstep. The humanitarian reason was the possibility of freeing the hostages.[7]

The Gulf War Against Iraq

Why did the United States go to war in 1990–1991 against Iraq? Using the classical, traditional mode of analysis, the answer is as follows.[8]

Iraq is the heart of the "fertile crescent," the area between the Tigris and Euphrates rivers where civilization based on agriculture first arose. It was occupied by Arabs in the seventh century A.D. and conquered by the Ottoman Turks in the seventeenth century. In World War I, the Ottoman empire was an ally of Germany, and after the war Britain created Iraq out of three Ottoman provinces.

Kuwait, which borders Iraq on the southeast, is largely desert. It must import almost all of its water, and it had no permanent inhabitants until 1710 when a band of Arabs settled near one of its few small springs. From 1775 until just after the end of World War II, Kuwait was a ward of Great Britain. It finally became independent in 1961.

In 1923 Britain drew the border between Iraq and Kuwait deliberately so as to deny Iraq a port, giving Kuwait two uninhabited islands that blocked Iraq's route to the open sea. Although the Rumaila oil field had not been discovered at the time, the border also put the tip of the field inside Kuwait.

---

[7]For further information on the Iran-Contra affair, see Jonathan Marshall, *The Iran-Contra Connection: Secret Teams and Covert Operations in the Reagan Era,* (Boston: South End Press, 1987); William S. Cohen and George J. Mitchell, *Men of Zeal* (New York: Viking, 1988); Donald T. Regan, *For the Record: From Wall Street to Washington* (San Diego: Harcourt Brace Jovanovich, 1988); Noam Chomsky, *The Culture of Terrorism,* (Boston: South End Press, 1988); Phillip Henderson, *Managing the Presidency* (Boulder, Colo.: Westview Press 1988). For an account of Lt. Col. North's testimony at the congressional hearings on the Contra affair, see Daniel Schorr, *Taking the Stand* (New York: Simon & Schuster, 1987); The Tower Commission report on the Iran-Contra affair is also available from Bantam Books, 1987, and from Times Books, 1987. In addition, twenty-seven volumes of source documents were published by the U.S. House of Representatives Select Committee to Investigate Covert Arms Transactions with Iran and the U.S. Senate Select Committee on Secret Military Assistance to Iran and the Nicaraguan Opposition.

[8]The analysis of the Gulf War given here and in Chapters 2 and 7 are adapted from my *George Bush vs. Saddam Hussein, Military Success! Political Failure?* (Novato, Calif.: Presidio Press, 1992).

After Britain pulled out of Iraq, a series of bloody coups finally settled power firmly into the hands of a new, pan-Arab nationalist party, the "Baathists."

Saddam Hussein joined the Baath party while he was still in high school and worked his way up until he became president of Iraq in 1979.

Then came the eight-year war with Iran. Iraq suffered 120,000 dead and 300,000 wounded—out of a population of 17 million. Iraq had racked up a foreign debt of $35 billion to Arab countries and another $35 billion to others.

Hussein tried to persuade Kuwait and other oil-rich Arab states to bail Iraq out of its difficulties. He had five demands: Arguing that Iraq had protected all Arabs by fighting Iran, (1) he wanted the Arab states to forgive their $35 billion loans; (2) he wanted them to grant Iraq new loans totaling $30 billion; (3) he demanded that Kuwait pay Iraq $2.4 billion for the oil stolen from Iraq through the slant wells dug into the Rumaila oil field on Iraq's side of the border; (4) he demanded that Kuwait cease violating Organization of Petroleum Exporting Countries (OPEC) quotas and prices; and (5) he urged that the price of oil be raised immediately to $18 a barrel. But Hussein's demands were ignored, exacerbating his domestic difficulties.

A few days before the Iraqi attack on Kuwait, Hussein called in the American ambassador, April Glaspie. He repeated his complaints about Kuwait, and Ambassador Glaspie, acting on instructions from President Bush and the State Department, replied that the United States had "no opinion" on Arab versus Arab conflicts such as Iraq's dispute with Kuwait.

Then, at 2:00 A.M. on August 2, 1990, Iraqi forces crossed the border of Kuwait in force. Within six hours they had occupied the whole country.

On her return to the United States, Ambassador Glaspie told the American press that the Bush administration had expected Iraq to take the islands blocking its access to the sea and the tip of the oil field but was surprised when Iraq took *all* of Kuwait.

President Bush spent the next few days on the phone with various heads of state, seeking allies and support for his plan to send U.S. troops to the Gulf. Once permission was granted, Bush ordered ground and air troops to Saudi Arabia and additional naval forces to the Gulf.

The United States also persuaded the members of the UN Security Council to vote to condemn the invasion of Kuwait and to call for worldwide economic sanctions against Iraq to pressure it to withdraw to its own borders.

As described by President Bush, the U.S. goals were to forestall an Iraqi invasion of Saudi Arabia and to put enough economic pressure on Saddam Hussein to force him to withdraw "unconditionally" from Kuwait.

Beyond those two immediate goals, Bush said he wanted to establish the principle that aggression should not be rewarded. Over the next few weeks, Bush compared Hussein to Hitler and said that the United States was not going to make the mistake of appeasing an aggressor a second time.

Bush also spoke of the strategic and military importance of oil. Iraq, Bush said, has the world's second largest reserves of oil, and the United States imports nearly half of the oil it consumes. If Hussein ever gained control of Saudi Arabia and its oil, Bush argued, it would threaten the American "way of life."

In an address to Congress on September 11, 1990, Bush also said that one of his goals in the Middle East was to establish a "new world order . . . in which nations recognize the shared responsibility for freedom and justice." This "new world order" was widely interpreted to refer to an overall strategic balance of power in which the great powers accepted responsibility for dealing with future threats by countries such as Iraq under Saddam Hussein.

A few weeks later, the Bush administration began to doubt that economic sanctions would be enough to force Iraq out of Kuwait. At the same time it changed its mind about U.S. goals. Even if Hussein did withdraw from Kuwait, he would still control Iraq's battle-hardened army of half a million men, 5,500 tanks, a formidable air force, a stockpile of chemical and biological weapons, and a potential for developing nuclear weapons. Bush concluded that if Iraq merely withdrew from Kuwait, the threat Hussein posed would remain and, because of Iraq's nuclear potential, would actually increase over time. So the goals were changed to include removing Saddam Hussein from power, forcing Iraq to reduce its armed forces, and destroying Iraq's chemical and biological facilities and weapons and its potential for building nuclear weapons.

In late October, President Bush ordered that the number of American troops in the Middle East be doubled—from 230,000 to almost half a million—to provide an "offensive" capability. The United States then vigorously lobbied the members of the UN Security Council to pass a resolution authorizing the use of force to drive Iraq out of Kuwait. On November 30, the UN Security Council did so, setting January 15 as the deadline for an Iraqi withdrawal. The vote was 12 in favor, Yemen and Cuba against, and China abstaining. Saddam Hussein responded by saying that Iraq would fight.

On January 8, Bush formally requested Congress to approve the use of military force against Iraq if it did not pull out of Kuwait by the deadline of January 15. The Senate approved Bush's request to use military force in the Gulf by a vote of 52 to 47. In the House of Representatives, the vote was 250 in favor to 183 opposed.

Saddam Hussein and Iraq remained unmoved, and the deadline of January 15 passed.

That next day, January 16, President Bush ordered an all-out air assault on Iraq and the Iraqi troops in Kuwait. The air campaign lasted forty days, with the aim not only of driving Iraqi troops out of Kuwait but also of destroying both Iraq's military and economic capabilities. The targets in Kuwait were Iraqi troop installations, road and rail networks, and bridges. But in Iraq, the targets also included communications facilities of all kinds (telephone, telegraph, radio, television), factories producing both military and civilian goods, warehouses, water purification plants, sewage plants—in fact, Iraq's entire economic base. The number of aircraft involved and the intensity of the bombing made it one of the largest air assaults in history.

The ground offensive was launched on February 25. Several columns attacked the Iraqi forces in Kuwait, but the main U.S. and Allied thrust was deep into Iraq, north of Kuwait, so as to cut off the Iraqi troops in both Kuwait and southern Iraq. The Iraqi forces defending the border, mainly second-line troops, were quickly overwhelmed. By the fourth day, American and British tanks met and engaged the Republican Guard, Iraq's elite troops who had been held in reserve just south of Baghdad. Almost immediately, Iraq sued for peace, and President Bush ordered an end to the offensive. The ground war had lasted 100 hours.

SUMMARY

Thus in all seven case studies the classical, or traditional, mode of analysis yields strategic, power-oriented answers, which seem logical and reasonably persuasive, to the question of why the states in question behaved the way they did.

2

COUNTERARGUMENTS

Chapter 1 offered explanations as to why the different states behaved the way they did in seven case studies. The explanations were based on the classical, traditional mode of analysis stressing strategic and geopolitical factors, and they seemed logical and reasonably persuasive. However, this chapter turns things around and tries to show that exactly the same mode of analysis can yield different but still plausible results.

THE CUBAN MISSILE CRISIS

In the Cuban missile crisis the members of the ExCom accepted two explanations of the motives behind the Soviet deployment of nuclear missiles to Cuba. The first was that the Soviets did so as a "quick fix" for their imbalance in ICBMs. The second was that the deployment was a cold war probe to test the will of the United States and its new president.

However, when it came time to decide what to do about the Soviet missiles in Cuba—especially when the discussion focused on the proposal to take out the Soviet missiles with a "surgical air strike"—some members of the ExCom turned the argument around, even though they continued to use the traditional, classical mode of analysis.

Rather than bomb the missiles, these ExCom members wanted the United States to blockade Cuba to ensure that no more missiles could be sent and to begin efforts to reach a negotiated settlement that would require the missiles already in Cuba to be withdrawn. This counterargument began with the point that MRBMs and IRBMs, of which the Soviet

Union had a huge surplus, were "soft," that is, not housed in silos of reinforced concrete. "Soft" missiles were vulnerable to attack by conventional weapons, even a man with a rifle. Further, the countdown time to launch MRBMs and IRBMs was rather long. For both of these reasons the Soviet missiles in Cuba were not really a substitute for the large-warhead ICBMs based in the Soviet Union in well-protected, "hardened" silos. In strategic parlance, the latter were "second-strike" weapons that were able to strike back at an attacker even after receiving a blow. The MRBMs and IRBMs were both too vulnerable and too slow to qualify as second-strike weapons.

In fact, the Soviet MRBMs and IRBMs did not even qualify as adequate "first-strike" weapons—capable of destroying the enemy's missiles and bombers before they can be launched. First-strike weapons must not only be fast in counting down but also extremely accurate. The MRBMs and IRBMs were deficient in both qualities, although they did have some first-strike capability (in the words of the official National Intelligence Estimate, the MRBMs and IRBMs would "begin to degrade the United States second-strike capability"). If they did not qualify as second-strike weapons and had only a marginal utility as first-strike weapons, how could the Soviets believe that the MRBMs and IRBMs were a "quick fix" when they did not offer much of a fix at all?

The second motive, a cold war probe of the will and determination of the United States and the new president, was even more easily turned around with the same strategic and geopolitical analysis. The counterargument began with the point that the Soviets knew all about the capabilities of the U-2 reconnaissance plane. They had shot down Gary Powers's U-2 over Russia in 1960, and they knew that it could take pictures from an altitude of 15 miles that could distinguish the 2-inch stripes in the parking lot of a supermarket. They must have logically assumed that the U-2 was flying regularly over Cuba before they decided to deploy the missiles. When the Soviet arms buildup in Cuba actually started in the summer of 1962, the director of intelligence and research at the State Department (the present author) was instructed to give regular background briefings to the press describing in great detail what was offloaded from each Soviet freighter that docked in Cuba. The Soviets had to realize that such information could only come from U-2 flights.

The Soviets must therefore have known that the United States would discover the missiles before they were fully operational. If so, the counterargument continued, it seemed inconceivable that the Soviets would think that the United States would sit idly by and watch the missiles being deployed. In prudence the Soviets had to assume that the United States would react strongly. There would be a formidable political and diplomatic crisis, and the United States might well resort to military force such as an air strike against the missiles, an invasion of Cuba, or even more drastic action. In light of all this, how could the Soviets possibly conclude that a cold war probe in Cuba was worth the extraordinary risk it created? As already mentioned, President Kennedy had wondered aloud why, if the Soviets "doubted our guts," they didn't just take Berlin?

Even if the United States backed down and confined its reaction to diplomatic and political moves, the argument against an air strike and for a blockade continued, it was axiomatic that any subsequent attempt to repeat the challenge in an important place such as Berlin would only mean that the U.S. reaction would be violent precisely because it had shown weakness earlier in Cuba.

Those who favored an air strike argued that a blockade might keep additional missiles from getting to Cuba but would do nothing whatsoever to force the Soviets to remove the missiles already there. Those who opposed an air strike and favored a blockade could only say that a blockade would just be the first step. If the combination of a blockade and negotiations failed to persuade the Soviets to remove the missiles, the United States could then consider options such as an air strike, an invasion, or some other kind of pressure.

Finally, the argument against an air strike and for a blockade concluded, the two explanations, a "quick fix" and a cold war probe, are logically inconsistent. How could the Soviets justify embarking on the adventurous policy of probing U.S. will and determination when at the very same time they perceived themselves at such a disadvantage in strategic missiles that they began a risky deployment of their surplus MRBMs and IRBMs? And indeed they *were* at a strategic disadvantage. If a showdown resulted, the Soviets would most likely be the losers. To probe U.S. will and determination in such circumstances would be madness, especially since the Soviets actually perceived themselves at a disadvantage.

Thus the Soviet motive could not really have been *both* a "quick fix" and a cold war probe. If the motive were one or the other, the "quick fix" is considerably more credible. Yet the counterarguments against the "quick fix" are rather persuasive considering the alternative that the Soviets could have pursued. If they were concerned about their strategic imbalance, a more logical and considerably less risky policy would have been to do what they finally did do after they withdrew the missiles: They eased tensions with the United States by accepting the olive branch Kennedy offered in his American University speech, negotiated the limited nuclear test ban agreement, and cooperated with Kennedy in bringing about what later became known as détente. Then, in the more relaxed climate that followed, they built up their defenses over the subsequent fifteen years until they reached parity with the United States in not only strategic weapons but other categories as well.

THE ESCALATION IN VIETNAM

The answer to the question of why the United States escalated the struggle in Vietnam into an American war yielded by the classical, traditional mode of analysis was threefold. First, Vietnam constituted a strategic route into Southeast Asia that was in turn strategically crucial to the interests of the United States in Asia. Second, the domino theory held that if Vietnam fell to a native, Communist-led insurgency, the other states of Southeast Asia would also fall. Here again the argument assumed that the other states were strategically crucial to U.S. interests. Third, as President Johnson argued, if the United States let Vietnam go "down the drain," then all other nations of the world, friend and foe alike, would have to reexamine their most fundamental assumptions, and the whole fabric of international politics would be ripped apart.

However, by using the same strategic and geopolitical mode of analysis, some opponents of the policy of escalation both inside and outside the U.S. government reached the opposite conclusion on every point. Consider a topographical map of Southeast Asia. The border between Laos and Vietnam is the spine of a mountain range, with subsidiary ridges coming off that spine perpendicular to the line from China south. The road and rail networks from China south into Vietnam must at places pass within a very few miles of the sea, which makes them extraordinarily vulnerable to interdiction by both air and naval power. It thus seems obvious that Vietnam has no strategic value as an invasion route from China into Southeast Asia, a fact that the Eisenhower administration implicitly acknowledged by its refusal to intervene in Vietnam at the time of Dienbienphu.

The only feasible route for a road from China south into Southeast Asia is through Laos. This route is well inland, screened by many miles of mountain ranges, and ends up in Thailand, at the very heart of Southeast Asia. The conclusion seems inescapable that if any country has significant strategic importance as a route into Southeast Asia, it is Laos and not Vietnam. The Chinese actually built such a road across Laos linking up to the roads to Thailand as part of their aid program to Laos in the latter part of the Eisenhower administration and the early part of the Kennedy administration. The Eisenhower administration did in fact consider intervening in Laos in 1960, partly because of the road building and partly because of Soviet support to the Communist guerrillas in both Laos and Vietnam. But in the end, the Eisenhower administration decided not to intervene. The Kennedy administration decided not only not to intervene but also to negotiate the neutralization of Laos, which was done by the Geneva Accords of 1962. If Laos is strategically more important than Vietnam, then why would the United States fight for Vietnam but not for Laos?

As for the domino argument, it was conceded by the opponents of escalation that if the Communists controlled all of Vietnam, both Cambodia and Laos might succeed in maintaining a technically neutral status but that they would most probably come under the domination of Vietnam. In 1960, the population of Laos was about 2 million and the population of Cambodia no more than 6, while the population of North and South Vietnam together was about 38 million. But the probability that Laos and Cambodia would come under the domination of Vietnam would make Thailand, Burma, Malaysia, and Indonesia even more determined to deal swiftly and ruthlessly with any foreign-stimulated insurgency. Thus the chance that Laos and Cambodia would fall like dominoes, the opponents of escalation argued, made it sharply less likely that the rest of Southeast Asia would do so as well.

As for President Johnson's argument that if the United States permitted Vietnam to go "down the drain," the fabric of international politics would be ripped apart, a number of his opponents argued exactly the opposite. If anything would rip apart the fabric of international politics, they claimed, it would be for the United States to intervene in Vietnam. None of the other nations of the world, Johnson's opponents argued, could see any strategic, political, or economic importance to Vietnam. If the United States turned the Vietnam conflict into a major war, the rest of the world would think it had gone mad. It is bad enough for your friends to think you mad, but if your enemies do, the world will become a much, much more dangerous place.

Thus, by using the same classical, strategic, and geopolitical mode of analysis, some of the opponents of escalating the struggle in Vietnam reached exactly the opposite conclusion from that of the government: The mistake would lie not in allowing Vietnam to go "down the drain" but in trying to prevent it.

CHINA'S INVITATION TO NIXON

Evidence about policy debates inside China is scarce. However, the charges presented by the Chinese government against Lin Piao, the former defense minister and once Mao's designated successor, and Mao's wife, Jiang Qing, have offered some insight. From this evidence it is clear that some Chinese leaders did in fact reason along the lines of the classical, traditional mode of analysis in deciding to invite President Nixon to visit. They did feel that the tension with the Soviet Union, Japan, and the United States isolated China, and they debated what to do about it. Some argued for the policy that was adopted, that is, easing tensions with the United States. But still others apparently favored easing tensions with the Soviets. Reconstructed, their argument seems to have been along the following lines:

First, the United States was too far away to constitute an immediate threat. It had found the Vietnam struggle a strain and was to some extent pulling back from what were actually its overcommitments in Asia. The United States, furthermore, would be of no help in dealing with the Soviet problem. Even if arms could be obtained from the United States, they would not be the most sophisticated weapons and would be a long time in coming.

Furthermore, the argument continued, normalizing relations with the United States might actually make the Sino-Soviet relationship worse, for the prospect of Chinese-American friendship would alarm the Soviets and might even cause them to step up tensions. Easing tensions with the Soviet Union, on the other hand, would defuse the most serious and immediate threat from a very powerful neighbor with whom the Chinese shared a long border that was difficult to defend.

Easing tensions with the Soviets would also help China in another way. The very act of normalizing relations with the United States would demolish the Chinese appeal to Third World Communist countries that China was more orthodox in its Communism than the Soviet Union. Of course, the argument continued, some concessions would have to be made to the Soviets on the ideological debate, but the Third World Communist countries would understand that such a move was prudent and expedient in the short run and would not impair the Chinese position in the long run. The wise policy, the argument concluded, was to ease tensions not with the Americans but with the Soviets.

THE SOVIET INVASION OF AFGHANISTAN

The Carter administration, using the classical, traditional mode of analysis, offered the following explanation of the Soviet invasion of Afghanistan: First, the Soviets were basically aggressive and expansionist, and the invasion represented still another move to extend their empire. Second, and more ominously, the Soviets' long-run intention was to secure Afghanistan as a base from which to "lunge" at the Middle East and its treasure of oil. The Carter administration announced to the Soviet Union that it considered the invasion a hostile act that threatened détente. It solicited other Western countries to join in a unified response and assured the countries bordering Afghanistan of U.S. protection from further Soviet aggression. It also began to lay the political groundwork for an increase in the defense budget. Carter asked the Senate to delay consideration of the Strategic Arms Limitation Talks (SALT II) treaty already negotiated. He embargoed the export of grain and high-technology goods to the Soviet Union, prohibited Soviet fishing in U.S. waters, put a moratorium on the opening of new U.S. and USSR consular offices, suspended cultural exchanges, and, some time later, announced a boycott of the Olympic games to be held in Moscow.

Using the same strategic and geopolitical mode of analysis, two other analysts—each unaware of what the other was writing—came to conclusions quite different from those of the Carter administration and at least slightly different from each other. Both analysts started from the proposition that ever since World War II, which had brought the Soviet Union such sickening casualties and the dreadful German occupation of so much of their country, the Soviets had worked to establish a belt of friendly states along their borders to serve as a buffer against future aggression. Because of this, the Soviets had long cast avaricious eyes on Afghanistan. So nothing had changed. As a writer for *The New York Times* editorialized, the only astonishing fact about the Soviet invasion was that President Carter was astonished. But even so, the question remained: Why did the Soviets invade Afghanistan at this particular time?

One of the analysts began to answer by saying that since World War II, the Soviets have recognized that they had much to gain from cooperating with the United States and much to fear from confronting it.[1] As a consequence the policy the Soviets have rather consistently followed is one of "low cost and low risk." However, the Soviets had spent the preceding fifteen years in a military buildup, while the United States had actually let its defenses slip until the military balance had changed from one of great American superiority to one of rough equality. Therefore, unlike the Carter administration, this analyst did not interpret the Soviet invasion as an indication that the Soviets were positioning themselves for a "lunge" at the Persian Gulf. On the contrary, he argued, the Soviets had always wanted Afghanistan as a satellite country.

What the Soviets had done, according to this analyst, was to reevaluate what constituted low cost and low risk for obtaining Afghanistan as a satellite. In their previous position of strategic inferiority, the Soviets assessed an invasion as a very-high-risk venture. But in 1979, when the Soviets had achieved a military balance with the United States, an invasion was assessed as a low risk. The desire to make Afghanistan a satellite had always existed; what had changed was the relative risk of doing so.

A second analyst agreed that the Soviets had always looked avariciously toward Afghanistan, and he also did not dispute the facts on the

---

[1]Seweryn Bialer, "A Risk Carefully Taken," *Washington Post,* January 18, 1980, p. A17.

Soviet military buildup.[2] But he did not conclude that the invasion was triggered by a reassessment of low cost and low risk based on the new military balance. His somewhat different analysis rested on the conclusion, shared by the other analyst, that the Soviets had always recognized that they had much to gain from cooperating with the United States and much to fear from confronting it. The implication for the United States was that its policy should be one of carrots and sticks. When the Soviet Union was cooperative, the United States should offer carrots; when the Soviet Union was confrontational, it should threaten with sticks.

This second analyst's explanation of the timing of the Soviet invasion of Afghanistan was based on these carrots and sticks. The United States never did have any sticks to act as a deterrent to such a move. Afghanistan is about as far away from the United States as possible. What is worse, to get there the United States would have to cross at least one other country, Pakistan or Iran. On the other hand, the United States did have carrots it could use, such as trade agreements and arms control negotiations. The Soviets had always wanted Afghanistan as a puppet but had refrained from invading, according to this analyst, because the value of the carrots they would lose seemed greater than the gain. But the Carter administration, whether through intention or bungling incompetency, had thrown away or lost all the carrots. It had failed to make any progress in getting Congress to ratify the SALT II arms control agreement so painfully negotiated in the previous two administrations, was determined to build the controversial MX missile that would give the United States a first-strike capability against the Soviets, and had decided to deploy the Pershing II IRBM missiles to Europe and flatly refused to negotiate this decision with the Soviets. What triggered the invasion, according to this view, was neither a Soviet decision to position itself for a lunge at the Persian Gulf nor a reassessment of low cost and low risk, but the fact that the United States no longer had any carrots.

IRAN AND THE AMERICAN HOSTAGES

One of the answers to the question of why Iran held the American hostages for 444 days yielded by applying the classical, traditional mode of analysis was that the Soviet military buildup over the preceding fifteen years raised questions about the wisdom of an Iranian alliance with the United States, especially since Iran's position bordering the Soviet Union left it so exposed. Expressing hostility toward the United

---

[2]Roger Hilsman, "Mumbles and Fumbles: Carter Abroad," *ADA World*, Vol. 35, no. 2 (Spring 1980).

States by holding the hostages would signal a concrete step toward neutrality. A second answer was that Iran aspired to leadership in the Muslim world, and holding the hostages demonstrated not only its independence of the United States but also that the United States was a "pitiful, helpless giant" when facing the ayatollah. A third was that confronting and defying a superpower by seizing the hostages carried the ideological message that the leaders of the Iranian revolution stood on the side of the downtrodden peoples of the Third World. Finally, a number of observers inside and outside the U.S. government suggested that still another motive for holding the hostages was revenge for U.S. support of the shah.

The same classical, traditional mode of analysis can yield a quite different policy conclusion, however. First, the new Iranian government was threatened not so much by a direct attack from the Soviet Union, which the shah seemed to fear, but from the internal opposition of the Communist Tudeh party, which might attempt a coup or, with Soviet help, start a guerrilla insurgency along the lines of that in Vietnam. A friendly United States could give massive aid to the government, which, combined with the ayatollah's religious and patriotic appeal to the Iranian people, could ensure a different outcome from that in Vietnam, where the leaders in the South lacked any such fundamental popular support. But expressing hostility to the United States by permitting the militants to continue to hold the hostages would make it difficult for the United States to give its support if the Tudeh party decided to move. Second, the ayatollah's regime was also in a precarious economic position. The Soviets might be pleased that Iran was establishing its neutrality, but this alone would probably not be enough to convince them to solve Iran's economic problems. The United States and the West, on the other hand, did have the resources to provide a solution, but if Iran continued to hold the hostages, they would find it politically impossible to offer such help. Finally, the argument concluded, defying a superpower might earn cheers from the Third World, but those cheers would not provide either the butter to solve Iran's economic problems or the guns to solve its security problems.

Thus the classical, traditional mode of analysis can lead to the conclusion that the logical course for Iran would have been not to confront the United States by permitting the militants to hold the American hostages but rather to cultivate U.S. support. The implications of this analysis for U.S. policy were that even if the Iranians persisted in holding the hostages, the United States should not have adopted the punitive measures followed by the Carter administration, such as freezing Iranian assets. Such moves only angered Iran and at the same time put it in a position in which agreeing to release the hostages would mean a loss of prestige. On the contrary, the United States should work behind the scenes to offer carrots such as help with Iranian economic problems, while quietly trying to persuade other Muslim countries to convince Iran that holding the hostages discredited Muslims worldwide.

THE IRAN-CONTRA AFFAIR

The Reagan administration offered two geopolitical and strategic reasons and one humanitarian reason for its actions in the Iran-Contra affair. First, they argued that selling arms to Iran would encourage moderates in the Iranian government and thus would help end the Iran-Iraq war, which in turn would restore stability in the Middle East and block an avenue for the Soviets to increase their political influence, if not their actual military presence, throughout the region. Second, Reagan officials thought that it would be a "neat idea" to use the money generated by selling arms to Iran to provide military aid to help the Contras overthrow the Communist government of Nicaragua, which if allowed to continue would provide both the Soviet Union and Communist Cuba with vital political opportunities in Central America and eventually lead to the establishment of Soviet submarine and missile bases right on the doorstep of the United States. The humanitarian reason was the possibility of freeing the American hostages in the Middle East.

Using the same mode of analysis, critics of the Reagan administration's action in the Iran-Contra affair came to opposite conclusions. First, they argued, there were no "moderates" in the government of Iran. All moderates had long since been eliminated, and the officials that remained were religious zealots. This was the one country in the world, the counterargument continued, where the priests truly ruled. Furthermore, even if there were moderates, selling arms to Iran, when the United States had been pressuring its allies and everyone else *not* to do so, would destroy the world's confidence in the U.S. government, its statements, its policies, and its integrity. As for the humanitarian motive, the counterargument responded that even if the United States did free a few hostages by trading arms to Iran, the Iranians would simply tell their minions to take a few more. Finally, according to the critics, any fool should realize that the fact that the United States was sending arms to Iran would leak, for the simple reason that the Iranians knew about the deal and would broadcast the details whenever it suited their purpose, as it surely would sooner or later.

For the Contra side of the affair, the Sandinistas, the argument asserted, were only superficially Communists; they were nationalists first and Communists second. They were fighting against the long exploitation of the peasants by the oligarchs and would seek help wherever they could find it. If all this was so, the counterargument continued, then the only hope for a solution to the problem of Nicaragua was negotiation, preferably multilateral, spearheaded by the Central American and Latin

American countries themselves. Finally, the critics concluded that even if no solution could be found, the worst that could happen was that Nicaragua would be a minor annoyance, as Castro's Cuba had been, and not a vital threat. The Soviets already had a submarine base in Cuba, the Cuban missile crisis taught them not to put nuclear weapons so near to the United States, and, even if the Soviets forgot that lesson, missile technology had advanced to the point where missile bases in the Soviet Union or on submarines lurking under the arctic and antarctic ice packs were more effective than missile bases in the Americas.

THE GULF WAR AGAINST IRAQ

The reasons for the U.S. decision to go to war with Iraq yielded by applying the classical, traditional mode of analysis were (1) to forestall an invasion of Saudi Arabia; (2) to establish the principle that aggression should not be rewarded by evicting Iraq from Kuwait; (3) to destroy Iraq's military capacity to threaten its neighbors, including its chemical, biological, and potential for building nuclear weapons in the future; (4) to prevent Iraq from controlling so much of the world's supply of oil as to threaten the American "way of life"; and (5) to establish a "new world order," which was understood to mean a strategic balance of power in which the great powers would join the United States in dealing with future threats by countries such as Iraq under Saddam Hussein.

Using the same classical, strategic mode of analysis, a number of critics of the Bush policy came to quite different conclusions. They argued that Bush had three ways of dealing with the problem of Iraq and Saddam Hussein other than using American military force. One of these was available *before* Iraq invaded Kuwait, and two were available *after* the invasion.

The first alternative was to midwife an Arab solution to the four problems facing Hussein that were described in Chapter 1 and so forestall the Iraqi invasion completely.

The problem of the two uninhabited islands could be met by either transferring sovereignty to Iraq or simply by internationalizing them.

The problem of Kuwait pirating oil from the Rumaila field was only slightly more complicated. Only a small tip of the field extends into Kuwait, and with all Kuwait's other oil fields, giving up this tip would not be a great sacrifice. If Kuwait balked at this solution, the problem could be solved by the other Arab states supervising operations at that field on both sides of the border to prevent piracy by either country.

The question of raising the price of oil and sticking to the new level would have required the Arab countries to develop a policing method. This would probably have required nothing more than the rest of the

Arab countries agreeing to isolate Kuwait if it again stepped out of line. If more pressure was required, it could have been supplied by oil-consuming states, such as Germany and Japan, agreeing to boycott Kuwaiti oil unless they adhered to the agreements.

Finally, the Arab states could easily have managed a loan to tide Iraq over the financial crisis resulting from the Iran-Iraq war. If not, the states most dependent on Middle East oil, such as Japan and Germany, could have helped. And if that were not enough, the United States and Great Britain could have been persuaded that a loan would be preferable – and cheaper – than war.

Such arrangements would have met Saddam Hussein's immediate needs. Once those needs were met, he would be unlikely to invade Kuwait and isolate himself from the other Arab states. His greatest ambition has been to be one of the principal leaders of the Arab world, and nothing would so quickly and effectively destroy that possibility as turning his back on a "brotherly" Arab solution.

Once Iraq invaded and annexed Kuwait, the critics conceded, the task became much more difficult. But, they argued, there were alternatives better suited to today's realities than invading Iraq with American troops.

To most observers familiar with the Middle East there was one absolutely fundamental criterion that any action had to meet. This criterion was that given the long history of Western countries oppressing Arabs, if anyone had to kill Arabs, it should be other Arabs.

Keeping this criterion central, the most promising policy open to Bush after Iraq invaded Kuwait, according to the critics, was threefold:

First, Bush could have said that any great power intervention in the Middle East was just as unacceptable as Hussein's annexation of Kuwait. The problem was an Arab problem and would have to be dealt with by Arabs. The United States could give both military and economic aid to the Arab countries opposing Iraq, but it would not send troops.

The rise of nationalism in the Third World, the argument continued, convinced most leaders in the West that the days of Western military intervention in Asia, Africa, Latin America, and the Middle East were over. It took a defeat by Vietnamese peasants "clad in black pajamas" to make Lyndon Johnson understand this elemental fact. One hopes, said the critics, that a similar disaster would not be needed to convince George Bush.

Second, the United States could have said that it should not be the architect of a boycott of Iraq, but that it could and would join such a boycott if the Arab states chose to organize one.

Third and most important, the critics argued, these policy statements should have been coupled with a far-reaching program to make the United States not only *less* dependent on Middle Eastern oil, but totally *independent* of it. Such measures, the critics argued, were necessary in any case, whether or not anything was done about Saddam Hussein.

Once Bush sent the troops to the Middle East, the critics shifted their ground. Recalling that Senator George Aiken of Vermont had once suggested that the way to end the Vietnam war was simply to announce that the United States had won and then withdraw, the critics said that Bush should announce that the American purpose had been to prevent the takeover of Saudi Arabia and that purpose had been successfully achieved. Accordingly, Bush could have continued, the United States would begin a phased withdrawal of its forces, turning the positions over to Arab and Third World states. At the same time, Bush could have promised that the United States would undertake both military and economic aid to support the replacement forces and the countries supplying them. He could have set the timetable for a complete American withdrawal from Saudi Arabia for, say, six months–although U.S. sea forces and sea-based air forces could be maintained for a much longer period.

Again, the economic boycott would continue. In fact, a boycott run by the Arabs would have considerably more credibility than would a boycott sponsored mainly by the United States.

The goal of an economic boycott sponsored by the Arabs would not have been an Iraqi withdrawal from Kuwait "without conditions," as Bush wanted, but an Iraqi withdrawal from Kuwait coupled with a settlement of Iraq's grievances along the lines described.

Suppose, however, that the Arab states were unwilling to take over. If so, the critics argued, Hussein might have waited until the U.S. forces had withdrawn and proceeded to invade and occupy Saudi Arabia and the various sheikdoms. The result, the critics admitted, would not be happy. But, they argued, it would not have been a world-shaking tragedy.

First, the critics argued, it is doubtful that Hussein would have been able to forge his conquests into a single homogeneous nation. Even if he did succeed in doing so, its population would be less than fifty million and its industrial capacity limited. Egypt and the rest of the Arab states would have been thoroughly alarmed and much more likely to take the major responsibility for containing any further Iraqi expansion.

As for Iraq's chemical and biological weapons, the critics argued, there is reason to believe that the other Arab states have enough similar weapons to deter Iraq from using theirs. As for Iraq's potential for developing nuclear weapons, the director of the Defense Nuclear Agency, General Gerald G. Watson, said that if Iraq ever did succeed in building a nuclear device, it "would weigh five tons and have to be carried on a flatbed trailer"–hardly a practical weapon of war.

More importantly, Israel has an estimated stockpile of about two hundred nuclear warheads and the missiles to deliver them, enough to destroy every living thing in Iraq in about 15 minutes—as effective a deterrent as can be imagined.

As for oil, if Iraq occupied Saudi Arabia and the sheikdoms, Hussein would then control 21.5 percent of the present global production of oil. In the short run, the critics admitted, Hussein could have forced a rise in price. But the rise would be limited—the oil would do Hussein no good if he could not sell it. In the short run a rise in the price of oil is limited by the production costs of other producers, such as Canada, Venezuela, and Texas. In the long run what determines the price is the cost of substitutes for oil as a source of energy—gasahol, solar power, hydrogen as a fuel, and so on. It has been estimated with oil at $25 a barrel, Venezuela, Canada, and Texas could supply all the oil that Kuwait, Saudi Arabia, and Iraq supplied before the war. If the price rose only a few dollars higher than $25 a barrel, substitutes would begin to be competitive. And since oil will not last forever, the world will have to come to substitutes sooner or later anyway.

SUMMARY

In these seven case studies, to sum up, analysts using the same classical, strategic mode of analysis can reach quite different conclusions! Thus it seems inescapable that the predictive power of this type of analysis that puts strategic and geopolitical factors central is limited and, as a result, so is its power as a guide to policy.

3

THE CLASSICAL MODEL ANALYZED: A BLACK BOX

Chapter 1 stated that the fundamental question asked by analysts of international affairs is, "Why do states behave the way they do?" The more "scientific" the answers, the better the ability of the analyst to (1) explain the past, (2) forecast the future, and (3) devise policies to influence the future or at least to prepare a country to adapt to what the future will bring.

Since at least the rise of the nation-state, people have answered this question when it is applied to a particular case by using what we have called the classical, or traditional, mode of analysis. This mode of analysis makes power relationships central. It assumes that states seek not only to survive and to defend what they have but also to add to their power. As a result strategic and geopolitical factors dominate such an analysis. Parenthetically it should be said that the expression "mode of analysis" is meant to be synonymous with the words "conceptual model" or simply "theory" as they are used in the physical sciences to indicate a set of hypotheses about how factors interact to produce a result.

Chapter 1 applied the classical, traditional mode of analysis to try to answer the question of why each state did what it did in each of seven case studies. Most of the explanations seemed logical and reasonably persuasive. Chapter 2 then applied exactly the same mode of analysis to the seven cases but reached quite different conclusions. These arguments were not always as persuasive as those presented in Chapter 1, although sometimes they were even more convincing, as, for example, in explaining the U.S. decision to intervene in Vietnam and the Chinese invitation to Nixon. All of the counterarguments were at least respectable.

Now if this can happen—that is, if the mode of analysis or conceptual model that puts power and strategic, geopolitical factors central can lead to quite opposite yet still reasonably persuasive conclusions—then the suspicion arises that something about this approach is seriously flawed. This chapter will attempt to do to the classical, traditional mode of analysis what Albert Einstein did to Isaac Newton—identify the implied assumptions behind Newton's theory. Einstein found that Newton had assumed that time and space were uniform, and when Einstein asked what would happen if time and space were not uniform, he was on his way to new insights about the universe and nature. Accordingly, this chapter will try to identify and lay out more or less systematically the implicit assumptions underlying the strategic, geopolitical mode of analysis—hoping for new insights into why states behave the way they do.

THE PHILOSOPHY OF SCIENCE

First, however, a digression is needed into what is usually called the philosophy of science to examine in more detail the nature and functioning of a conceptual model or theory.

Practical men and women of affairs are frequently contemptuous of "theory" and demand only the "facts." The implied assumption behind this attitude is not only that understanding what is likely to happen is impossible without facts but also that the obstacle to understanding is solely the lack of facts and that once all the facts are known any difficulty in making a prediction will disappear. Thus the assumption is not only that a set of facts contains a self-evident answer (and that every problem does ultimately have an answer) but also that such facts hold only one true answer, which any reasonable person cannot help seeing. In the final analysis it would seem that the facts admit of only one interpretation, that is, that false interpretations are possible only if the facts are incomplete, if the "facts" are not really facts (i.e., false), or if the person who studies the facts is actually irrational. But however much "practical" men and women may despise "theory," they too think in terms of theory, conceptual models, modes of analysis, or whatever other name is used.

The Role of Theory

What is a theory or conceptual model? First, both of these terms have the same meaning, for they both assert that certain aspects of reality supply the conditions necessary for a given result, that other factors supply the causal forces bringing about that result, and that there is a dynamic relationship between the conditions and the causal factors on the one hand and the results on the other. In short, a theory or conceptual model describes an "if/then" relationship connected by a dynamism. If certain conditions exist and certain factors are at work, then certain results will follow. Newton's law of gravitation is such a theory or conceptual model: If two bodies have mass, then they will attract each other directly in proportion to their masses and inversely in proportion to the square of the distance between their centers of gravity. Although this example is from one of the "hard" sciences, the same kind of theories and conceptual models are used in everyday nonscientific life, as typified by the proposition, "If I see a black cloud racing across the sky toward me, then I can expect rain."

To be able to forecast what will happen, one does not need to assemble the facts about all the conditions and factors present but only those that the theory says are decisive in causing the result. To be able to forecast the pull of two bodies on each other, for example, one does not need to know exactly what they are composed of but only their mass. To predict rain one does not need to know whether the cloud is passing over land or water or whether it is night or day.

The statement "A black cloud racing toward me means rain" is a theory. The facts are the existence of the black cloud and its rapid movement; they supply the "if" in the "if/then" proposition. The "then" is the predicted outcome, rain. The "if" and the "then" are connected by a dynamism—the one leads to the other. The black cloud moving rapidly toward me means rain.

The policy indicated by the theory is what is to be done about the situation. In the case of the black cloud a policy to influence the future is beyond our technological means (except for seeding the cloud with iodide crystals to produce rain immediately rather than later). A rational policy suggested by this interpretation is to adapt: to get out an umbrella or to take shelter.

A theory or conceptual model first tells the analyst what facts to look for and then what will happen if certain kinds of facts are found. In our example the theory tells the analyst to look for a racing black cloud and to expect rain if one is seen. A theory or conceptual model permits the analyst to select the facts that set the necessary conditions and have a causal effect from the welter of facts available.

Certainly the number of facts available on most problems is simply overwhelming. On a problem in American relations with France, for instance, an investigator could begin by collecting all the facts in the history of American and French relations, and then consider all the facts about the history of French relations with other countries, the French economy, the amounts and kinds of French goods produced and sold, the people and factories producing each item, the market patterns, the financial system behind the markets, and so on to infinity. Next our investigator could gather facts about French technology, science, literature, geography, and political and social institutions. Still more facts could be piled on about French politicians and public officials and how they think, as well as their backgrounds, dislikes, likes, and predilections. Then our investigator could begin to gather the countless billions of facts about the millions of people who are merely citizens of France.

By this time our problem solver would have more facts than any human mind could possibly grasp, but there would still be no reason to stop. The real difficulty is that any or all of these facts might have some bearing on the problem. Not so long ago, for example, it would have seemed ridiculous to think that humankind would have to study the stars before it could build a superbomb or study thunder and lightning, among other things, to learn that an obviously firm and solid table is actually composed of countless numbers of moving particles.

To solve a problem, either in everyday living or in Franco-American relations, a certain number of facts are obviously needed. But an investigator cannot begin by attempting to collect all the facts, for that person would soon be intellectually buried in a mountainous pile of data, most of which would be either irrelevant or of only marginal significance. A problem solver must thus find some device for selecting those facts that have a direct and causal relationship to the question being asked. The device that rational problem solvers use is the conceptual model, for it establishes what will happen if certain facts are present and thereby indicates which facts to look for.

A Parable About a Dog

Let us use a parable to demonstrate the conceptual model. Suppose that while out driving I miss a turn and end up on an isolated road. However, there is one house on the road, so I decide to go up to it to ask for directions. The yard of this house is fenced, and in the yard is a dog. My problem is whether the dog will bite me if I open the gate. To make a decision, I need some facts. But which of the billions available will be useful?

I reason that if a dog is tied by a rope or chain stout enough to resist its strength, tough enough to resist its teeth, and short enough to prevent it from reaching the path I must follow to get to the door of the house, it will not be able to bite me even if it wants to. I thus look again at the dog, but this time for a specific fact: whether it is tied. I see that the dog is not and now know that all further facts connected with chains and ropes have become irrelevant to this problem. I quit looking for rope and chain facts and also abandon the theory that sent me looking for them.

If I were an expert on dogs, I would know which breeds tend to be friendly and which tend to bite. This knowledge would direct me to facts about the color of the dog's hair, the shape of its body, head, and tail; its height and weight; and so on. These facts constitute the "if" in the "if/then" relationship, with the "then" being the conclusion that this particular set of facts means that the dog is, say, a boxer, which bites, or a golden retriever, which is friendly. It is the "if/then" relationship, or the theory, that gives the facts meaning. But since I am not an expert on dogs, I have no knowledge of the theory. The facts are available, but without the necessary theory I am as helpless as if I lacked the facts.

However, although I am not an authority on dogs, I do have one theory that may help me reach a decision: the "common sense" theory that friendly dogs wag their tails while vicious dogs growl. I may recognize that this is a very crude theory, but crude or not, it is the only conceptual model I have at the moment, and, I reassure myself, it has been at least informally tested by several hundred generations of human beings.

Armed with this concept, I look again for specific facts: tail wagging and growling. To my dismay, I observe that this dog neither wags its tail nor growls. I thus have a theory but no facts, and I am just as helpless as I was before and still cannot decide whether to open the gate.

I have exhausted my stock of knowledge about the behavior of dogs, so I fall back on my original theory, the one that I used in recognizing that I was faced with a problem.

When I first looked into the yard, a simple fact—movement—forced itself on my consciousness. With many alternative sets of theories simultaneously in mind, some concerned with movement caused by animals and others by movement caused by wind or similar phenomena, I began to look for the facts indicated by those theories, working, like a person playing "Twenty Questions," from the general to the specific. Finding certain facts rather than others, I concluded that the movement was animal rather than vegetable or mineral. I then looked for facts indicated by the concept "animal" and decided that what was before me was the animal I call "dog."

But notice that the idea "dog" fits my definition of a theory or conceptual model since it is an "if/then" relationship and contains a dynamism. The concept "dog" contains the notion that such animals bite, and so I was faced with a problem. Here then is another important point: The recognition that one has a problem in the first place also requires a theory or conceptual model.

After going through my entire stock of theories about dogs in a vain effort to solve the problem, I finally return to my original theory: This is a dog. Dogs tend to bite. So I decide to try to find another house, preferably one with no animals in its yard.

In this example, my expectations, assumptions, and theories or conceptual models served as guides not only about what to expect if faced with certain kinds of facts but also about what sorts of facts to look for and where to look for them. Look for tail-wagging facts and growling facts, the theory said, and look for tail-wagging facts at one end of the dog and for growling facts at the other.

Suppose, however, that the problem one faces is new. When the first human met the first dog, what did that first human do? If the first human had known other animals, he or she would have had some ideas about teeth and claws and what happens when they are used. These ideas would have led our first human to start looking for teeth and claws facts. Even if the person recognized that this particular animal was different from those previously encountered and that the ideas might therefore be inappropriate, both the facts and the theory that animals use teeth and claws to hurt other animals would have helped in making the decision about what to do when he or she found teeth and claws.

On the other hand, if this first human had never seen an animal of any kind, the first facts about the dog he or she would have noticed would probably have been those that are obvious to the senses: movement, color, and shape. The course of action this person followed would probably have had very little relation to whether the facts could forecast how the animal would react. The human would have been cautious if he or she had once been hurt by something similar in movement or color or bold if he or she had not been hurt and was delighted with the movement or color. In any event, whether the human based his or her actions on assumptions about other animals or simply reacted to the anomalous facts that pressed upon the person's senses, the dog might have behaved in unexpected ways. It might have started biting, running away, barking, or acting more friendly than other animals had done. This new behavior might have led the human to think about the problem and to wonder, for example, if it was the color or something else that enabled the animal to make the strange sound of barking. In doing so the human might have worked out a new theory or conceptual model to account for these new facts, perhaps by distinguishing between this and other kinds of animals.

How Scientists Work

Scientists presumably work in similar fashion. Their interest in a problem may be roused in one of several ways. It may be stimulated by new and compelling events. A star may suddenly increase its brilliance many times, a new disease may strike, a great economic depression may settle on the world, or a new totalitarianism may rise to plague us all with war and terror. The scientists' interest may be piqued by a puzzling fact, uncovered either in research or by accident, that simply does not fit into prevailing theory. It may also be roused by some concept in an apparently unrelated field that seems to point to a body of facts that had previously been ignored.

After the scientists' interests are awakened, their first step is to formulate a question that is both meaningful and researchable. This necessitates bringing existing knowledge to bear on the problem not only to make sure that the answer is not already available but also to see that the question is pointed in a direction that seems likely to lead to a worthwhile conclusion. Since the mass of possible data on almost any subject is so vast as to demand selection, investigators will be forced to start with some sort of tentative hypothesis. Ideally they should also make their assumptions explicit, although some assumptions, like Newton's theories about the uniformity of time and space, may elude even the greatest of scientists until later investigations and thought permit a fresh approach.

Having formulated their questions and hypotheses and tried to make their assumptions explicit, scientific investigators finally begin to look for facts. They logically try to deduce what facts can be found in what places under what conditions if the hypothesis is correct, and what other facts can be found in what other places under what other conditions if it is not. They then carefully search for facts of both kinds. If they find only those that fit the hypothesis, they assume it to be correct; if they find only facts that do not fit, they assume it to be incorrect. If, as usually happens, they find some of both kinds, their next task again calls for thought. They must either modify the hypothesis to account for the facts or find a new hypothesis. They then once again look for evidence. If they are finally satisfied with their results and reasonably sure that they have covered an adequate range of material, they publish their findings.

This procedure is the ideal. In practice scientists are much like other people; they stumble and bumble around, making hundreds of false starts, and finally begin their work with two or three half-formed and probably conflicting hypotheses that trap them into collecting a lot of useless information that obscures rather than reveals the truth. They struggle with a problem endlessly, think and think until their heads ache, discard a dozen hunches that at first seemed to be nothing less than revelation, and, likely as not, come up with a conclusion that is neither very useful nor very surprising. Only if they are very lucky do they somewhere along the line glimpse an interrelationship that is excitingly new and significant. But nothing in these observations in either the schematically economic ideal or the meandering reality implies that the facts alone contain the answer. If they did, people could have simply immersed themselves in the facts, and human knowledge would have grown much faster than it has. Certainly most of the great discoverers had no more facts available to them than were available to anyone.

Although some facts were hidden until the development of tools such as the microscope, most have been in plain view but went unnoticed until some insightful mind forged the tools of thought that revealed their importance.[1] The facts currently known about human psychology have existed for at least hundreds of years, but no one paid very much attention to them until Sigmund Freud produced the insights, the hypotheses, and the seminal ideas that could be tested and have been partly rejected, partly modified, and partly accepted, achieving closer and closer approximations of a fully reliable intellectual tool at each step. All the readers of *The New York Times* and the *London Times,* to give another example, had in front of them the facts necessary for predicting the economic consequences of the Versailles peace treaty, which ended World War I. Yet only John Maynard Keynes and a few others were able to see the meaning of those facts.

Certainly the role of thought in the creation of new knowledge is vital. If the problem is new, something is necessary beyond prevailing theory and the stock of facts whose relevance is pointed up by that theory. Consider, for example, the development of Einstein's theory of relativity. Numerous experiments have demonstrated that light is a wave motion. Waves need a medium through which to travel, but light travels through outer space, which is a more nearly perfect vacuum than anything that can be produced in the laboratory. But even the rather imperfect vacuum that can be produced in the laboratory demonstrates the phenomenon. Most of us remember the high school experiment in which an electric bell is rigged inside a jar and the air is then pumped out of the jar. When the bell's switch is thrown, the clapper bangs vigorously against the bell but no sound is heard. Light, however, travels through the near vacuum inside the jar without any change at all.

How can this be? A wave motion must have a medium through which to travel, but here light, a wave motion, is traveling through a near vacuum. Scientists therefore hypothesized that space was filled with some kind of substance, which they named ether, through which the waves of light but not the waves of sound could travel.

Then, in 1881 Professors Albert A. Michelson and Edward W. Morley reasoned that the earth's movement would generate a flow of ether. Since ether was a substance that transmitted light's waves, then moving ether would affect the motion of light. Therefore a ray of light projected perpendicularly to the flow of the ether generated by the earth's motion would be slightly retarded. Michelson and Morley designed equipment that split a beam of light into halves, one of which was bounced back and forth between mirrors perpendicular to the path of the earth through space, while the other bounced back and forth in line with it. The amaz-

---

[1]More often than not it was a conceptual tool, such as the idea that minuscule organisms exist, that showed the need for the mechanical one, in this example, the microscope.

ing result was that when the two beams were brought back together they were still perfectly in phase.

Other scientists repeated the experiment many times, but the results were always the same. The conclusion was inescapable: The velocity of light is not affected by the earth's motion, a fact that could not be reconciled with the prevailing theory that light is a wave motion. For twenty-four years scientists all over the world pondered this paradox and sought hypotheses to explain it. Although many of these men and women were highly trained, none found a satisfactory hypothesis until in 1905 Einstein evolved an entirely new theory by altering the Newtonian assumptions of time and space that had been so fundamental that they seemed the essence of common sense and even sanity.

Even though formal training does not seem to guarantee success in developing new theories, one should not assume that it is unimportant. The trained investigator will always have an advantage over the untrained, even the untrained genius. The trained investigator is versed in the accumulated knowledge of humankind and is thus less likely to rediscover known territory or stumble into old traps. The trained investigator is also in a better position to make the most of lucky accidents and to evolve meaningful hypotheses. In science at least, serendipity is the monopoly of the trained.[2] Being familiar with theory, the trained investigator knows not only what is unknown territory but also what needs to be accounted for when altering prevailing theory as well as how to go about doing these things.[3]

---

[2]In 1754 Horace Walpole coined the word *serendipity* after reading a fairy story about the travels of three princes of Serendip (Ceylon, now Sri Lanka) who had a happy faculty for discovering things they were not seeking. Serendipity, according to Walpole's definition, is the gift of finding, by chance or sagacity, unsought valuable or agreeable things. After World War II the word came to be used to describe happy accidents in research and to emphasize the role of the theoretically prepared mind in making the most of such accidents (see Robert K. Merton, *Social Theory and Social Structure* [Glencoe, Ill.: The Free Press, 1949]). For example, when some growing bacteria were killed by a mold that had come into the laboratory through a window left open in carelessness, an untrained mind might have merely thrown out the contaminated culture and started over. But to the trained mind of Sir Alexander Fleming, this accident was highly significant and led eventually to the discovery of penicillin and the whole family of antibiotics. However, the word has unfortunately sometimes been used carelessly to describe the flash of inspiration that leads to a final, significant hypothesis after research has been going on for some time. The danger of this usage is the confusion it would cause if it were understood to mean that in research one could plunge oneself into the data, seize the hypotheses abounding there, and never have to think at all.

[3]Training, of course, is also the main source of objectivity. In their training scientists acquire techniques for recognizing bias; a conviction that they will be "found out" very quickly if they are only a little careless in collecting data, much less if they deliberately ignore bodies of facts; and a set of moral values and a superego. All these are usually effective in preventing at least the grosser forms of bias; the more subtle forms are probably inevitable and disappear only as conceptual tools grow more precise.

However, even though answers seem to come more from the mind of the investigator than from the facts themselves, one should not assume that facts do not convince in some circumstances. If two persons agree on a "theory" but disagree on the evidence, a new fact of the right kind will settle the question. If we both agree that dogs that wag their tails do not bite but disagree about whether a particular dog will bite, the arrival of a fact (we both see the dog in question suddenly wag its tail) will settle the dispute.

Furthermore, if a person's assumptions are explicit, and if he or she recognizes that a certain kind of fact will demonstrate that those assumptions are wrong, then a fact that is obviously of this certain kind will convince the person to alter his or her assumptions. The problem is that since many facts will fit rather neatly into two or more theories, such happy circumstances do not occur as often as one might wish. We have all had the experience of thinking that some new fact will certainly convince an opponent of the error of his or her ways, only to find that our opponent has attached a quite different meaning to the same fact and is dismayed to find that it does not convince us of the error of *our* ways. The point of all this seems to be that although people say that the truth lies in the unvarnished facts, in a sense the opposite seems to be the case, and the meaning is, so to speak, not in the facts themselves but in the varnish. But even though facts do not contain self-evident answers, the whole truth of course is that all the ingredients, facts, theory, training, and brains are equally necessary. Each would be useless without the others, but each has its separate role.

In sum, a theory or conceptual model tells the analyst first, what facts to look for; second, where to look for those facts; and third, what to expect when certain kinds of facts are found. There are, however, other things that one needs to know about theories. The first is that theories are not necessarily true or false. It is a mistake to think that one theory is an accurate description of reality and another is not. Newton thought that light was made up of streams of tiny particles, which he called corpuscles, traveling from the source of the light to the eye. Later, in the early nineteenth century many experiments showed "conclusively" that light was a wave motion. However, the puzzle remained, as mentioned earlier, that a wave motion needs matter through which to travel but light nevertheless travels through a vacuum. Early in the twentieth century, as a result of the work of Max Planck, Einstein, and others, humankind came to understand that light was composed of photons, or little packages of energy. Although it seems logically impossible, light somehow manages to act as if it were both a wave motion and a corpuscular motion at one and the same time.

But here is the point: Even though light is not really a wave motion, the wave motion theory should not be abandoned and in fact is very useful. By using the theory, for example, humankind can make a host of such marvelous machines as eyeglasses, telescopes, and cameras. Newton was superseded by Einstein, but we should be careful not to throw the Newtonian baby out with the Einsteinian bath. It is noteworthy that the equations by which the American spaceships were guided to the moon and back were worked out in the eighteenth century on the basis of Newtonian physics.

Two other points about theories are worth discussing. The first concerns what is necessary for a theory to be generally accepted. The second focuses on the essential differences, if any, between the role of theories in the "hard" sciences, such as physics, and in the "soft" sciences, such as economics and the other social sciences. Both points can be illustrated by considering the problem of predicting eclipses of the sun and moon.

Predicting Eclipses

Of all the many predictions regularly made by humankind, those about eclipses are among the most precise and consistently accurate. Humankind can predict within microseconds when and where not only the *next* eclipse will occur but also all the eclipses that will occur thousands or even millions of years in the future. We can even "predict" backward; that is, we can calculate with complete confidence when eclipses occurred so remotely in the past that no member of *Homo sapiens* existed to observe them.

The accuracy of these predictions is rooted in certain scientific discoveries. About A.D. 150 in Alexandria, Egypt, the Greek astronomer Ptolemy developed a theory of the solar system in which the sun, moon, and planets revolved around the earth. His equations for these orbits were enormously complicated; the planets were supposed to pirouette in loops as they traveled the basic circle around the earth. But what is extraordinary is that as complicated as they were, Ptolemy's equations actually permitted astronomers to predict eclipses rather accurately. It was not until 1543 that Nicolaus Copernicus offered a theory in which the sun was at the center of the solar system and the planets, including the earth, circled it.

In fact, however, the Copernican model was no more accurate than the Ptolemaic. There were two basic reasons for this. First, the planets do not travel in circles, as Copernicus believed, but in ellipses, and this difference introduced almost as great an error into the Copernican calculations as existed in the Ptolemaic equations. Second, the telescope had not been invented in 1543, and the instruments of the time were not precise enough to detect the differences.

What is particularly instructive is that Copernicus's theory came to be generally accepted by scientists before it was known that the planets traveled in ellipses and before the telescope had been invented, that is, before the facts to prove it became available. This occurred because the Ptolemaic theory was messily complicated and the Copernican was elegantly simple, yet the results were about the same. Calculating an eclipse with the Copernican theory was much quicker and easier than with the Ptolemaic theory. There was also an essentially esthetic or perhaps religious reason for its acceptance: Scientists like to believe that nature is fundamentally simple and straightforward. The simple and therefore elegant reason is thus to be preferred over the convoluted. Einstein's theory of relativity, for example, was generally accepted long before any of its propositions could be tested empirically. After all, what could be more elegant than $E = MC^2$?

Theory and the Social Sciences

All these examples have been from the "hard" sciences. In the social sciences, human achievement is considerably less impressive, although a certain amount of rather reliable knowledge of the workings of different aspects of human society has been developed and can be used to change and improve our lot. For example, psychology has something useful to say about human motivations and emotions; sociology can tell us something of the consequences of different social arrangements; economics can predict the results of certain kinds of monetary, trade, or other economic policies with fairly useful accuracy; and political science can make helpful statements about voter behavior.

But even if "science" is defined rather loosely as an "organized body of knowledge," there is some question whether the social sciences are really "scientific." Our knowledge of social psychology may be sufficient to demonstrate the "scientific" validity of the Supreme Court decision on segregating schools by race—that "separate" simply cannot be "equal"—but we obviously have not yet learned how to eliminate racial prejudice itself. We now seem to understand the workings of the economy well enough to avoid a major depression like that of the 1930s, but we certainly have not learned enough to eliminate even a majority of our economic troubles. Are the social sciences therefore sufficiently "scientific" for what we have been saying about theories to apply to them too?

Albert Einstein once identified at least one difference between the "hard" and "soft" sciences. When asked why humankind had done so much better with physics than with politics and the other social sciences, he replied that it was because politics and the other social sciences were so much more difficult than physics! Some of the reasons for this can be found by looking again at our example of predicting eclipses. To be able to do so, we must be armed with two analytical models: first, the Copernican model of the solar system, as modified by Johann Kepler, that puts the sun in the center and recognizes that the planets travel in ellipses rather than circles; and second, Newtonian physics, particularly Newton's law of gravitation, which says that two bodies are attracted to each other directly in proportion to their mass and inversely in proportion to the square of the distance between them. To predict eclipses, one does not need to know anything about either Einsteinian physics, for example, or the kind of nuclear chemistry that explains why the sun is hot.

Now the first thing to notice is that the model for predicting eclipses works only if the system remains closed, that is, only if the solar system remains isolated from any outside force strong enough to alter the internal forces determining the orbits of the earth and moon. If a wandering star intrudes into the system in some future aeon, all bets are off. Second, notice that predicting eclipses requires one to deal with only one operating force—gravity. Making predictions that involve two or more forces is much, much more complicated. Thus one reason that the "soft" sciences are more difficult than physics is that in social affairs closed systems are extremely rare. Intruders are the rule rather than the exception. Another reason is that in social affairs a system in which only one force operates is almost unheard of; the norm is a system in which several forces operate simultaneously.

There are other reasons for the difficulty in acquiring knowledge of social affairs for which the example of eclipses offers no help at all. One is the fact that the act of investigating a social phenomenon can alter it. Economists have discovered to their sorrow that predicting a fall in the stock market can sometimes be a self-fulfilling prophecy. Similarly, the sociologist who interviews student activists may alter their behavior by the nature of the questions he or she asks. The only consolation for social scientists is that physicists have at last reached a similar situation in certain of their inquiries. As pointed out in the Heisenberg principle of uncertainty, the act of determining the position or velocity of an electron will in fact alter its position or velocity.

Of course, the ultimate reason that social affairs are more difficult than physics is what philosophers have called "free will." In social affairs, there are many different and frequently competing actors. While one actor or group of actors attempts to shape events in one direction, another may be working to shape them in the opposite direction. In the language of systems theory, social affairs are not a zero-sum game, and the outcome is thereby less predictable.

In sum, a theory, conceptual model, or mode of analysis is not a description of reality, or not even a version of reality. Instead it describes certain conditions and causal factors of certain aspects of reality and then simplifies them. The conditional and causal factors are then expressed as a dynamism, again simplified, as to how they interact and what the outcome will be. In a sense, a conceptual model is a little machine. When the analyst turns the crank, it produces hypotheses that can then be tested against reality. The hypotheses will tell the analyst what facts to look for, where to look for them, and what to expect if the specified facts are present. If the tests confirm the hypotheses, the analyst can take the action indicated if he or she is acting as an individual; recommend a decision if he or she is a government official; or publish the results if he or she is a researcher. If the facts do not support the hypotheses, the analyst must return to the conceptual model or use a different one to develop alternative hypotheses, remembering that any given model might produce hypotheses that meet the test of reality on one occasion but not on another.

For these reasons a theory, conceptual model, or model of analysis should not be thought of as true or false but rather as useful in certain circumstances and not in certain others. The wave theory of light, for example, should be considered helpful in making eyeglasses and telescopes but not in thinking about the nature of interstellar space. Newtonian physics should be looked upon as useful in calculating the orbits needed to put astronauts on the moon but not in calculating the trajectory of light from distant galaxies. The strategic, geopolitical model of why states act as they do is likewise flawed, although at times the available facts will not permit the use of any other mode of analysis. And, for all its flaws, the strategic, geopolitical model is a better tool for analyzing international politics than flipping a coin. So again the analyst must be careful not to throw the strategic, geopolitical "baby" out with the bath.

THE STRATEGIC MODEL ANALYZED

Now let us do to the strategic, geopolitical model what Einstein did to Newton: Try to identify the assumptions, both explicit and implied, that lie behind the model. First, according to the model, the actors in international affairs are not men and women but states. Second, the model assumes that states have goals. Survival of course is paramount. From survival flows the goal of national security in all its aspects. Thus the industry, raw materials, skilled labor, and all other requirements for building weapons, armies, and navies become national security goals, as do strategic territories or geographical positions. Great Britain in the age of sea power, for example, used national security to justify its acquisition of Gibraltar, Aden, and Singapore, each of which dominated a narrow sea. Russia under both the czars and the Communists sought a warm-water port for similar, essentially strategic reasons. Such political contributions to security as alliances likewise become national security goals.

Power too is a paramount goal. States seek power, the strategic, geopolitical model assumes, partly for reasons of national security and partly for its own sake. In analyzing the causes of World War I, for example, Hans Morgenthau, a foremost analyst who was very closely identified with the realpolitik school, said flatly, "The First World War had its origins exclusively in the fear of a disturbance of the European balance of power." Prestige is an aspect of power. Power brings prestige, and prestige brings power. Even such seemingly irrelevant contributions as winning gold medals in the Olympics are regarded as enhancing power in some subtle way. From these major goals flow a number of subsidiary goals, including economic prosperity, trade and trade routes, and scientific achievement.

Third, the model assumes that states seek relatively few goals that can be arranged in order of priority without too much difficulty. Survival and national security come first. Power is next. Historically states have given up power when seeking it came to threaten their survival. Sweden was once a great power actively pursuing empire; but then its rivals grew much larger, and after decades of disastrous wars Sweden decided to be content with a lesser status and adopted a policy of neutrality. The Netherlands followed the same course but made its decision to accept secondary status without having to endure the cycle of disastrous wars.

Subsidiary goals and concrete manifestations of paramount goals, such as acquiring a Gibraltar, Aden, or Singapore, are balanced against their costs and the possible loss of other subsidiary goals. Whether a Gibraltar, Aden, or Singapore is worth a war, for example, would be the subject of debate.

Fourth, the geopolitical, strategic model assumes that the state examines the alternative means for achieving its goals systematically. The state, or its leaders in the name of the state, outline different ways of accomplishing a particular goal, such as increasing power, and compare the alternatives to determine the most effective.

Finally, the model assumes that the examination of the means for achieving the state's goals is conducted through rational analysis that is both objective and without emotion. This fulfills the three criteria for a rational action set out by Max Weber, the German political economist.[4] For a decision to be rational, objective consideration must first be given to the relative effectiveness of alternative means for achieving a goal. This entails bringing to bear all available, relevant knowledge, both facts and theory. If increasing the state's power by acquiring Singapore is the goal, the alternative means would include war, political maneuvering, and purchase.

---

[4]See Max Weber, *The Theory of Social and Economic Organizations,* trans. A.M. Henderson and Talcott Parsons (New York: Oxford University Press, 1947), pp. 115–118; and idem, *Methodology of the Social Sciences,* trans. E. A. Shils and H. Finch (Glencoe, Ill.: The Free Press, 1949), pp. 52–53.

Second, there must be an objective calculation of the effects of each alternative on subsidiary goals, that is, on values other than those that would be fulfilled by achieving the immediate end. Again, the calculation must consider all available facts and theory. If acquiring Singapore is the goal, the consequences of war, political maneuverings, and purchase for economic prosperity must be estimated as well as the possible effects on less tangible values such as the militarization of the society.

Third, there must be objective consideration of alternative ends. Thus in the light of the costs in terms of other values, a judgment must be made as to whether the original objective is worth the costs or whether some other objective should be sought. This step can be considering whether to seek Aden or Gibraltar, say, as a substitute for Singapore, or to give up the idea of seeking power, as Sweden and the Netherlands did.

The systematic examination of the alternative means for achieving a particular goal rules out those means that are ineffective and arranges the rest in order of effectiveness. The rational examination of the alternative means compares the costs of achieving a particular goal with the cost of substituting other goals or giving up the goal entirely.

In sum, the assumptions underlying the strategic, geopolitical model are as follows. States are the actors. States have goals. These are few in number and can easily be arranged in priority. Alternative means for achieving goals are analyzed both systematically and rationally. A state chooses the alternative that is most economical and effective. If that alternative entails excessive cost, the state modifies the goal, substitutes another goal, or gives up the goal entirely.

The behavior of a state reflects purpose and intention. The action chosen is a calculated solution to a strategic problem. Explanation consists in showing which goal the state was pursuing by a particular action and why that action was a reasonable choice in terms of the state's goals.

In discussing the utility of this mode of analysis, Hans Morgenthau said that the model "provides for rational discipline in action and creates that astounding continuity in foreign policy which makes American, British, or Russian foreign policy appear as an intelligible, rational continuum . . . regardless of the different motives, preferences, and intellectual and moral qualities of successive statesmen." When using the strategic, geopolitical model, the analyst does not need to know anything about the leaders of a state; they will behave the same no matter who they are. The czar of Russia will behave the same as the chairman of the Communist party of the Soviet Union. It does not really matter that one state was a monarchy and the other a communist dictatorship, for both behaved the same. Both sought a warm-water port, both tried to balance the powers of Europe, both tried to build a wall of buffer states between Russia and Europe. The personalities of the different leaders were irrelevant in the view of the strategic, geopolitical model, as were their abilities and ideologies.

Thus strategic analysts speak as often of China, the United States, and the Soviet Union as they do of Mao, Deng, Roosevelt, Kennedy, Reagan, Bush, Stalin, Khrushchev, or Gorbachev. Analysts talk in shorthand: "Moscow thinks this, Washington wants that, and Peking is angry about something else." The actors in international politics are like black boxes. The analyst has no need to know what goes on inside them. Some of the boxes are big, some small. Some have good economic resources to build military power, some poor. Some have good strategic locations, some do not. But these things are all that the analyst needs to know about them.

The black box has goals. It has means for achieving those goals. It examines the alternative means available systematically and rationally, and it picks the one that is most effective and economical. Or, if the cost is excessive, it shifts its goals. Working outside the black box and not knowing what goes on inside it, the analyst can deduce from its actions on the world scene the nature of its motives and intentions, and what it will do in the future. Thus the analyst can also design policies for his or her own state to counter the moves of the other state or to adjust and adapt to them. All black boxes are the same in terms of motives, goals, and actions. The only differences are in how big the black boxes are, how strong they are, and where they are located in a strategic sense.

4

PINK, PURPLE, BROWN, AND BLUE BOXES

In the strategic, geopolitical model, states are the actors. States have goals that are few in number and can easily be arranged in priority. States analyze the alternative means for achieving a goal both systematically and rationally and choose the most effective and economical alternative. If the available alternative entails excessive cost, states modify the goal, substitute another, or give it up entirely. The behavior of a state reflects its purpose and intention. The action chosen is a calculated solution to a strategic problem. Explanation consists in showing what goal the state was pursuing by a certain action and why that action was a reasonable choice in terms of the goal sought.

States may be thought of as black boxes. Analysts do not need to know what goes on inside them. Working outside the black box and not knowing what goes on inside it, analysts can deduce from its actions on the world scene the nature of its motives and intentions and what it will do in the future. Thus analysts can also design policies for their own state to counter the moves of another state or to adjust and adapt to them. All black boxes are the same in terms of motives, goals, and actions. The only differences are in their size, strength, and strategic location.

Quite obviously the strategic, geopolitical, "black box" model is not "true" because it is not really a description of reality. The temptation is strong, of course, to think of a nation as an entity and to assume that it has its own goals and that it chooses one course of action over another. But however difficult the animistic structure of our language may make it to avoid personification, a nation is not a living organism; it has neither a nervous system nor a personality. Although people who were reared in the same culture exhibit regularities in their behavior, the existence of these regularities offers no support for an approach that treats states as beings capable of making a decision or taking action. Neither does it support a belief that a group of people has goals of its own or a mind of its own above and beyond the individual goals and minds of its leaders and members.[1] Concepts that treat states as if they had these capabilities are not "scientific" theories but mere analogies. In foreign affairs, as in all human action, individual or group, a choice must be made among different courses of action, and this choice can be made only by individual human beings and not by nations or institutions. At all levels of international events and in each state of development, men and women are making choices. Power, geography, resources, and population all present both obstacles and opportunities and may limit the choices available as well. But it is the choices themselves that make up the body of international affairs.

But even though the black box model is not "true," it is frequently useful as an analytical tool. The men and women who do in fact make the decisions in the name of the state often pursue state goals. Explanations and forecasts made using the black box model are thus at least acceptably accurate fairly often. What is particularly important is that the information required by this model is likely to be available, whereas the information required by some other conceptual models is not.

REFINEMENTS OF THE BLACK BOX MODEL

Because of its usefulness, a number of scholars have worked to improve the black box model rather than look for an entirely different one. Some of this work has focused on the international system and how states interact within that system.[2] In a bipolar system, for example, the two dominating states would behave differently from the lesser states, and all would behave differently from states in a multipolar system.

Ideology, Culture, and National Character

Still other scholars have explored whether differences in ideology result in differences in state behavior. Do fascist states, Communist states, and

---

[1]On the group mind fallacy, see Floyd Henry Allport, *Social Psychology* (New York: Houghton Mifflin, 1924), pp. 4–10.

[2]See, for example, Morton A. Kaplan, *System and Process in International Politics* (New York: John Wiley, 1967); Richard Rosecrance, *Action and Reaction in World Politics: International Systems in Perspective* (Boston: Little, Brown, 1963); Stanley Hoffmann, *The State of War: Essays on the Theory and Practice of International Politics* (New York: Praeger, 1965); and Kenneth N. Waltz, *Theory of International Politics* (Reading, Mass.: Addison-Wesley, 1979).

democratic states behave in ways that differ importantly?[3] Others have pursued a variation of the ideological approach, asking whether differences in culture result in differences in state behavior. Does France act differently from other democratic states, such as Great Britain and the United States, because of differences among the French, English, and American cultures? Another version of this culture question is the notion of national character. Do differences in culture and life-style reflect themselves in personality? Is it possible to say that there is an American personality type, and does this affect the policies adopted by the U.S. government?[4]

Still another approach is to ask whether the leaders and citizens of a state are so emotionally affected by its historical experience as to influence the way the state itself behaves. It has been argued, for example, that the humiliating defeat that France suffered in 1940 at the hands of Nazi Germany caused an emotional reaction among its leaders and citizens that led to state decisions after the war that tried to compensate by clinging to France's empire in Indo-China and Algeria, when most of the other Western colonial powers were giving up their possessions with much less struggle. Similarly, analysts talk about the "Munich psychology" and suggest that after the bitter failure of the policy of appeasing Hitler at Munich, the Allies were emotionally blocked from considering concessions in negotiations, even when it was logical and reasonable to do so.

Elements of National Strength

Another approach to enhancing the usefulness of the strategic, geopolitical model has been to focus on the factors that determine national strength, such as population, industrial base, and raw materials.[5] In the case of strategic, geographical position, this work sometimes assumed a deterministic form. Alfred Mahan concluded that a state having an island position dominating the approaches to a continent, which was the case of both Great Britain and Japan, would lead the state to develop sea

---

[3]See, for example, Seweryn Bialer, *Stalin's Successor: Leadership, Stability, and Change in the Soviet Union* (New York: Cambridge University Press, 1980); Cyril E. Black, ed., *The Transformation of Russian Society: Aspects of Social Change Since 1861*, Joint Committee on Slavic Studies (Cambridge, Mass.: Harvard University Press, 1967); and Marshal D. Shulman, *Beyond the Cold War* (New Haven, Conn.: Yale University Press, 1966).

[4]Gabriel A. Almond, *The American People and Foreign Policy* (New York: Praeger, 1960).

[5]Harold Sprout and Margaret Sprout, *Foundations of International Politics* (Princeton, N.J.: Van Nostrand, 1966); and idem, eds., *Foundations of National Power: Readings on World Politics and American Security* (Princeton, N.J.: Princeton University Press, 1945).

power and give it such great strategic advantage that it would inevitably become a great power.[6] Later Halford J. Mackinder, noting the rise of the railroad, argued that the balance had shifted to land power.[7] He coined the aphorism, "He who commands the heartland of Eurasia, will dominate Eurasia; he who commands Eurasia will dominate the world." Still later, Nicholas J. Spykman, discussing the development of air power, argued that the strategic position had shifted once again to the "rimlands," the lands along the rim of Eurasia, from which air power could dominate both the heartland and the sea.[8]

Improving the Rationality of Policy Decisions

Other analysts have used game theory and other tools to improve the rationality and logic of policy moves. Thomas C. Schelling, for example, did some landmark work on bargaining.[9] Other work by Schelling stemmed from Secretary of State John Foster Dulles's "brinkmanship" policy, the device of moving quickly to the "brink" of war as a negotiating ploy that would force the other side to choose between making the concessions demanded or actual war. For insights into the logic of brinkmanship, Schelling looked at the teenage game of "chicken," in which two cars are driven straight toward a head-on collision or a cliff to see which driver will turn off or jump out of the car first.

Another example of efforts to improve the logic of policy grew out of the policy of unconditional surrender that the Allies adopted toward Germany and Japan in World War II. A number of scholars thought that such a stand would prolong the war and that a willingness to negotiate the conditions for surrender would give the Germans and Japanese an incentive to end the conflict sooner. This belief led to studies of the kind of policies that would make it easier to end war in the nuclear age.[10] For example, it might be wise to avoid striking at the enemy's command,

---

[6]Alfred Mahan, *The Influence of Sea Power upon History: 1660*–1783 (Boston: Little, Brown, 1890).

[7]Halford J. Mackinder, "The Geographical Pivot of History," (London: Royal Geographical Society, 1904).

[8]Nicholas J. Spykman, *America's Strategy in World Politics: The United States and the Balance of Power* (New York: Harcourt, Brace, 1942).

[9]Thomas C. Schelling, *The Strategy of Conflict* (Cambridge, Mass.: Harvard University Press, 1960); and idem, *Arms and Influence* (New Haven, Conn.: Yale University Press, 1966).

[10]Paul Kecskemeti, *Strategic Surrender, The Politics of Victory and Defeat* (Stanford, Calif.: Stanford University Press, 1958); Stephan Cimbala and Keith Dunn, *Conflict Termination and Military Strategy* (Boulder, Colo.: Westview, 1987); and Herman Kahn, "Issues on Thermonuclear War Termination," *The Annals of the American Academy of Political and Social Sciences* (November 1970).

control, and communications system so that the enemy commanders would have the means to order their subordinates to cease firing.

Deterrence theory. A particularly instructive example of how analysts have gone about trying to improve the logic within the strategic, geo-political model is the dilemma of deterrence in a nuclear age. Given the destructiveness of nuclear weapons and the speed and accuracy of ballistic missiles, defense is simply impossible. Therefore the only way to avoid war is through deterrence or arms control or a combination of the two. Strategists quickly came to understand that this situation poses a most peculiar problem, which has been most vividly stated by a fable concocted by Professor Warner R. Schilling of Columbia University. Visualize a sort of fortresslike squash court with ceilings 14 feet high and divided down the middle by a heavy concrete wall 10 feet high. On one side of the wall is a totally evil person armed with a single hand grenade. With him are ten innocent babies. On the other side is a man who is totally good. He also has a grenade, and with him are another ten innocent babes. If either one throws his grenade, the other will have just enough strength before dying to pull the pin and throw his.

Both the good guy and the bad guy will soon realize that their strategic situation is highly unstable. If the bad guy throws his grenade, the good guy and his ten babies will die. All that will be accomplished by the good guy retaliating is the death of the bad guy at the cost of the lives of ten more innocents. Deterrence having failed, the only motive for retaliating is revenge, which is not a moral motive; a truly good person would not retaliate. In strategic parlance this is known as the problem of credibility. How do you make the other side believe that you will launch a second strike no matter what?

What can the good guy do? The only effective strategy is to build a "doomsday machine." In this case it would be a catapult, held down by a string. If the bad guy tosses his grenade, it will sever the string and automatically launch the good guy's grenade. The good guy can now say to the bad guy, "I no longer have any control. Moral or not, retaliation will be automatic." Deterrence is once again established, and the strategic situation stabilized.

With gallows humor, analysts at the RAND Corporation, the think tank for strategy in Santa Monica, California, conceived a way of making a real-world doomsday machine in the days before missiles, when the manned bomber was king. They proposed making General Curtis L. LeMay the lifetime commander of the Strategic Air Command. LeMay was a hard-line Air Force general who had wanted to bomb North Vietnam "back to the Stone Age." No one in the world would doubt that he would retaliate, even if he had to fly the last surviving B-52 bomber himself.

For the second half of the problem—that a second strike was pointless if deterrence failed—the RAND analysts suggested a second lifetime appointment. This person would be LeMay's deputy, and he would have secret orders that if in spite of everything deterrence failed, he was to shoot LeMay! By using these Byzantine illustrations analysts have been able to state the essential nature of strategic problems in stark and dramatic terms and thus pave the way for improving the logic entailed in using the strategic, geopolitical model.

SUMMARY

In sum, recognizing that the strategic, geopolitical, black box model is useful, a number of scholars have worked to improve its utility. Some study the international political system and ask how states interact within that system. Others ask if ideology affects state behavior: Do fascist, communist, and democratic states behave differently as a result of their different ideological commitments? A variation of this approach is to ask if cultural differences alter state behavior: Do Asian states behave differently from European states? Some psychologists, for example, maintain that the Western guilt complex is not found in Asia, where the psychological function of the complex is served instead by a "shame complex" that is triggered by discovery. If this is so, would this culturalpsychological difference cause differences in the behavior of Western and Asian states?

Still another approach asks if there is such a thing as national character, and, if so, how it affects state behavior. Other scholars investigate whether a state's historical experience emotionally affects its leaders and citizens in a way that alters the subsequent behavior of the state. Some study the factors that determine national strength, such as population, industrial plant, and raw material supply, on the assumption that well-endowed states would behave differently from those less well endowed. A variation of this approach focuses on strategic geographical position and occasionally results in deterministic theories. Finally, other scholars try to refine the logic of policy moves, studying the process of bargaining and working out the moves in various political strategies such as "brinkmanship."

The starting point for all of these approaches is the strategic, geopolitical, black box conceptual model. The assumption has continued to be that states are the actors in international affairs, that states have goals that are few in number and can easily be arranged in order of priority, that alternative means for achieving goals are analyzed both systematically and rationally, that a state chooses the most effective and economical alternative for achieving a goal, and that if the alternative available entails excessive cost, the state modifies the goal, substitutes another, or gives it up entirely. Other assumptions also remain, including that the behavior of a state reflects its purpose and intention, that the state action chosen is a calculated solution to a strategic problem, and that explanation consists in showing what goal the state was pursuing by a certain action and why that action was a reasonable choice in terms of the goal sought.

States, in other words, continue to be boxes in the sense that the analyst does not need to know what goes on inside them. The differences, however, are not just in their size, strength, and strategic position but also in their motives, goals, and actions. Fascist, communist, and democratic boxes have different motives and behave differently, as do Asian and European boxes. The boxes, in other words, are not all black. Some are pink, some are purple, some are brown, and some are blue.

5

OPENING UP THE BOXES

In both the strategic, geopolitical, black box conceptual model and its refinements that produce pink, purple, brown, and blue boxes, the analyst does not need to know what goes on inside the boxes. Working outside the boxes, analysts can deduce the nature of their intentions from how they act on the world scene and so design policies for their own state to counter the moves of the others or to adjust and adapt to them. Some scholars, however, have been unhappy with both of these conceptual models and have opened up the boxes to see if a better explanation of state behavior can be developed by studying what goes on inside.

When an analyst opens the U.S. box, he or she finds an executive headed by a president, a legislature, and a judiciary whose power and authority is specified by the Constitution. The president is elected directly by the people for a four-year term and cannot be removed from office except by impeachment for "high crimes or misdemeanors." In certain domestic matters Congress or the judiciary has greater power than the president. Congress, for example, has greater power in both constitutional and practical political terms in both taxation and spending than does the president, and the courts have greater power in many aspects of liberties and rights than do either the president or Congress. But in foreign policy the president's power is not approached by either Congress or the courts.

When an analyst opens up the British box, however, he or she finds a constitutional monarch, a prime minister, a cabinet, and a Parliament with the rules of the game laid down not by a written constitution but an unwritten code of custom and tradition. The members of Parliament are elected by the people in the district they represent. The prime minister, however, is elected not by the people but by the members of Parliament.

The prime minister then appoints the members of the cabinet from among members of his or her party who are also members of Parliament. But the prime minister is far from free in making appointments even from among this limited group. If the prime minister wishes to remain in the position, he or she must take care to see that the cabinet members represent the different factions in his or her party, or the parliamentary party will remove the prime minister and get one who does.

In the British parliamentary system, the cabinet is extremely powerful. The American cabinet is composed of the heads of the major departments, who have power as individuals, but as a collective body the cabinet is almost powerless. President Lincoln once polled his cabinet and found every member voting against a proposal but himself. "The ayes," Lincoln announced with a twinkle, "have it."

In Britain the cabinet members are also heads of major departments, but there the similarity ends. Unlike their American counterparts, they are also members of Parliament and, more importantly, are usually leaders of factions of their party. British constitutional tradition provides that major government decisions are taken by the cabinet as a collegiate body. Its members actually vote on questions of policy, and the cabinet is collectively responsible. The prime minister is sufficiently powerful to ensure that he or she is rarely outvoted. But the practical political consequences of these two differences mean that if the prime minister is outvoted on a serious issue in the cabinet, he or she can be replaced by a caucus of the party's members of Parliament, or the cabinet members can bring about a vote of no confidence in Parliament and thus automatically a general election. As a result the prime minister is more powerful on domestic issues than an American president but not nearly as powerful on issues of foreign affairs.

Thus analysts who look inside the boxes find differences in the actual legal and constitutional workings of governments that result in differences in the way the states behave. The product of their efforts is called a "constitutional law" or "internal workings" conceptual model of state behavior.

THE ORGANIZATIONAL PROCESS MODEL

A variation of the internal workings model that focuses on organizations and their behavior is known as the "organizational process" model. The aphorism adopted by analysts using this approach is, "Where you stand (on policy issues) depends on where you sit (that is, where you are organizationally situated)."

The basic assumption of this model is that governments are made up of large organizations. The major leaders do sit formally on top of these organizations, but the information they receive is processed by organizations, the policy alternatives from which they choose are analyzed by organizations, and their decisions are carried out by organizations. Government behavior can thus be understood less as deliberate choices than as the outputs of organizations. The responsibility for different policy areas is divided among organizations. For example, the State Department is responsible for political matters, and the Defense Department for military matters. The work of these organizations requires that the efforts of a large number of people be coordinated, which is accomplished by standard operating procedures (SOPs).

The major points of the organizational process model may be outlined as follows.[1] First, the events of international politics are the outputs of organizations. Second, the actors in international affairs are not nation-states but rather "a constellation of loosely allied organizations on top of which government leaders sit." Third, both problem areas and the responsibility for particular problem areas are divided among the different organizations concerned; for example, the State Department is responsible for diplomacy and thus has more power over diplomatic policy than the other organizations of government, while the Defense Department is responsible for military problems and thus has more power over military policy. Fourth, because the different organizations are responsible for narrow subject areas, their attitudes tend to become parochial. The preeminent characteristic of organizational outputs is their programed character, which results from the need to deal with problems according to SOPs. Fifth, the need for organizations to decentralize if they are to do their work is in constant tension with the need for central control to achieve coordination. Sixth, although intervention by top officials is successful less frequently than might be expected, these leaders do have techniques for changing government policy without having to fight the major battle that would be required to change an organization's SOPs. For example, officials might be able to give responsibility for a new policy to a different organization or to create a new organization to deal with it.

An important criticism of the organizational process model is that the examples given to illustrate how organizations affect decisions as organizations have not been of the same order as the examples given for the other models. Thus the examples used to demonstrate the black box model have been such major policy decisions as the Cuban missile crisis, the American escalation of the Vietnam war, and the Soviet invasion of Afghanistan. On the other hand, the three most familiar examples of the organizational process model are the Soviet production of MRBMs and

---

[1]What follows is drawn from Graham T. Allison, *Essence of Decision: Explaining the Cuban Missile Crisis* (Boston: Little, Brown, 1971).

IRBMs far in excess of any possible use, the failure of the Soviets to camouflage their missile sites in Cuba, and the decision of the U.S. Air Force to begin bombing Vietnam at the twentieth parallel rather than creeping up on it as President Johnson had intended.

According to the organizational process model, the Soviet massive overproduction of missiles is explained by the fact that in the Soviet Union control of missiles was given to the artillery rather than to the Air Force, as in the United States. Air forces are accustomed to providing a finite number of planes with which to fight a war, while the artillery is accustomed to maintaining a production capacity of so many millions of rounds of ammunition per month of fighting, rather than a finite number for an entire war. The Soviet failure to camouflage the missile sites is explained by the fact that the construction battalions were following the SOP for constructing sites in the Soviet Union and did not consider that the different situation in Cuba demanded camouflage. The American decision to begin bombing at the twentieth parallel is explained with the argument that the Air Force wanted to prove that air power was decisive by making a maximum effort at the outset.

These examples all show how organizations changed policies or skewed them to another direction rather than how policies are made from the beginning. The criticism is that the organizational process model therefore does not really qualify as a model, although the notion of organizational SOP does offer insights that make it a useful corollary to the other models. For example, the way that a particular army is organized, trained, and equipped will make it appropriate for certain kinds of fighting and not for others. Hence an army presents the leaders of a state with a limited set of policy options. At the time of Vietnam the American army was organized, trained, and equipped to fight the Soviets on the North German plain, which was then the major strategic threat. It was not prepared to fight a guerrilla war in the jungles of Asia. It was Army Chief of Staff General Matthew B. Ridgway's great achievement at the time of Dienbienphu in 1954 not only to understand this but also to have the political knowledge and skill to keep the United States out of the war, contrary to the opinion of top civilian leaders. Analysts, it seems obvious, should keep these limitations of organizations constantly in mind, but it would be a mistake to elevate such insights to the status of a model.

LESSER VARIATIONS

There are numerous lesser variations of the internal workings model. One example seen occasionally in the press, which might be called the "Svengali" theory, holds that the president is the puppet of the bureaucrats of the State Department and the Pentagon, who really determine foreign and defense policy in their own parochial interests. Another variation is the "power elite" theory. A number of political analysts have argued that the United States is ruled by a power elite.[2] The term "power elite" implies first that members of a particular social stratum monopolize the principal power positions in the major institutions of the society. In feudal Europe the aristocracy was a power elite, as were the Prussian Junkers. In nineteenth-century Great Britain the upper middle classes and titled aristocrats together formed a power elite. These were the people who attended such schools as Eton and Harrow, then went on to Oxford and Cambridge, and eventually rose to occupy the top positions in government, the armed services, the church, and the other major institutions of society. Second, the phrase implies that the members of this top social stratum coordinate their activities and policies. Third, it assumes that the purpose of their coordination is to govern society in such a way as to benefit themselves and the other members of the elite at the expense of everyone else. Finally, the term implies that the elite is self-perpetuating, that is, that it passes power on to its own children. Although a few analysts who are concerned with domestic issues, particularly social justice, continue to debate whether the United States is run by a power elite, the theory has not enjoyed much popularity among analysts concentrating on the behavior of states on the international scene.

THE POLICY-MAKING PROCESS

To summarize the argument so far, the strategic, geopolitical, black box model continues to be useful, especially when the information available to an analyst is limited. The refinements that have turned the black box

---

[2]C. Wright Mills, *The Power Elite* (New York: Oxford University Press, 1956), sparked the contemporary interest in this theory. Among those associated with earlier versions are Gaetano Mosca, *The Ruling Class* (New York: McGraw-Hill, 1939), originally published in 1896; Vilfredo Pareto, *Sociological Writings,* ed. S. E. Finer (London: Pall Mall, 1966), originally published in 1902; and Robert Michels, *Political Parties: A Sociological Study of the Oligarchical Tendencies of Modern Democracy* (New York: Collier, 1962), originally published in 1911. Others who have argued along the same lines as Mills include G. William Domhoff, Floyd Hunter, Gabriel Kolko, and Thomas R. Dye and L. Harmon Ziegler. See also Kenneth Prewitt and Alan Stone, *The Ruling Elites, Elite Theory, Power, and American Democracy* (New York: Harper & Row, 1973). Other relevant works are those of Henry S. Kariel, T. B. Bottomore, and Peter Bachrach. For rebuttals, see the works of Geraint Parry, Arnold M. Rose, and Nelson W. Polsby and especially Robert A. Dahl, "A Critique of the Ruling Elite Model," *American Political Science Review* (June 1958); pp. 463–469. See also Ian Shapiro and Grant Recher, eds., *Power, Inequality and Democratic Politics: Essays in Honor of Robert A. Dahl* (Boulder, Colo.: Westview, 1988).

into pink, purple, brown, and blue boxes have created more useful tools for analyzing state behavior. Scholars who have opened the boxes and studied the internal workings of different governments have refined the tools of analysis even further. But others who have opened the boxes have developed still another model based on the theory that government decisions are made in a process that is essentially political.

The interest of the analysts who have developed this "political process" model was aroused by a number of "puzzlements" and inconsistencies. Consider the following. Vice President Charles G. Dawes, who served under President Calvin Coolidge, once remarked that the "members of the Cabinet are a president's natural enemies." Yet how can this be, when the members of the cabinet are appointed by the president, with the advice and consent of the Senate, and "serve at the president's pleasure"? President Harry S Truman, as he contemplated turning over the office to General Dwight D. Eisenhower in 1952, said, "He'll sit here and he'll say, 'Do this! Do that!' *And nothing will happen.* Poor Ike – it won't be a bit like the Army."[3]

John F. Kennedy discovered similar puzzlements. In the midst of the Cuban missile crisis of 1962, much to Kennedy's disgust, the Soviet Union said it had decided to put its missiles in Cuba because the United States during the Eisenhower administration had deployed medium-range Jupiter missiles in Turkey. The Soviet statement was probably made more for propaganda reasons than out of true concern, since the Eisenhower administration's decision had been made in response to the Soviet deployment of missiles aimed at Western Europe and since by 1962 the Jupiters were obsolete and virtually useless. Kennedy was annoyed, however, because he distinctly remembered directing the State Department to reach an agreement with Turkey to remove those missiles in 1961. He also remembered telling Secretary of State Dean Rusk to raise the issue with the Turks at a NATO meeting early in 1962, and that he and the National Security Council had issued the most formal kind of order, a National Security Action Memorandum, directing the removal of the missiles, and he had personally ordered the State Department to carry it out. But the missiles were still there! As the president's brother Robert later wrote, "The President believed he was President and that, his wishes having been made clear, they would be followed and the missiles removed. He therefore had dismissed the matter from his mind.

---

[3]Richard E. Neustadt, *Presidential Power: The Politics of Leadership* (New York: John Wiley, 1960), p. 9, emphasis in original. (As a matter of interest, a family disagreement over whether Truman's middle name was Shippe or Solomon, the names of his two grandfathers, led him to use only the initial S – usually without a period following it. But sometimes, as in his memoirs, he used the period.)

Now he learned that the failure to follow up on this matter had permitted the same obsolete Turkish missiles to become hostages to the Soviet Union."[4]

Another such puzzlement occurred in the administration of Lyndon B. Johnson. Johnson had long felt that efficiency would be better served if the departments of Labor and Commerce were merged into one. He also thought this move would have maximum effect if it could be kept secret until he dramatically revealed it in his State of the Union message. Only minutes before the speech quick telephone calls to the secretaries of labor and commerce obtained their agreement. The president did get his surprise headline, but he never got his merger. Union leaders set their heels against losing what they regarded as labor's own representative, for which they had fought hard and long. Business leaders set their heels just as emphatically, fearing that their interests would be submerged in an agency dominated by those they saw as their opponents.[5] The president is powerful, and Johnson was a president who knew how to use his power. But he was not powerful enough to go against the combined strength of labor and business.

President Richard M. Nixon received a similar rebuff, not from powerful interest groups but from one of his supposed subordinates. He directed J. Edgar Hoover, head of the FBI, to put the agency to work on certain surreptitious operations, but Hoover flatly refused the president's order. The irony is that Hoover's refusal contributed to Nixon's eventual downfall. To get the job done that Hoover had refused to do, Nixon set up a special unit in the White House, the so-called plumbers (because their job was to stop "leaks" of information to the press). This was the group who were later linked to the burglary of the Democratic National Headquarters in the Watergate Building, which was the ultimate cause of Nixon's resignation under threat of impeachment.

When Jimmy Carter had been president for six months, he announced his decision to cancel the plans for the B-1 bomber, and so fulfilled one of his campaign promises. But to many members of Congress, a very large number of Air Force generals, powerful interest groups in the aircraft industry, and many other people and organizations, Carter's decision was only a signal to fight harder to get the B-1 into production. Almost immediately after Reagan was elected, in fact, the Air Force proposed a new and improved version of the bomber, and before the end of the first year of his administration, Reagan approved that

---

[4]Robert F. Kennedy, *Thirteen Days: A Memoir of the Cuban Missile Crisis* (New York: W. W. Norton, 1969), p. 73.

[5]George E. Reedy, *The Twilight of the Presidency* (New York: World Publishing, 1970), p. 13.

proposal. This and similar puzzlements have led one authority on the presidency to note, "Underneath our images of Presidents-in-boots, astride decisions, are the half-observed realities of Presidents-in-sneakers, stirrups in hand, trying to induce particular department heads, or congressmen, or senators to climb aboard."[6]

The Policy-Making Ideal

The preceding series of anecdotes suggests that our image of the process by which the government makes decisions may not represent the way it really happens. Americans have a flair for the mechanical and a love of efficiency that are combined with a Puritan heritage. Consequently, we like to think that the decisions of government are the conscious and deliberate result of analyzing problems and carefully studying alternatives. We also like to think that government decisions are aimed at achieving great ends that will serve a high moral purpose. Puzzlements such as those described are disquieting, for they seem to suggest that there is confusion about the goals and that some of the goals themselves might be mutually incompatible.

As Americans, we think it only reasonable that the procedures for making national decisions should be orderly and that there should be clear lines of responsibility and authority. We assume that what we call the "decisions" of government are in fact decisions, that is, self-contained acts with recognizable beginnings and sharp, decisive endings. We like to think of policy as rationalized, in the economist's sense of the word, with each step leading logically and economically to the next. We want it to be clear who makes the decisions and to be assured that they are the proper, official, and authorized persons. We also want to know that the truly important decisions will be made at the top, by presidents and their principal advisers in the formal assemblage of the cabinet or the National Security Council and with the Congress exercising its full and formal powers. We feel that the entire decision-making process ought to be a dignified, even majestic progression and that all participants should have their roles and powers so well and precisely defined that they can be held accountable for their actions by their superiors and eventually by the electorate.

The Realities of Policy Making

The reality of policy making is quite different. Few if any government decisions are either decisive or final. For example, during the Johnson, Nixon, Ford, and Carter administrations, Congress passed and the var-

---

[6]Richard E. Neustadt, "White House and Whitehall," *The Public Interest*, Vol. 2 (Winter 1966).

ious presidents signed a number of laws designed to clean up pollution by restricting the kinds of fuel that industry can burn. Industry objected that these regulations hurt business, and the Reagan administration loosened many of the regulations. Carter canceled the B-1 bomber program, as mentioned, and then Reagan restored it. Similarly, Carter approved an MX missile-basing plan that involved using railroads to shuttle two hundred missiles among forty-six hundred launching pads in Western states as a way of fooling the Soviet Union, and Reagan reversed the decision. Public policy, in a word, is rarely final but almost always continuously unfolding.

Policy is often the sum of a congeries of only vaguely related or even entirely separate actions. Sometimes momentous policies seem to be the result not of conscious decision but of bureaucratic momentum. At the outbreak of World War I, the former German chancellor Prince Bernhard von Bülow is supposed to have said to his successor, "How did it all happen?" The reply was, "Ah, if we only knew!"[7] Even as awesome a decision as the one to drop atomic bombs on Hiroshima and Nagasaki was apparently not really a "decision" but the result of this kind of "bureaucratic momentum." (See *Case Study: Dropping the Atomic Bomb in World War II—A "Decision" by Bureaucratic Momentum,* pp. 73–75.) At times a decision is an uneasy, internally inconsistent compromise among competing goals or an incompatible mixture of alternative means for achieving a single goal. Decisions are not based on the systematic and comprehensive study of all the implications of all the alternatives, nor can they be. A government does not decide to inaugurate the nuclear age but only to try to build an atomic bomb before its enemy does. It does not formally decide to become a welfare state but only to meet specific needs such as alleviating the hardship of people who have lost their jobs, lightening the old age of workers, and providing a minimum of health care for the elderly. Policy changes seem to come not through grand decisions on grand alternatives but through slight modifications of existing policy. The new policy emerges slowly and haltingly, by small and usually tentative steps. It is a process of trial and error in which policy zigs and zags, reverses itself, and then moves forward in a series of increments.[8] Some policies are formulated and duly ratified only to be skewed to an entirely different direction and purpose by those carrying them out. Others are never carried out at all, and still other issues

---

[7]As quoted in Kennedy, *Thirteen Days,* p. 128.

[8]See Charles E. Lindblom, "The Science of 'Muddling Through,'" *Public Administration Review,* Vol. 19 (1959); and idem, *The Policy-Making Process* (Englewood Cliffs, N.J.: Prentice Hall, 1968).

continue to be debated with nothing being resolved until both the problem and the debaters disappear under the relentless pyramiding of events.

The "half-observed realities" are that the decisions of government are made in a convoluted process that involves both conflict and consensus building. Even presidents seem to spend most of their time maneuvering, persuading, and arm twisting, using whatever levers, influence, and power they can muster to persuade or pressure the people concerned. Sometimes presidents end up doing what they never really wanted to do. During the Nixon administration, for example, Congress passed a law empowering the president to control wages and prices. The Democratic majority in Congress did not really want such controls; they wanted to build a public record that would let them say it was the Republican administration and not the Democratic Congress that was to blame for continued inflation. Nixon swore that wage and price controls were against his deepest philosophic commitments to "free enterprise" and that he would never, ever use them. A year later he ordered them into effect.

On some occasions presidents clearly make decisions, even if they cannot make the exact decisions they might wish. At other times decisions are just as clearly made by Congress. But in action after action the responsibility for decisions is as fluid and restless as quicksilver; there seems to be neither an individual nor an organization on whom it can be fixed. At times the point of a decision seems to have escaped into the labyrinth of government machinery, beyond layers and layers of bureaucracy. At other times it seems never to have reached the government at all but to have remained in either the wider domain of public opinion, which may or may not have been influenced by the press, or a narrower domain dominated by the maneuverings of special interests.

Turmoil and Confusion

Just as our desire to know who makes a decision is frustrated, so is our hope that the process of policy making will be dignified and orderly. In fact, a decision may be little more than the start of a public brawl by the people who want to reverse it. This has been especially obvious in defense policy, for the Army, Navy, and Air Force at times seem to regard each other as more dangerous enemies than foreign powers. The weapon frequently used in these interservice battles has been the leak of secret information, which is often distorted to present a special view. Out of Washington flows a continuous stream of rumor, tales of bickering, speculation, stories of selfish interest, charges, and countercharges. Abusive rivalries arise between government agencies engaged in making policy. Even within a single agency different factions battle, each seeking allies in other agencies, among members of Congress, from interest groups, and among the press. Officialdom, whether civilian or military, is hardly neutral. It speaks, and inevitably it speaks as an advocate. The Army battles for ground forces, the Air Force battles for bombers, and the Navy battles for ships. The Department of Labor fights for the rights of workers, the Department of Commerce looks after the interests of business, and the Department of Agriculture struggles to keep farm prices high. Consumers, lacking a central organization or clearly recognized leaders, try to put pressure on their representatives in Congress or perhaps organize a boycott. Many interests, organizations, and institutions both inside and outside the government are joined in a struggle over the goals of government policy and the means by which they shall be achieved. Instead of unity there is conflict. Instead of majestic progression there are erratic zigs and zags. Instead of clarity and decisiveness there are tangle and turmoil; instead of order, confusion.

Sources of the Turmoil

In part the turbulence of policy making results from the nature of the Constitution itself. As scholars have pointed out, the Constitutional Convention of 1787 really created not a government of "separated powers" but a government of separate institutions sharing powers.[9] The executive is part of the legislative process, and so is the judiciary. Congress has a role to play in carrying out the laws, and so do the courts.

Another reason for the turmoil is the large number of people who take part in policy making. The president, the White House staff, the cabinet, and other political appointees make up what we think of as an administration. Below them are a host of civil servants as well as Congress and the courts. Also, because the United States has a federal system, many decisions are made by state and local governments. In addition, a lot more people are involved in policy making than just those who hold official positions. It is no accident that the press is called the fourth branch of government. Lobbies, interest groups, political parties, "attentive publics," and the mass electorate all on occasion also have a role in the policy-making process.

Policy Convictions

The turmoil has other sources as well. Among the principal conclusions of a British government committee appointed to study the powers of ministers was that most people find it easier to go against their own economic

---

[9]Neustadt, "White House and Whitehall," p. 33.

and pecuniary interest than to go against their deep convictions on policy. In the business of government the stakes are high and the issues fundamental. In such circumstances it is not surprising that passions run strong and full. It is not even surprising that people occasionally feel so deeply that they take matters into their own hands, leaking secret materials to the Congress or the press to try to force the government to adopt what they are convinced is the only right path, the salvation of the nation. In the late 1950s, for example, intelligence officials leaked to sympathetic members of Congress and the press secret information foreshadowing a U.S. missile gap in relation to the Soviet Union. They did not do this because they were disloyal citizens but rather because they had failed to convince the Eisenhower administration to increase missile production and felt completely justified in going over the president's head to Congress, the press, and the public.

The same kind of deep conviction was also undoubtedly behind the leak of the so-called Pentagon Papers, the top-secret collection of documents showing how the United States became involved in the Vietnam conflict. A similar belief deeply pervaded the work on SALT II in the late 1970s, when senior government officials frequently leaked detailed information about the evolving U.S. negotiating posture, particularly to *The New York Times.* One government analyst felt so strongly about the course the government was pursuing that he leaked highly sensitive material to the staff of the Senate Armed Services Committee. He was subsequently fired for doing this but promptly hired by sympathetic senators as a staff member. And, after Reagan was elected, he was given another job in the executive branch! Similar leaks in almost every administration since World War II have driven each of the presidents to order investigations by the FBI. Just a few days after his election, George Bush announced that in his administration leaks would not be tolerated! But of course they occurred in the Bush administration as in all others. Bush was infuriated, but there was little he could do about it.[10]

Inadequacy of Knowledge

Another cause of the confusion and turbulence of the policy-making process is the complexity of the problems and the inadequacy of our knowledge of the how and why of social affairs. More and better under-

---

[10]See the comments of the columnist William Safire quoted in Chapter 15, The Press and Television, p. 237.

standing will not always lead us to sure solutions of knotty problems, but it often does. If our understanding of the workings of a modern industrial economy had been better in the 1920s, for example, the depths of the Great Depression might have been avoided. When knowledge is inadequate, when problems are complex, and especially when they are new, there is much room for disagreement, conflict, and turmoil.

Policy Making Is Politics

These facets of policy making in government were also the point of the anecdotes with which this discussion began. The nature of the process is what Dawes was alluding to when he said that members of the cabinet were a president's natural enemies, what Truman had in mind when he laughed about Ike finding that being president would not be anything like being a general, and what Kennedy, Johnson, Nixon, and all the rest found frustrating. Understanding the process also helps to explain the turmoil of decision making and flags a warning to those who would be cynical about government or who are disgusted with the hurly-burly of policy making.

But these points about the nature of the turmoil are not a complete explanation of even the surface phenomena of how government works, nor are they completely satisfying. Our hope is for a rationalized system of government and policy making, which implies that a nation can pursue a single set of clearly perceived and generally agreed-upon goals, just as a business organization is supposed to pursue profits. But is this realistic? Is the problem of making policy in a highly diversified mass society really one of relating the steps of making a decision to a single set of goals? Or is it precisely one of choosing goals, not in the abstract, but in the context of ongoing events, with inadequate information, incomplete knowledge and understanding, and insufficient power? Is it also one of choosing goals while pitted against opposition not only from outside one's own particular group or organization but from within it as well? If so, the making of national decisions is not a problem for the efficiency expert or a matter of assembling different pieces of policy logically as if the product were an automobile. The test of a policy is not whether it is in fact the most rational means for achieving an agreed-upon objective or whether the objective agreed upon is in the true national interest, but rather whether enough of the people and organizations having a stake in the policy and holding power agree to the policy. Policy faces inward as much as outward, seeking to reconcile conflicting goals, to adjust aspirations to available means, and to accommodate to one another the advocates of competing goals and aspirations. It is here that the essence of government and policy seems to lie, in a process that is essentially political.

CASE STUDY: DROPPING THE ATOMIC BOMB IN WORLD WAR II–A "DECISION" BY BUREAUCRATIC MOMENTUM

When Soviet missiles were discovered in Cuba in 1962, President Kennedy ordered all the major departments of the government to lay out systematically the alternative courses of action open to the United States and to explore the probable consequences of each. Numerous meetings of the National Security Council were then held to discuss each alternative; after full discussion, the president decided to blockade Cuba. If a "national decision" can be defined as one that follows from this kind of procedure, two points can be made. First, a number of important decisions are indeed made in this deliberate and systematic way. Second, however, some equally important decisions are not made in a deliberate and systematic fashion at all. Some such decisions in fact seem merely to happen by default or by bureaucratic momentum. One example was the "decision" to drop atomic bombs on Hiroshima and Nagasaki. Here is what happened.

A number of physicists in the United States heard through the scientific grapevine that scientists in Hitler's Germany had split the atom, which they knew made it theoretically possible to build an atomic bomb. They persuaded Albert Einstein, the most prestigious physicist of all, to write to President Franklin D. Roosevelt and urge him to order the United States to try to build such a bomb as soon as possible.

One of Roosevelt's economic advisers was his friend Alexander Sachs, who was also a friend of the physicists, and in October 1939 they asked him to take the letter to the president. The letter alone would probably not have convinced Roosevelt, but after Sachs talked and talked, the president's face finally "lit with comprehension." He saw that the physicists might be wrong and that a bomb could not be built. He also saw that they might succeed but not in time to help the war. But he also saw that the United States could not take a chance that Hitler would get such a mind-boggling weapon first. Roosevelt authorized the Manhattan Project, charged with making an atomic bomb.

I. I. Rabi and Leo Szilard at Columbia University did much of the theoretical work. Enrico Fermi, working under the old football stadium at the University of Chicago, built the first uranium pile and achieved a chain reaction. In the meantime J. Robert Oppenheimer and many others worked on top of a remote mesa in New Mexico called Los Alamos to put all the pieces together to make a bomb. General Leslie Groves, who knew nothing of physics but was a good organizer, was named project administrator.

Over the next few years the physicists worked hard, and on July 16, 1945, they were ready to test a bomb in the desert at Alamogordo, New Mexico. As they were setting up the test Fermi announced that he had been studying the possibility that the incredibly intense heat of the bomb might ignite the atmosphere. He said he was prepared to handicap the odds on two bets: One was that the heat would spread to destroy all life on the earth; the second was that it would dissipate and thus only destroy life in New Mexico. General Groves had anticipated that the bomb might generate more energy than planned and therefore had prepared a press release explaining that Oppenheimer and the other physicists had been vacationing at Oppenheimer's ranch and were killed when an ammunition dump nearby had exploded accidentally. But he was not prepared for the total catastrophe that Fermi was suggesting. Finally, Groves decided that Fermi was joking. A number of senior physicists present, however, felt that Fermi was *not* joking.

The bomb worked. Watching it, Oppenheimer thought of the words of Krishna in the Bhagavad-Gita: "I am become Death, the Shatterer of Worlds."

But the bomb did not ignite the atmosphere. What next? Oppenheimer said later, "We always assumed that if bombs were needed they would be used." Bureaucratic momentum took over the process of making that decision. President Harry S Truman had been informed of the progress of the bomb. A committee chaired by Henry L. Stimson, secretary of war, former secretary of state, and undoubtedly the most prestigious member of Truman's administration, had been set up in May 1945 to consider how a bomb should be used if the test worked. About one hour of a six-hour session was devoted to the question of dropping bombs on Japan; Germany had already been defeated. At the meeting Oppenheimer played the role of the pure scientist. On the question of whether the Japanese should be warned, he testified that either or both of the two bombs that they expected to have ready if the test worked might be a dud—and that in any case he could not guarantee the force of the next explosion. The consensus of the committee was that the two bombs should be dropped without warning, for they reasoned that if warning were given and the bombs failed, the Japanese would be encouraged to fight even harder and longer. The committee decided that the bomb should *not* be used on purely civilian areas. However, it also decided that to make the greatest possible psychological impact, the bombs should be used on a "vital war plant employing a large number of workers and closely surrounded by workers' houses."

Bureaucratic momentum continued. Stimson told Truman that if the bomb worked, it might make an invasion of Japan unnecessary. Although no one knows where he got his figures, Stimson said that an invasion, scheduled for November 1945, would cost a million American casualties, not to mention Japanese losses. Truman raised no objections to the use of the bomb.[11]

The target-selection people in intelligence were given the guidelines and recommended Hiroshima and Nagasaki as targets. Two bombers were readied and their crews briefed.

In the meantime a number of the physicists were becoming uneasy about

---

[11]Certain "revisionist" historians have suggested that the real motive for dropping the atomic bombs on Japan was to intimidate the Soviet Union. I have found no evidence that this possibility was ever raised in the high-level discussions, although some lower-level speculation along these lines may have taken place. Politicians would have been acutely aware that evidence of such a motive would have leaked and that the political consequences would have been horrendous. At the same time, the evidence is that, right or wrong, the high-level officials concerned were convinced that an invasion would bring enormous casualties, both American and Japanese, and that using the atomic bombs would make an invasion unnecessary.

the morality of using the bomb. Several working at Chicago signed a petition that was sent to Groves and Stimson. Groves's reaction was to bury it. He was convinced, as he said, that if the bomb was not used, Congress would launch an investigation that would blame them all "for the blood of our boys shed uselessly." No one knows exactly what Stimson thought, except that he believed the bomb might render unnecessary an invasion that would cost a million casualties. Other physicists and Under Secretary of the Navy Ralph Bard, however, also raised questions about the use of the bomb.

At this time Truman was preparing to go meet with Churchill and Stalin at Potsdam, and thus without firmer assurances that the bomb would work, Stimson hesitated to fire up the government to the effort needed to make a true "national decision" of the kind that was made years later in the Cuban missile crisis. He sent the physicists' petition to Oppenheimer and Fermi at Los Alamos, asking again for confirmation that the bomb would work before he raised the issue with Truman.

If the effort for a "national decision" had been made, it would have shown that Army Chief of Staff General George C. Marshall did not agree that an invasion would cost one million casualties; he thought it might cost forty thousand. After the Potsdam conference he also told General Maxwell D. Taylor (at that time acting as one of Marshall's aides) that he believed that the bomb might make an invasion unnecessary. It would also have shown that General "Hap" Arnold of the Army Air Corps and Admiral William Leahy, Truman's personal military adviser, both believed that even without the bomb an invasion would not be needed. It would also have shown that Japan had already approached both Switzerland and Russia about negotiating a peace.

Oppenheimer and Fermi had no knowledge of the military situation and thus no reason to challenge the need for an invasion and either of the estimates on casualties. In their response to Stimson they said that the physicists were divided and that they had no special competence on the moral question. They then reaffirmed their judgment that because on technical grounds the bombs could not be guaranteed to work, there should be no warning if they were used.

Because Stimson did not have the government gear up to make a "national decision," bureaucratic momentum continued to rule. In reality Roosevelt's decision to try to make the bomb was the only one approaching a "national decision" that was ever made in this issue. From that time on the only decision was not to disturb the inevitable, massive, irresistible progress of bureaucratic momentum.[12]

---

[12]The major source for this account is Nuell Pharr Davis, *Lawrence and Oppenheimer* (New York: Simon & Schuster, 1968). Others are Fletcher Knebel and Charles W. Bailey, *No High Ground* (New York: Harper, 1960); Alice Smith, "Behind the Decision to Use the Atomic Bomb: Chicago 1944–45," *Bulletin of the Atomic Scientists* (September 1958); Michael Amrine, *The Great Decision: The Secret History of the Atomic Bomb* (New York: Putnam's Sons, 1959; Peter Wyden, *Day One: Before Hiroshima and After* (New York: Simon & Schuster, 1984); and McGeorge Bundy, *Danger and Survival: Choices About the Bomb in the First Fifty Years* (New York: Random House, 1988)

6

THE NATURE
OF POLITICS

If the process by which governments make decisions is essentially political, what then is politics? The ancient Greek philosopher Aristotle, writing four centuries before Christ, declared that human beings are political animals. He said that nature intended them to live in groups and that politics concerned the governance of such groups. Aristotle also said that politics was humankind's most noble invention! Nineteen centuries later Niccolò Machiavelli, writing in the period of the Italian city-states, defined politics as the process of seeking, maintaining, and exercising power. Since then, most political thinkers have also felt it necessary to give power some place in their definitions of politics.

Later political thinkers such as John Locke, Montesquieu, Jean Jacques Rousseau, and Karl Marx focused on how humankind might achieve the best possible government. This was true even of Thomas Hobbes, to whom power was as central as it had been to Machiavelli. They all tried to discern the essential nature of humankind and society and to deduce from that the elements of a truly good society and government.

TWENTIETH-CENTURY CONCEPTS

Modern definitions of politics frequently cite Max Weber, a German scholar of the early 1900s. Weber's concept of politics rested on his definition of the state as a "human community that [successfully] claims the *monopoly of the legitimate use of physical force* within a given territory." Since the state is the sole source of the right to use violence, for Weber politics "means striving to share power or striving to influence the distribution of power, either among states or among groups within a state."[1] Thus he, like Machiavelli, saw power as central to politics: "He who is active in politics strives for power either as a means in serving other aims, ideal or egoistic, or as 'power for power's sake,' that is, in order to enjoy the prestige-feeling that power gives."[2] Thus some people dominate and others are dominated, and it is important, Weber argued, to understand why people obey.

The point Weber was making rests on the thinking of Aristotle: "Authority," or "Rule," is power that people recognize as legitimate. Weber identified three forms of authority that make the domination of other people legitimate and therefore acceptable.[3] The first is the authority of the "eternal yesterday," or ancient tradition and custom: "My father was the king [or caliph, khan, maharajah, or tribal chieftain]. He is now dead. I am therefore king, and you must obey me." The second is "rational-legal" authority: "I was elected president by legal and constitutional procedures, and therefore you must obey me (or at least you must obey all my commands that are legal and constitutional)." The third is the authority of an "extraordinary and personal gift of grace," to which Weber gave the name *charisma*, which was derived from the Greek word for spirit. "God [or history or the spirit of the nation] has laid His hand upon me to make me the leader, and therefore you must obey." The Ayatollah Khomeini of Iran claimed that his authority to rule after the shah abdicated was legitimate for this reason, as did Hitler, Lenin, and most revolutionary leaders.

More recent analysts of politics have stressed different aspects of these major themes. Some have emphasized the territorial base of political groups.[4] Some talk about the purpose of politics: "Who gets what, when, and how."[5] Others have restricted their definition of politics to the search for and exercise of power only with respect to the process of government.[6] Some have limited the concept of politics to the making and executing of authoritative or legally binding decisions.[7] Still others have

---

[1]*From Max Weber, Essays in Sociology,* ed. and trans. H. H. Gerth and C. Wright Mills (New York: Oxford University Press, 1946), p. 78. Weber's emphasis.

[2]Ibid., p. 78.

[3]Ibid., pp. 116–117.

[4]Charles E. Merriam, *Political Power: Its Composition and Incidence* (New York: McGraw-Hill, 1934).

[5]Harold D. Lasswell and Abraham Kaplan, *Power and Society* (New Haven, Conn.: Yale University Press, 1986); and Harold D. Lasswell, *Politics: Who Gets What, When, How* (New York: McGraw-Hill, 1936).

[6]V. O. Key, Jr., *Politics, Parties, and Pressure Groups* (New York: McGraw-Hill, 1936).

[7]David Easton, *The Political System* (New York: Alfred A. Knopf, 1953); idem, "An Approach to the Analysis of Political Systems," *World Politics* (April 1957); and idem, *A Systems Analysis of Political Life* (New York: John Wiley, 1965).

combined these ideas to say that politics is any persistent pattern of human relationships that involves power, rule, or authority.[8]

POLITICS AS A FORM OF GROUP DECISION MAKING

For our purposes it seems most useful to say that (1) politics is concerned with power, (2) in larger systems it is concerned with government, and (3) the most important political decisions are concerned with the ordering and regulating of society itself. Politics involves the activities and relationships of groups of people that are organized as societies. Thus a political process may be seen as a device for making group decisions. It is a set of peaceable and more or less orderly procedures by which a group of people can decide what they should do as a group, which goals they should seek and how they should achieve them, or how they should divide among themselves the benefits available. Politics is thus concerned with both the making of such decisions and the maneuvering to acquire the power and influence to affect them.

CHARACTERISTICS OF A POLITICAL SYSTEM

There are of course devices other than the political system by which groups can make decisions. One example is the marketplace. By buying certain products and not others, people in a market economy determine how the resources of their society will be allocated and how the economic pie will be divided. However, four characteristics distinguish a political decision-making process from other decision-making devices: (1) disagreement or conflict, (2) shared values (especially a belief in the need to preserve the system itself), (3) competing groups, and (4) power.

Disagreement or Conflict

Politics implies a diversity of goals and values that must be reconciled before a decision can be reached. What goals should the United States pursue as a country? For some people the main goal is a high standard of the consumption of such material goods as color televisions, fancy cars, and vacations. Others argue for holding back on increased consumption to permit a larger investment in basic industry such as steel, heavy

---

[8]Robert A. Dahl, *Modern Political Analysis,* 2nd ed. (Englewood Cliffs, N.J.: Prentice Hall, 1970), pp. 5 ff; and David Easton, *The Analysis of Political Structure* (New York: Routledge, Chapman and Hall, 1990).

machinery, and electronics to give the country a stronger economic base. Still others are willing to make sacrifices in both consumption and industrial development out of concern for the environmental and ecological balance. Other people emphasize even less tangible values. All of these goals require the expenditure of resources.

What kind of society shall the United States try to be? Shall the goal be more freedom from government surveillance, even at the risk of less law and order? Do we want the government to take an active role in assuring equality for minorities in jobs, education, and housing? Or would we prefer to let people work this out by themselves, even if it means tolerating certain inequalities for a longer time?

In a political process there can be disagreement or conflict not only about goals and values but also about the means for achieving them. There are more ways than one to reach any particular goal, and the precise effects of different policy alternatives are frequently in dispute. Almost everyone agrees on the goal of a prosperous economy that would give all Americans a decent standard of living, but not everyone agreed that President Reagan's "supply-side" economic program of cutting both taxes and government spending was the best policy for achieving this goal. Similarly, at the time of the Vietnam war most Americans agreed on the goal of a peaceful, stable, non-Communist Vietnam, but they disagreed violently about the means to that end. The hawks thought the goal could be achieved only by defeating the Communists on the battlefield, whereas the doves thought it could be accomplished by negotiation. Neither side had enough "scientific" knowledge to guarantee that their policy was better. Such lack of "scientific" knowledge is the source of much turmoil and dispute about which policy to adopt.

Disagreement can also arise over the allocation of benefits. Shall senior citizens receive pensions? Shall veterans? Shall the disabled? Shall the money for these benefits be raised by sales taxes (which fall most heavily on those who are less well off) or by graduated income taxes (which fall most heavily on those with higher incomes)? Disagreement on this issue was another reason for the controversy over Reagan's economic program.

Dividing a society's economic pie can be accomplished indirectly by the kind of rules adopted for governing the relationships between people and groups of people. Thus the nature of the rules of competition is the subject of much political argument, but competition alone does not produce politics. If, for example, there is a consensus that unrestrained economic enterprise shall govern the distribution of material benefits in the society, competition will take place in other than political terms. But if there is disagreement about the rules for economic competition, politics takes over the decision-making process.

In sum, politics comes to the fore when there is disagreement about (1) the goals the group should seek, (2) the values and the kind of society the group wants, (3) the effects of alternative policies for achieving the goals or values sought, (4) the sacrifices required from different segments of society, (5) the allocation of benefits among different segments of society, and (6) the rules governing competition among individuals and subgroups within the society.

A "Strain Toward Agreement" and Shared Values

A second characteristic of a political process is that, along with disagreement, struggle, and conflict, there is simultaneously and paradoxically a "strain toward agreement."[9] By this is meant an effort to build a consensus or a push to reach an accommodation, compromise, or some sort of agreement on policy decisions. There are independent participants in the process who may be able to block, sabotage, or at least snipe away at a policy from the sidelines. There may be other people whose active, imaginative support and dedicated efforts are required if the policy is to succeed. To enlist this kind of willing cooperation may take concessions aimed directly at these people and their interests. Finally, all the participants in a working political system share an intuitive realization that prolonged intransigence, stalemate, and indecision on urgent and fundamental issues might become so intolerable as to threaten the very form and structure of their system of governance. Thus successful–that is, working–political systems are characterized by a general consensus that the system itself is worth preserving.

Most of the citizenry of a successful system believe the system is worth preserving for one of two reasons. Some believe that the overall political system or society is of more value than the particular goal they have been unsuccessfully seeking. Others believe that the political system is sufficiently malleable to enable them to get what they want through the system sooner or later. Dispute over policies can be bitter (such as those over Roosevelt's New Deal and Reagan's economic program), but even the most bitter opponents do not resort to violence.

The fact that most members of a working political system share a desire to preserve it implies that they share other values and goals as well, such as concepts of right and wrong and fairness. Thus solutions to problems that bring even profound social change are more often than not consistent with traditional goals and notions of legitimate authority. Communist China under Mao Zedong, for example, probably underwent the most radical revolution of any country in recent times. But it is often

---

[9]The phrase is Warner R. Schilling's. See his "The Politics of National Defense: Fiscal 1960," in *Strategy, Politics, and Defense Budgets,* eds., Warner R. Schilling, Paul Y. Hammond, and Glenn H. Snyder (New York: Columbia University Press, 1962), p. 23.

observed that Communist China is as much the child of Confucius, the philosopher of ancient China, as it is of Karl Marx.

Competing Groups

A third characteristic of a political process is the presence of competing clusters of people with alternative goals or policies. Although one thinks immediately of the traditional political parties, even on the national level there are many other groupings, including organizations of farmers, labor unions, manufacturing and business organizations, liberals, conservatives, and a vast array of special interests such as the National Rifle Association (which fights against gun control), antiabortion groups, and antinuclear groups. Within the policy-making arena itself there are not only the principal departments and agencies such as Treasury, Commerce, Labor, Health and Human Services, Justice, Defense, and State but also subgroups throughout the executive branch and even within departments. Entirely informal alliances frequently cut across departmental or institutional lines, such as the division between the executive and Congress. Consider the issue of foreign trade, for example. The United States cannot sell abroad unless other countries earn the dollars to buy our goods by selling their goods to us. Those people in the Department of Agriculture who are concerned with wheat farmers are in favor of international trade, but those who are concerned with cattle raisers are less enthusiastic and instead want to protect the beef industry from too much competition from Argentina.

On every major policy dispute, domestic or foreign, the same pattern of subgroups and informal alliances is to be seen. This was certainly clear in the struggle over Reagan's economic program, which sometimes made for very strange bedfellows indeed. For example, lobbyists for the dairy industry, which had supported Reagan in the election, approached staff members of the congressional subcommittee responsible for the food stamp program to form an alliance to prevent Reagan's proposed cuts in both food stamps and dairy subsidies. Sometimes this pattern of informal alliances is more prominent and sometimes less. But it is almost always there.

Power

The final characteristic of a political process is power. In a political process the relative power of the people and groups involved is as important to the final outcome as the appeal of the goals they seek or the cogency and wisdom of their arguments. The arguments for workers' rights, including decent wages, safe working conditions, unemployment benefits, and retirement pensions, were just as valid in the late nineteenth century as they are today. But it was not until the labor movement organized workers and so made them a political power that conditions began to change fast enough and fundamentally enough to make a real difference. For generations farmers in the Middle West, Southwest, and West had complained of their exploitation by eastern bankers, farm equipment manufacturers, and railroads. But it was not until those complaints could be expressed through the levers of political power that conditions truly changed.

The powerful, however, must sometimes bow to countervailing power. When Lyndon B. Johnson was majority leader of the Senate, he was one of the most powerful men in the country. But he was also a senator from Texas, and as such even he could not dare to vote against the oil depletion allowance. "What Senator [Paul] Douglas needs," Johnson once said in weariness over one of Douglas's more sanctimonious speeches, "is a few oil wells in Illinois."[10] Only then, Johnson felt, could Douglas learn true humility. But what Johnson was forgetting was that if he had oil producers in Texas, Douglas had corn growers in Illinois. John Kennedy, as senator from Massachusetts, had the textile industry to teach him humility, and the liberal Frank Church of Idaho could never really vote for gun control, no matter how persuasive the facts might be. In a political situation, who advocates or opposes a policy is thus just as important as what they advocate or oppose.

Policy Making Is Politics

It may be difficult to agree with Aristotle's statement that politics is humankind's most noble invention, but when government is viewed as a political process, some of the puzzlements—conflict and struggle, consensus building, bargaining, alliance forming, and compromise—are explainable. Politics may not be humankind's most noble invention, but it may well be one of its most fascinating games.

THE NATURE OF POLITICAL POWER

Viewing policy making in government as political process illuminates the diversity and inconsistency of the goals that national policy must serve and calls attention to the strong but sometimes hidden forces through which competing goals are reconciled. It also helps explain why the push and pull of these crosscurrents are sometimes dampened or obscured and sometimes so fiercely public. The roles of such "unrational"

---

[10]Quoted in Harry T. McPherson, *A Political Education* (Boston: Little, Brown, 1972).

procedures as bargaining also become more clear, as does the peculiar place of power in a political system.

What is power? All great social thinkers have considered this question. As Robert A. Dahl has pointed out, the existence of so much comment arouses two suspicions.[11] The first is that where there is so much smoke, there must be some fire, and therefore some "Thing" that can be called power must exist. The second suspicion is that "a Thing to which people attach many labels with subtly or grossly different meanings in many different cultures and times is probably not a Thing at all but many Things."[12] If Dahl is right, power need not necessarily be the motive force behind politics nor the cause of politics nor even a necessary condition of politics. It may well be the single most pervasive and perhaps decisive of the instrumentalities of politics, but it may be no more characteristic of politics than persuasion or bargaining or compromise. Certainly many observers have noted that although power seeking may be one of the motives of people involved in politics, it is certainly not the only motive, and sometimes it is not even a part of their motivation.

Sources of Power

But power is obviously a part of politics. At certain times and in certain places military power, for example, may be starkly central in domestic affairs. Civil war is the case that first comes to mind. Mao Zedong said that power grows out of the barrel of a gun. But to the extent that military strength is a source of domestic power, the mechanics hardly seem so crude. In the making of foreign policy on such issues as arms control, Vietnam, and bases in the Philippines, the domestic "military-industrial complex," as President Eisenhower called it, has a large stake and expresses its position. On the questions of the size of the defense budget and the kinds of weapons to be procured, its stake has been equally large. But even on these issues the military-industrial complex has been loosely organized, amorphous, and more potential than structured. On other matters bearing more or less directly on security, it has been exercising its power even more ambiguously. Finally, on a broad range of issues ranging from welfare to civil liberties, it appears to wield no discernible power at all.

---

[11]Robert A. Dahl, "The Concept of Power," *Behavioral Science* (July 1957). See also, Harold D. Lasswell, and Abraham Kaplan, *Power and Society* (New Haven, Conn.: Yale University Press, 1986); David Baldwin, "Power Analysis and World Politics: New Trends Versus Old Tendencies," *World Politics,* Vol. 31 (1979). For a different view from Dahl's, see Peter Bachrach and Merton S. Baratz, "Two Faces of Power," *American Political Science Review,* Vol. 56 (1962).

[12]Dahl, p. 6. See also the works cited therein.

Great inherited wealth is another obvious source of power, one typified by names like Rockefeller, Harriman, Du Pont, Morgan, and Vanderbilt. Power is also inherent in top positions at corporations like General Motors, American Telephone & Telegraph, and U.S. Steel. Social position is another foundation of power. Members of the Cabot, Lodge, Lowell, and Adams families, for example, have exercised power in the city of Boston, the state of Massachusetts, and the nation at large to some extent simply because they belonged to the top social strata. But power in the American political system clearly has more varied and subtle sources, for it grows not only out of the barrel of a gun, as Mao would have it, or out of economic control, as Marx would have it. Power also comes from legitimacy, legal authority, expertise, and the accepted right to speak for a special interest, such as the interest of the farmer in agricultural policy or that of the banker in monetary policy. Indeed, the sources of power are so varied and subtle that one wonders whether the concept can be expressed with just one word.[13]

Examples of Power

Power can be expressed negatively as when Congress makes life difficult for a president if one of its treasured views is ignored or as when the chairs of congressional committees used to frustrate the rest of Congress and prevent action on a bill by simply refusing to consider it. Power can also be the constitutional right to decide in a formal sense, which belongs to presidents in some matters and to the Congress or the courts in others. Or it can be influence, in the sense of having the ear of the president or the leaders of Congress without holding any office at all. Andrew Jackson had his "Kitchen Cabinet," Truman had his so-called bourbon-and-branch-water cronies, Eisenhower had his golf-playing friends from the business world, Kennedy had his brothers and the so-called Irish Mafia, Johnson had his pals from his days in the Congress, Carter had his "Georgia gang," Reagan had his rich and conservative friends from California, and Bush had his friends from Texas and his earlier years in government. All had power.

Power can also be the ability to have your views taken into account because the world has come to believe that you speak for a wider public and that there will be political consequences if you are ignored. Ralph Nader, who wrote a book charging that automobile manufacturers were careless about the safety of the automobiles they built, established this

---

[13]For a further discussion of the values that comprise the bases of power, see Lasswell and Kaplan, *Power and Society*.

sort of power.[14] After his book had attracted widespread attention, Nader broadened his horizons and began to investigate other issues, especially those affecting the consumer. Before long he came to exercise impressive power in the areas of food and drug standards, safety, ecology, and consumer interests.

Presidents and Power

No one person, group, or subgroup is all powerful, not even the president. At times presidents may merely preside. However, if presidents want decisions to go their way, they cannot merely order it so but must engage in the politics of policy making and build a consensus for their policies among the different power centers. They must bring along enough of the factions in Congress to forestall revolt and contend for the support of wider constituencies among the press, interest groups, and attentive publics. Even within the executive branch itself the policies of presidents will not succeed merely at their command. Presidents must cultivate cooperation and support and obtain approval from certain people, acquiescence from others, and enthusiasm from still others. This is the truth that Vice President Dawes alluded to when he said that members of the cabinet were a president's natural enemies and that so amused President Truman when he said Eisenhower would find that the presidency was not "a bit like the Army." It is the truth that President Kennedy discovered when he realized that State Department foot-dragging about the missiles in Turkey had given the Soviets a club to beat him with and that President Johnson ran up against when he was blocked from merging the departments of Labor and Commerce. It is the "half-observed realities" underneath our images of "Presidents-in-boots, astride decisions"—the realities of "Presidents-in-sneakers, stirrups in hand, trying to induce particular department heads, or congressmen, or senators to climb aboard."

A POLITICAL PROCESS CONCEPTUAL MODEL

What then would be the assumptions on which a political process conceptual model is based? The first is that a wide variety of people are involved in the making of government decisions. Those most directly involved hold government office: the president, members of Congress, bureaucrats in the Department of State and the Pentagon. But some of those actively trying to influence policy decisions do not hold office, including members

---

[14]Ralph Nader, *Unsafe at Any Speed* (New York: Grossman, 1956).

of interest groups, academics, the press, attentive publics, and the mass of the voters.

Most of the people directly involved, both officials and nonofficials, act through organizations, such as the Congress, Department of State, Pentagon, interest groups, or the press. Even the president acts more often through the institution of the presidency—the "White House"—which includes several hundred people, than as an individual. But some of the participants do act as individuals all of the time, and all of the participants act as individuals some of the time.

Second, each of these participants, both the individuals and the organizations, exercises power, some more than others. The president has more power over the full range of governmental policy than any member of Congress. The source of that power is basically the Constitution, but as we shall see some is also derived from the nature of a political process.

The power that each participant wields also varies with the subject matter. In some specific policy areas, the president is not the most powerful of the power centers. He is paramount in foreign affairs but not in some aspects of agricultural policy, for example, when compared to chairs of the House and Senate Committees on Agriculture. Power also varies with the circumstances. Even though the president is the most powerful in foreign affairs, a coalition of other power centers could and often does defeat him on specific issues.

Third, each power center, whether an individual or an organization, has different motives and goals. All presumably share to a greater or lesser extent a number of "state goals." That is, they all presumably value the United States and count its survival high in their own personal list of goals. At least some of the time, they all would also presumably share the goal of preserving the power and prestige of the United States, possibly at times solely for the sake of power and prestige. And some of the time at least certain participants would share all the other state goals of the strategic, geopolitical model: national security in all its aspects, such as industrial development, access to raw materials, skilled labor, and all the other requirements for building weapons, armies, navies, and air forces; acquisition of strategic territories or geographical positions; political alliances; and such subsidiary goals as prosperity, high standards of living, and trade advantages.

Parenthetically, it should be repeated that the fact that a high percentage of the men and women participating in the policy-making process share a commitment to such state goals is why the strategic, geopolitical, black box model works as well as it does. States do not have goals, rationally examine alternatives, and choose the most effective means of accomplishing the goals. But to the extent that the individuals who act in the name of the state agree about state goals and the policy for achieving them, the result is very much the same.

However, even though most power centers share a commitment to state goals, each power center also has other goals. Power centers that are organizations have organizational goals. The Air Force, for example, has Air Force goals, including a commitment to the well-being of the organization itself, often a belief that air power, such as strategic bombing or interdiction, will win wars more quickly and economically than land or sea power, and sometimes the "bureaucratic imperialism" goal of enlarging the responsibilities of the Air Force at the expense of the Army and Navy. And, of course, exactly the same thing can be said of the Army, the Navy, and the Department of State.

The people in these organizations also have personal goals. Secretaries of state, for example, share in the state goals of the United States and in the organizational goals of the Department of State but also have individual goals. They will want the good opinion of their colleagues and fellow citizens, they would like to have a place in history, and they might also entertain further ambitions, perhaps to run for president. Henry A. Kissinger, Cyrus R. Vance, Alexander M. Haig, Jr., George P. Schultz, and James A. Baker are only the most recent to follow this pattern. The same is true of presidents, for even though they have achieved the highest office, they will be ambitious for a place in history. The individual men and women within a power center may also have more specific goals. For any of a variety of reasons stemming from their background or experience, they may share the goals of some special interest group, such as farmers or manufacturers or the labor unions, or have ideological convictions, such as a commitment to conservatism or liberalism. Furthermore, not only does each power center, whether an individual or an organization, have different motives and goals, but each may have a different view about how to achieve a particular goal. In fact, historically it seems that policy disagreements are more frequently over means than goals, although this in no way lessens the bitterness of the disagreement.

Third, because the power centers differ in their goals and in their judgments about the effectiveness and cost of alternative means to those goals, there is conflict and struggle over policy. Certain power centers seek allies among others less involved in the particular issue. They try to build coalitions, making concessions as they do. "Logrolling" is typical, as the various power centers maneuver and manipulate in their political wheeling and dealing.

At the same time, because the power centers share so many values, including a commitment to the political system itself, there is a "strain toward agreement." Except in extremely rare circumstances, the struggle stops well short of violence. The United States has gone through a number of social upheavals that were revolutionary in their effects but has seen only one civil war. Not only does the struggle stop short of violence, but it also usually stops short of measures that threaten severe damage to the system itself or that make cooperation on other issues impossible. Hence persuasion, compromise, and consensus building are as characteristic of the policy-making process as conflict. This is the basis of the political process conceptual model.

The Bureaucratic and Political Models Compared

Notice that the political process model differs from the bureaucratic politics model as laid out in the works of Graham Allison, Morton Halperin, I. M. Destler, and Alexander George.[15] The bureaucratic politics model implies that the organization is the single most important determinant of the policy the participants espouse and that the great bureaucracies are the most important determinant of the policy outcome. The political process model regards the organization as only one determinant of the policy the participants espouse and the great bureaucracies as important but not nearly the most important determinant of the policy outcome.

Thus Allen S. Whiting, in criticism of the bureaucratic politics model, points out that much of the policy struggle cuts across institutional lines and that factions in a department like State are often allied with like-minded factions in Defense against rival State factions who are also allied with still other Defense factions.[16] Whiting goes on to say that these factions within a single large department do not even form around smaller organizations within the larger one but around potential or actual leaders on the basis of ideological or personal affiliations.

Another critic, Robert J. Art, points out some of the other important differences between the models.[17] First, the political process model puts more emphasis on Congress and the pressures exerted on it from lobbies and interest groups. Second, this model assumes that the single most important determinant of what the participants espouse is their fundamental perspective on international affairs. The bureaucratic politics model instead suggests that the nature of the process is more important than these perspectives. The political process model does not deny that

---

[15]Graham T. Allison, *Essence of Decision: Explaining the Cuban Missile Crisis* (Boston: Little, Brown, 1971); Morton H. Halperin, *Bureaucratic Politics and Foreign Policy* (Washington, D.C.: Brookings, 1974); I. M. Destler, *Presidents, Bureaucrats, and Foreign Policy* (Princeton, N.J.: Princeton University Press, 1972); and Alexander L. George, "The Case for Multiple Advocacy in Foreign Policy," *American Political Science Review* (September 1972).

[16]Personal communication. See also my own statement about factions cutting across bureaucratic and institutional lines in "Congressional-Executive Relations and the Foreign Policy Consensus," *American Political Science Review* (September 1958).

[17]Robert J. Art, "Bureaucratic Politics and American Foreign Policy: A Critique," *Policy Sciences* (December 1974).

the process has an effect but places the effect of the perspectives above that of the process.

Third, the political process model credits the participants with realistic expectations about the final outcome and intelligent choices about their strategies to affect the outcome. In Art's words, the "participants frame their actions with a view toward what is required to get a policy adopted." In political bargaining you have to anticipate what the others will do and shape your position accordingly. As Art says, this is what the first wave of theorists on policy making meant when they said, "The test of a policy is not that it will most effectively accomplish an agreed-upon value but that a wider number of people decide to endorse it."[18] On the other hand, the bureaucratic politics model suggests that the outcome is largely the result not of the intentions of the participants but of the force diagram of their pulling and hauling.

Finally, the political process model does not neglect the influence of domestic politics on foreign policy but gives it a prominent place. The most dramatic example concerns the Vietnam war. It was not pressure from the great bureaucracies that forced the U.S. government to withdraw from Vietnam but student demonstrations, public opinion, and the clear probability that the general electorate had come to think the war was a mistake and that it would take its revenge at the next election.

---

[18]In Roger Hilsman, "The Foreign Policy Consensus: An Interim Research Report," *Journal of Conflict Resolution,* Vol. 3 (December 1959).

7

THE POLITICAL PROCESS
MODEL APPLIED

The question now is, will applying the political process model to the seven cases with which we began resolve either the puzzlements that arose in using the classical, black box model that put strategic and geopolitical factors central or the differences between analysts who used that model?

The political process model, to repeat, sees a number of individuals and organizations involved in the policy-making process. Each of these has power. Some have more than others, and the power of each varies with the subject matter. Each power center shares a commitment to state goals, such as power, prestige, and survival, but each may also have different views of the exact nature of the goals and even more frequently about how to achieve those goals. In addition, each power center has goals of its own, including the power and well-being of the organization, the success of the individual members, and certain ideological commitments. They decide not only what policy they want but what policy they think they can succeed in having adopted as the state's policy. Power centers then attempt to build coalitions among like-minded power centers as they persuade, bargain, make mutual concessions, logroll, attempt to outmaneuver and manipulate each other, and, at a certain point, apply whatever naked power they can muster.

Sometimes a power center succeeds in getting its ideal solution adopted, but sometimes it achieves only partial success. At other times the outcome is a policy that none of the power centers really wanted but rather a compromise. The resultant policy is also not always completely logical or internally consistent.

THE CUBAN MISSILE CRISIS

Analysts using the political process model must first look for power centers. They would assume that a variety would be involved in a decision and that they shared a commitment to state goals but also had different organizational and personal goals. In applying this model to the Cuban missile crisis, the hypothesis would be that the various power centers of the Soviet leadership supported or at least acquiesced in the decision to put missiles in Cuba because they came to believe the move would not only serve the interests of the Soviet state but also either meet their overall policy preferences in terms of ideology, philosophy, or simply expectations about the nature of international politics or fulfill some parochial personal or organizational interest. The most obvious of these power centers in the Soviet Union would be the party *apparatchiks*, the military, the KGB, other government bureaucracies, the bureaucracies of the various economic enterprises, and the party apparatus and government in the different regions. (Khrushchev, for example, had his original power base in the Ukraine, where he was the party boss for years.)

Analysts would next look for disagreements over goals or the means to achieve them. In the case of the decision to deploy missiles to Cuba, the American superiority in missiles coupled with the American awareness of this fact presented the Soviets with a problem. Outside analysts could safely assume that the Soviet military would argue for a crash intercontinental ballistic missile (ICBM) program to close the missile gap as fast as possible. It seems likely that the leaders of the Soviet economic bureaucracies would argue instead for a more stretched-out program to avoid disrupting the economy and growth in heavy industry, a view the party *apparatchiks* and some of the other power centers would likely share. The Soviet Union, however, had a huge oversupply of MRBMs and IRBMs, and at some point in the debate someone must have pointed to Castro's insistent appeals for military assistance and suggested deploying missiles to Cuba as a temporary solution to both problems.

Western analysts could now craft the following hypotheses about positions of the various Soviet power centers. First, the military would not be entirely happy with the deployment decision, but having MRBMs and IRBMs in Cuba would be at least half of what they wanted: Deployment would partly redress the immediate missile imbalance until a buildup of ICBMs could take place. To the economic power centers, this notion provided a real victory: a stretched-out program that did not disturb the plans for long-term growth. If deploying missiles to Cuba would placate both the military and the industrial leaders, the party leaders would obviously regard the policy as a plus. Beyond that, deployment would score a victory against the United States that would be useful in the Sino-Soviet dispute and at the same time provide tempting opportunities to use Cuba as a base to advance the political interests of the party in Central and South America. The bureaucracies dealing with foreign affairs in general and with the Western powers in particular, including the KGB, could be expected to think of the leverage the new strategic balance would bring, especially on the problem of Berlin and Germany. The regional party *apparatchiks* and local government officials would find the proposal appealing because it offered the prospect of avoiding a cutback in consumer goods by providing both guns and butter. Party hardliners could be expected to see the decision as appropriate to their view of the world since it would foil the imperialists who would otherwise inevitably and ruthlessly exploit the U.S. superiority in nuclear ICBMs.

As it happened, two groups of U.S. government officials actually did use what amounted to a political process model during the Cuban missile crisis. The first was the Sovietologists in the State Department's Bureau of Intelligence and Research (INR).[1] In the midst of the crisis they circulated a memorandum to the ExCom analyzing Soviet motives that began with a proposition expressly recognizing multiple power centers with differing motives: "As with the major policy decisions of all governments, whether dictatorial or democratic, different segments of the Soviet leadership undoubtedly saw particular advantages and disadvantages in putting missiles in Cuba according to their own parochial interests and responsibilities." The memo then went on to argue that "the Soviet government as a whole seems to have hit upon putting missiles in Cuba as a generalized, strategic response to a whole set of problems, military, economic, and political." The memo pointed out that because of the Gilpatric speech and the NATO briefings (as described in Chapter 1), the Soviets now knew that the United States realized that it had superiority in missiles. For the Soviets the implications of this were "horrendous."

The memo argued that the Soviets must have quickly recognized that the Americans had made an intelligence breakthrough by finding a way to pinpoint where and how many Soviet missiles had been deployed. The Soviets' "soft" ICBM system, with its somewhat cumbersome launching techniques, was an effective weapon for both a first strike, such as that at Pearl Harbor, and a second, retaliatory strike so long as the

---

[1]See Roger Hilsman, *To Move a Nation: The Politics of Foreign Policy in the Administration of John F. Kennedy* (Garden City, N.Y.: Doubleday, 1967), pp. 159–181. It might be added that their analysis has been supported by the evidence that has since become available, including Khrushchev's memoirs.

location of the launching pads could be kept secret. However, if the enemy had a map of all the launching sites, the system would retain some of its utility as a first-strike weapon but almost none as a second-strike weapon. Thus, the memo concluded, the whole Soviet ICBM system was suddenly obsolescent.

The memo also accepted the evidence that Castro had been clamoring insistently for military protection and magnifying the threat of an American invasion. In any case, the memo continued, among the Soviet leadership all these problems, fears, and demands somehow converged on the thesis that at least a temporary and expedient solution would be to install some of their older, more plentiful medium- and intermediate-range missiles in Cuba. It would give them a cheap and immediate substitute for the newer, more expensive ICBMs and let them stretch out the ICBM program to ease the pressure on resources. It also would meet Castro's demands and protect what had become, since his self-proclaimed membership in the Communist bloc, not just another "war of national liberation" but also the first opportunity to project Soviet power into the western hemisphere.

Thus the motive for the deployment decision, the memo argued, was strategic in the broad sense that a general improvement in the Soviet military position would affect the entire political context, strengthening their hand for dealing with the whole range of problems facing them as well as unanticipated problems. But even though general rather than specific security and foreign policy goals were the principal motives, the memo also argued that the deployment promised enticing prospects for specific gains in foreign policy and ancillary benefits that would appeal to various segments of the Soviet leadership. If the move in Cuba were successful and the overall Soviet position strengthened, their leverage on Berlin would indeed be improved. NATO would surely be shaken and the chances of the United States successfully creating a multilateral nuclear force reduced. In Latin America, the memo concluded, other potential "Castros" would be encouraged. U.S. power would seem less impressive and U.S. protection less desirable; and some of the Latin American states would move in the Soviet direction even if their governments were not overthrown. Then, too, a successful deployment in Cuba would cut the ground from under the Chinese Communists and go far toward convincing Communists everywhere that Soviet leadership was strong and that Soviet methods in dealing with the "imperialists" were effective.

In sum, the State Department Sovietologists argued that a variety of individuals and organizations were involved in the Soviet decision to send missiles to Cuba. They all shared an interest in the strategic goals of the Soviet state, but each interpreted those goals somewhat differently and each also had goals of their own.

The second group who used a political process model was Kennedy and the policy makers around him, once they had finished trying to interpret why the Soviets had deployed the missiles and started devising their moves to meet the crisis as it progressed. When they were engaged in trying to decide what motives lay behind the deployment, they thought in black box terms. But when they began to devise a policy to deal with the situation, they shifted to a political process mode of thinking. Quite clearly they envisioned their opponents as individual human beings and groups of human beings working within different organizations. Kennedy repeatedly said that U.S. moves should be gradual and paced so as to avoid backing the Soviets into a corner or placing them in a position where they might have what he called a "spasm reaction." Consideration was given at each stage of the effect the U.S. move under consideration would have on the Soviet military, the KGB, and other power centers so that the hand of those likely to favor negotiations and accommodation would be strengthened and the hand of those likely to oppose such tactics would be weakened, at least to the extent that U.S. moves could have such influence.

The first point is that an analysis based on the political process model does in fact resolve one puzzlement created by the black box model: the internal inconsistency between the hypothesized Soviet goals of trying to overcome the "missile gap in reverse" and probing the will of the West and the new American president. In an analysis based on the political process model, probing the will of the West is simply not a consideration. It is assumed that the various Soviet power centers share the state goal of wanting to right the imbalance in missiles, so sending the IRBMs and MRBMs for this purpose is not a puzzle. Although they do not really solve the problem, they would give the military and the other hawks some satisfaction because they would at least, in the words of the American National Intelligence Estimate (NIE), "begin to degrade the American second-strike capability." In addition, the deployment would fulfill the economic power centers' demand for a stretched-out buildup in ICBMs.

Second, to the extent that an analysis based on the political process model is correct, the basic Soviet motives were not in fact belligerent or aggressive per se, and thus the Kennedy administration decision to blockade Cuba and negotiate rather than bomb the missile sites was by far the better policy. The Soviet state goal was defensive—to right the missile imbalance—and their other motives flowed from an attempt to reconcile the disagreements among their own contending factions. Thus a blockade—or as Kennedy chose to call it, a quarantine—prevented more missiles from coming in to Cuba.[2] What is more, the quarantine sent a signal to the rest of the world that the United States took the Soviet Union's deployment of nuclear missiles to Cuba very seriously. The tension alarmed governments everywhere, and they added their own pressure on the Soviets to withdraw the missiles. Some members of the ExCom, to repeat, believed that a blockade would keep more missiles from coming into Cuba but would do nothing to pressure the Soviets to remove the ones already there. But in fact the blockade, added to the public protests by the president and others, actually exerted considerable leverage on the Soviets, not only through world opinion but very probably through opinion among power centers within the Soviet Union itself.

In any case, the first real break in the crisis came on Friday, October 26. Aleksander Fomin, whom the Americans knew to be head of the Washington office of the KGB, sought out ABC correspondent John Scali and asked him if he could find out if the highest levels of the U.S. government would be interested in a solution in which the Soviets would withdraw the missiles in Cuba in exchange for a public U.S. promise not to invade the island. Scali, who was a friend of Roger Hilsman, the present author, then the director of the Bureau of Intelligence and Research, had said that he thought that if the message were genuine and had originated at the top of the Soviet government, I would be willing to convey it to the secretary of state and the president. This was done.

That evening a long, rambling, cable—a letter from Khrushchev to Kennedy—began to arrive. It was conciliatory but contained nothing specific. One key passage, for example, likened the crisis to a rope with a knot in the middle, with Kennedy pulling on one end and Khrushchev pulling on the other. The more they both pulled, the more the knot tightened, until finally it could be cut only with a sword. But if they both stopped pulling, the knot could be untied. When this vague but forthcoming message was compared with the short but very specific message received through Fomin, a solution seemed possible. It was Robert F. Kennedy who con-

---

[2]Many years later, the Soviet representatives to a meeting in October 1987 to discuss the Cuban missile crisis claimed that twenty nuclear warheads actually did arrive in Cuba on the Soviet ship *Poltava*. It makes the Soviets look good, of course, if the warheads were actually in Cuba but not used because of Soviet restraint. However, there are grounds for skepticism. The heavy bunkers being built to house the warheads, which were necessary for safety reasons, were never completed. Also, to send warheads by ship would have risked their capture and thus the revelation of the secrets of their construction. Although the possibility that the warheads arrived by ship along with the missiles themselves should not be ruled out, it was for these two reasons that the United States at the time decided that it was more likely that the warheads would be sent by air. Hence the United States asked the African states on the route to Cuba to deny Soviet aircraft landing and refueling rights, which they did.

ceived a brilliant diplomatic maneuver that was later dubbed the "Trollope ploy," after the recurrent scene in Anthony Trollope's novels in which the girl interprets a squeeze of her hand as a proposal of marriage. Robert Kennedy's suggestion was to pick out of the message received through Fomin and out of the long cable from Khrushchev only those points that were acceptable to the United States, send Khrushchev a cable saying that this is what the United States understood that he was proposing, and that if this understanding was correct, the United States was prepared to accept. Such a message was sent, and the next morning Khrushchev broadcast from Moscow that he agreed. The crisis was over.[3]

---

[3]In an article in *Foreign Policy* (Fall 1988) entitled "Cuban Missile Crisis: The Soviet Story," Raymond L. Garthoff reported on a conference in 1987 between three Soviet officials who had knowledge of the crisis and some American scholars at Harvard. Although the Soviet officials had occupied lower-level positions at the time and so were involved only at the periphery, two of the points they made were new and different from what the Americans had understood in 1962 and also seemed credible. The Soviet representatives said first that it was Khrushchev and the Soviets who had requested the deployment, whereas Washington was uncertain whether the request for missiles had come from Castro or whether Castro had asked for arms and perhaps troops, which the Soviets had seized as an opportunity for a temporary solution to the "missile gap in reverse." Their second credible point was that whereas U.S. intelligence had estimated the total Soviet military personnel in Cuba at twenty-two thousand, the actual figure was forty-two thousand. (In 1979 U.S. intelligence discovered that a Soviet brigade of twenty-six hundred men had stayed on in Cuba after the crisis.)

However, two other points the Soviet representatives made were less believable. One was their assertion that the decision to shoot down the U-2 was made on the spot by a Soviet brigadier general without authorization from Moscow. It is frightening to imagine that the Kremlin had such little control over its troops in the field, although its very admission that this was the case does lend the assertion credibility. If so, it is one more reason to worry that deterrence alone cannot avoid nuclear war.

Their second assertion was that Fomin's approach was his own idea—and this is certainly not believable. Fomin asked Scali if he had a contact in the government who could get a message to the president himself. As described, Scali said that he was a friend of the present author and that he was absolutely certain that I would be able to get the message to Kennedy. Fomin stressed several times that the message had come directly from Khrushchev and that he was acting on Khrushchev's personal instructions. Without these emphatic assurances, it is doubtful that the message would in fact have been forwarded to the secretary of state and the president. What was also convincing at the time was that the Soviets had used similar unofficial channels on many occasions in the past. It is also extremely doubtful that a KGB chief would act on his own.

As for their later assertion, the Soviets have an obvious interest in insisting that they were *not* using Fomin in an official approach. They had a large stake in keeping the approach unofficial and "deniable" at that time. If the United States refused the deal, they could simply say that Fomin had not been authorized to make it. At the same time, the Soviets have a continued interest in holding to that position in case such a channel might be useful again. In addition, I have been told by a Soviet official who was a personal aide to Foreign Minister Andrei Gromyko that the approach had indeed been instituted by Khrushchev. Another conference between Americans and Soviets, which included people

(footnote continues on page 97)

THE ESCALATION IN VIETNAM

The U.S. government considered intervening in Southeast Asia on three separate occasions: at the time of Dienbienphu in the Eisenhower administration, in Laos in the Kennedy administration, and in Vietnam in the Johnson administration. Let us apply the political process model to all three decisions.

At the time of Dienbienphu, the French government asked the United States to bomb the Communist forces surrounding the French troops. Admiral Arthur W. Radford, chairman of the Joint Chiefs of Staff, and General Nathan Twining, chief of staff of the Air Force, developed a plan to drop three small tactical nuclear weapons on the forces surrounding the French.[4] Although the record is not clear whether they all thought the strike should be nuclear, Vice President Richard M. Nixon, Secretary of State John Foster Dulles, and Admiral Radford all favored some sort of air strike. The only one of the top Eisenhower officials who was strongly opposed to an air strike of any kind was General Matthew B. Ridgway, chief of staff of the Army. The general public, being unfamiliar with Southeast Asia, exerted no pressure either for or against the bombing.[5]

Ridgway proceeded to fight the proposal in every way he could.

---

who had held higher-ranking positions at the time, was held in Moscow in 1988. At this meeting, the Soviet representatives said that the motive for the deployment of missiles to Cuba was the fear that the United States was about to launch an invasion to make up for the failure of the Bay of Pigs. However, since the Soviets knew that Kennedy had adamantly refused to give in to the pressure to use American forces at the time of the Bay of Pigs, it seems very doubtful indeed that fear of an American invasion was the reason for the 1962 deployment.

Also, an invasion fleet takes an enormous number of landing craft. The United States had not assembled those landing craft at the time the Soviet decision was made to send the missiles to Cuba, and Soviet intelligence had excellent means to make that determination. It is simply not credible that they failed to use those means before making such a fateful decision if it was based on fear of an American invasion.

If there are any doubts that the Soviet representatives to these meetings were acting under instructions, a rather amusing incident will dispel them. During a coffee break at the Moscow meetings, a young Soviet representative was overhead by an American who speaks Russian asking one of the senior Soviet representatives, "Well, sir, did we follow the line correctly?" (Source: personal communication to the author by one of the American participants.)

[4]McGeorge Bundy, *Danger and Survival, Choices About the Bomb in the First Fifty Years* (New York: Random House, 1988), pp. 266–267.

[5]This account is drawn from Melvin Gurtov, *The First Vietnam Crisis: Chinese Communist Strategy and United States Involvement, 1953–54* (New York: Columbia University Press, 1967), p. 80 and pp. 92–115.

First, he piled up memo after memo citing his reasons. He argued that air power alone could not be decisive and that if the United States became involved by bombing, it would have to take the further step of introducing ground forces to complete the job. He assembled a team of military experts of all kinds and sent them to Vietnam with instructions to investigate all aspects of the terrain, port facilities, road and rail networks, and so on and to report back in a matter of days on the feasibility of an American intervention and its prospects for success. The report stated that more ground troops would be needed than the United States currently had and that the terrain and logistics backup was so unfavorable that even if the United States did have the requisite number of troops, victory would still be questionable.

It was clear to everyone concerned that what General Ridgway was doing ensured that if the U.S. intervention was not successful quickly, the fact that he had opposed it would inevitably become known. Even though the president was Dwight D. Eisenhower, who had been the supreme allied commander in Europe in World War II, the political repercussions of going against the advice of the Army chief of staff would be severe if the intervention dragged out or became costly in lives and treasure. Any decision to intervene therefore had to have very wide political backing, including that of the leaders in Congress, whom Eisenhower insisted be called into the discussions.

However, Ridgway had not only submitted his memos to the president and members of the National Security Council but also made his views known to key leaders in Congress. As a result, the congressional leaders were skeptical and insisted that allies such as Great Britain be a part of the intervention. The British government sided with Ridgway, however, and the proposal to intervene was defeated. The only alternative was to negotiate a settlement at Geneva.

The second major Southeast Asian crisis concerned Laos. Eisenhower had warned Kennedy that he might have to send American troops to Laos and that, if so, he would come to Washington and stand beside Kennedy in support. This was the kind of political support that Eisenhower himself would have liked to have had at the time of Dienbienphu. The crisis in Laos came late in 1961, when the Communists broke the cease-fire, and continued into early 1962. Again the general public had little knowledge of the situation and exerted no influence either way. In Washington, the power centers concerned were not so sharply divided as they had been at the time of Dienbienphu. Most of the military, the hardline faction in the State Department, and others who had been hawkish during Dienbienphu still favored intervention, but they were considerably less confident of such a solution. Similarly, those who had favored negotiations before still did so, but they too were hesitant and unsure. As a result, unlike Eisenhower at the time of Dien-bienphu, Kennedy was essentially free to go either way, since the pressures on him from the different power centers in effect canceled each other out. Given a free choice, Kennedy chose to negotiate.

In the Johnson administration, the issue was Vietnam. During the first year of his administration, the situation there had steadily worsened. Johnson gradually increased the number of military advisers until by the beginning of 1965, they numbered over 25,000. The final decision to bomb North Vietnam came in February 1965, but the president had laid the political groundwork for the decision much earlier. Again the general public exerted no significant influence either way.

Inside the government the officials involved in policy making were sharply divided—and Johnson had become very familiar with the individuals and organizations on both sides. On the White House staff, McGeorge Bundy, the national security adviser, and Michael V. Forrestal, the NSC staff specialist on Asia, were very skeptical of military intervention. In the State Department, Secretary Dean Rusk was hawkish. George W. Ball, the undersecretary, W. Averell Harriman, the undersecretary for political affairs, and Roger Hilsman, the present author who was the assistant secretary for Far Eastern affairs, were decidedly dovish. Secretary of Defense Robert S. McNamara was hawkish. CIA Director John A. McCone was hawkish, whereas Attorney General Robert F. Kennedy, the president's brother, was decidedly dovish. In the Congress, both the Senate and House committees dealing with foreign affairs tended to be dovish, while the members of the armed services committees tended to be hawkish.

The members of the Joint Chiefs of Staff were a special case. After the Korean conflict, the military in general felt that they should never again be required to fight a limited land war in Asia. Their feelings were so strong that around Washington they were jokingly dubbed the "never again club." In its extreme form their position was that before being sent into an Asian war, the military should be guaranteed permission to do whatever was necessary to win, including using nuclear weapons.

Thus President Johnson found himself in a position more like that of Eisenhower than Kennedy. Although the general public exerted no pressure, whichever path he chose would be opposed by powerful groups within the government.

There seems to be no doubt that Johnson did not plan in advance to escalate the war in Vietnam. But there also seems to be no doubt that he was determined not to lose the war, even if winning it required escalation. Kennedy used to say, "In the final analysis, it is their [the South Vietnamese people's] war. They are the ones who have to win it or lose it."[6] What seemed clear in the days following Kennedy's assassination was that Johnson had dropped the last three words. He did not want to escalate the war if it could be won without escalating. But if escalation was necessary for victory, he intended to escalate.

Given this conviction, the clever course for Johnson was to remove any dovish opposition in advance, which he proceeded to do with consummate political skill. His first target was the assistant secretary for Far Eastern affairs, Roger Hilsman, the present author. When President Johnson wanted to remove John Gronouski as postmaster general yet keep him in government to prevent him from criticizing the administration from a position in private life, he offered him the ambassadorship to Poland. Sure enough, Gronouski found the prospect of being the first Polish-American ambassador to Poland irresistible. In my case, the president found that I had spent part of my childhood in the Philippines, so Johnson offered me the post of ambassador to that country. As it happened, however, I preferred to return to private life and so resigned.

As for W. Averell Harriman, the president shifted him from undersecretary to roving ambassador with particular responsibility for African affairs. Harriman remarked privately that if he had been twenty years younger, he would have resigned. He also went on to say that Johnson would escalate the Vietnam war, that the escalation would fail, that the United States would have to negotiate, and that the president would have to choose him, Harriman, to be the negotiator because of his past record of negotiating with the Soviets. It was a remarkably prescient set of predictions, all of which came true.[7]

In dealing with George W. Ball, Johnson made him feel as if he would be the only spokesperson for the dove position that would be permitted to remain. For almost two years Ball was content at this job of being the "house dove," but he then came to feel that he was being used and left for private life.

Members of the White House staff could not exercise independent power, so Michael V. Forrestal was not a serious problem. He was encouraged to stay on but eventually returned to private life. However, McGeorge Bundy's position as national security adviser did make him a problem. For reasons known only to himself, Johnson seems to have felt that Bundy could be tempted to go along with a policy of escalation, perhaps because of the possibility of eventually replacing Rusk as secretary of state. In any event, after Johnson had tentatively decided to bomb North Vietnam, he persuaded Bundy to go to Vietnam for a final check and recommendation. Bundy was reluctant but did go and in fact acqui-

---

[6]Quoted in an interview with Walter Cronkite on CBS television, September 2, 1963.

[7]Personal conversation with Harriman, January 1964.

esced in the decision, and this acquiescence effectively accomplished Johnson's purpose.

Robert F. Kennedy was a much more formidable political problem. What Johnson did first was to announce to the public that he would not choose as his running mate in the election of 1964 anyone serving in his present cabinet, which was a roundabout way of saying that he would not choose Robert Kennedy. It had already become clear that as attorney general Kennedy was not going to be allowed to play a very important role in the Johnson administration. Privately Johnson suggested that the wisest course for Kennedy would be to resign and run for the governorship of Massachusetts. In the end, Kennedy decided to run for senator from New York.

The most difficult problem of all, however, was the Joint Chiefs of Staff. The way that Johnson removed them as an obstacle was to divide them. During the period between the two world wars the doctrine of air power had become increasingly prominent. The theory was that strategic bombing alone could win wars without the bloody attrition of battlefield combat. Bombing factories would destroy an enemy's capacity to build weapons and other materiel. Bombing cities, including workers' housing, would destroy civilian morale and thus erode support for the war. Any materiel that the enemy managed to produce despite the bombing would be prevented from reaching the front by interdiction bombing—striking the road and rail networks leading to the war zone. It was this strategy that the United States followed against both Germany and Japan in World War II.

Following World War II, the United States mounted a huge research effort to assess the effectiveness of the bombing. To the despair of the Air Force, the report, *The Strategic Bombing Survey,*[8] concluded that strategic bombing was not decisive and that resources would have been better spent in close support for the ground forces.

The Korean conflict gave the doctrine of air power one more chance. The U.S. Air Force had almost total air superiority over Korea and bombed the factories and towns of North Korea and the road and rail networks virtually at will. But again after the war the conclusion was that the bombing alone had not been decisive, even though it had undoubtedly slowed the enemy's preparation for an offensive and made such a buildup more costly. In effect, the enemy had to put 3 tons of supplies into the logistical pipe line to get 1 through to the front.

At the time of Vietnam, Johnson held out to the Air Force the prospect of one more chance to prove that strategic bombing could by

---

[8]*The U.S. Strategic Bombing Survey Report: European and Pacific Wars* (Washington, DC.: U.S. Government Printing Office, 1945–1947), 319 volumes.

itself win wars. The initial proposal for escalation was thus not for making the struggle an American war but only for bombing North Vietnam. This proposal, code named "Rolling Thunder," divided the Joint Chiefs of Staff and nullified their resistance to anything that seemed likely to lead to another limited war in Asia. The United States began bombing North Vietnam and the supply routes leading to South Vietnam in February 1965. A few weeks later some regular combat ground forces were introduced to defend the airfields used by the bombers. The situation in South Vietnam continued to deteriorate in spite of the bombing, and in July 1965 the United States introduced ground forces on a large scale, eventually numbering over half a million men.

Thus the political process model does clear up at least some of the puzzlement over why the Eisenhower and Kennedy administrations chose not to fight in Southeast Asia while the Johnson administration did. It also resolves some of the differences between the hawks and the doves on strategic factors. Eisenhower was not really free to escalate the war without significant political cost, and since there were strategic arguments both for and against escalation, the high political cost seems to be a plausible explanation of why he chose not to do so.

Nor was Johnson free to escalate, but he very cleverly outmaneuvered the opposition. Although he eventually had to pay a high political cost for failing to win the war, he was able to escalate without any immediate cost. Of course Johnson could just as easily have made himself free to negotiate by the same kind of skillful political maneuvering. Kennedy, unlike Johnson and Eisenhower, was free to go either way. He chose to negotiate.

Thus one puzzle remains: If the strategic factors can be argued either for or against intervening in Laos and Vietnam and if the political factors also tended to cancel out in Kennedy's case and were nullified in Johnson's case, why did Kennedy negotiate and Johnson escalate? On this essentially psychological point, the political process model, like the others, is silent.

CHINA'S INVITATION TO NIXON

Why did China invite President Richard M. Nixon to visit China and so begin the process of normalizing relations between China and the United States? The black box explanation for the invitation was as follows: China and the Soviet Union found themselves increasingly at odds over ideology, over power within the Communist bloc, over how decision making was organized within the Communist world and whose national interests would be given priority, over policy toward the "in-between" world, and finally over grand strategy and how aggressive the Communists should be in their dealings with the West and how much risk of nuclear war should be run. The tension between China and the Soviet Union actually resulted in rather large-scale fighting along the Ussuri River on the long border between the two.

At the same time, China also faced tensions with Japan, with the Chinese becoming convinced during the late 1960s that Japanese militarism was on the rise again. Finally, China had tension with the United States, with many Chinese leaders believing that the United States actually intended to invade China in the future.

Thus China found itself isolated and surrounded by hostile powers: the Soviet Union, Japan, and the United States. Since a grand alliance, the classical answer to such a situation, was impossible, the only alternative was to lessen tension on one front or the other. If relations could be eased with the United States, they would automatically be eased with Japan and what was essentially a three-front conflict would be reduced to one.

The counterargument, using the same black box mode of analysis, was that if all these strategic arguments were valid, the logical course of action was not to ease tensions with the United States but with the Soviet Union, with which China shared a long border that was difficult to defend. Easing tensions with the Soviets would also help China on other matters, such as its relations with the Third World.

An explanation using the political process model begins by looking for power centers and then for differences between them on goals, means to the goals, parochial interests, and the like. In China, as in the Soviet Union, major power centers include the party hierarchs, the military, the industrial bureaucracies, and the various regional and local government organizations. However, in the case of China, Western analysts have actually identified a number of other possible candidates, for in the speeches, articles, and various official statements that have become available, the Chinese themselves have talked about "factions."

Since we are interested in these factions only to show that a political process model has some utility, no attempt will be made to survey the Chinese literature. Instead, only the work of one particularly prominent analyst will be used: Lucian Pye's study for the RAND corporation. Pye's study was actually done several years after the events with which we are concerned took place, but there is reason to believe that the groups existed in the earlier period, although they had different names. In any case, we will assume that these groups did exist earlier, and we will also use the names by which they were known during Pye's research.[9] Pye

---

[9]Lucian Pye, *The Dynamics of Chinese Politics* (Cambridge, Mass.: Oelgeschlager, Gunn & Hain for the RAND Corporation, 1981).

found that at least four factions were described and given names in the Chinese materials. Some had members concentrated in one or another place in the Chinese government and political bureaucracies, whether in the party, the government, the economic enterprises, the military, or the regional centers (such as the Shanghai party and local government, which were prominent for their ultraleft stance during the Cultural Revolution). However, to some extent these factions cut across organizational and even regional lines. The names of the factions are those used by the Chinese.

One faction was made up of Mao loyalists. Later it was called the "whatever" faction because it supported "whatever Mao said." Its most prominent leader was Huo Guofeng. This faction was particularly strong among rural party officials.

The second faction was composed of cadres who had survived the Cultural Revolution and wanted to hold on to their positions. Later it was called the "veteran cadres" faction or, by its opponents, the "opposition" faction. The members were essentially opportunists who would risk either a leftist or a rightist tide if it meant they could retain their jobs.

The third and fourth factions were essentially two wings of a broader faction of "rehabilitated cadres," that is, people who had been purged in the Cultural Revolution and rehabilitated in its aftermath. Deng Shaoping was the overall leader, although he was more closely identified with the second wing, or fourth faction.

The first wing, or third faction, believed the party should return to the policy of the 1950s, especially the policy that immediately followed the Great Leap Forward. This faction, in other words, favored essentially conservative economic and social policies. Later, it was called the "restoration" faction because it wanted to restore the policy of the 1950s.

The second wing, or fourth faction, was composed partly of veteran cadres who had made the Long March but mainly those who had been accused and sent to reeducation centers during the Cultural Revolution and had since been rehabilitated. Because its position was that all that had gone before had been disastrous and that new practices were needed, this was later called the "new practices" or simply the "practices" faction.

In the strategic debate over whether to ease tensions with the Soviet Union or the United States, the Mao loyalists were strongly opposed to the former alternative, although they were probably not really enthusiastic about the latter either. Mao's position had been that both were enemies. He called the Soviets "revisionists" who were unfaithful to Communist doctrine and the Americans "imperialists" who were out to conquer the world. The "opposition" faction apparently had no strong ideological position on the question but would favor whichever policy seemed to help most in their own survival. This was a "swing" faction. The "restoration" faction seemingly favored easing tensions with the Soviets in an attempt to return matters to their former status. Finally, the "new practices" faction apparently leaned slightly toward easing tensions with the United States. There seems to have been no inherent ideological reason for this tendency other than that friendlier relations with the United States fit better with the faction's ideas about economic development. However, the suspicion is that the main reason that the "new practices" faction favored this policy was because it was thought to be the most useful in gaining allies in the struggle they regarded as much more important—the struggle over who would succeed to power when Mao died.

The hypothesis is therefore that the Chinese debate over whether to ease tensions with Russia or the United States became mixed up with the power struggle over Mao's successor. The historical parallel would be the Soviet dispute over economic policy between Stalin and his faction and Trotsky and his supporters that became tangled up with a power struggle. That Stalin's opposition to the economic policy Trotsky proposed was tactical rather than substantive is demonstrated by the fact that when Trotsky fled into exile, Stalin adopted his economic policy. If this hypothesis is correct when applied to the Chinese debate, then the puzzle over which policy was more logical disappears. It may have been more logical strategically to ease tensions with the Soviets, but if the decision to ease tensions with the United States had instead been an element in building the coalition that succeeded in replacing Mao, then politics, not strategic logic, was the central consideration.

THE SOVIET INVASION OF AFGHANISTAN

The Carter administration's analysis of the Soviet invasion of Afghanistan argued that the Soviets were basically aggressive and expansionist and that the invasion represented a move both to expand their empire and to secure Afghanistan as a base for a lunge on the Middle East and its treasure of oil. Based on this analysis the Carter administration adopted a series of hard-line policies: a public statement that the United States considered the invasion a hostile act that threatened détente, an attempt to persuade other Western countries to join in a unified response against the Soviets, assurances to the countries bordering Afghanistan of U.S. protection from further Soviet aggression, the laying of the domestic political groundwork for an increase in the defense budget, a delay in Senate consideration of the SALT II treaty, an embargo of the export of grain and high-technology goods to the Soviet Union, a prohibition of Soviet fishing in U.S. waters, a moratorium on the opening of new U.S. and USSR consular offices, suspension of cultural exchanges, and a boycott of the Olympic games to be held in Moscow.

By applying the same black box model used by the administration, one analyst opposing the Carter position argued that since World War II, the Soviets have followed policies of "low cost and low risk." They had always wanted Afghanistan as part of the Communist bloc of buffer nations but considered both the cost and risk too high. However, the military balance between the Soviets and the Americans had shifted in the Soviets' favor after their arms buildup over the preceding 15 years and led to their reassessment of what constituted both low cost and low risk, which explained their decision to invade Afghanistan.

A second analyst agreed that the Soviets had always cast an avaricious eye on Afghanistan and did not dispute the facts on the Soviet military buildup. But he came to a quite different conclusion: The United States never did have any sticks that would deter an invasion of Afghanistan, which had previously been prevented by the Soviets' fear of the possible loss of carrots. What triggered the invasion, according to this analyst, was neither a Soviet decision to position itself for a lunge at the Middle East nor a reassessment of what constituted low cost and low risk, but the fact that the United States under the Carter administration no longer had any carrots.

In applying the political process model to the question of why the Soviets had invaded Afghanistan, analysts could begin by listing the power centers used in determining Soviet motives for deploying the missiles to Cuba: the party *apparatchiks,* the military, the KGB, other government bureaucracies, the economic bureaucracies, and the regional party apparatus and local governments. The problem in the case of the Soviet invasion of Afghanistan, unlike the Cuban missile crisis, was that there was little or no evidence of the position of these various power centers on the issue. There was neither hard information available about any differences among the power centers nor any reason to suppose that the alternative policies would impinge on the various power centers in ways that would permit Western analysts to deduce useful hypotheses. As a result, the political process model was useless in trying to provide additional light on Soviet motives or to help resolve the differences among the black box analyses of both the Carter administration and its two critics. As in the case of the dog that neither growled nor wagged its tail, there was a theory but none of the facts needed to make it work.

Some years later, Gorbachev indicated in public that the decision to invade had been made not by the full Politburo but by Brezhnev together with a very small number of the top military officers and his top civilian colleagues. If Gorbachev's revelation is true, which the circumstances seem to indicate, it explains why Western analysts had so little information about which factions favored intervention and which did not. Both Gorbachev's revelation and the fact that the Soviets under his rule announced a plan for withdrawal from Afghanistan suggest that the decision to invade did not reflect the true interests of the various factions but rather some as yet unknown personal or subgroup goals.

In any case, the lesson of applying the political process model to the Soviet invasion of Afghanistan is that analysts of international affairs must be careful not to throw the black box baby out with the bath water. When the information required for this model is unavailable or inadequate, the black box, rational-actor model is obviously better than merely tossing a coin because the people who act in the name of the state share at least some commitment to state goals and at least some of the time agree on what those goals are and the best means for achieving them.

IRAN AND THE AMERICAN HOSTAGES

The black box model's answers to the question of why Iran held the American hostages for 444 days were threefold. First, taking and holding the hostages was a step toward neutrality and away from the alliance with the United States that was no longer wise in the light of the Soviet military buildup. Second, the move established Iran's leadership in the Muslim world by demonstrating that the United States was a "pitiful helpless giant" when facing the Ayatollah Khomeini. Third, by confronting and defying a superpower Iran sent an ideological message to the Third World. A number of analysts also suggested that an additional motive was revenge for the American support of the shah, including allowing him to come to the United States for medical treatment.

The counterarguments, also based on a black box analysis, started with the proposition that the Iranian revolution was threatened not so much from a direct attack by the Soviet Union as from Iran's precarious economic and financial situation, a coup by the Communist Tudeh party, a guerrilla war led by the Tudeh party along the lines of Vietnam, or a combination of all these factors. Thus the logical conclusion, according to the counterargument, would be not to confront the United States by permitting the militants to go on holding the American hostages but to cultivate the United States. The implication of this analysis for U.S. policy was that even if the Iranians persisted in holding the hostages, the United States should not adopt the punitive measures followed by the Carter administration, such as freezing Iranian assets, but should behind the scenes offer carrots while working quietly to get other Muslim countries to try to persuade Iran that holding the hostages damaged the reputation of them all.

In applying the political process model to Iran analysts did not lack information, as they did in trying to understand the Soviet invasion of

Afghanistan. The contending groups were quite obvious. Ayatollah Khomeini and his immediate supporters were the most prominent. The old business, commercial, industrial, military, and government elites also all continued to exercise some power, even though they had been weakened by the purges of both the shah and the new revolutionary government.

In addition, it was clear that a struggle for power was going on inside the revolutionary government among a variety of groups. The overthrow of the shah had been accomplished by a coalition of militant Muslim religious leaders (mullahs), of whom Ayatollah Khomeini was the most prestigious and the acknowledged leader. Other contending power centers included more moderate mullahs, mostly in outlying districts; a group of mullahs who were fanatically Muslim but at the same time extremely left wing, almost Marxist; and moderate laymen of the national front. Prime Minister Mehdi Bazargan was the leader of one of the latter groups. A rival group was headed by a man who had been a close lay adviser to Khomeini during his exile, Abol-Hassan Bani-Sadr, who was elected president of Iran under the new constitution in January 1980.

The Carter administration saw Iran as a state like all the other states. In the terms of the political process model, the administration viewed it as a country with a working government and political system. They would negotiate with what they assumed was the government of Iran, reach an agreement with it, and then be infuriated when the government did not live up to its side of the agreement and produce the results it had promised. The fact is, however, that at this time Iran did not have a working government and political system in which policies were bargained out among the power centers, agreement reached, and policies then implemented more or less as they were decided upon. Thus when the United States reached an agreement with what was ostensibly the government of Iran, the other contending groups proceeded to do something that would in fact nullify the agreement. The militants, for example, refused to obey orders from President Bani-Sadr on several occasions and from the Revolutionary Council, the highest body of the government, at least once. The militants may well have been able to ignore a direct order to release the hostages from Ayatollah Khomeini himself, their professed leader. The truth is that when the hostages were being held, Iran was an anarchy. Rival power centers were struggling over power with no one of them yet certain of the extent of its power or authority. As Gertrude Stein said of her birthplace, Oakland, California, "There was no there there."

The story of the struggle for power inside Iran reveals that the hostages were taken and held not for strategic, geopolitical reasons but for use as a weapon in this struggle.[10] In the months following his appointment as prime minister, Bazargan attempted to pursue a moderate course. He called for calm, emphasized reconstruction, and opposed extreme antagonism toward the United States. He said that the benefits of the revolution could come only when the economy was back on its feet, and he deplored the preoccupation with American "conspiracies." Khomeini, however, continued to preach violent anti-Americanism.

While visiting Algeria for its independence day celebrations in 1979, Bazargan met with Zbigniew Brzezinski, Carter's national security adviser. Rivals of Bazargan in Iran arranged for pictures of the meeting to appear on Iranian TV. There was a mass demonstration in protest, during which a group of militants broke off from the march and staged a sit-in at the American embassy. Violence ensued, and in the struggle the militants occupied the embassy and took the hostages.

The evidence is that their action had not been directed by either the government or Khomeini. The militants made a public appeal for Khomeini's approval, which he gave the next day, saying that the embassy was a "lair for spies" and that the Americans had expected to bring the shah to the embassy and "engage in plots." Apparently the militants' only intention at the time was to take advantage of the pictures of the Bazargan and Brzezinski meeting to stage a sit-in to demonstrate against the Bazargan group. They seem to have had no plan actually to occupy the embassy and hold the hostages for any length of time.

However, the militants apparently ended up holding the hostages for 444 days because the worldwide publicity, especially on TV, made it a useful tactic in the power struggle inside Iran by giving the militants backing the Khomeini group a prominence of which they never dreamed. In fact, the American press itself realized that it had been a primary reason the hostages were held so long. During the entire 14 months that the Americans were held captive, Walter Cronkite, anchor of the CBS evening news, ended each broadcast with a solemn and sonorous intonation: "This is the umpteenth day of the captivity of the American hostages

---

[10]Information on this struggle was readily available at the time in American newspapers. For a rundown, see Robert D. McFadden, *No Hiding Place: The New York Times Inside Report on the Hostage Crisis* (New York: Time Books, 1981). For a very full account of what went on inside the policy councils in Washington, see Warren Christopher and colleagues, under the editorial guidance of Paul Kreisberg, director of studies, Council on Foreign Relations, *American Hostages in Iran: The Conduct of a Crisis* (New Haven, Conn.: Yale University Press for the Council on Foreign Relations, 1985). This book is a prime historical record of the crisis. Seven of its nine authors were direct participants in its resolution as policy makers and negotiators. See also Gary Sick, *All Fall Down: America's Tragic Encounter with Iran* (New York: Random House, 1985); and Robert Parry and Peter Kornbluh, "Iran-Contra's Untold Story," *Foreign Policy* (Fall 1988).

in Iran." Following the aborted rescue attempt James Reston of *The New York Times* criticized President Carter for giving in to the pressure to "do something" rather than being patient and letting the inevitable factionalism within Iran bring about the release of the captives. But Reston quickly added that the pressure on Carter had been enormous, with not the least coming from "my old buddy, the Ayatollah Walter Cronkite."[11] The most biting criticism of the role of the press during the hostage crisis was made by still another news reporter, Digby Whitman:

> The hostages fully deserve our sympathy and respect. . . . They have been callously exploited by the Iranian [government] . . . for political, mercenary, and venal purposes. But it seems to me that they have also and equally cynically been exploited for the same purposes in their homeland.
>
> During the fourteen months of their internship [*sic*], the plain fact is that there have been exactly three pieces of hard news. The first was the news of their seizure. The second was the news of the imbecilicly bungled attempt by our military to bring them away by force. The third was the news of their release.
>
> These three islands of actual, factual news have been almost submerged in a 400-day sea of wildly speculative, usually inaccurate, and often flatly wrong newspaper blather and noisy network commentary: it has been authoritatively reported, it has been learned from reliable sources, an unidentified official at the State Department (or the White House) has said, it is believed in the Pentagon that—with every week's reportage contradicted or reversed next week, and in its totality nothing being reported at all.
>
> The whole fourteen-month "crisis" has been ruthlessly utilized to attract and hold readers and viewers and listeners.
>
> Even today, in the happy hour of the hostages' homecoming, it is worth noting that while they pushed the regular programs off the channels, they didn't displace any commercials. They are simply perceived and used as a vehicle superior to "Ironsides" or "Captain Kangaroo" for the movement of beer and toilet tissue, toothpaste and pantyhose.[12]

In any case, as part of a power struggle the militants' move was successful. The Bazargan government had promised to protect the American embassy and criticized its occupation. Thus when Khomeini gave public approval to the action, the government resigned.

In January 1980 Bani-Sadr was elected president. In February he began to try to assert his authority over the militants by saying that the "government within a government" that they were attempting to create was "intolerable." As a result of negotiations, a UN commission was appointed to investigate the shah's regime as part of an agreement to

---

[11]*The New York Times,* April 27, 1980.

[12]Digby Whitman, "52, Yes but How About the 52,000?" *The New York Times,* February 8, 1981.

bring about the release of the hostages. Bani-Sadr then told an interviewer that the hostages would be released as soon as the commission reported. Ayatollah Khomeini immediately announced that the decision on the fate of the hostages would be made by the Islamic assembly, which was not scheduled to meet until May. The UN commission arrived in Teheran shortly thereafter, and on March 6 it was announced that the hostages would be turned over to the custody of the government of Iran. The militants refused. Khomeini then seemed to uphold their decision by announcing that the UN commission would not even be allowed to see the hostages until their report was submitted to and approved by Iran. The next events were the Carter administration's decision to break diplomatic relations and its aborted rescue attempt, following which it was announced that Secretary of State Cyrus Vance had resigned because he had opposed the raid.

Bani-Sadr had been elected president in January by 75 to 80 percent of the vote. But in May, when the results of the election to the Islamic Assembly were announced, the Islamic Republican party, the party of the militant leaders of Iran's 180,000 mullahs, took a clear majority of the seats. Although Bani-Sadr was still nominally in charge, Khomeini's group had won the power struggle. They launched a purge of all but the most devout fundamentalists in the bureaucracies, the universities, the army, and elsewhere. There were many executions, public stonings of sinners, and so many arrests that the jails were as full as they had been under the shah at the worst of times.

By the end of the summer, the power struggle was over. Although some extremists talked of putting the hostages on trial as spies to humiliate the United States even more, now that the power struggle was over the hostages were no longer useful. All that was needed was a graceful way out, which the defeat of President Carter in the election provided. The negotiations began to make headway immediately after Carter's loss, although they were probably deliberately slowed down so that the actual release did not occur until after he had left office.

Thus in the case of Iran and the American hostages, not only was the information available to make the political process model work, but the use of this mode of analysis removes the puzzlements that arose from the black box model.

THE IRAN-CONTRA AFFAIR

The black box analysis of the Iran-Contra affair began by stating that Iran was vital to the West because it was an important crossroad of world communication routes, an avenue for a Soviet invasion of the Middle East and its oil reserves, and itself a rich source of oil. The mullahs dominating Iran were hostile to the United States, and providing arms to Iran through a dialogue with "moderate" mullahs promised to lessen this hostility. At the same time, the deal might also accomplish the humanitarian goal of freeing the three or four American hostages being held by groups under Iranian control. Then, when the sale of arms generated a surplus, that money could be used to buy arms for the Contras, since Congress had expressly forbidden the use of appropriated U.S. funds for such purposes. Administration officials maintained that President Reagan had not been informed of the Iran-Contra affair to avoid a potential embarrassment to him. Here the historical parallel is King Henry II's rhetorical outburst, "Is there not one who will rid me of this low-born priest?" which two Norman knights promptly proceeded to do in order to please the king.

The counterarguments were that there were no "moderates" left in Iran and that for the United States to sell arms to Iran when it had been urging its allies not to do so would be dishonorable – and would surely be revealed by the Iranians whenever it suited their purpose. The opponents also argued that the Sandinistas were nationalists first and Communists only second, that the Contras were venal and ineffective, and that the only hope for a solution to the problem of Nicaragua was multilateral negotiations, spearheaded by the Central American and Latin American countries themselves.

When the political process model is applied to the Iran-Contra affair, the decision begins to resemble the Bay of Pigs invasion. The policy was determined by a very small number of power centers who had successfully excluded those that had legitimate responsibilities and knowledge that might have shown the weaknesses of the operation. It was led not by the NSC, which is composed of the secretaries of the major departments such as State, Defense, and Treasury, but by the *staff of the NSC,* principally Robert C. McFarlane, the NSC adviser at the beginning of the affair, his successor Admiral John Poindexter, and Lieutenant Colonel Oliver North. McFarlane and Poindexter seem to have been motivated by both ideological convictions and personal ambitions to play as large a role in the NSC as their predecessors, Henry A. Kissinger and Zbigniew Brzezinski. North, on the other hand, apparently was not only highly ideological but also what the military call a "can-do" personality or a "loose cannon" – a highly energetic person, eager to please, who charges off in all directions to accomplish what he thinks his leaders want but exercises little judgment.

As for the role of President Reagan, the Henry II analogy seems to have been only partly true. It has been suggested that the whole affair reminded him of an old movie plot that had all the elements for a box office success: anti-Communist fervor, intrigue, and, most important, the sentimental human element provided by the hostages. It was precisely the kind of operation, the argument runs, that would pique Reagan's interest.

But the limited evidence so far available is that all this is only part of the story. What is known hints that the person who was in control, who knew all the details and pulled all the strings, was William Casey, the director of the CIA. Casey had served in a very active post in the Office of Strategic Services, the World War II predecessor of the CIA. He was a hardline anti-Communist and a firm believer in the covert actions and behind-the-scenes maneuvering of secret intelligence. However, his exact role in the affair may never be known. He died of cancer in the middle of the investigation.

But even though Casey's role may be obscure forever, the political process model explains most of the ambiguities of the Iran-Contra affair left when the other models are used.

THE GULF WAR AGAINST IRAQ

Why did the United States go to war to reverse Iraq's invasion of Kuwait? To repeat the points outlined earlier, President Bush compared Saddam Hussein to Adolf Hitler and argued that he should not be "appeased." Second, Bush said that if Hussein controlled Middle Eastern oil, it would threaten the American "way of life."

As time went on, Bush added two more goals. The first was to destroy Iraq's military capacity, including its potential for building nuclear weapons in the future. The second goal was to establish a "new world order."

Using the same classical, black box theory, critics of the Bush's decisions argued, first, that the United States should midwife an Arab solution to the four problems facing Hussein and Iraq and so forestall an Iraqi invasion before it happened.

After the invasion, the critics argued that if anyone had to kill Arabs, it should be other Arabs. They said that the United States and the Western Allies should supply sea and sea-based air forces but the Arabs and the Third World should supply the ground forces. The boycott should be run by Arabs.

At the same time, the critics urged that the United States adopt a far-reaching policy to make itself independent of Middle Eastern oil.

After President Bush sent American troops to Saudi Arabia, the critics argued that war could still be avoided. Since an immediate takeover of Saudi Arabia had been forestalled, the United States should turn responsibility over to Arab and Third World states. Again, the economic boycott would continue under Arab auspices.

If the Arabs refused to fight and Iraq ended up taking Saudi Arabia as well as Kuwait, Bush's critics argued, the long-term political consequences would not be good, but they would be better than if it was Americans who did the killing.

Applying the Political Process Model

In looking at the decisions made by the United States, what strikes the observer first is that the goals President Bush laid out seem to be rationalizations—"good" reasons rather than "real" reasons.

On the first point, not permitting aggression, the United States fought in Korea and Vietnam on the grounds that the ultimate enemy in both cases was the Soviet Union and world Communism. But the United States did not fight when Soviet troops invaded Czechoslovakia, Hungary, or Afghanistan. The United States has tolerated dozens of aggressions like that of Iraq against Kuwait in recent history—such as the Indian takeover of Goa; the Vietnamese invasion of Cambodia; the Israeli occupation of the Gaza strip and the West Bank, its attack on Lebanon, and its occupation of the Golan Heights; the Indonesian attack on East Timor; and the Iraqi attack on Iran. The United States has even invaded a few countries itself—such as Cambodia, Grenada, and Panama.

As for the assertion that Saddam Hussein is a new Hitler, it is obvious that while Hitler was a threat to the entire world, Iraq was not. With a population of eighteen million people, with only an embryonic industry, and with weapons not made in Iraq but imported from abroad, Iraq could never be a threat to anyone except its immediate neighbors.

As for the question of Iraq's potential for building nuclear weapons, experts are unanimous on two points. The first is that although Iraq in a few years might be able to build two or three nuclear bombs similar to the 14-kiloton bomb dropped on Hiroshima, it would be decades before it could develop the means to deliver them anywhere except in its immediate neighborhood. In the words of the director the Defense Nuclear Agency (DNA), General Gerald G. Watson, if Iraq ever did succeed in building a nuclear device, it "would weigh five tons and have to be carried on a flatbed trailer"—hardly a practical weapon of war.

The second point is that several other countries pose a similar threat of developing nuclear weapons. In November 1991, for example, American, Japanese, and South Korean officials announced that North Korea's enormous effort to develop a nuclear capability would soon succeed. The only real hope for a long-term solution to such threats is not unilateral military action by the United States but some sort of international control—through the UN or some other international body.

On the question of the American dependence on Middle East oil, it need only be said that even if Saddam Hussein did come to control a large share of the oil produced in the Middle East, it would do him no good unless he could sell it. He would undoubtedly have raised the price, but if he raised it too high, the United States and the other industrial nations would have turned to other sources of oil—such as Canada, Venezuela, Mexico, and Texas—and to other sources of energy, such as coal, water, the sun, and the atom.

The point is simply that the reasons President Bush offered for going to war are not really persuasive and that the real motive must have been something deeper. The evidence suggests the following sequence of events. First, Iraq had a genuine complaint against Kuwait. Second, a misunderstanding developed between the United States and Iraq about what Iraqi actions against Kuwait the United States would tolerate. Finally, this misunderstanding escalated into a full-scale war because it became a personal struggle between two men, Saddam Hussein and George Bush.

George Herbert Walker Bush

Because of his two years as ambassador to the UN, his slightly more than one year as ambassador to China, and his year as the director of the CIA, President Bush clearly thought that his major expertise was in foreign affairs. He had met and talked with the leaders of most of the other countries of the world. In the process, he developed a personal style in dealing with foreign affairs that was totally different from that of any previous president in history. Essentially it was based on personal contact—on making *"friends"* with the leaders of other countries. It is said, for example, that during the Gulf War he made over 30 telephone calls to the president of Turkey alone and many more to some of the other leaders.

There are obvious advantages if a president knows other leaders. But there are also disadvantages to a person-to-person approach. Countries whose leaders a president regards as personal friends tend to be treated well even if the state behaves in ways contrary to American interests. For example, during his year as ambassador to China, Bush got to know and make "friends" with the country's top leaders. Later these same leaders ordered the massacre of Chinese students protesting in Tiananmen Square. The world was outraged, and most democratic countries took some sort of concrete measures to give meaning to their feelings. But the Bush administration confined itself to a rather mild expression of disapproval, and since then President Bush has lobbied the Congress to grant China most-favored-nation status in trade. Many members of Congress regard such a move as rewarding tyrannical and brutal behavior and fear that this is exactly the way that the Chinese would interpret it.

Weighing leader-to-leader relationships more heavily than state-to-state relationships works the other way as well. The evidence is that Bush thought he had at least made some progress in making a "friend" of Saddam Hussein. He also seems to have concluded that Saddam Hussein had given some sort of assurance that if he used force in dealing with his problems with Kuwait, it would be limited. So when Hussein took *all* of Kuwait, Bush seems to have felt that Hussein had lied to him and betrayed their budding friendship. This personal, emotional reaction seems to have been fundamental to President Bush's decision to turn his back on the alternatives and to make the Gulf conflict an American war.

The View from Iraq

Saddam Hussein's decisions also seemed to be based on personal traits as well. As Saddam Hussein saw it, he had three choices. First, he could order his troops to resist. If he did, according to several American generals and outside experts, something like ten thousand Americans would probably have been killed and two or three times that many wounded. Allied casualties would have been just as high. But even so, Hussein seems to have understood that if Iraq did fight, it would only be a matter of time – a rather short time – before Hussein's troops would have been defeated.

What Hussein also seems to have realized is that the Americans and their Allies would then have had both the excuse and the incentive to drive on to Baghdad and occupy the whole of Iraq. If so, the result may well have been the breakup of Iraq as a state and certainly the end of Saddam Hussein himself.

Second, Saddam Hussein could have acceded to the U.S. and Allied demands and promptly withdrawn from Kuwait. If he had done so, Iraq would have been spared both the enormous, mind-boggling physical destruction of the weeks of constant bombing and the 200,000 or 300,000 military and civilian casualties – killed, wounded, and dead from malnutrition and disease.

But the thought of Iraqi casualties has never bothered Hussein in the past, and what must have seemed more important to him was that if he gave in at the outset, Hussein himself would not be the hero to the Arab masses that he has apparently since become. As it is, most Arabs see Saddam Hussein as one more victim of the brutality of the western infidel, but a victim who at least tried to stand up and resist. In Jordan during one week in January 1991, for example, over 400 newborn males were given the name "Saddam."

Hussein's third alternative was neither to accede to the Allied demands nor to fight, but to retreat without either surrendering or putting up any more than a token resistance to cover the withdrawal.

Adopting this course of action offered Hussein a chance for a sort of moral victory. A few days before the invasion he told some Palestinians that he was in a "lose-lose" position. If he fought, he would surely lose militarily. On the other hand, if he capitulated and withdrew from Kuwait without fighting, he would lose politically. "Shall I lose militarily or politically?" he asked rhetorically. "I shall lose militarily."[13]

His reasoning seems to have been along the following lines. Although their motives were different, neither America's Arab nor European Allies relished the idea of the Americans occupying Iraq. So Hussein could be fairly confident that they would probably succeed in persuading the United States to stop short of driving on to Baghdad. Withdrawal with only minimal resistance would mean high Iraqi casualties, but, again, Hussein would not care.

This third alternative of refusing to surrender but withdrawing with only token resistance would give Iraq a very good chance of surviving as a state. Bush publicly encouraged both the Shiites and the Kurds to rebel. But none of America's Allies and friends in the Middle East—whether Arab, British, French, or Israeli—wanted to see Iraq balkanized into separate Kurdish, Sunni, and Shiite states. They much preferred a united Iraq to stand between them and the 55 million Iranians led by religious zealots, even if the cost was that Iraq's leader continued to be Saddam Hussein. As it turned out, both the Arab and European Allies opposed continuing the offensive to Baghdad and strongly urged Bush to halt well short of it. The Turks, for example, went even farther, warning that they would invade Iraq themselves to prevent the formation of an independent Kurdish state.

Hussein also seems to have reasoned that this third alternative offered the possibility not only of letting Hussein himself evade a hangman's noose or a firing squad, but of giving him a fairly good chance of surviving as the ruler of Iraq.

So far, it looks as if Hussein's judgment from his own, personal point of view was sound. The fact that he was able to put down both the Shiite and the Kurdish rebellions indicates that the military casualties were confined to reserve and second-line troops and that a substantial proportion of the tanks, helicopter gunships, and other military equipment needed to put down the rebellion survived. The Republican Guard, his elite force, was damaged, but not enough to prevent them from dealing with the rebellion. Some of Hussein's air force was destroyed, and he sent some to Iran. But a substantial number seem to have survived in bun-

---

[13]Elaine Sciolino, *The Outlaw State, Saddam Hussein's Quest for Power and the Gulf Crisis,* (New York: John Wiley, 1991), p. 31.

kers, especially the helicopter gunships, which were vital in putting down the rebellion.

Iraq suffered terribly, both in terms of physical damage and casualties. But it avoided being dismembered and survives as a state, a state that still has a significant military capacity. And as for Saddam Hussein himself, he not only remains the dictator of Iraq, but he seems to be more strongly in power than he was before. What is more, to many of the Arab masses, Saddam Hussein seems to have become a hero—an Arab leader who defied the United States and the entire industrialized world and survived.

On the other hand, the Arab peoples looked aghast at the 150,000 to 200,000 Iraqi dead. They looked at the ruins of Iraq's road and rail networks, manufacturing industry, water purification plants, and electrical capacity and asked if such wholesale destruction had any real military significance. They noted that several months after the war ended an estimated 500 Iraqi children were still dying each day because of the lack of pure water and medicines that need refrigeration. And they said that it seemed that Americans do not put as much value on Arab lives as they do on the lives of other peoples.

Many people in the Third World shared the Arab dismay about the casualties and the seemingly needless destruction. Bush's talk of a "new world order" also bothered them. To many, the phrase suggested a "New American Imperialism." It sounded especially ominous because of the turmoil inside the Soviet Union. When there were two superpowers, the developing world speculated, one restrained the other. When there is only one, what will happen?

SUMMARY

In all of the seven case studies, using the political process model cleared up most of the puzzlements unaccounted for in using the other models. But not all. In some cases some puzzlements remain. The different ways that Kennedy reacted to the Laos crisis in 1962 and Johnson reacted to the situation in Vietnam in 1965 seem to lie more in the realm of psychology than political science. So did the way that the mutual dislike between Saddam Hussein and George Bush came to override other considerations and lead to the war in the Persian Gulf. In other cases, such as the Soviet decision to intervene in Afghanistan in 1979, the information needed to make a political process model work was simply not available to anyone outside the inner circle of the Kremlin.

8

ELECTING
THE PRESIDENT

The president of the United States is a power center. Since our focus is the politics of policy making in defense and foreign affairs, we are mainly concerned with presidential power in these two areas. But to understand the power of presidents in defense and foreign affairs we need to know something of their power in other subject areas and how their power compares with such power centers as the Congress and the bureaucracies.

The first question to ask in assessing the power of presidents is: Where do they come from? Are presidents chosen from a particular strata of society or profession that will influence how they act in dealing with foreign affairs and defense? The second question to ask is: To whom are presidents obligated? Do presidents incur debts in the process of being nominated and elected that give others power over them in defense and foreign affairs?

THE FORTY PRESIDENTS

Of the forty people who have been president, not one has been a woman, an African-American, a Jew, a Hispanic-American, or a Native American.[1] Furthermore, not one has been a doctor, a scientist, a police officer, a fireman, a carpenter, or an artisan or craftsperson of any kind. Not one

---

[1]George Bush is counted as the forty-first president because Grover Cleveland's two terms were interrupted by Benjamin Harrison's one term. Thus Cleveland is counted as both the twenty-second and the twenty-fourth president.

has been an artist, a novelist, or a musician, although one actor finally did make it. That no one in these jobs or professions has been president may not be surprising, since their work is so different from the work of presidents. But neither has the head of a large business corporation become president, nor has the head of a bank, railroad, manufacturing concern, or other large-scale economic enterprise of the kind that gives a person administrative or executive experience. Jimmy Carter did manage his family's peanut farm and warehouse and made them a financial success, but he had also been a naval officer, a member of the state legislature, and governor of Georgia.

The only president with extensive business experience was Herbert Hoover, who had been an engineer and a principal officer of an international business engaged in mining and other forms of engineering. But it was not his business background that brought Hoover to national prominence and gave him the opportunity to run for the presidency but rather his positions as chair of the American Relief Commission, which sent food and medicine to Europe after World War I, and as secretary of commerce in the Harding administration.

Three presidents were professional soldiers: Zachary Taylor, Ulysses S. Grant, and Dwight D. Eisenhower. Other presidents had been war heroes, but only those three had made careers of military life. Three other presidents, George Washington, Thomas Jefferson, and Andrew Jackson, thought of themselves as plantation owners. They may have made their fortunes in this way, but none spent very much time at the job. Two presidents, James A. Garfield and Woodrow Wilson, worked for many years as professors and then as college presidents. Andrew Johnson was a tailor for a brief period, and Harry S. Truman was a storekeeper for an equally short time. Ronald Reagan was a film actor for twenty-seven years. George Bush was in the oil business for a while, but for only a fraction of the time that he spent in government office. Twenty-four of the forty presidents (including the planter Jefferson and the storekeeper Truman) were lawyers, although at least two of them, Theodore Roosevelt and Franklin D. Roosevelt, never practiced law as either attorneys or judges.

But the most significant fact about the careers of the presidents is that thirty-six of the forty spent substantial parts of their lives as practicing, professional politicians. This includes Jimmy Carter, Ronald Reagan, and George Bush. After Carter's seven years in the Navy and his return to his family's peanut business, he almost immediately entered local politics. In 1962 he was elected to the Georgia legislature, where he served two terms. In 1966 Carter ran for governor of Georgia and lost. After campaigning almost full time for the next four years, he was elected governor in 1970. Upon leaving the governorship in January 1975, he immediately launched a full-time campaign for the presidency. Thus

Carter was involved in politics for about eight years part time and about fourteen years full time, or a total of twenty-two years by the time he was elected president.

Reagan had become president of the Screen Actors Guild in 1947 and for a number of years was politically active as a union leader. He spent most of 1960 campaigning for Richard M. Nixon and from that time on was continuously engaged in politics. In 1964 he started his own campaign for governor of California and won in the election of 1966. He served eight years as governor and then spent virtually all of the next five years running for the presidency, which he won in 1980. Thus Reagan spent at least twenty years as a professional politician in addition to his thirteen years part-time participation as head of the Screen Actors' Guild.

George Herbert Walker Bush was born into an old, upper-class New England family and grew up in Connecticut. His father was an investment banker for most of his career, later serving as U.S. senator from Connecticut from 1962 to 1972. Bush attended an exclusive private primary school in Connecticut and then went to Andover, an equally exclusive secondary school in Massachusetts, where he was an athlete and the president of his senior class. On graduating from Andover, Bush enlisted in the Navy, became its youngest pilot, and, after seeing considerable action in the Pacific during World War II, was shot down, although he escaped injury. After the war, he followed family tradition by going to Yale, where, also following family tradition, he was tapped for the exclusive Skull and Bones Society.

Rather than follow his father to Wall Street after graduating from Yale, Bush took his wife and infant son to Texas to enter the oil business. In 1950, he and a friend formed a company of their own, which developed into the Zapata Petroleum Corporation, shortly thereafter based in Houston. Bush, who had apparently always wanted to follow his father into national politics, quickly became active in Houston's Republican party. In 1964, he won the Republican nomination to challenge incumbent Democratic U.S. Senator Ralph Yarborough. Bush ran as a conservative, enthusiastically supporting the Republican nominee for president, Barry Goldwater. He was defeated, but considering that Lyndon B. Johnson won the presidency that year in a landslide, Bush did rather well, getting 43.5 percent of the vote, the highest a Republican had ever received in Texas.

In 1966, Bush ran for a seat in the House of Representatives from a district in Houston that included its wealthiest—and most Republican—neighborhood. Four years later, he gave up his safe House seat and tried again for the U.S. Senate, but was overwhelmingly defeated by a conservative Democrat, Lloyd M. Bentsen, Jr., who much later would be the nominee for vice president on the Democratic ticket that Bush defeated.

From that time until Ronald Reagan chose him as his running mate in the 1980 election, Bush, like both Herbert Hoover and William Howard Taft, followed the path of appointive rather than elective office. Hoover, as mentioned, served as chair of the American Relief Commission and as secretary of commerce. Taft had been elected judge of the Superior Court of Ohio, but the rest of his offices were appointive: local offices in Ohio, governor general of the Philippines, and secretary of war under Theodore Roosevelt. President Nixon appointed Bush ambassador to the United Nations after his Senate defeat in 1972 and a year later named him chair of the Republican National Committee. When Nixon resigned, Bush tried hard to persuade President Ford to choose him as vice president, but when Ford chose Nelson Rockefeller instead, Bush was appointed ambassador to China, serving from 1974 to December 1975, when Ford appointed him director of the CIA.

After the Democrats won the White House in 1976, Bush spent the next four years campaigning for the Republican nomination for president. Defeated in the primaries of 1980 by Ronald Reagan, he eagerly accepted Reagan's offer to be his running mate. Although Reagan appointed Bush chair of both the "crisis management team" of the National Security Council and a task force on illegal immigration, crime, and drug smuggling, these positions carried little power. Like most recent vice presidents, Bush spent the next eight years representing the United States at the inaugurations and funerals of foreign leaders and cultivating local "pols" by faithful attendance at Republican fund-raising events throughout the country.

Thus historically three main roads have led to the White House. One was to win worldwide fame relieving human suffering and then spend a highly successful tour of duty as head of a government department (Hoover). A second was to be a popular general in a victorious war (Taylor, Grant, and Eisenhower). The third was to be a professional politician who climbs the ladder of elective and appointive office. It may well be that Hoover's business background influenced the way that he behaved as president and that their military background influenced the way that Taylor, Grant, and Eisenhower behaved. But these were exceptions rather than the rule. Most presidents, to repeat, have spent a large part of their lives as professional politicians.

One would presume that a political background would not influence the way a president would deal with foreign affairs and defense. It does seem reasonable, however, that presidents with a political background would be sensitive to how the American electorate is structured: whether it forms and expresses its opinions through the various power centers, or whether the electorate functions as an incoherent mass influenced mainly by the media. We will return to this issue later in the chapter.

THE NOMINATING POWER

The nature of the obligations that presidents incur in the process of being nominated and elected has changed over the years. In the early years of the republic, the nominating power lay solely with the caucus of the party's members in Congress, but this system ended with the revolt against "King Caucus" in 1832. As more than one political observer has remarked, this removed forever any possibility that the United States would become a parliamentary democracy along the lines of Great Britain.

From after the Civil War and until the days of Franklin D. Roosevelt, the power to nominate the president was at the local level. U.S. senators and representatives shared in this power, but their power was no greater than that of governors, state legislators, mayors and other town officials, and local politicians and party activists. This was the era of party bosses, and in states ruled by bosses they chose the delegates to the national convention, although they would normally take care to see that various factions within the party were represented. In states that did not have a boss or where the nominal boss was weak, delegates were usually chosen at caucuses or conventions. Bargaining among the factions determined who would go to the national convention, with the leaders of each faction having the largest say. In the few states dominated by a single industry the power to name delegates lay in some periods with the heads of that industry (an example would be the copper industry in Montana), but at no time in recent decades has this been so. None of these people involved in nominating presidential candidates were much concerned with foreign affairs and defense, however, so presidents rarely incurred any obligation on either issue during the process of getting the nomination.

Franklin D. Roosevelt's New Deal ended the rule of bosses. The sources of their power were the benefits that holding office could bring. At the lowest level the benefits were patronage jobs; sewer, road, and other contracts; and various forms of kickback—"honest graft" as well as not so honest. A proportion of what was skimmed off went into the pockets of the top politicians and the contractors allied with them. But a large proportion of both the honest and not-so-honest graft actually served a social function. In the days before Social Security, unemployment compensation, Medicare, Medicaid, and the other benefits of the welfare state, political parties were one of the few places to which the poor, the unemployed, the sick, widows and orphans, and the elderly could turn for help. This help took the form not only of jobs in the city or county government but also of such things as a ton of coal, a basket of food, and assistance with funeral costs. In return the beneficiaries, both the rich and the poor, voted and worked for the party. What was skimmed off was the oil that made the party machine work.

Roosevelt's New Deal social programs took over the functions that boss rule had served and so destroyed it. A poignant evocation of the way a boss-led party worked and how the New Deal destroyed the city machine and its bosses is given in Edwin O'Connor's novel of Boston city politics, *The Last Hurrah.*

From the New Deal until 1972, however, the party still played the central role in the presidential nominating procedures, which included nonbinding primaries in a few states, caucuses in other states, and state conventions in still others. The power was local, centering in the party and its elected officials and members who were willing to do the party's work. Here again, those who held the power to nominate were by and large uninterested in either foreign affairs or defense, and presidents were essentially free of obligations in either field.

Beginning in 1972 both parties began to institute reforms such as increasing the number of primaries, making them binding, establishing proportional representation, and limiting the amount of contributions. Some of these reforms had unforeseen effects, and following the election of 1980 an effort was made to reverse certain of the changes. For the 1984 Democratic primaries, 55 percent of the delegates were chosen in twenty-five primaries. Party caucuses, in which party officials have a larger role, picked about 31 percent of the delegates. The remaining 14 percent were made up of "super-delegates," that is, party and elected officials who went to the convention with no advance commitment to any candidate. However, the committed delegates were not formally or legally bound to their candidates. Under these rules, if it becomes clear by the time of the convention that one or another candidate really has no chance of winning, his or her delegates are free to vote for someone who does. Finally, the 1972 rule requiring proportional representation was altered drastically. In 1984, states had the right to retain proportional representation if they wished. Most of the caucus states did so, but about half of the primary states and most of the large primary states went back to the winner-take-all system.

But in spite of the attempt to reverse the worst effects of the reforms, the final result was still to lessen the power of the party in choosing candidates. Since candidates in primaries are contending against members of their own party, the party has traditionally stayed neutral. Thus the more influence that primaries have in picking candidates, the less that party leaders, officials, and activists have.

At the same time the changes in primary rules gave more power to special interest and single-issue groups. The turnout of voters for most primaries (at all levels) is usually between 15 and 30 percent. For hotly contested presidential primaries, the mean turnout from 1948 to 1968 was 39 percent, while the turnout for presidential elections in the same period was 69 percent.[2] This means that a dedicated minority of 15 to 20 percent of the registered voters of a particular party can usually determine who wins the nomination, even though the ideological or policy views to which they are dedicated may be repugnant to the majority of their party.

The changes in the primary rules also gave more power over the nomination to single-issue groups, such as those opposed to abortion, nuclear power, gun control, and prayers in the schools, and increased the influence of special interest groups. Before the New Hampshire primary of 1980, for example, leading chiropractors in the state told President Carter's son Chip that they would help get out the vote for Carter if he would change his mind and include chiropractic services in Medicare and Medicaid and in his proposed national health legislation, a change that would mean $30 million a year to chiropractors. Carter did make the change, and the chiropractors were an enormous help in Carter's primary victory.[3]

In the same way the changes in primary rules also gave more power to organized ideological groups, both of the right and the left. Too much of this kind of influence in the primaries, however, can sometimes backfire in the general election. Candidates with sharp ideological views bring out dedicated ideologues to vote in the primaries, but this can antagonize the middle-of-the-road voters who are needed to win the general election. This is clearly what happened in the Goldwater campaign of 1964 and the McGovern campaign of 1972. The Republican Goldwater's views attracted dedicated right-wingers, and the Democratic McGovern's views brought out the dedicated left-wingers. Both won their party's nomination but in the process so alarmed moderates that they lost the general election by wide margins.

Another group that has gained power to influence nominations in recent years consists of those the professional politicians somewhat disparagingly refer to as "hobbyist amateurs." The fact that the party organizations stay neutral in primaries means that candidates must recruit anyone they can to create a personal organization. Frequently the recruits are people who have not been involved in politics but are flattered by the candidate's personal appeal for help. They become active during that one campaign but then return to their usual activities when it is

---

[2]Austin Ranney, "Turnout and Representation in Presidential Primary Elections," *American Political Science Review* (March 1972).

[3]Timothy B. Clark, "As Long as Carter's Up He'll Get You a Grant," *The New York Times,* April 21, 1980, p. A19.

over. The hobbyist amateur's political participation is essentially epi-
sodic—in and then out.

The media of mass communication—especially TV but also the print
press—likewise increased its influence over nominations, although this
was due to changes in technology rather than changes in the rules.
Driven by its need for novelty in the form of new faces, in 1976 TV was
the main force that catapulted Jimmy Carter from being almost totally
unknown with a recognition factor of only 2 percent to winning the
Democratic nomination. Long before Ronald Reagan became a presidential candidate, someone remarked that as TV became a more important
vehicle for news, "Politicians will have to become actors—or actors will
become politicians."

The power to nominate thus remains at the local level of the state,
county, city, town, and village. But in states with primaries the professional politicians, elected officials, and party activists exercise less power
than they once did and special interest and single-issue groups, ideological groups, and hobbyist amateurs exercise more.[4]

THE ELECTORAL COLLEGE

Both before and since the dominance of television, one other determinant
of electoral strategy has been central—the electoral college, which is
governed by the winner-take-all unit rule. On the one hand, a bare
majority of the popular vote in California, the largest state, wins all of its
electoral votes, which in the 1988 election were 47 of the 270 needed to
win the election. On the other hand, even if a candidate by some miracle
gets 100 percent of the vote in a small state such as Alaska, Wyoming, or
Vermont, that candidate wins only 3 electoral votes. Consequently, the
strategy of most presidential candidates is to concentrate on states with
large populations, which means the industrialized states with large urban and suburban areas.

---

[4]On the nominating process and elections, see also Gerald M. Pomper, ed., *The
Election of 1988: Reports and Interpretations* (Chatham, N.J.: Chatham House, 1989);
William Crotty and John S. Jackson III, *Presidential Primaries and Nominations* (Washington, D.C.: Congressional Quarterly Press, 1985); Michael Nelson, ed., *The Presidency and
the Political System* (Washington, D.C.: Congressional Quarterly Press, 1984); Howard L.
Reifer, *Selecting the President: The Nominating Process in Transition* (Philadelphia: Uni-
versity of Pennsylvania Press, 1985); Robert E. DiClerico and Eric M. Uslauer, *Few Are
Chosen: Problems in Presidential Selection* (New York: McGraw-Hill, 1984); David R. Run-
kel, ed., *Campaign for President: The Manager's Look at '88* (Dover, Mass.: Auburn House,
1989); Pomper, *Voters, Elections, and Parties: The Practice of Democratic Theory* (New
Brunswick, N.J.: Transaction Books, 1988); and Nelson W. Polsby and Aaron Wildavsky,
Presidential Elections: Contemporary Strategies of American Electoral Politics, 7th ed. (New
York: The Free Press, 1988).

Two experts on elections, Richard M. Scammon and Ben J. Wattenberg, have pointed out that if you draw a quadrangle extending from Massachusetts and Washington, D.C., to Illinois and Wisconsin and then add to it California, you will have embraced a majority of Americans.[5] They call this country within a country "Quadcali." It includes Boston, New York, Philadelphia, Baltimore, Pittsburgh, Cleveland, Chicago, Detroit, San Francisco, Los Angeles, San Diego, and a host of smaller cities such as Hartford and Milwaukee.

OBLIGATIONS INCURRED IN GETTING NOMINATED AND ELECTED

Because most of the groups that are influential in primaries are not particularly interested in foreign affairs and defense, presidential candidates incur few obligations on such issues in the process of getting nominated and elected. Of those that are interested, the largest number are concerned with economic matters such as trade barriers and similar issues. Industry and labor unite in trying to keep out foreign competition. Walter Mondale incurred such obligations to unions in the 1984 election, although their assistance did not help him in the general election. Ethnic groups are interested in particular countries, the most notable being Jewish organizations' concern with Israel and Irish groups' concern with Northern Ireland. Beyond these particular groups, it seems obvious that at least the potential influence in foreign affairs and defense is there, especially among ideological groups of both the right and the left. When and if it is manifested, presidents will indeed incur obligations. (It should be said that interest groups have power and influence quite apart from that which they can exercise on the president. This will be dealt with in Chapter 14.)

The effect of the electoral college is to make presidential candidates pay careful attention to the needs and interests of urban areas, but the consequences of this for foreign affairs and defense seem to be general rather than specific. Today all presidential candidates have to appear competent on such matters. The most important result of this has probably been to make the Congress and especially the Senate a better platform for running for the presidency than a governorship. From 1900 to World War II, five presidents attained the office via a governorship compared to one via Congress, while two, Hoover and Taft, served in a variety of appointive offices. In contrast, beginning with Truman, four

---

[5]Richard M. Scammon and Ben J. Wattenberg, *The Real Majority* (New York: Coward McCann, & Geoghegan, 1971), p. 70.

presidents came to the office via the Senate, Ford came from the House, two came from governorships, one, Bush, came through appointive offices as did Hoover and Taft, and one, Eisenhower, via some other route. Among the reasons for the large number from the Senate are senators' greater access to national press exposure, mainly TV, and the ease with which they can build an image of competency in foreign affairs and defense as compared to governors.

However, the pattern may be changing, for governorships gave both Carter and Reagan the platforms for their successful campaigns.

9

THE PRESIDENT'S ROLE AND POWER

"The Presidency is the toughest job on earth," two authors of a well-known book assert, "it is the most powerful position in the Free World."[1] The president, another scholar wrote, is "a kind of magnificent lion who can roam widely and do great deeds so long as he does not try to break loose from his broad reservation."[2] Theodore White, author of the popular series *The Making of the President,* sees the president as an even more "magnificent lion": "So many and so able are the President's advisers of the permanent services of Defense, State, Treasury, Agriculture, that when crisis happens all necessary information is instantly available, all alternate courses already plotted."[3] Arthur M. Schlesinger, Jr., goes further still, at least in terms of assessing the president's power on questions of defense and foreign policy. He terms the office the "imperial presidency," and says that "by the early 1970s the American President had become on issues of war and peace the most absolute monarch (with the possible exception of Mao Tse-tung of China) among the great powers of the world."[4] Joseph A. Califano, Jr., who served as President Johnson's

---

[1]James McGregor Burns and Jack Walter Peltason, *Government by the People: The Dynamics of American National Government,* 7th ed. (Englewood Cliffs, N.J.: Prentice Hall, 1969), p. 359.

[2]Clinton Rossiter, *The American Presidency,* 2nd ed. (New York: Harcourt, Brace and World, 1960), p. 73.

[3]Theodore H. White, *The Making of the President, 1960* (New York: Athenaeum, 1964), p. 369.

[4]Arthur M. Schlesinger, Jr., *The Imperial Presidency* (New York: Popular Library, 1973), p. 11.

special assistant for domestic affairs and in 1976 became secretary of health, education, and welfare in Carter's administration, offers an even broader view of the president's powers:

> Men like Abraham Lincoln, Woodrow Wilson, and the two Roosevelts have been among our strongest presidents and have exercised enormous power at the peaks of their careers in office. . . . But even those men, to say nothing of the founding fathers, could hardly have conceived the total power that would be vested in the modern presidency at the time of our nation's bicentennial.[5]

In sum, many observers see presidents as very much like old-time kings: Their power may not be absolute, but it is very, very great indeed. On the other hand, it was mentioned in Chapter 6 how Truman was amused at the thought that Eisenhower would find out that the presidency would not be a bit like the Army, how Kennedy was exasperated over the State Department's failure to obey his orders to remove the missiles from Turkey, and how Johnson was frustrated in his attempt to merge the Labor and Commerce departments. It also has been noted that Vice President Dawes believed that the members of the cabinet are a president's natural enemies and that Richard Neustadt observed that "underneath our images of Presidents-in-boots, astride decisions, are the half-observed realities of Presidents-in-sneakers, stirrups in hand, trying to induce particular department heads, or congressmen, or senators to climb aboard."[6]

How can these conflicting views about the power of presidents be reconciled? One way to begin is by looking at what presidents actually do. By analyzing the roles they play and how they spend their time, it should be possible to understand both their functions and their power.

THE PRESIDENT'S ROLES AND FUNCTIONS

Looking at both the responsibilities that the Constitution assigns to the president and the presidents' actual activities, scholars over the years have tried to describe the president's job as a series of roles.[7] For our

---

[5]Joseph A. Califano, Jr., *A Presidential Nation* (New York: W. W. Norton, 1975), p. 7.

[6]Richard E. Neustadt, "White House and Whitehall," *The Public Interest* (Winter 1966).

[7]Edwin S. Corwin, *The President: Office and Powers,* 4th rev. ed. (New York: New York University Press, 1957); Rossiter, *The American Presidency;* Dorothy Buckton James, *The Contemporary Presidency* (New York: Pegasus, 1969); and Rexford G. Tugwell and Thomas E. Cronin, "The Presidency: Ventures in Reappraisal," in *The Presidency Reappraised,* ed. idem (New York: Praeger, 1974), p. 5. Erwin C. Hargrove and Michael Nelson,

(footnote continues on page 131)

purposes, these several roles can be consolidated into four: chief of state, chief legislator, chief administrator, and chief decision maker.

Chief of State

Most presidents are probably bored by their ceremonial activities as chief of state, such as signing bills, delivering speeches at graduations and other solemn occasions, and throwing out the first baseball of the season. But such functions do give the people, all of us, a sense of national identity and unity. Most political analysts argue that the role of chief of state carries little power; it is equivalent to the position of king or queen in a constitutional monarchy. However, the aura, prestige, and symbolism of being chief of state must inevitably contribute to a president's power of legitimacy, of being the constituted authority of the state.

Chief Legislator

To examine the president's role as chief legislator, the origin of legislative ideas must first be considered. Just after World War II a careful, scholarly study was made of the roots of ninety pieces of major legislation that Congress had passed between 1880 and 1940.[8] The study found that seventy-seven of the laws could be traced to bills that had been introduced in Congress without the sponsorship of the president and the administration. Additional studies have since confirmed that Congress has not relinquished its legislative role to the president at all.[9]

Presidents, Politics, and Policy (Baltimore: The Johns Hopkins University Press, 1984); Michael Nelson, ed., *The Presidency and the Political System*, 3rd ed. (Washington, D.C.: Congressional Quarterly Press, 1990); James G. Benze, Jr., "Presidential Management: The View from the Bureaucracy," *Presidential Studies Quarterly*, (Winter 1986); James G. Benze, Jr., *Presidential Power and Management Techniques* (Westport, Conn.: Greenwood Press, 1987); John Hart, *The Presidential Branch* (Elmsford, N.Y.: Pergamon Press, 1987); Stephen Hess, *Organizing the Presidency* (Washington, D.C.: Brookings, 1988); Theodore J. Lowi, *The Personal President: Power Invested, Promise Unfulfilled* (Ithaca: Cornell University Press, 1985); Kenneth W. Thompson, ed., *The Presidency and The Constitutional System* (Lanham, Md.: University Press of America, 1989); and Richard E. Neustadt, *Presidential Power and the Modern Presidents,* rev. ed. (New York: The Free Press, 1990).

[8]Lawrence H. Chamberlain, *President, Congress, and Legislation* (New York: Columbia University Press, 1946).

[9]Ronald C. Moe and Stephen C. Teel, "Congress as Policy-Maker: A Necessary Reappraisal," *Political Science Quarterly*, Vol. 85 (September 1970), pp. 443–470. See also such case studies as Stephen K. Bailey, *Congress Makes a Law: The Story Behind the Employment Act of 1946* (New York: Columbia University Press, 1950); Robert L. Peabody et al., *To Enact a Law: Congress and Campaign Financing* (New York: Praeger, 1972); Daniel M. Berman, *A Bill Becomes a Law: Congress Enacts Civil Rights Legislation,* 2nd ed. (New York: Macmillan, 1966); idem, *In Congress Assembled* (New York: Macmillan, 1964); David A. Baldwin, "Congressional Initiative in Foreign Policy," *Journal of Politics,* Vol. 28 (November 1966), pp. 754–773. John Roland Johannes, "When Congress Leads: Cases and Patterns of Congressional Initiation of Legislation" (Ph.D. dissertation, Harvard University, 1970); and James L. Sundquist, *Politics and Policy: The Eisenhower, Kennedy, and Johnson Years* (Washington, D.C.: Brookings, 1968).

The process by which ideas are originated, developed, and transformed into laws is usually extraordinarily complicated. The original idea is often only the germ of the final legislation. Its source, which may be impossible to pinpoint, can be an academic, a lobbyist, a member of the press, a congressional aide, a member of Congress, a bureaucrat in an executive department—in short, almost anyone. The idea usually reappears many times, developing and maturing as it progresses. It is discussed among members of Congress and their staffs, in the bureaucracies, among interest groups and the constituencies affected by the legislation, and on television and in the press. More often than not it is only at a very late stage that the White House becomes involved by a decision to include the bill in the president's program. Of course, doing so may perform the enormously important task of giving the bill the publicity and momentum needed for its passage. But this in no real sense entitles the president to be called chief legislator. We speak of Kennedy's space program, of Johnson's War on Poverty, of Carter's energy program, and of Reagan's economic program, but not because they deserve the sole credit for originating an idea or obtaining its passage as law. To give the name of a president to a major piece of legislation is often just a kind of verbal shorthand, just as we speak of Victorian architecture and Queen Anne furniture although neither woman had anything whatever to do with designing buildings or manufacturing furniture. President Kennedy once remarked impishly at the end of a meeting on a complicated issue of foreign policy, " 'I hope this plan works. If it does, it will be another White House success. If it doesn't, it will be another State Department failure.' "[10]

So what is it that presidents actually do when it comes to legislation? Mostly, when they support a piece of legislation, they seem to spend their time trying to persuade members of Congress to vote for it, leaders of interest groups to support it, and the general public to believe that it is in their best interests. Occasionally, of course, presidents have an original idea or read or hear about one. They may then ask a staff aide or cabinet member to see that the idea is developed into a bill, which they add to their legislative program. And then they begin to try to persuade. When they oppose a bill they *begin* with trying to persuade.

In sum, techniques that presidents usually use in the legislative process are persuading, bargaining, making concessions and deals, trading, threatening, arguing, maneuvering, manipulating, and even begging. They wheel and deal, in a word, politick. As one observer has

---

[10]Quoted in Harlan Cleveland, *The Future Executive* (New York: Harper & Row, 1972), pp. 95–96.

remarked, "The President of the United States has many titles. Chief Legislator is one of them. It is a paper title."[11]

Because presidents cannot impose their view of what legislation should be, they cannot gain dictatorial power over legislation. Indeed, it is so rare that bills come out exactly as presidents wish them to, it cannot even be said that presidents are the chief legislators. But they have formidable capacities to persuade, to bargain, and to manipulate. So they greatly influence legislation even though they cannot dictate it, and this is power.

Chief Administrator

It is often said that we need presidents with experience as managers. The implication is that the government must be "managed" in much the same way that a business or industry is managed. For this reason some political observers regret the fact that the background of several presidents since World War II has been chiefly in the Congress (Truman, Kennedy, Johnson, Nixon, and Ford). "A Senator has no responsibility for organizing, managing, or directing large-scale enterprises," two such commentators write. "The Presidency requires a highly skilled executive adept in the art of delegating responsibility to people often superior to the chief executive himself in specialized matters."[12]

But except for Herbert Hoover and Jimmy Carter, no president has ever managed a business. Three had been generals, but all the rest—and even Hoover and Carter—had been professional politicians for a large proportion of their lives. Many were governors, and thus had experience dealing with legislators, interest groups, the press, and the voters. But it is doubtful that either governors or presidents administer or manage in the sense that a business executive does.

The executive branch of the federal government is an organization (really a group of organizations) with over three million civilian em-

---

[11]Hugh G. Gallagher, "Presidents, Congress, and the Legislative Function," in *The Presidency*, ed. Tugwell and Cronin, p. 231. Other works that explore the relationship between the legislative and executive branches include Nigel Bowles, *The White House and Capitol Hill* (Oxford: The Clarendon Press, 1987); Louis Fisher, *Constitutional Conflicts Between Congress and the President* (Princeton, N.J.: Princeton University Press, 1985); Cecil V. Crabb, Jr. and Pat M. Holt, *Invitation to Struggle: Congress, the President, and Foreign Policy* (Washington, D.C.: Congressional Quarterly Press, 1984); Nelson M. Polsby, *Congress and the Presidency* (Englewood Cliffs, N.J.: Prentice Hall, 1986); Mark A. Peterson, *Legislating Together: The White House and Capitol Hill from Eisenhower to Reagan* (Cambridge, Mass.: Harvard University Press, 1990); Jon R. Bond and Richard Fleisher, *The President in the Legislative Arena* (Chicago: University of Chicago Press, 1990); and Thomas E. Mann, ed., *A Question of Balance: The President, Congress and Foreign Policy* (Washington, D.C.: Brookings, 1990).

[12]Tugwell and Cronin, *The Presidency*, p. 9.

ployees and two million military personnel. These organizations deal with subjects covering every aspect of national life, including health, education, the economy, agriculture, energy, the environment, civil rights, crime, defense, and foreign affairs. Even a person with a staff of two thousand extraordinarily able people could not hope to "administer" or "manage" the federal government in the same sense that heads of small- or medium-sized businesses or manufacturing enterprises administer and manage.

Managers of small- or medium-sized businesses can pay attention to detail. They can keep close watch on who is hired and how well they do their jobs. They can keep tabs on the purchase of raw materials. They can inspect the manufacturing process, looking for inefficiencies and waste. They can make sure that the shipping departments fill orders promptly. They can constantly check to see that the sales force is doing an efficient and imaginative job. They can watch the market for the company's product, detecting when new models are needed and when production should be stepped up or cut back. Presidents of the United States have little hope of maintaining this kind of close control of the activities of the vast federal bureaucracies. In fact, almost all presidents have complained bitterly about their troubles in getting the bureaucracies to do what they wanted them to do. One of the most vivid complaints was from Franklin D. Roosevelt, who had been assistant secretary of the Navy under Woodrow Wilson:

> The Treasury is so large and far-flung and ingrained in its practices that I find it is almost impossible to get the action and results I want. . . . But the Treasury is not to be compared with the State Department . . . [and] the Treasury and the State Department put together are nothing compared with the Na-a-vy. . . . To change anything in the Na-a-vy is like punching a feather bed. You punch it with your right hand and you punch it with your left until you are finally exhausted, and then you find the damn bed just as it was before you started punching.[13]

If there are people in the business or industrial world who have jobs similar in any way to that of the president, they are not the presidents or the chief operating officers of small- or medium-sized concerns but rather those who chair the boards of directors of huge corporate conglomerates such as General Dynamics and General Motors or giant multinational corporations engaged in a wide range of unrelated activities. Such people would find it fruitless to try to "administer" or "manage" their organization (or really the group of organizations). The most they can hope to do is

---

[13]Quoted in Marriner S. Eccles, *Beckoning Frontiers* (New York: Alfred A. Knopf, 1951), p. 336.

to supervise the planning and decision making of overall policy, choose the heads of the various subsidiaries who carry out ("administer") the policies, watch the results, and move in when the results are bad and change both the top personnel and the policy. If what presidents and the heads of large corporate conglomerates do is similar, it is not because either one "administers" or "manages" in the sense that the head of a small- or medium-sized business does but because the corporate officers must often behave like politician-presidents!

Chief Decision Maker

Many of the comments that were made about the role of the president as chief administrator and chief legislator can be made about the role of chief decision maker. The Constitution gives presidents the sole right to make certain decisions, many of which deal with foreign affairs and defense. It is also the president to whom the Constitution assigns the task of conducting foreign affairs. In addition, from time to time presidents have claimed the right to make certain kinds of decisions under the implied powers of the Constitution or under the "prerogative" powers of any head of a state.

Implied powers. The Constitution gives the president the right to appoint cabinet officials with the advice and consent of the Senate, which "implies" that he also has the right to direct the work of those cabinet officials. President Andrew Johnson asserted this implied power to give orders to a cabinet member and to fire that member when he did not obey them, even when a majority of the Congress disagreed. This conflict between President Johnson and the Congress led to his impeachment, but he was saved from conviction by a single vote in the Senate. Since then no one has ever questioned the power of a president to give orders to a cabinet member even though Congress disagrees, at least as long as those orders are constitutional. President Truman, for example, used implied powers when he ordered the armed services to carry out the integration of black and white soldiers into the same units.

Prerogative powers. A prerogative power is even broader than an implied power. The notion originated with John Locke, the seventeenth-century English political theorist, who argued that the legislature could not always foresee all contingencies and that the executive had the power to act and by "the common law of Nature a right to make use of it for the good of society. . . ." In fact, Locke argued, in some cases the public good might require the executive to act in violation of the laws. Although it was never spelled out, it was presumably prerogative power (exercised on the premise that the nation's safety was threatened) rather than implied powers that Truman was invoking when he ordered American soldiers to fight in Korea in 1950 without a declaration of war by Congress and that Johnson was invoking when he ordered troops into Vietnam in 1965, again without a specific declaration of war.

Delegated powers. From time to time Congress passes a law that delegates to presidents the right to make certain decisions without further legislation. During the Nixon administration, Congress empowered the president to invoke wage and price controls whenever the economic situation seemed to warrant it. Originally Nixon vehemently opposed the law, but in the summer of 1971, when inflation was running very high, gold was pouring out of the U.S. Treasury, and the dollar was in danger of collapse, he used the powers to impose such controls.

In these and similar circumstances, the president is indeed the chief decision maker. But several aspects of presidential decisions in such cases are worth considering. First, the decision must be on a matter that either the Constitution, Congress, or custom has assigned to the president. Second, in a number of respects such a decision, like putting a bill into the presidential program, is only the opening shot of a long battle. In the wage-price decision, for example, President Nixon convened a meeting of his top economic advisers—and his speech writers. William Safire, then his chief writer, has published an extensive account of what was said at the meeting.[14] What is most striking is how little time was devoted to considering which policy to follow and how much time was devoted to tailoring the policy so as to enlist the support or head off the opposition of Congress, the press and TV, various special interests and constituencies (such as bankers and the labor unions), and allied and other nations who use the dollar as their reserve currency.

Decision Making in Foreign Affairs and Defense

In foreign affairs and defense, on the other hand, presidents have fewer limits on their power, as the following examples demonstrate. Before the Japanese attack on Pearl Harbor and the formal declaration of war against Japan and Germany, President Roosevelt had placed the United States firmly on the side of the Allies, sometimes without the approval of Congress. President Truman ordered American troops into the Korean conflict without a declaration of war by Congress. President Eisenhower sent troops into Lebanon without congressional authorization. President Kennedy permitted the Cuban brigade trained by the CIA to land at the Bay of Pigs. President Johnson, without authorization from Congress, ordered the bombing of North Vietnam and sent 550,000 American

---

[14]William Safire, *Before the Fall: An Inside View of the Pre-Watergate White House* (Garden City, N.Y.: Doubleday, 1975), pt. VII, Chap. 5 passim.

ground troops to fight in South Vietnam. President Nixon, without congressional authorization, ordered the mining of Haiphong Harbor and the invasion of Cambodia. President Ford took policy positions on détente with the Soviet Union, the SALT talks, and several other initiatives, all without consulting Congress. President Carter, when the American hostages were seized by Iranian militants, froze $8 billion in Iranian assets, imposed trade sanctions and pressured our allies to join in, dispatched a fleet to the Persian Gulf, ordered the deportation of certain categories of Iranians living in the United States, and ordered a commando raid by helicopters in an aborted attempt to rescue the hostages, all by his own decision. President Reagan, without consulting Congress, ordered American troops to invade Grenada, an action that many charged violated both international law and the UN charter. President Bush ordered the invasion of Panama without congressional approval—although he did get such approval for the war against Iraq.

These decisions—made by presidents without authorization from Congress—illustrate the power that presidents wield in foreign affairs and defense. And many, many more examples could be given. The framers of the Constitution gave the president more power over such decisions because they recognized that the survival of the nation might require quicker and more decisive action than could be expected from the cumbersome and time-consuming procedures of debate and argument characteristic of a legislative body.

These constitutional powers are reinforced by present-day political considerations that stem from exactly the same argument. Almost everyone, from members of Congress to journalists, agrees that the president has too much power in foreign affairs. Yet members of Congress hesitate to use the powers they do possess, and other observers are reluctant to propose reforms that would limit the president's war powers. Members of Congress agree with the framers of the Constitution that in times of peril the president may have to act quickly and often secretly, and that there might be neither time nor opportunity for the open and lengthy procedures by which Congress and the public could be brought into the deliberations. They point to the Cuban missile crisis as an example. As described in Chapter 1, Soviet missile sites were discovered under construction in Cuba on October 14, 1962. To be effective, action had to be taken before the missiles became operational. In the case of the medium-range missiles this would have been on about October 26, and in the case of the intermediate-range missiles it would have been some time in November. This meant that Kennedy had only a week or so to explore the alternatives and decide what to do; whatever he decided had to be done in secrecy to prevent the Soviets from taking countermeasures. Most members of Congress doubt that there is a practical way in which Congress could participate in such a decision.

Thus it is as much the realities of international politics as the provisions of the Constitution that give presidents their extraordinary power in defense and foreign affairs. They are more powerful in foreign affairs than in domestic affairs, and their power increases as the issues of war and peace become more central. Congress can participate in decisions on foreign aid, a test-ban treaty, or a trade agreement with the Soviet Union without fear of being accused of risking the nation's survival. Congress has often cut or turned down requests for aid to other countries, and it has gone against presidents on matters even dearer to their hearts. In 1974, for example, Congress approved amendments (proposed by Senator Henry M. Jackson of Washington) to the trade agreement with the Soviet Union that required the Soviets to liberalize their policy toward emigration of Jews as a condition of the deal, which the Soviets found so objectionable that they canceled the agreement. But when it comes to war—to sending troops to Korea, Lebanon, Vietnam, Cambodia, Grenada, or Panama—Congress has been reluctant to exercise even the powers it already has, much less reach for more.

Domestic politics present other limits on the use of congressional power in foreign affairs. Foreign affairs lack the play of rival interests that characterizes debate on domestic policy. The issue can too easily be turned into one of simple patriotism, when to object to the president's course of action can be branded an act of disloyalty to the nation itself. The power of the purse, which the framers of the Constitution counted on to be an effective check on the powers of the president in so many areas, is not a practical limitation of the president in time of war, even during a limited, undeclared war. Members of Congress are too vulnerable to the charge that they are taking weapons and ammunition out of the hands of soldiers who are already being shot. "You may be right in thinking this particular war is wrong," the critics can say, "but that does not justify your voting to deprive the soldiers in the field of the means of defending themselves." That is why Abraham Lincoln, when he was a member of Congress, was so careful to promise not to vote against appropriations for the Mexican war, even as he spoke against it. It also explains why only two senators, Ernest Gruening of Alaska and Wayne Morse of Oregon, actually voted against appropriations for the Vietnam war, even though several dozen senators publicly opposed the war. Significantly, both senators were defeated in the primaries of 1968, despite the fact that antiwar sentiment was stronger then than it had been when they had voted in Congress.

The War Powers Act of 1973

In 1973, the frustrations of the Vietnam war and President Johnson's decisions to bomb North Vietnam and to send more than half a million Americans to fight in South Vietnam without consulting Congress led to the passage of the War Powers Act over President Nixon's veto. The Watergate scandal solidified congressional support for such an act out of a desire to constrain "Imperial Presidents." The law provided that a president could commit U.S. armed forces to hostilities only under a declaration of war, a specific statutory authority, or a national emergency created by an attack on the United States or its possessions. The law required the president to report any commitment of U.S. troops to Congress within 48 hours. It also required that the troops be withdrawn within 60 days of the report unless Congress approved their continued use, although it did permit the president to extend the commitment for another 30 days if it was a military necessity. It also authorized Congress to terminate the troop commitment by concurrent resolution. Finally, the law required the president to consult with Congress before committing U.S. troops overseas "in every possible instance."

The first real test of this law came with the so-called *Mayaguez* affair in May 1975. The U.S. merchant ship *Mayaguez* was seized by Cambodian Communists off a disputed island in the Gulf of Siam on May 12, 1975, and its crew of thirty was taken prisoner. President Ford ordered an assault on the island by U.S. marines and the bombing of Cambodian patrol boats, which took place on May 14. The crew and the ship were recovered, but ground fighting occurred and forty-one Americans were killed. President Ford reported his action to Congress on May 15. This fulfilled the provisions of the War Powers Act concerning reporting, but many members of Congress believed it did not fulfill the provision requiring consultation.

When President Carter ordered an attempt to rescue the hostages in Iran by helicopter, he neither asked nor informed congressional leaders of the operation. The legalities of his failure to do so are murky, but the fact that the White House filed a report to Congress after the raid seems to be an admission that the action did come under the purview of the War Powers Act.

In 1983 President Reagan insisted that his decision to order American marines to Lebanon did not require invoking the War Powers Act, even though they were under fire, suffered casualties, and fired back. Finally, a compromise was worked out in which the president agreed that the act was applicable, and Congress agreed to the marines remaining in Lebanon for 18 months. Early in 1984, however, the president ordered their withdrawal to ships standing offshore.

By order of President Reagan, on October 25, 1983, about 5,000 American troops invaded Grenada, a tiny, 100-square-mile Caribbean island-state with a population of just over 100,000. The island had been controlled by a hard-line Marxist group with close ties to Communist Cuba that had been overthrown only two weeks earlier by an even harder-line Marxist group. The president justified the invasion on the grounds, first, that the lives of 1,000 Americans attending medical school there were in jeopardy and, second, that four of the seven members of the Organization of Eastern Caribbean States had requested it. When stockpiles of Cuban rifles and other arms were discovered on Grenada, the additional justification of preventing Cuba from making the island a base was claimed, although the airfield being constructed in Grenada was clearly for civilian purposes and the supervising engineers were from Great Britain. Later evidence raised questions about whether the students were in any real danger and about the significance of the numbers of arms discovered. A number of members of Congress and other observers also pointed out that the action in fact violated international law, the UN charter, and the treaty of the Organization of the American States, which the United States had signed.

President Reagan notified Congress of the invasion after it had taken place "in accordance with my desire that the Congress be informed on this matter, and consistent with the War Powers Resolution." This "consistent with" formulation had been used by other presidents to avoid conceding that the War Powers Act was in effect or even valid. Resolutions were promptly introduced in both houses invoking the act and asserting that in accordance the troops must be withdrawn within 90 days unless the Congress approved a longer stay.

As it became clear that the cheap, quick, and easy U.S. victory in Grenada was very popular with the general public, congressional criticism died down. Over the next few weeks most of the troops were withdrawn, and most members of Congress assumed that the issue had become moot. More recently in the Gulf War, the War Powers Act was not invoked even when the resolution in support of President Bush's decision to take military action came before the House and Senate. President Bush sought congressional approval in order to strengthen popular support, not to be consistent with the guidelines of The War Powers Act. In all likelihood, his course of action would have been the same whether or not Congress voted in favor of the resolution.

Political Limits on the President's War Powers

The conclusion seems inescapable: Despite the War Powers Act of 1973, Congress and the general public cannot participate as effectively in the management of foreign affairs as they can in that of domestic affairs. Presidents are consequently more powerful in foreign affairs than they are in domestic.

But this does not mean that presidents are all powerful in defense and foreign affairs. In any major decision in defense and foreign affairs, presidents must have the support or at least the passive acquiescence of most and sometimes all of the principal officers of the executive branch, the main congressional leaders, and the members of Congress who chair key committees. They must also have the support of significantly substantial numbers of the opinion leaders in the news, business, and academic worlds.

Consider again the historical record. In the Eisenhower administration at the time of the French defeat at Dienbienphu in 1954, most top officials favored an American intervention in Vietnam of the kind that Johnson actually decided on in 1965. But one official within the administration was vehemently opposed, and he occupied a position that as a practical political matter gave him a veto. The man was General Matthew B. Ridgway, chief of staff of the Army. General Ridgway was convinced that an American intervention would be a mistake. He sent a team of experts to Vietnam to look at the situation and then prepared a report for the president arguing that bombing would not work, that if the United States did decide to bomb it would have to follow it with an invasion of at least six army divisions, and that the American forces could expect heavy casualties because the terrain in Vietnam was ideal for guerrillas. The implication was that even six divisions might not succeed.

President Eisenhower found his power to decide on this issue greatly restricted. Although it is not entirely clear that Eisenhower wanted to intervene in Vietnam, it is true that a president whose military advisers are hawks and whose civilian advisers are doves has great freedom in such a decision. But any president, even a former five-star general who was the victor in World War II, would be very hesitant to decide in favor of a military intervention that the Army chief of staff insisted would be a disaster. If the adventure failed, the fact that the chief of staff had objected to it would inevitably become known, and the political consequences for the president, for the administration, for the party, and for the president's place in history would be overwhelming.

Presidential Decision Making: A Summary

Presidents thus do make decisions, sometimes on very great issues indeed. But the lesson to be learned is that making a decision is not enough. In the decision-making process, as in the legislative process, presidents must also work to persuade, cajole, and prod those who must carry out the decision. They must enlist the support of the bureaucracies, members of Congress, the media, and, through them, the general public. Again, presidents must wheel and deal. They must politick. Presidents may thus not be the chief legislators or even the chief decision makers, but they are certainly the chief politicians.

PRESIDENTIAL POWER

What can now be said about the power of presidents? Clearly they do have power—great power. But equally clearly their power has many limits.

The debate on just how much power presidents exercise has continued for years. One of the more thought-provoking and influential theories was put forward in a book by Richard E. Neustadt, a political science professor who had been an aide to President Truman. The book appeared just before the 1960 election, and between the election in November and the inauguration in January 1961, when Kennedy was resting in Palm Beach and planning what to do after he took office, someone gave him the book and urged him to read it, describing it as a "how-to book for presidents." Neustadt's argument was provocative because it stated that a president's constitutional powers, implied powers, prerogative powers, and status as chief of this and that really did not mean very much:

> In form all Presidents are leaders nowadays. In fact this guarantees no more than that they will be clerks. Everybody now expects the man inside the White House to do something about everything. Laws and customs now reflect acceptance of him as the Great Initiator. . . . But such acceptance does not signify that all the rest of the government is at his feet. It merely signifies that other men have found it practically impossible to do *their* jobs without assurance of initiatives from him. Service for themselves, not power for the President, has brought them to accept his leadership in form. They find his actions useful in their business. The transformation of his routine obligations testifies to their dependence on an active White House. A President, these days, is an invaluable clerk. His services are in demand all over Washington. His influence, however, is a very different matter. Laws and customs tell us little about leadership in fact.[15]

Neustadt argued that a modern president has to face demands for aid and service from the executive branch, from Congress, from his partisans, from citizens at large, and from abroad. In effect these are constituency pressures, and the presidency's clerkship is expressive of these pressures: *"The same conditions that promote his leadership in form preclude a guarantee of leadership in fact."*[16] Neustadt was saying that all the discussion and debate about the power of presidents just described dealt with only their potential power. If presidents are actually to exer-

---

[15]Richard E. Neustadt, *Presidential Power: The Politics of Leadership* (New York: John Wiley, 1960), p. 6, Neustadt's emphasis. See also the revised edition of this work, *Presidential Power and the Modern Presidents* (New York: The Free Press, 1990).

[16]Ibid., p. 7, Neustadt's emphasis.

cise their potential, he insisted, they must consciously and deliberately seek to add to their personal power and influence. "The search for personal influence is at the center of the job of being President."[17]

The Sources of Presidential Power

In the public debate that has continued since Neustadt's book, no one has seriously questioned his point that presidents do not automatically receive power but rather must consciously and deliberately cultivate it. There has, however, been considerable debate about the sources of presidential power.

One view is that although presidents must indeed engage in the politicking described, the ultimate source of their power is the constitutional prerogatives.[18] The politicking is necessary to assert these prerogatives successfully, but the source of the power is the prerogatives themselves. The counterargument is that although constitutional prerogatives are the source of the power presidents exercise in time of crisis, they are not the principal source of the power presidents use in dealing with day-by-day matters. A crisis can be defined as a situation in which all the major participants in the decision agree that continuing the present policy will certainly bring failure as great as the potential failure of a new, relatively unpredictable, alternative policy. In such circumstances there is inevitably some sort of confrontation between the president and those who oppose his proposed solution to the crisis. But such situations are relatively rare. What is the source of presidential power in the day-by-day making of public policy?

Political Brokering

Almost all "president watchers" implicitly recognize what seems to be the true source of the day-by-day power of presidents, but none really spell it out in any detail. They seem to regard it as crucial and yet too obvious to name. The name it probably should be given is political brokering.

Political brokering in fact is central to any political process, whether it is totalitarian, authoritarian, monarchic, aristocratic, oligarchic, or democratic. A political process is a device by which a society decides what it shall do. It concerns the goals the society should seek and the means for achieving them, how the members of the society should divide among themselves those benefits already available, the rules guiding economic and other competition, and the rules governing the rela-

---

[17]Ibid., p. 8.

[18]Richard M. Pious, *The American Presidency* (New York: Basic Books, 1979).

tions among elements of the society, whether minority groups, geographical regions, men and women, or teenagers and adults. Politics is concerned with the making of such policy decisions and with the maneuverings to acquire the power and influence to affect them.

Politicians engage in three types of activities, all of which overlap and interweave. The first is working to attain office or some less formal position in which they will have influence and power. The second activity—the true center of any political process—is the business of brokering. Brokering is mediating, trying to work out compromises, bargaining, negotiating, pressuring, threatening, dangling tempting baits and prizes, and using both sticks and carrots. All of this is done to reach some kind of decision that will be acceptable to all the many and varied power centers that make up American society: Congress, the cabinet, powerful bureaucrats, generals and admirals, leaders of interest groups, governors, and other state and local leaders. Only when politicians have attained some degree of success in the first two activities are they occasionally able to afford the luxury of the third activity: exercising power to suit their own purposes by tilting policy in the direction that they personally favor or that will benefit them in some way, changing the world to meet their preferences, or taking an initiative to establish something entirely new for which they can take the credit and to which their name will be attached.

Presidents are inevitably and inescapably involved in, and indeed in the midst of, the second, most central role of the political process—brokering. Political brokering is as much a tactic as a role, a way to enable presidents to be more than clerks who carry out other people's desires and to impose their own preferences and those of their supporters on the policies and decisions of the government. The job of political brokering comes to presidents because they are at the hub of all the many kinds of governmental decision making, both legislative and executive. The White House is the only place where all issues cross and converge. Thus the function and role of political brokering entails mediating among the conflicting demands of the competing power centers of the Congress; cabinet members; agency heads; individual senior bureaucrats; generals and admirals; press barons; interest groups; labor; industry; bankers; governors; and state, local, and regional leaders.

The role of political broker quite obviously includes mediating the conflicts among competing interests and power centers. Many of these conflicts are simple disagreements. Others are more dramatic, including strikes, riots over school desegregation and busing, and the fiscal collapse of cities. The role of political brokering, whether day by day or more dramatic, is central to the entire political process. It is the essence of the job of presidents, and performing it occupies most of their time.

Political Brokering as a Source of Power

Thus the role of political broker is not only the inevitable essence of the president's job but is also the principal source of the president's power. It gives presidents the right to be involved in the major issues that are the object of political struggle, legitimizes their participation, and allows them to take part in the debate even though they do not represent the power centers involved in the same sense as the head of an interest group. It makes presidents the central mediator among rival power centers. They are the ones on whom pressures are brought to bear, and the people who apply those pressures look to them for compromises and bargaining. In short, it is the main source of what has been called the president's only true power: the power to persuade.

Presidential Power: A Summary

Presidents thus do have power, great power. Its sources are varied and are rooted in their constitutional authority—explicit, implied, and prerogative; their right to participate in the legislative process; their right, granted either by the Constitution or Congress, to make certain kinds of decisions; the fact that it is a world of sovereign nation-states in which each must look to its own security; their personal reputation and prestige; the attention that the media give to the White House; and their central position in the political process and the function of political brokering that this position confers.

But presidents are not kings. To understand the power that they wield we must distinguish between foreign and domestic affairs and specify what kind of power over what kind of issues and in what circumstances and against the opposition of which other centers of power. We must also consider how well the particular president understands the political process itself, how deeply that person feels about achieving the goals being sought, and how much political skill the president brings to the job.

10

THE PRESIDENT'S STAFF AND ADVISERS

The president's staff and advisers constitute still another power center. Although their power is exercised through the president and is dependent on his continued confidence in them, they obviously have power.

An organizational chart of the White House, the Executive Office of the President, and various commissions reporting directly to the president—not to omit the cabinet and the National Security Council—shows the following arrangement. First, there is the White House staff, which has numbered about five hundred in recent years. Generally included are the national security adviser and the staff of the National Security Council (as opposed to the members of the NSC), which the adviser administers. Second, there is the so-called Executive Office of the President, which embraces a number of rather large, semi-independent bureaus and agencies such as the Office of Management and Budget as well as a number of almost completely independent agencies, such as the CIA. It also includes a variety of special commissions and other organizations, such as the Council of Economic Advisers.

Then there is the cabinet, consisting of the secretaries of the large departments, such as State, Defense, and Treasury. A similar body, set up by the National Security Act of 1947, is the National Security Council, consisting of the vice president, the secretaries of state, defense, and the treasury, the director of emergency planning, and a number of others concerned with foreign affairs and defense.

Finally, there is the office of the vice president. The Constitution laid down only two duties for the vice president. One is to be the presiding officer of the Senate, which as a practical matter he performs only when his presence is necessary to break a tie. The only other is to take over if

the president dies or, since the Twenty-fifth Amendment, becomes inca-
pacitated. However, a few presidents have tried to use the vice president
in special ways.

THE WHITE HOUSE STAFF

Franklin D. Roosevelt was the first president to have a White House staff
of significant size. Earlier presidents had one or two secretary-clerks and
sometimes as many as a half dozen senior aides on loan from the various
departments. President Roosevelt appointed the Brownlow Commission
specifically to remedy this situation, and the commission duly recommended, and the Congress and the president established, two major
changes. The first was to provide presidents with six senior, full-time
aides. The second was to create an Executive Office of the President and
to transfer from the Treasury Department to the new organization the
Bureau of the Budget, later renamed the Office of Management and
Budget (OMB). Since then, both the White House staff and the Executive
Office of the President have grown steadily.

In organizing the White House staff, Roosevelt avoided giving continuing assignments to particular people. He preferred to keep the organization loose and the jurisdiction overlapping. A staff person might work
on domestic affairs one day and foreign policy the next. Roosevelt believed that in this way no one would develop a proprietary interest in any
particular subject and that he would be able to keep the power to make
policy choices to himself.

If Roosevelt's White House was the most loosely organized, the most
tightly organized was probably Eisenhower's. For Eisenhower the model
was a military headquarters, with which he had been familiar all his
working life. Since the commanding general must often be in the field, a
high military headquarters revolves around a chief of staff who is always
present to "run the store." The general meets with the staff in the
morning to set the tasks for the day, leaves the headquarters to spend the
day with the troops in the field, and returns at the end of the day to decide
among the alternative choices the staff has laid out in his absence. In the
first part of the Eisenhower administration, this chief of staff was Sher-
man Adams, through whom everything had to flow. The single exception
was foreign policy, over which John Foster Dulles, the secretary of state,
kept tight control.

None of the other recent presidents has organized his staffs either as
loosely as Roosevelt or as tightly as Eisenhower. Truman had no chief of
staff, but he tended to give his staff permanent assignments and to divide
responsibility along clear lines of authority and jurisdiction. Under Kennedy the model was Roosevelt's White House, but in practice it was more

like Truman's. Johnson also dispensed with a chief of staff, but he drew lines of jurisdiction among members of the staff more sharply than Kennedy had.

Under Nixon the White House was organized more like Eisenhower's. H. R. Haldeman was chief of staff, but unlike the Eisenhower White House, he and four other senior assistants constituted a sort of inner circle or group of "supersecretaries." One dealt with domestic affairs, one with national security, one with "executive management," and one with economic affairs. Ford had a chief of staff, while Carter first tried a system without a chief but after several changes ended up appointing one.

In his first term, Reagan organized the White House more like Nixon's than any of the others. At first he assigned overall responsibility to three people—Edwin Meese, James A. Baker, and Michael Deaver. Although Deaver held the title of chief of staff, he did not have the usual responsibilities of that position. Actually each of the three acted as a sort of chief of staff for a particular subject matter, and only they could walk into the Oval Office without an appointment; all others (and all pieces of paper coming from others) had to go through one of the three to reach the president.[1]

However, the White House staff was organized quite differently in Reagan's second term. Meese became attorney general, and Deaver went back to private life. James Baker and the secretary of the Treasury, Donald T. Regan, traded jobs, and Regan became a true chief of staff. For a time he had no apparent rivals, but then Regan fell into disfavor with other White House staffers, and particularly with the president's wife, and he was replaced by Howard Baker.

Bush began his administration by following the organization of the later Reagan White House. John H. Sununu, a very conservative former governor of New Hampshire with a reputation for being both tough and blunt, was appointed chief of staff. Brent Scowcroft was appointed national security adviser and given increased power by chairing interdepartmental committees of which both the secretary of state and the secretary of defense would be members. Scowcroft was a retired Air Force general who had been an aide to Henry A. Kissinger when he was national security adviser and then national security adviser himself under President Ford. His reputation was that of a self-effacing team player. The other White House aides were long-term associates of Bush with reputations as moderate Republicans.

---

[1]For a brief period when William P. Clark, Jr., was Reagan's national security adviser, these "big three" became a "big four."

Whether presidents adopt one or another of these staff systems or some combination of them, these days most presidents have about two dozen personal assistants, including a confidential secretary, an appointments secretary, a press secretary, and a special assistant for congressional relations. Each of these in turn might also have two or three assistants as well as stenographers and clerks. Recent presidents have also found it necessary to have a special assistant for economic affairs, and some have found it desirable to have one for noneconomic domestic affairs as well, such as civil rights and minority group relations.

Certain presidents have also had personal assistants who played highly important and very intimate roles. For a time Woodrow Wilson felt he needed Colonel Edward House in a position that came near to being the president's alter ego. Harry Hopkins played a similar role for Franklin Roosevelt and for a time actually lived in the White House. He was the president's eyes and ears on vital matters, both domestic and foreign, and on many occasions served as Roosevelt's representative with extraordinary powers in meetings with Churchill and Stalin. Robert F. Kennedy performed such a role for his brother and at the same time served as attorney general.

The National Security Adviser

The National Security Act of 1947 created the National Security Council (discussed in the paragraphs that follow), consisting of the secretaries of State, Defense, Treasury, and Commerce and the director of the CIA, among others. It also provided for a special assistant to the president for national security affairs. In the Truman administration, the job amounted to little more than being a glorified clerk-secretary to the NSC, overseeing its agenda and following up on the president's decisions.

The job was only slightly more important in the Eisenhower administration. Eisenhower had the NSC meet weekly, and he set up a series of interdepartmental committees to prepare recommendations for the NSC to consider and to coordinate the various departments in carrying out the decisions made by the president. The national security adviser (Robert Cutler and later Gordon Grey) was responsible for supervising this rather large amount of committee activity.

The Eisenhower system was heavily criticized by Congress, the press, and academics on the grounds that the committee system tended to paper over differences between the contending departments. The president, the critics argued, ended up rubber-stamping compromises that were often internally inconsistent rather than actually choosing between true policy alternatives. The result, they felt, was that the government tended to drift along until an international crisis finally forced the departments and the president to face up to the problems that had caused the crisis.

President Kennedy and McGeorge Bundy. A major change in the role of the national security adviser came with the Kennedy administration. Responding to the criticism of the Eisenhower system, President Kennedy abolished most of the interdepartmental committees. His idea— following Roosevelt's example—was to have each of the major departments come to NSC meetings with their own proposals and to insist that they be fully prepared to argue their point of view. Kennedy believed that in this way he would better understand what the true alternatives were and thus be able to make more intelligent choices. Under this system the role of the national security adviser became much more important.

President Kennedy and his national security adviser, McGeorge Bundy, worked out an arrangement of what the adviser's job would be, and by and large it worked rather well. First, Bundy was not to be an advocate of any particular policy at any time in any way. This meant that his professional staff should be kept small and that he would not recommend a policy to the president or come to an NSC meeting with a proposal. If the adviser became an advocate, the reasoning went, tension would inevitably develop between the adviser on the one hand and the secretary of state or the secretary of defense on the other. The Congress, the press, the general public, and other countries would naturally learn of the rivalry and of the rival policies and become confused as to who really spoke for the administration and just what U.S. policy really was. The second part of the Kennedy-Bundy arrangement was that the adviser would avoid being a public spokesperson for foreign policy. He would severely limit his contacts with the press, even in so-called background sessions in which the official is not identified. Finally, the arrangement provided that the adviser would not engage in the implementation of foreign policy. This meant that Bundy would keep both his trips abroad and his contacts with foreign ambassadors in Washington to a minimum.

All of the foregoing were the don'ts that Kennedy and Bundy worked out. As for the do's, there were five. First, Bundy would attempt to make sure that the president was kept fully informed on developments abroad by using intelligence, diplomatic, and press sources. Second, he would keep the president aware of what was going on inside the U.S. government and between its departments, of what people at State, Defense, Treasury, and the CIA were thinking, and of any developing disagreements among them. Third, whenever Bundy or anyone else saw the need for a decision that might prevent trouble or saw a crisis coming up, Bundy would endeavor to get all the departments and agencies concerned to work to develop proposals and recommendations. He would then schedule an NSC meeting at which those proposals could be discussed and a decision made. Fourth, Bundy would try to follow through on any decisions the president made to see that the departments and agencies did their part to carry out such decisions. Finally, he would undertake to make sure that senior officials outside the White House understood the president's thinking and that the president understood theirs. As Bundy himself put it, ". . . a good national security assistant works for Cabinet officers as well as for the President."[2]

It is hard to find an instance in which Bundy violated the don'ts of this conception of the job of national security adviser, and most of the time he also complied with the do's. The notable exceptions were two. The first was his failure in the early months of the administration to stand up to Allen Dulles, the director of the CIA; Dulles's chief deputy, Richard Bissell; and the chairman of the Joint Chiefs of Staff, General Lyman L. Lemnitzer, when they insisted on excluding almost everyone but themselves from the meetings that finally authorized the attempted invasion by the brigade of Cuban exiles that ended in the Bay of Pigs fiasco. The second was his failure to follow through energetically enough on the

---

[2]McGeorge Bundy, "Mr. Reagan's Security Aide," *The New York Times,* November 16, 1980, p. E21. On the NSC in general, see I. M. Destler and Stanley L. Falk, *The National Security Structure* (Washington, D.C.: Industrial College of the Armed Forces, 1972); Clark A. Murdock, *Defense Policy Formation* (Albany: State University of New York Press, 1974); U.S. Congress, Senate, Committee on Government Operations, Subcommittee on National Security and International Operations, *The National Security Council: New Roles and Structure,* 91st Cong., 1st sess., S. Res. 24; Ralph Sander, *The Politics of Defense Analysis* (New York: Dunellen, 1973); Henry M. Jackson, ed., *The National Security Council* (New York: Praeger, 1965); R. Gordon Hoxie, *Command Decision and the Presidency* (New York: Reader's Digest Press, T. Y. Crowell, 1977); Karen Elliot House, "Mr. Zbig," *The Wall Street Journal,* October 3, 1979; Edward A. Kolodziej, "The National Security Council: Innovations and Implications," *Public Administration Review* (November–December 1969), pp. 573–585; John F. McMahon, Jr., "Revitalization of the National Security Council System," *Air University Review,* Vol. 21 (March–April 1970), pp. 28–36; Frederick C. Thayer, "Presidential Policy Processes and New Administration: A Search for Revised Paradigms," *Public Administration Review,* Vol. 31 (September–October 1971), pp. 552–561; Roy M. Melbourne, "The Operations Side of Foreign Policy," *Orbis,* Vol. 15 (Summer 1971); pp. 544–560; Etan Gilboa, "Intellectuals in the White House and American Foreign Policy," *Yale Review,* Vol. 65, (June 1976): 581–597; Dom. Bonafede, "Brzezinski–Stepping Out of His Backstage Role," *National Journal,* Vol. 9 (October 15, 1977), pp. 1596–1601; U.S., Congress, Senate, Committee on Foreign Relations, *The National Security Adviser: Role and Accountability,* 96th Cong., 2nd sess., April 17, 1980, Hearing; and Dick Kirschten, "Beyond the Vance-Brzezinski Clash . . . ," *National Journal,* Vol. 12 (May 17, 1980), pp. 814–818. See also Cyrus R. Vance, *Hard Choices: Four Critical Years in America's Foreign Policy* (New York: Simon & Schuster, 1983); Zbigniew Brzezinski, *Power and Principle; Memoirs of the National Security Adviser, 1977–1981* (New York: Farrar, Straus, Giroux, 1983); Joseph G. Bock, *The White House Staff and the National Security Assistant* (Westport, Conn.: Greenwood Press, 1987); Karl Inderfkurth and Loch K. Johnson, *Decisions at the Highest Order: Perspectives on the National Security Council* (Pacific Grove, Calif.: Brooks/Cole, 1988); Carnes Lord, *The Presidency and the Management of National Security* (New York: The Free Press, 1988); and Constantine C. Menges, *Inside the National Security Council* (New York: Simon & Schuster, 1988).

president's order to the State Department, which had been delivered on three separate occasions several months apart, to arrange for the removal of the U.S. Jupiter missiles deployed in Turkey. The Jupiter missiles were obsolete, unreliable, inaccurate, and very vulnerable; they could be knocked out by a sniper with a telescopic rifle. The Turks knew all this, but they wanted to delay their withdrawal until a time that seemed to them politically propitious. But the Jupiters were still in Turkey when the Soviets deployed their missiles to Cuba and were an extreme embarrassment for both Kennedy and the United States.

Henry Kissinger. Except for these few exceptions, however, the arrangement between Kennedy and Bundy about the role of the national security adviser worked very well. In the Nixon and Carter administrations, however, the advisers became rivals to the secretaries of state and defense and their role became extraordinarily controversial.

In the Nixon administration the secretary of state was William P. Rogers, an old friend of the president. Rogers was a lawyer who had been attorney general in the Eisenhower administration, but he had little knowledge of or experience in foreign affairs and even less stomach for the kind of bureaucratic and political infighting that is necessary to win battles over policy. The national security adviser, on the other hand, was Henry A. Kissinger, who had about twenty-five years of experience in international politics as a professor at Harvard and as an adviser to Nelson Rockefeller in his several attempts at winning the Republican nomination for president. Kissinger not only had the requisite knowledge of foreign affairs and defense but also a zest for and considerable skill at policy infighting.

Kissinger's first step was to increase the size of the NSC professional staff. In Bundy's time the staff numbered about a dozen; under Kissinger it rose to about 150.[3] This put Kissinger in a position to submit policy recommendations that were as fully worked out as those submitted by the State Department. Next, he instituted the practice of regular "background" sessions with members of the press. He also began to see foreign ambassadors on a regular basis. Finally, he began to make trips abroad as special negotiator for the president.

Bundy, in comparison, had made no official trips abroad as an official negotiator during Kennedy's administration. During Johnson's administration he made four, which Johnson had insisted upon for special reasons of his own, mainly to ensure that the remaining Kennedy man in the White House endorsed the policy Johnson wanted to pursue.

---

[3]Vincent Davis, "Henry Kissinger and Bureaucratic Politics: A Personal Appraisal," *Essay Series,* 9 (Columbia: Institute of International Studies, University of South Carolina, 1979), p. 25.

When Kissinger was adviser, on the other hand, his foreign trips numbered in the dozens. He became the principal negotiator for the endlessly drawn-out Middle East talks, inspiring the term "shuttle diplomacy" to describe his almost continuous trips around and around from Israel to Egypt to Washington. He was the *sole* negotiator in the normalization of relations with Communist China, which culminated in Nixon's visit in 1972 and produced the unforgettable spectacle of Nixon and Kissinger conferring with Mao Zedong while Secretary of State Rogers remained in his hotel room.

In the latter part of the Nixon administration, Kissinger replaced Rogers as secretary of state, and for the rest of the Nixon administration and the first part of the Ford administration, he also kept the job of national security adviser—making no secret of the fact that he did not want another "Kissinger" as adviser to the president in the White House while he, Kissinger, was secretary of state. Finally, pressure from Congress and the press did lead President Ford to fill the post of adviser, but at Kissinger's insistence he chose a career military officer, Colonel (later General) Brent Scowcroft, who had been Kissinger's deputy when he was adviser.[4]

Zbigniew Brzezinski. For his national security adviser Carter appointed a political science professor specializing in Soviet studies from Columbia University, Zbigniew Brzezinski. Carter and Brzezinski promised publicly that, unlike Kissinger, Brzezinski would keep a "low profile," meeting with neither the press nor ambassadors from other countries. But Secretary of State Cyrus R. Vance had no taste for dealing with the press or for public appearances, and the White House staff began to complain that the administration's positions were not getting the proper treatment in the news media. It was not long before Brzezinski was meeting with the press in "backgrounders."

Gradually, Brzezinski increased the NSC staff to over one hundred and soon began meeting with ambassadors and making public speeches and press appearances; he also began to make negotiating trips abroad. Soon it was well known in Washington, to the general public, and to other countries that Vance and Brzezinski were recommending quite different policies, especially toward the Soviet Union.

Vance had been prominent in defense and foreign affairs during the Kennedy and Johnson administrations and was highly respected by members of Congress, the press, academics, and other countries. Basically, he advocated a continuation of détente with the Soviet Union and

---

[4]One of George Bush's first acts after being elected was to appoint Brent Scowcroft his national security adviser, as mentioned.

further negotiations on the range of issues between the two countries. Brzezinski, on the other hand, was recommending hard-line policies toward the Soviets, demanding further concessions on arms control and the like.

Brzezinski also developed a somewhat flamboyant public image. On a visit to China, for example, he wisecracked about the "Great Polar Bear" (Russia) and the common interest that China and the United States should have in opposing it. Later, after the Soviet Union had sent troops to Afghanistan, Brzezinski went on a mission to offer arms to Pakistan. While there he visited the Khyber Pass, on the border between Pakistan and Afghanistan, and posed for photographers ostentatiously brandishing a submachine gun in the direction of the Soviet occupying forces.

The final confrontation between Vance and Brzezinski came over the aborted attempt to rescue the fifty-three American hostages in Iran by American commando troops in helicopters. Vance opposed the operation because he believed that the chances of success were so low that negotiations continued to be the more promising route. Brzezinski favored the plan. Vance told the president that even if the raid succeeded, he, Vance, could not publicly support it, and so he submitted his resignation before the raid took place, to be effective immediately after the raid, whether or not it was successful.[5]

The Reagan administration. President Reagan seemed determined to avoid the problem created by the overly ambitious national security advisers in the Nixon and Carter administrations. His first adviser was not authorized to report directly to the president. His second adviser, William P. Clark, Jr., had been Reagan's chief of staff when he was governor of California, and for a time it appeared that some of the same problems that plagued Nixon and Carter would arise again. However, following the resignation of the controversial secretary of the interior, James Watt, President Reagan transferred Clark to the interior job and named as adviser Clark's deputy, Robert C. McFarlane, a career Marine officer and an expert on the Middle East who had served on the NSC staff under Kissinger. McFarlane was not nearly so powerful in the post as Clark had been. Still later McFarlane left for civilian life and was replaced by Admiral John M. Poindexter. Poindexter became implicated with Lieutenant Colonel Oliver North in the Iran-Contra scandal and was replaced by Frank C. Carlucci. Shortly afterward, Carlucci was appointed secretary of defense and he was replaced by General Colin L.

---

[5]As mentioned in Chapter 1, the raid was aborted after three of the helicopters developed mechanical troubles at the assembly point in a remote area of Iran, and six American servicemen lost their lives when one of the helicopters collided with one of the cargo airplanes involved.

Powell, a career Army officer with a reputation for no-nonsense efficiency.[6]

The Bush administration. In dealing with questions in foreign affairs and defense, President Bush developed a style that was entirely different from any of the other modern presidents. On both defense and foreign affairs, he relied for advice on an inner circle consisting of Brent Scowcroft, the national security adviser; John A. Baker III, the secretary of state; Richard B. Cheney, the secretary of defense; and John H. Sununu, the White House chief of staff. However, on defense policy, Bush sometimes relied solely on Scowcroft. After Iraq invaded Kuwait, for example, the decision to increase the number of American troops so as to provide an offensive capability was apparently made without any consultation with the Joint Chiefs of Staff.[7] As mentioned earlier, to the apparent dismay of the State Department, Bush also consulted directly with other heads of state more than any other president in history.

THE EXECUTIVE OFFICE OF THE PRESIDENT

In addition to the president's personal staff is the Executive Office of the President. In terms of the power of the president and the White House, the most significant organization of the Executive Office is the Office of Management and Budget (OMB), which is headed by a director appointed by the president and staffed by career civil servants, professionals, and experts in various fields.

The main task of the OMB is to prepare the budget for the entire government, a complicated document that is two years in the making. The preparation process is not one of straightforward accounting and book balancing but of political bargaining, negotiating, manipulating, maneuvering, and pulling and hauling.[8]

The OMB's second responsibility is to make recommendations on any request for appropriations by any department or agency of the government. Before it does so, the OMB demands detailed plans and programs that specify the personnel and materials required. The OMB is also the clearinghouse for all legislation. Bills that the various departments and agencies propose to Congress, even if they do not require appropriations, must be cleared by the OMB. Bills passed by Congress on

---

[6]General Powell, incidentally, was the first African-American to serve in the post.
[7]Bob Woodward, *The Commanders,* p. 261.
[8]See Aaron Wildavsky, *The Politics of the Budgetary System,* 3rd ed. (Boston: Little, Brown, 1979).

its own initiative go to the OMB for its recommendation as to whether the president should sign or veto.

Finally, the OMB has a kind of "inspector general" role. It is required to maintain a continuous watch on the organization and management of each of the government departments and agencies and to recommend changes to improve efficiency and economy and to prevent one department or agency from duplicating the work of others. For example, the Veterans Administration runs health and welfare programs for veterans, while the Department of Health and Human Services runs other health and welfare programs. The OMB is responsible for seeing that the efforts of the two agencies do not overlap or duplicate one another.

Because the OMB is responsible for watching for inefficiency, overlap, and duplication, many presidents have tried to use it to control at least some aspects of the work of the departments and agencies. In general, these attempts have worked poorly if at all.[9] When the departments and agencies want for themselves what the OMB recommends, all goes well. But when they do not want what the OMB recommends, they almost always find ways to circumvent those recommendations. The exceptions are when the issue becomes national and so important that the president and the Congress become protagonists.

The main responsibility of the OMB, of course, is to prepare the budget. A very large part of the budget cannot be changed by presidents. Veterans' pensions, Social Security, and retirement for civil servants, which today amount to about $336 billion,[10] are among the items that, as a practical political matter, neither the president nor the Congress can change very radically. Many other programs, such as Medicare, Medicaid, food stamps, and certain kinds of agricultural subsidies, can only be changed with extraordinary political difficulty. The great bureaucracies also have ways of getting around presidential orders to increase or decrease some of the expenditures over which presidents supposedly have full legal control. The money can be shifted to different accounts, for example, or the bureaucracies can stimulate their constituencies, who are the people affected by the programs, to bring pressure on the president through their representatives in Congress or through the press.

---

[9]See, among others, Richard Rose, *Managing Presidential Objectives* (New York: The Free Press, 1976); idem, "Implementation and Evaporation: The Record of OMB," *Public Administration Review*, Vol. 37 (January–February 1977); Allen Schick, "A Death in the Bureaucracy: The Demise of Federal PPB," *Public Administration Review*, Vol. 33, (March–April 1973); and Lawrence Berman, "The Office of Management and Budget That Almost Wasn't," *Political Science Quarterly*, Vol. 92, no. 2 (Summer 1977).

[10]*Budget of the U.S. Government, 1991.* Social Security amounts to $299 billion, retirement for civil servants comes to $32 billion, and $15 billion is spent on veterans' pensions.

There does, however, remain a portion of the budget of almost every department and agency that presidents can change. But since it is difficult to ferret out possible savings in each of a host of bureaucracies, the usual technique presidents follow is to impose an arbitrary cut across the board—say, 10 percent—in the expenditures of every department and agency and force them to decide for themselves just where that 10 percent should be. In such ways presidents do find the OMB a useful tool for accomplishing their purposes, albeit a crude one.

Even when presidents call for cuts across the board, the bureaucracies can often find ways to circumvent their orders. For example, on several occasions when the National Park Service was told to make an across-the-board cut, they saved a good part of the money by closing the Washington Monument to visitors. Because the monument was a particular favorite of school groups on their yearly visit to Washington, almost every member of Congress was the target of howls of protest from their constituents. The Congress in turn raised hell with the OMB and the White House, and the cuts demanded of the National Park Service were usually reduced. The so-called Washington Monument ploy finally became such a notorious joke that the Park Service abandoned the practice.

Other Offices of the Executive Office of the President

The Executive Office includes about three dozen other offices, boards, and councils, some of which are established by statute and thus are permanent and some of which are the creatures of a particular president and thus are temporary. Among the more noteworthy are the Council of Economic Advisers, set up by the Employment Act of 1946, and the Office of Science and Technology Policy, established by law in 1976. Presidents have generally added to the Executive Office by setting up special offices, councils, or advisory boards whenever a particular problem or issue assumed crisis proportions.[11]

With the exception of the OMB, these various offices, boards, and councils are little different from those that are not lodged in the Executive Office. The Council of Economic Advisers would have about the same relationship with presidents and give them about the same advice

---

[11]On the White House staff, see also Samuel Kernell and Samuel L. Popkin, *Chief of Staff: Twenty-five Years of Managing the Presidency* (Berkeley: University of California Press, 1986); Alfred Dick Sander, *A Staff for the President: The Executive Office, 1921–1952* (Westport, Conn.: Greenwood Press, 1989); Joseph G. Bock, *The White House Staff and the National Security Assistant* (Westport, Conn.: Greenwood Press, 1987); Bradley H. Patterson, Jr., *The Ring of Power: The White House Staff and its Expanding Role in Government* (New York: Basic Books 1988); and Stephen Hess, *Organizing the Presidency* (Washington, D.C.: Brookings, 1988).

whether or not it appeared on the chart as part of the Executive Office. Similarly, large agencies such as the CIA, which has several thousand employees and its own huge building in Langley, Virginia, would act the same and have the same relationship with the president if it were an independent agency.

THE CABINET

The cabinet was not mentioned in the Constitution or in any legislation until 1907. George Washington simply called the principal secretaries to meet, and people, following the custom in Great Britain, called it the cabinet. Today the cabinet is composed of the secretaries of the major departments: State, Treasury, Defense, Justice, Interior, Agriculture, Commerce, Labor, Health and Human Services, Housing and Urban Development, Transportation, and Education. As a sort of sop to Adlai Stevenson, who had twice run unsuccessfully against President Eisenhower, President Kennedy gave cabinet rank to the ambassador to the United Nations to entice Stevenson to take the job. Each of these individuals has power and influence, but the cabinet as a collective body has almost none.

The American cabinet differs fundamentally from the cabinet in a parliamentary system, such as that of the British. In both Britain and the United States the members of the cabinet are also heads of major departments, but there the similarity ends. Unlike their American counterparts, members of the British cabinet are also members of Parliament and, more importantly, frequently leaders of factions of their party. British constitutional tradition provides that major decisions of the government are taken by the cabinet as a collegiate body. Its members actually vote on questions of policy, and the cabinet is collectively responsible. The prime minister is sufficiently powerful to ensure that he or she is rarely outvoted. But the practical political consequences of these differences are that if the prime minister *is* outvoted on a serious issue, he or she can be replaced by a caucus of the party's members of Parliament, or the cabinet members can bring about a vote of "no confidence" in Parliament, which automatically triggers a general election.

The American cabinet has no such power. As described earlier, President Lincoln, after casting the only "aye" vote, declared that the "ayes have it," and no one challenged him. Presidents can call meetings of the cabinet for whatever benefit they might derive from just listening to the discussion. But meetings for this purpose are rare, for secretaries of major departments would much prefer to speak to the president alone about anything that is important to their departments, and they are usually reluctant to oppose something affecting another department in front of the others.

More often, presidents convene meetings of the cabinet for quite different reasons. Sometimes presidents convene the cabinet to explain a policy they have chosen. Another reason is to "read the riot act"—to make sure that the cabinet members understand that on this particular issue the president wants a united front before Congress and the press and that anyone who strays from the president's line will suffer. A third reason is to use the meeting as a way of lending dignity and authority to a policy by creating a public impression that the decision has the approval of the cabinet.

Because of the disparate and often conflicting interests of the members of the cabinet, it is rare indeed that presidents use it as an advisory body.

The Twenty-fifth Amendment

If the cabinet holds any power at all as a collective body, it derives from the Twenty-fifth Amendment:

> Whenever the Vice President and a majority of either the principal officers of the executive departments or of such other body as Congress may by law provide, transmit to the President pro tempore of the Senate and the Speaker of the House of Representatives their written declaration that the President is unable to discharge the powers and duties of his office, the Vice President shall immediately assume the powers and duties of the office of Acting President.

Even this power of the cabinet is uncertain, for the amendment does not say whether the "principal officers of the executive departments" are in fact the members of the cabinet.

THE NATIONAL SECURITY COUNCIL

Another advisory body, similar in many ways to the cabinet, is the National Security Council. It was created by the National Security Act of 1947, in the wake of World War II. The law specifies that its members shall include the president, the vice president, the secretary of state, the secretary of defense, the director of emergency planning, and any others the president might desire. In practice most presidents have "desired" that the secretary of the treasury, the director of the CIA, and the chairman of the Joint Chiefs of Staff shall be included. They have also "desired" that the national security adviser at least be present, if not a member. President Kennedy also "desired" that his brother, the attorney general, be a member.

Everything said so far about the cabinet's lack of power applies to the NSC: Presidents can make life difficult for members of the NSC in a variety of ways, but members of the NSC cannot vote presidents down on a particular question, replace them with another president, or bring about a special presidential election.

There are, however, two ways in which the NSC differs from the cabinet, and both of them give the NSC somewhat greater significance. First, unlike the cabinet, the NSC is concerned with a single, rather narrow issue: national security, which means defense and foreign policy. Second, each of the departments whose heads are members of the NSC have some responsibility in implementing policy on this issue. The State Department must carry out the diplomatic aspects of the decisions, the Defense Department must provide any military backup that is required, Treasury must provide money, and the CIA must gather the necessary intelligence. For these two reasons the members of the NSC are somewhat less reluctant to discuss problems in front of each other than are the members of the cabinet. Because all members are involved in the implementation of the final decisions, the president too has a stake in winning their approval and building a consensus, since this will mean they will cooperate more willingly. Hence most presidents call meetings of the NSC more frequently than they call cabinet meetings, and they listen more attentively to what its members have to say.

THE VICE PRESIDENT

Can the vice president be said to be a power center? At the Constitutional Convention of 1787, the office of vice president was proposed only at the last minute and then just to break the deadlock over the process of choosing the president. The electoral college was conceived as a way around the objections to all the other means of choosing a president. The framers of the Constitution knew that the pressure on electors to vote for a leading citizen of their own state would be overwhelming. As a way of overcoming potential localism, they specified that each of the electors, without consulting the others, should vote for two people he or she considered best qualified to be president, "of whom one at least shall not be an Inhabitant of the same State with themselves." Thus the second choice of a majority of the electors would be the person with the greatest national standing and would therefore, the framers reasoned, become president.

However, the framers also realized that it would help in maintaining national unity if a job could also be found for the person who got the next largest number of votes. A member of the committee that came up with the notion of the electoral college told the convention that the office of vice president was not wanted but that it "was introduced only for the sake of a valuable mode of election which required two be chosen at the same time." Vice presidents were apparently then given the job of presiding over the Senate because no one could think of anything else for them to do. The Senate itself quickly adopted rules that denied the presiding officer any possibility of exercising power, so the job is usually rotated daily and even hourly among the most junior senators. Historically, the vice president has actually presided only when a tie vote is anticipated, so that he may cast the deciding vote.

Throughout most of the history of the United States, the vice presidency has been held in some contempt—as unnecessary as a "fifth wheel." John Adams called it "the most insignificant office that ever the invention of man contrived or his imagination conceived. . . ." Jefferson said it was the "only office in the world about which I am unable to decide whether I had rather have it or not have it." John Nance Garner, FDR's salty vice president from Texas, declared that the office wasn't worth a "bucket of warm spit." Thomas R. Marshall, vice president to Woodrow Wilson, stated that the "only business of the vice-president is to ring the White House bell every morning and ask what is the state of health of the president." On another occasion, he remarked that the vice president "is like a man in a cataleptic state: he cannot speak; he cannot move; he suffers no pain; and yet he is perfectly conscious of everything that is going on about him."

With nothing to do but preside over the Senate—a task that could hardly be called taxing—vice presidents have filled their days in ways that range from the unimaginative to the downright ingenious. Richard M. Johnson, vice president to Martin Van Buren, ran a tavern. On occasion vice presidents have tried to promote alternative policies. Charles G. Dawes advocated legislation that his president, Calvin Coolidge, finally vetoed. Jefferson and Calhoun spent much of their time as vice presidents launching attacks on the power of the national government, against the wishes of their presidents.

Partly to keep vice presidents out of such mischief and partly to avoid the anomalous situation in which the second-ranking officer of the government has nothing to do, a number of presidents have tried to give the vice president additional duties. One of these has been to perform ceremonial functions deemed to be of minor political importance, such as attending inaugurations and funerals in foreign countries. Vice presidents have also done much traveling on the "chicken-and-peas" circuit of party fund-raising banquets.

But these jobs are just as unimportant as presiding over the Senate. In recent times three presidents—Roosevelt, Ford, and Carter—tried to give their vice presidents duties of real importance. Franklin Roosevelt made Vice President Henry A. Wallace head of the Board of Economic Warfare, a very important job indeed. But as all agency heads inevitably do if they are conscientious, Wallace got into fights with other agency heads—the most acrimonious being with Jesse Jones, the secretary of commerce. It is always embarrassing to an administration to have cabinet members fighting, and to have a vice president and a cabinet member fighting is doubly so. Presidents can fire cabinet members, if need be, but not an elected vice president. When Wallace charged publicly that Jones had obstructed efforts to stockpile critical war materials, Roosevelt was furious. He would undoubtedly have fired Wallace if he could. But he could not, so he dissolved the Board of Economic Warfare and transferred its functions to the Office of War Mobilization, headed by James F. Byrnes.[12]

When Vice President Ford assumed the office of president on the resignation of Richard M. Nixon, he promised to give the man he appointed to fill the job he vacated, Nelson A. Rockefeller, substantial responsibilities in domestic affairs. But by the summer of 1975, it was clear that the White House staff had succeeded in preventing Rockefeller from getting the authority he had expected. A few weeks later Rockefeller made a slip in public that illustrates the peculiar poignancy of the vice president's job. At a meeting of Republican governors he remarked that it was not enough for Republicans to berate the Democratic Congress for overspending and for budget deficits. Waxing enthusiastic, Rockefeller went on to say that the question Republicans had to answer was this: "If we were in power, what would we do?" Then, belatedly remembering that the Republicans *were* in power, at least in the White House, he caught himself. "But the President is in power," he added lamely, "so I'm sure he will come up with solutions."[13]

In spite of the Wallace and Rockefeller experiences, President Jimmy Carter attempted to give Vice President Walter F. Mondale important work. The job was that of "senior adviser," in the words of one member of the press, and "general adviser, trouble-shooter, and mover-and-shaker without portfolio," in the words of another.[14] Some memoirs written by members of the Carter administration suggest that this arrangement caused confusion as to who was actually speaking for the president. But on balance the experiment seems to have been reasonably

---

[12]Robert E. Sherwood, *Roosevelt and Hopkins, An Intimate History.* (New York: Harper & Row, 1948), pp. 740–741.

[13]Christopher Lydon, "In a Brief Slip, Rockefeller Describes His Situation," *The New York Times,* November 24, 1975.

[14]*The New York Times,* April 29, 1977, p. A1; and Brock Brower, "The Remaking of the Vice President," *The New York Times Magazine,* June 5, 1977, pp. 38 ff.

successful in the sense that Mondale does seem to have done some important work in addition to the usual ceremonial functions and the "chicken-and-peas" party fund-raising duties.

The reasons for Mondale's success were twofold. First, he was self-effacing and avoided appearing to compete with the president for publicity, while Carter was apparently less bothered than some people might be at President Lyndon Johnson's description of the vice president: He is "like a raven, hovering around the head of the president, reminding him of his mortality." Second, the work that Carter gave Mondale did not carry any continuing responsibilities that might have brought him into repeated or steady conflict with one or another cabinet member or White House aide. Wallace's job as head of the Board of Economic Warfare did have continuing responsibilities, as did Rockefeller's as "czar" for domestic affairs. The job Mondale was assigned shifted from subject to subject and was much more like that of a personal troubleshooter. It was, in a word, much more like the job that Colonel House did for President Wilson or Harry Hopkins did for President Roosevelt.

Between George Bush's election in 1988 and inauguration in 1989, both the press and Vice President-elect Danforth Quayle speculated about what role Quayle might play. Before the inauguration, the press suggested that Quayle would be the spokesman within the administration for the right wing of the Republican party, a suggestion probably inspired by the right wing itself. But Quayle quickly denied that he would play such a role and himself speculated that he might be able to use his constitutional position as presiding officer of the Senate to work out an important part in the Senate's business—an idea that died at birth. As it turned out, Quayle did what vice presidents have usually done: chaired some unimportant interdepartmental committees, attended the inaugurations and funerals of foreign leaders, and spoke at Republican party fund raisers that the president regarded as not worth doing himself.

It is no accident that presidents either have not taken the risk of giving great responsibilities to their vice presidents or have taken back what they had begun to give when they realized the potentialities for trouble. Since vice presidents are the heirs apparent and since they cannot be fired, the possibility exists that they will use any power they are given to try to unseat the president at the next election. During the Constitutional Convention one delegate worried that the president and the vice president might develop a "close intimacy" that would be dangerous. Gouverneur Morris replied that the vice president "then will be the first heir apparent that ever loved his father."

Why then would anyone want the job of vice president? Recently, at least, the answer has been that the vice presidency is a good place from which to run for the presidency—or at least to get the nomination. (Although a number of sitting vice presidents got their party's nomination, George Bush was the first who was actually elected since Martin Van Buren in 1837. Nixon, of course, was defeated in 1960, when he was the sitting vice president, but was later elected, in 1968.)

The reason vice presidents are successful in getting their party's nomination is not because the office is a good training ground for the presidency. During the 1960 campaign, Nixon claimed that his experience as vice president and his participation in making national decisions made him especially qualified to be president. But when President Eisenhower was asked about the national decisions Nixon was supposed to have helped make he hesitated and then said, "Well, if you give me a week or two I might think of one."[15]

Mondale's work seems to have been more useful than that of any other recent vice president, but it did not really give him much experience that was relevant to the job of being president. What makes the vice presidency attractive is that it offers opportunities for building name recognition and for accumulating "due bills" from local "pols" by attending fund-raising events, two assets that can help in getting the nomination for president some day. And of course there is another factor often remarked upon: The vice president, after all, is only a heartbeat away from being president.

The vice president, thus, is not a power center. In fact he has almost no power. But his potential for power – if he succeeds to the presidency – is high.

---

[15]Press conference of August 24, 1960, *Public Papers of the President, Dwight D. Eisenhower* (Washington, D.C.: U.S. Government Printing Office, 1961), p. 658.

11

THE POLITICAL
APPOINTEES

On the surface, the men and women whom presidents appoint as members of their administrations—the political appointees—appear to have power. But do they constitute power centers?

Who are the members of an administration? When President Nixon was putting together his administration, *The New York Times* defined an administration as being "one President, one Vice President, 12 Cabinet appointees, 300 sub-Cabinet officials and agency heads, 124 ambassadors, and 1700 aides, assistants and confidential secretaries."[1] Another guide to the definition of an administration is the document *United States Policy and Supporting Positions,* which is published each election year as a public service by one of the committees of the Senate.[2] It lists not only the jobs that make up an administration but all of the patronage and Schedule C jobs available to a new administration (a Schedule C job is one that is "political" in the sense that the occupant has no tenure and is expected to change with each new administration). Variously called the green book and the shopping list, it is usually called the plum book because it describes the available political "plums." The *Times* article and the plum book, however, are only rough guides to a definition. A number of other points should be underlined.

---

[1]Max Frankel, "Priorities for the Nixon Team," *The New York Times,* November 15, 1968, p. A32.

[2]U.S. Congress, Senate Committee on Governmental Affairs, *United States Policy and Supporting Positions* (Washington, D.C.: U.S. Government Printing Office).

Most of the top jobs filled by presidents require Senate confirmation. Cabinet members, deputy secretaries, undersecretaries, assistant secretaries, agency heads, and members of regulatory boards and commissions all require such approval, as do certain members of the Executive Office of the President, such as the director of the Office of Management and Budget, members of the Council of Economic Advisers, and the director of the Office of Science and Technology. All of these are obviously candidates for the label of power center.

However, commissioned officers of the Army, Navy, Air Force, Marine Corps, Coast Guard, Foreign Service, and certain other officials also require Senate confirmation, but they are not members of an administration. If these officers become power centers, it is because of their position in the national security bureaucracies rather than because of their appointment by the president and confirmation by the Senate.

White House aides do not require confirmation, presumably on the theory that they are personal aides to the president. But they are obviously very likely to be part of power centers quite apart from presidents themselves.

Of the more than two thousand appointments that a president makes, only about five hundred are to policy-making jobs. It is these jobs that are potential power centers and that are occupied by appointees that are truly political. Political appointees quite obviously do not constitute a single power center. But it is equally obvious that they are key elements in quite a number of power centers.

THE IMPORTANCE OF POLITICAL APPOINTEES

Political appointees are people who come in and out of government with a president, and they are of crucial importance. Many, for example, think that the problem of government is a problem of bureaucracy, but V.O. Key, Jr., an eminent political scientist, argued that the problem of government is not really a problem of bureaucracy at all:

> It is rather a question of attracting into party service an adequate supply of men competent to manage and control the bureaucracy from their posts as transient but responsible heads of departments and agencies. ... It is through such persons who owe their posts to the victorious party that popular control over government is maintained.[3]

---

[3]V. O. Key, Jr. *Politics, Parties, and Pressure Groups,* 5th ed. (New York: Crowell, 1964), pp. 711–712.

While one might at first assume that Key is proposing a return to the spoils system, in fact he is not. One might also assume that he is proposing a parliamentary system on the British model in which the party is the central mechanism and party discipline is the oil that makes the mechanism work, but this would be equally wrong. Key is talking about the people who make up an administration: the secretaries, under-secretaries, assistant secretaries, and all the others appointed to policy-making jobs. He thus is talking about the political appointees, the men and women whom some observers have called the "president's people," others have called the "in-and-outers," and still others have called the "front people" of government.[4] These are the people who provide the vital link between a president and the bureaucracies, and to some extent between the executive and the press and between the executive and the general public. They also share with the top bureaucracies the responsibility for providing the link between the executive branch and Congress. Key was saying that these people play a crucial role in making the government more efficient, more controllable, more responsive, and more accountable. And he was absolutely right.

CHOOSING POLITICAL APPOINTEES

In theory, presidents are free to choose the members of their administrations—with the "advice and consent of the Senate"—and almost all presidents are intensely interested in having the freedom to choose. They understand that their own success or failure, and hence their place in history, will depend on the caliber and philosophy of the men and women who hold the top jobs in their administrations. But presidents are not really as free in making their choices as one might think.

One reason for the limitations on their freedom is the fact that presidents have not won the nomination and election on their own. A lot of people have worked very hard for a very long time for their victory, frequently without pay or with very little pay. As suggested in Chapter 8, these people do not come from a single power center or even from a small group of them, so presidents have not incurred a policy debt. But they do

---

[4]Credit for the term "in-and-outers" seems to belong jointly to Richard E. Neustadt and Adam Yarmolinsky, both of whom are in-and-outers themselves. See Neustadt's "White House and Whitehall," and Yarmolinsky's "Ideas into Programs," both in *The Public Interest*, Vol. 2 (Winter 1966). The term "front people" is my own, from *To Move a Nation: The Politics of Foreign Policy in the Administration of John F. Kennedy* (Garden City, N.Y.: Doubleday, 1967), pp. 469 ff.

owe these people a personal debt, and many want to serve in some sort of important position in the government.

Government jobs do not pay enough for money to be the motivation for most of these people. Instead, most want the positions to be able to influence policy. They may want to serve in the State Department or Defense Department because they believe in a tougher foreign policy or, alternatively, in one that puts more emphasis on negotiations and the reconciliation of international disputes. They may also want more or less spending on defense. They may want to serve in the Department of the Interior because they are concerned with the environment or natural resources. They may want to be involved in agencies concerned with education or the poor. On the other hand, they may like the feeling of power that an important office gives, or they may have further ambitions, such as running for Congress or a governorship, and believe that the publicity and prominence of appointive office will further those ambitions. Whatever their motives, many people who worked to elect a president want a job, and presidents are under pressure to satisfy as many of them as they can.

But these are only the beginnings of the pressures on presidents about appointments, for presidents owe their election not only to the hard work of many individuals but also to the support of various organizations, constituencies, and interest groups. Many of these want to see their own people in top jobs and thus suggest particular candidates. Even if they do not push for a particular person for a particular job, they want people appointed who are sympathetic to their interests. At the very least, these organizations and constituencies will try to veto the nominations of those they believe are *not* sympathetic to their interests.

The first of such organizations that comes to mind is the political party. If a Democrat is elected, the national, state, and local Democratic party organizations and the mass of voters who think of themselves as Democrats expect to see Democrats fill the top posts in the new administration. The same is true if it is the Republican who is elected. The Democrats will not object if the president they elect appoints a few Republicans to top jobs, and again the same applies to the Republicans. Willingness to tolerate appointments from the other party is high in time of crisis, whether domestic or international, when a few outstanding appointments from the other party can help to unify the country. With World War II looming on the horizon, for example, President Roosevelt thought it wise to appoint two Republicans, Henry L. Stimson and Frank Knox, to be secretary of war and secretary of the navy, respectively. In 1960 President Kennedy won by a very narrow margin, the cold war was in full swing, and the dollar was under frightening international pressure. Understandably, he thought it expedient to appoint two Republicans to cabinet posts, Robert S. McNamara as secretary of defense and C. Douglas Dillon as secretary of the treasury, and another, McGeorge Bundy, as his national security adviser. Ronald Reagan appointed Jeanne J. Kirkpatrick, a Democrat with a tough-minded view on foreign affairs, as ambassador to the United Nations (she later decided to switch parties and became a Republican). But after winning an election, party activists expect the bulk of the appointees to be members of their party most of the time.

Typical constituencies who would expect a voice in decisions on presidential appointments whenever they could claim that their votes had helped elect a particular president would be conservatives, liberals, farmers, blacks, and environmentalists. Conservatives from the right wing of the Republican party were enthusiastic supporters of Ronald Reagan, and they felt strongly that people who shared their views should hold top positions. They pushed hard for David A. Stockman to be director of the Office of Management and Budget, a position essential to carrying out their desires for tax cuts and reductions in government spending. They also pushed for Donald T. Regan as secretary of the treasury and Richard V. Allen as national security adviser, both of whom they believed to be their kind of conservatives. At the same time Reagan's conservative supporters, especially those in the Senate led by Jesse Helms of North Carolina, tried to exercise a veto over Reagan's nominees in the second level of the State Department who were believed to have more moderate views.

The same sort of thing happened when George Bush was elected. The right wing of the Republican party, for example, made a particular issue about having former Senator John G. Tower appointed as secretary of defense. Tower had a reputation as a very right-wing conservative with hard-line views on both the Soviet Union and defense policy, and conservatives thought of him as their representative—and their reward for having supported Bush. The Senate rejection of Tower was more a slap at conservatives than at Bush.

Both interest groups and constituencies expect that top-level posts will be filled by people who represent their interests or who have a special sympathy with and understanding of their interests. The secretary of agriculture is expected to be a farmer or to come from an agricultural college or some industry related to agriculture. The secretary of the treasury is expected to come from Wall Street, the financial community of some other city, or the banking world. The secretary of labor is expected to be a union person, a labor economist from a university, an official from a relevant office of government such as the Federal Mediation and Conciliation Service, or at the very least a business leader with a reputation for getting along with the unions.

Some of the positions to which presidents make appointments are by tradition reserved for career bureaucrats. In the Veterans' Administration, for example, the post of deputy administrator is by custom held by a career official; for many years in the State Department so was the post of deputy undersecretary for political affairs.

Debts to people who helped in the election, rewards for loyal members of the victorious political party, and recognition of special interests and constituencies all must be considered in the choice of presidential appointees. Beyond these, presidents must also consider the nominee's qualifications and whether his or her philosophy or ideology will be generally acceptable to the Congress, the press, and the general public. For secretary of state, for example, presidents must choose someone who has the appropriate education and experience and whose known views are not too "radical." These limitations mean that the pool of candidates is relatively small.

Who Are the Political Appointees?

From the beginning of the Roosevelt administration in 1933 to the beginning of the Bush administration in 1989, about seven thousand policy-making officials were appointed. Although no definitive study has been made of all these political appointees, not even those of cabinet rank alone, the Brookings Institution, a private, nonprofit research organization, has sponsored two studies on political appointees—a total of eight hundred people.[5]

The notion that political appointees are "in-and-outers" suggests that political appointees have some well-known ladder to high office. The implication is that young people come into government as a Schedule C special assistant or aide, depart when the administration ends, pursue private careers for a while, and then return as secretary of one of the great departments or director of an important agency. The impression is also that the American system permits top policy makers to be educated progressively in the workings of government, acquiring higher and higher levels of experience as they move up. To some extent this is true. Of the eight hundred people studied by Brookings, four out of five had had some prior service in the national government. The overall pattern for those who had had government service outside the career service was to have moved from one subordinate executive position to a presidential appointment. "This has often meant the promotion of an assistant to the

---

[5]Dean E. Mann and Jameson W. Doig, *The Assistant Secretaries* (Washington, D.C.: Brookings, 1965); and Hugh Heclo, *A Government of Strangers* (Washington, D.C.: Brookings, 1977).

secretaryship or of a politically appointed bureau chief to a position at the secretarial level." The few who had not previously held a full-time government job usually had had some experience on advisory boards or as government consultants.[6] About one-third of the eight hundred had been public servants for a large proportion of their working lives. This figure is probably misleading, however, because in many administrations the political appointees tend to leave a year or two before the administration ends to take an attractive job offer that comes their way, and the balance of their terms is temporarily filled by career bureaucrats.

Many of the eight hundred appointees had already achieved considerable success and prestige in their own occupations and communities. As a consequence, they tended to be a little older than their counterparts in private life. Each administration appointed women to high-level posts, but none appointed very many. The number of black and other minority appointees was even smaller. As would be expected, political appointees tended to be better educated and from higher socioeconomic strata than the general population.

CAREER PATTERNS OF POLITICAL APPOINTEES

How does one become a top-level policy maker? In some countries there are clear-cut routes to such jobs. But in the United States the roads to positions of responsibility are murky and confusing; one description of the process is "complex pandemonium."

Recently, the most common route to a policy-making job has been through building a national reputation in a particular field. Appointees tend to be prominent Wall Street lawyers; well-known, successful bankers; labor union leaders or lawyers for a prominent union; leaders in the agricultural community; nationally known professors in economics, urban planning, or international affairs; presidents of major industries such as General Motors or the Ford Motor Company; presidents of universities or major charitable foundations; or prominent figures in any one of several dozen other areas with some direct relevance to the work of one of the departments or agencies of government.

Appointees also participate in public affairs in their own and related fields. They attend meetings and conferences, volunteer to sponsor causes that have widespread public support and approval while avoiding those that are radical and unpopular, publish thoughtful papers in respected journals, and send helpful advisory letters to potential presidential candi-

---

[6]Mann and Doig, *Assistant Secretaries*, p. 29.

dates, senators, members of the House, governors, secretaries of departments and agencies, and the like. Then, during a presidential election year, they often become active politically, working hard for their party's nominee. Presidents will naturally give preference to people who supported them early. Franklin Roosevelt favored those who had supported him "before Chicago," where the nominating convention was held. For Eisenhower the watershed was also the nominating convention. For Kennedy the magic phrase was "before Wisconsin," the state primary in which he first began to look as though he might really win. Nixon's preference went to people who had supported him when he was vice president and had stood with him when Senator Barry M. Goldwater dominated the party in the dark days between Nixon's defeat in 1960 and his victory in 1968. Carter's staff jokingly divided themselves into three categories: the "Chosen," those who had joined the Carter team before 1972; the "Anointed," those who had joined in 1975; and the "Converted," those who had joined after the New Hampshire primary. For Reagan the people who had been with him in his fight for the governorship of California and worked with him when he served as governor obviously had a special place in his heart, as did those who had worked for him in the primary campaign of 1976, when he lost the nomination to President Ford. Bush was particularly grateful to the people who had encouraged him during his eight, long, frustrating years as vice president.

Another strategy for obtaining appointive office has been to become established in elective politics. A significant proportion of secretaries of departments, directors of agencies, undersecretaries, and similar officials have been senators, governors, and members of the House. In the early days of the republic, almost all political appointees had held elective office, usually in one of the states. Today it is slightly less common, but it does happen. Several members of Carter's administration had held elective office, the one drawing most attention being Andrew Young, the African-American Congressman from Georgia who became UN ambassador. In the Reagan administration, David Stockman, director of the OMB, had been a member of Congress; James B. Edwards, secretary of the Department of Energy, had been governor of South Carolina; and Richard S. Schweiker, secretary of health and human services, had been senator from Pennsylvania. In the Bush administration, former New Hampshire governor John H. Sununu, who was appointed White House chief of staff, and former Senator John Tower, who was appointed secretary of defense but failed to win confirmation, have already been mentioned. Another such appointee is John F. Kemp, secretary of housing and urban development, a right-wing conservative who served nine terms in the House.

Other Ladders to Appointive Office

For women and men just out of college, law school, or graduate school, who are still in their twenties or thirties and have not yet built a national reputation, there is still another route to appointive office. Their first appointive jobs will hardly be those of secretary of one of the major departments, director of an agency, or even assistant secretary. But it may well be a job as a White House aide or as special assistant to a secretary, director, or assistant secretary. The experience gained may well lead to the higher post in later years.

The first step for young people who choose this ladder has been to become involved in the organization of one of the political parties. Many a White House aide and later high-level political appointee started out sweeping the floor and making coffee at a local party headquarters. Ringing doorbells, stuffing envelopes, answering telephones, and performing all the other boring but necessary jobs are part of getting started. In time such volunteers progress to running a local campaign headquarters or acting as advance person for a candidate for mayor, member of the assembly, member of Congress, senator, or governor.

Some young people have begun their political careers by working in a presidential campaign. In all recent elections—from 1960 to 1988—young people in and just out of college joined the staffs of every candidate. Many started out as volunteers and, after showing their talent and willingness to work hard, moved into paying jobs. Only one candidate in either party can win the nomination, and when their favorite dropped out, many of these young people moved over to the staff of another candidate whose views were compatible with their own, often on the recommendation of the person they had first served.

Some young people have followed a variation of this career strategy in years in which there is no presidential election. At least two or three thousand young men and women hold jobs as aides to senators or representatives or on the staffs of committees and subcommittees.[7] Frequently but not always they hold law or other graduate degrees. They work on legislation, write speeches, do research, handle publicity, mend political fences in the member's state or district, help with constituents' problems, and perform the numerous chores of running a congressional office. Many take the job in the hope that their boss will run for president. Many more have come to learn the political ropes, and in an election year they will go

---

[7]Harrison W. Fox, Jr., and Susan Webb Hammond, "The Growth of Congressional Staffs," in *Congress Against the President*, ed. Harvey C. Mansfield, Sr. (New York: Praeger, 1975).

to work for someone whose views they support. Others are acquiring experience because they want to run for political office themselves. Lyndon B. Johnson, for example, started out as an aide to a member of the House, then ran for the House himself, then went to the Senate, and later became vice president and president.

THE ROLE OF POLITICAL APPOINTEES

What is the function of political appointees? V. O. Key, Jr., was quoted as saying that their function was to control the bureaucrats. It has also been said that their function is to be transmission belts—to transmit the wishes of presidents and Congress to the bureaucracies and to transmit the specialized knowledge in the bureaucracies to presidents and the Congress. But is this the whole story?

Appointees: The Presidential Ideal

For presidents who want to achieve the policies that they believe in and put their mark on the government, the ideal political appointee would be their personal representative to the bureaucracies who would argue for the presidents' views. For staff aides in the White House, presidents would probably want this to be their only function. Presidents would want them to jab and prod and push the bureaucracies to help the president make and implement policy decisions. Their job would be to make sure that the bureaucracies produced the data, analyses, and recommendations that presidents need to make decisions. They would also follow up on decisions, making sure that the bureaucracies took timely and effective action in their implementation.

For political appointees who head departments, agencies, or bureaus, or who serve in a line job in one of them, presidents would want something more: to shape and mold the bureaucracies to presidential needs. Ideally, such appointees should represent political management, the top level of the administration. Truly wise presidents, however, would want their political appointees to be not only the president's representatives to the careerists but also the careerists' representatives to the president. Political appointees must judge whether what the experts have to say deserves to be laid before the highest councils of government. When they do decide that the experts' views should be heard, they should be the experts' unrelenting champion. Wise presidents recognize that the heads of departments, bureaus, and agencies and the presidential appointees who serve under them should run interference for their organizations and their careerists. Otherwise the only bureaucratic experts whose views would be heard would be those with political power in their own right.

Presidents usually want their political appointees to serve three other, related functions. The first is to represent the president before Congress. The tradition of executive privilege excuses White House aides from the requirement to testify before congressional committees, but this exemption does not apply to appointees in the departments and agencies. Because they must testify, presidents would like them to be ardent, articulate representatives of the presidents' views rather than their own or their departments'.

A second additional function of appointees is to meet with the press and the public. Here again, presidents want them to represent the president rather than themselves or their departments. Finally, political appointees must deal with special interest groups and clientele constituencies, make speeches at their conventions, and negotiate with them. Here too presidents want their political appointees to be their ardent and articulate supporters.

Political Appointees: The Reality

If the foregoing represents the presidential ideal for political appointees, what is the reality? In practice, appointees have or will develop motives that cause them to be more than just the selfless servants of the president. In working with the careerists in the departments and agencies, they come to know and respect the careerists, and to understand their problems, goals, motivations, and loyalties. To manage a department or agency well, which is important to their own self-esteem, appointees must win the willing and enthusiastic cooperation of careerists. Thus they frequently come to identify with the men and women in the organization they head and defend its views with passion and conviction. This is one source of the tension between presidents and members of the cabinet that has so often been noted. It is also why presidents must go consensus building in the executive branch as well as in the wider rings of policy making.

Personal Motives

Political appointees have goals, ambitions, moral principles, and needs of their own. As mentioned, many entertain notions of moving up in their business or profession as a result of having served in a high position in government, and others may think of running for elective office. These ambitions as well as their policy convictions and moral scruples may often make it difficult to be as selfless as presidents might like. The temptation to garner a little publicity for themselves may be just too great. In addition, their need for good relations with both the careerists with whom they work and the communities from which they have come at times may make it impossible for them to support certain issues as ardently as presidents might wish.

Their own self-regard is central to the manner in which appointees behave. Not infrequently they may like the presidents they serve and actually be their friends, they may approve of the presidential program and the general goals of the administration, and they may find the policies of the department or agency in which they serve equally to their liking. Nevertheless, a time may come when they disagree fundamentally with a particular policy. When this happens, they will try to get the policy changed. Should they fail, what can they do? They can resign and attack the policy publicly, but this probably will not change the policy and may hurt the president and the administration. Also, people who resign in this manner can be sure that they will have no future influence with the president and the administration. Resignation is a card that can be played only once. An alternative course of action is to swallow their disagreement and stay on in the government, hoping at least to shift the emphasis of the policy or to promote some other policies. They can also resign quietly. In this way, they will not only retain their own self-respect and escape association with the policy of which they disapprove but also preserve the chance for some future influence with the administration.

Personal Constituencies

The earlier discussion of the limitations and pressures on presidents in choosing political appointees explains another reason for the differences that arise between presidents and their appointees. As pointed out earlier, everyone expects that some top-level posts will be filled by people from the relevant special interest groups, constituencies, and related fields. When presidents adopt policies unfavorable to one of these groups, it is not surprising that the appointees oppose the policies.

Functions

Almost all presidents understand that the success of their administrations will depend on the caliber of the people they appoint. Presidents can both give broad guidance over the entire range of policy and manage a particular crisis, as Kennedy managed the Cuban missile crisis and Lyndon Johnson managed the railroad strike crisis in 1964. But the detailed management of policies for all governmental issues is too great a task for one person, even someone with a staff as large as that of the White House. Presidents thus must delegate, as must the secretaries of major departments. The quality of the people chosen for their top-level appointments is crucial to the success of the administration.

For political reasons, however, there are limits on how far down the line the delegation of responsibility can go. Many policies cannot be managed at a level lower than that occupied by a person appointed by the president, who can at least begin to inject into policy the broad political concerns of the president, such as what effect a policy will have on various segments of society and on special interest groups; what Congress, the press, and the general public will accept; and what effort will have to be made to develop the necessary consensus and public support. Although ultimately only presidents can apply this kind of broad political judgment, assistant secretaries occupy the first level in government at which these essentially presidential considerations can be applied to policy. Presidents experienced in the ways of Washington are thus concerned about the quality of the second and third levels of their appointees as well as the cabinet secretaries at the very top.

Policy advocates. Most political appointees probably try to mold the bureaucracies to the policies of the president they serve by explaining those policies and trying to persuade and prod the bureaucracies into doing what the president wants. But appointees also face up and out: up to the White House and inside the government, and out to Congress, the clientele constituencies, special interests, and attentive publics. Thus they rarely represent only the president who appoints them.

The function of political appointees is to analyze problems in their area of responsibility, to recommend policy to deal with those problems, and to attempt to build support for their recommendations—in a word, to be the advocates of policy. It is their role to force an issue to decision, to try to make the government confront an emerging problem, and to develop and offer alternative policies and become identified with those policies. They are the "front people," the people who lead the way. If they are not already public figures, they soon will be.

The front people need not be specialists in a particular subject, but those who last will become specialists in using specialists by being able to sense when the specialists are right and should be backed and when they are the prisoners of their own parochialisms. It is the front people who push for a particular policy at different places in and out of the government, with high officials and low, with other departments and agencies, in congressional hearings, in background press conferences, in public speeches, and in endless struggles over countless pieces of paper. They are the leaders of constituencies, the sponsors of policies, and the principal builders of consensus. Career men and women down the line may push a particular policy with unrelenting passion and be committed to the core of their being, but the front people are the advocates. Theirs is the function of advocacy. The very nature of their job is to run interference, to take the political heat.

Instruments of popular control. These unique functions of political appointees clarify what V. O. Key, Jr., had in mind when he suggested that "it is through such persons who owe their posts to the victorious party that popular control over government is maintained." Presidents who do not have a team bound to them in the various ways described may not be able to get enough of a grip on the great bureaucracies to put through the programs on which they were elected. This is especially true if they were elected on a platform of new policies.

Ordinary bureaucrats, people from interest groups, members of Congress, newspaper people, and such outside needlers as Ralph Nader all play the role of advocate, kicking and pushing and shoving to get the government to recognize a problem and to face up to the policy choices. Any one of them may do the work of sponsoring alternatives, enlisting support, arguing, selling, persuading, and building a consensus around a particular course of action. But even when others do the job, the responsibility for the task belongs to the political appointees. It is their leadership—or lack of it—that determines whether a decision will be made and whether it will be carried out indifferently or vigorously. Most important—and this is what Key was driving at—if it is left to chance whether a bureaucrat, member of Congress, or someone else does or does not pick up these functions, the president and the administration simply will not be able to carry out a consistent policy program. It is only through a team of political appointees that a president's program can be brought to life and "popular control over government" can ever really be established.

THE POWER OF POLITICAL APPOINTEES

What is the power of the front people? The secretary of a department, the director of an independent agency, an assistant secretary, or any presidential appointee who heads a bureau has the power—at the very minimum—to cause papers to be written, information to be amassed, and recommendations to be made. If these political appointees can win over to their side the bureaucracies they head, their power will be great. A person who commands a great bureaucracy has the power to develop ideas and proposals and to have them prepared in the form of position papers. At meetings of various organizations those who arrive armed with such papers determine the frame of reference of the discussion and in many cases can dominate the final decision itself. For only when the issue cuts deeply into the interests of the other organizations will their representatives find the time to develop position papers of their own. Heads of bureaucracies who have the support of their organizations have power by virtue of their day-to-day direction of their activities, including the problems they will study, the policies they will recommend, and the manner in which they will be implemented.

The authority of their offices confers some power on secretaries and assistant secretaries, even though they were appointed by the president. When presidents oppose their views, they have at least the right to be heard and the power to be persuasive. Should word get out that the president refuses even to listen to the views of the official responsible for a particular policy area, such a refusal may backfire on the president himself.

On specific matters that carry the presumption of special expertise, the power of the political appointee may be great enough to cause presidents to go along with a decision even though they do not agree. Suppose that an unimaginably vast oil field were discovered in Kansas and that the president proposed a law that Americans could no longer use any oil but Kansas oil. But suppose that the science adviser of the time discovered that Kansas oil had a high sulfur content and opposed the policy on the grounds that it would damage health and the environment. Most presidents would hesitate to act against such advice, even if they doubted its accuracy, and most would be doubly reluctant to act if no outside scientist stepped forward to take the opposite view.

Thus at one extreme political appointees always carry the implicit threat of resigning with a public flourish if the president goes directly against their advice or refuses to let them be heard. But this card, as we have said, can be played only once. At the other extreme are political appointees who enjoy the support of the bureaucracy, key members of Congress, interest groups, and influential segments of the press. If these people also enjoy the confidence of the president, they have power that is enormous.

12

THE CONGRESS

Although Congress is obviously a power center, the exact nature of its power, especially in foreign affairs and defense, is elusive. The framers of the Constitution clearly intended Congress to be the first branch of government. It was to represent both the people and the states. The framers took care to make sure that Congress had both the power and the incentive to protect the rights and liberties of the people from the potential tyranny of the executive. Although the power of the executive has grown enormously in modern times, many scholars agree that the American Congress remains the most powerful legislative body in the entire world.

Yet as public opinion polls for many years have shown, a majority of the American people do not share this view and are skeptical that members of Congress or Congress as a whole can really accomplish very much of anything. This opinion is shared by many members of Congress themselves. One senator, for example, in a book with the revealing title *Congress: The Sapless Branch,* said, "Since the foundation of the Republic, Congress has rarely initiated anything, rarely faced up to current problems, even more rarely resolved them."[1] In the face of such diametrically opposed opinions, it is not surprising that the truth is hard to determine.

WINNING A HOUSE NOMINATION

As we considered in examining the power of the president, the first question is whether members of Congress incur obligations in winning

---

[1]Joseph Clark, *Congress: The Sapless Branch* (New York: Harper & Row, 1964), p. 24.

the nomination and the election that affect their power in foreign affairs and defense.

Aspiring candidates for a nomination for a House seat need to make themselves known to the party regulars, the chairs of town and county party organizations, the active members of the party, and as many of the enthusiastic amateurs as possible. In states where the nomination is by caucus or convention in each congressional district, these people have the power to grant or withhold the nomination. In states with primaries, they influence the votes of the party members who are most likely to turn out. It is also among such people that aspiring candidates are most likely to find volunteers for their own organizations. Quite obviously, people who have been active in party affairs in their congressional district for a number of years will have built up a wider range of friends and acquaintances than the newcomer.

Money

In states with primaries, money is more important in winning the nomination than in states with caucuses or conventions. Winning a primary may require a lot of money for TV and other forms of advertising. Having a private fortune is thus a huge advantage.[2]

Time

A person with a private fortune can also afford to campaign full time without worrying where the next paycheck is coming from. The freedom to campaign full time can also come from the nature of one's job. In every democracy the profession that has the highest proportion of its members in the legislature is the law. Lawyers, of course, do have skills that are particularly appropriate to the job of writing laws, but the fact that they do not have to put in regular hours may be even more important. Running for office is also good advertising for a lawyer. In fact, before the recent changes that permit lawyers to advertise, running for office was about the only way that they *could* advertise!

WINNING A SENATE NOMINATION

Aspiring candidates for a Senate seat have a much more difficult time than do candidates for the House in getting to know the party regulars because they are dealing with an entire state. Doing so is easier for

---

[2]For more on campaign financing, see Gary Jacobson and David Magleby, *The Money Chase* (Washington, D.C.: Brookings, 1990); David Magleby, *Direct Legislation: Voting on Ballot Propositions in the U.S.* (Baltimore, Md.: The Johns Hopkins University Press, 1984).

people who have held statewide office, such as governor or attorney general, or a House seat for a number of years.

Money

In states with primaries, especially in large states, money becomes even more important in Senate races, since TV and other advertising will be so much greater. A statewide primary means that many more voters have to be reached, and name recognition is both more important and more difficult. TV is vital. It is probably this need for money that accounts for the fact that there are significantly more senators with private fortunes than members of the House. At the very least, an aspiring senator must have access to large contributors, either individuals or organizations.

Money is not the only solution to the problem of name recognition, however. Holding elective office at the state and local level is probably the most common way of increasing recognition, but anything that makes a person well known will help. Being a Roosevelt in New York or a Kennedy in Massachusetts, for example, is a wonderful asset. The fact that John Glenn was a famous astronaut helped him enormously in winning a seat in the Senate from Ohio.

Time

Again what is important for aspirants in gaining time to campaign for a House seat is doubly so for anyone aspiring to the Senate, simply because in most states there are so many more people to be reached.

WINNING THE ELECTION

Once nominated, candidates must work hard to be elected. Until elections for Congress, like presidential elections, are federally subsidized, candidates will continue to spend much of their time raising money. Of course this does not apply to a very wealthy candidate. In 1976 John Heinz, heir to the "Heinz 57 Varieties" fortune, spent $2.93 million in his successful campaign for a seat in the Senate from Pennsylvania. The amount is not unusual, but in this case it was all his own money.[3]

The Campaign Reform Act of 1974 set limits on what candidates could spend on their own election, but the Supreme Court struck down

---

[3]*The New York Times,* November 18, 1976, p. A31; May 4, 1977, p. A21.

that portion of the bill on the grounds that it was an infringement of free speech. The Court permits a limitation only on presidential candidates who accept a federal subsidy of their campaign. Similar legislation to finance congressional campaigns has so far been defeated. Members are reluctant to adopt such a system because it would reduce the present advantage that incumbents enjoy.

In the 1990 congressional elections, the candidates for both the House and the Senate spent a total of $360 million, up from $310 million in 1988. The average spent for a House seat was about $263,000 and for the Senate about $2 million. But a hot Senate campaign in a large state might easily cost each candidate $4 million. To spend as much as $500,000 for a House seat is not unusual—and this does not count the money spent in any preceding primaries.

Three other factors heavily affect the outcome of an election: party registration, the "coattail" effect, and incumbency.

Party Registration

In a contest between two people who are equally well known or unknown for a vacant seat, party affiliation is generally the single most important influence. On the other hand, a candidate who has a winning personality, popular views on the burning issues of the day, and lots of money can win without too much trouble over an opponent whose party has a larger registration.

"Coattail" Effect

A second factor is the so-called coattail effect: A popular presidential candidate who wins by a large margin will bring in senators and representatives "riding on his coattails." However, this effect is greatest when two relative unknowns are running for an unoccupied seat and least when a challenger, no matter how well known, is running against a well-entrenched incumbent, especially for the House.

The coattail effect exists because many voters simply vote for the straight party ticket if they like the presidential candidate. This happened often when Franklin D. Roosevelt was the candidate for president. But when the candidate at the top of the ticket is unpopular, the effect can be the reverse. In 1964, when the Republican Goldwater lost so heavily, many Republican candidates for Senate and House seats also lost. The same thing happened to the Democrats in 1972 and again in 1980, when McGovern and then Carter lost so badly.

However, splitting one's ticket by voting for a Republican, say, for president and Democrats for senator and representative is becoming more common. In 1956, the Republican Eisenhower won the presidency, but the Democrats won a majority in both the Senate and the House. The same thing happened with the Republican George Bush in 1988.[4]

Incumbency

Although incumbency helps both representatives and senators, it is much more important for the former. From 1946 to 1986, over 90 percent of the members of the House seeking reelection won, compared to only 74 percent of the senators. In 1988, 98 percent of House incumbents were reelected. In the Senate, an unusually large number of incumbents chose to retire, so a similar comparison is not possible. However, of Senate incumbents who did run, four were defeated. This is consistent with the trend of the past few years. By contrast, house incumbents, even first-term incumbents, are particularly difficult to dislodge.[5]

One reason that incumbency helps is that a senator or representative has innumerable opportunities to build name recognition and to perform services for constituents. The Scandinavian countries have a government official, called an ombudsman, whose job it is to receive and investigate complaints from ordinary citizens and to help them in dealing with the government bureaucracy. None of the other democracies has a

---

[4]On ticket splitting, see Walter De Vries and Lance Tarrance, Jr., *The Ticket Splitters: A New Force in American Politics* (New York: Erdmans, 1972); Walter Dean Burnham, "Insulation and Responsiveness in Congressional Elections," in *American Political Institutions in the 1970's: A Political Science Quarterly Reader,* ed. Demetrios Caraley (New York: Columbia University Press, 1976); and Gary Jacobson, *The Electoral Origins of Divided Government Competition in U.S. House Elections, 1946–1988,* (Boulder, Colo.: Westview, 1990).

[5]On the downtrend for senators, see David R. Mayhew, *Congress: The Electoral Connection* (New Haven, Conn.: Yale University Press, 1974); and John F. Bibby, Thomas E. Mann, and Norman J. Ornstein, *Vital Statistics on Congress, 1980* (Washington, D.C.: American Enterprise Institute, 1980), pp. 14–15. On House incumbents, see Nelson W. Polsby, "The Institutionalization of the U.S. House of Representatives," *American Political Science Review* (March 1968); and Charles W. Bullock III, "House Careerists: Changing Patterns of Longevity and Attrition," *American Political Science Review* (December 1972). See also Alan I. Abramowitz, "Name Familiarity, Reputation and Incumbency Effect in a Congressional Election," *The Western Political Quarterly* (December 1975); David Mayhew, "Congressional Elections: The Case of the Vanishing Marginals," *Polity* (Spring 1974); Robert S. Erikson, "The Advantage of Incumbency in Congressional Elections," *Polity* (Spring 1971); Edward R. Tifte, "The Relationship Between Seats and Votes in Two-Party Systems," *American Political Science Review* (June 1973); Warren Lee Kostroski, "Party and Incumbency in Postwar Senate Elections," *American Political Science Review* (December 1973); John A. Ferejohn, "On the Decline of Competition in Congressional Elections," *American Political Science Review* (March 1977); Morris P. Florina, "The Case of the Vanishing Marginals: The Bureaucracy Did It," *American Political Science Review* (March 1977); J. Bond et al. "Explaining Challenger Quality in Congressional Elections," *Journal of Politics* (May, 1985); Christopher J. Bailey, *The U.S. Congress* (New York: Basil Blackwell, 1989); and Morris P. Fiorina, *Congress: Keystone of the Washington Establishment* (New Haven, Conn.: Yale University Press, 1989), especially Chap. 6.

formal office charged with such responsibilities, but in the United States members of Congress have taken over this role. If a constituent is having trouble getting a Social Security check or a Medicare payment, the member's office knows how and where to get the matter settled. In this ombudsman role, members stand between government and the individual, ready to guide the citizen through the maze of bureaucracy, to open doors, to counsel, and to explain. All this earns the gratitude of constituents—and their spouses, their voting-age children, and, in the words of Gilbert and Sullivan, "their sisters and their cousins and their aunts."

For all these reasons, being a member of Congress has become a career. At one time most members served only a term or two. Today over half have served at least four terms.[6]

In the past few years a grass-roots movement to restrict the terms that elected officials could serve succeeded in getting limited measures adopted in three states, but in 1991, a much stricter measure to limit the terms of members of Congress came to a vote in the state of Washington. A rather high percentage of the state's members of Congress had served for enough years to have been affected, including the speaker of the House, Thomas S. Foley. Passage would have reduced the influence that Washington state has on national legislation, and Foley himself campaigned hard against the idea. It was defeated, and even if it had passed there is some question whether such legislation is constitutional. But voter dissatisfaction with government in general and Congress in particular indicates that the idea will reappear in other states.

Obligations of Winning

The conclusion from all this is that the obligations that members of Congress incur in winning the nomination and the election are almost exclusively to their constituents and to organizations, such as labor unions, that contribute workers and money to their campaigns.

Although members indeed have obligations to these people, two points must be made. First, the contributions were probably made because the individuals and organizations like the candidate's views. Thus such obligations rarely force a member to go against prior convictions. Second, these individuals and organizations are usually not all that interested in foreign affairs and defense, except for the exceptions described in the paragraphs that follow.

---

[6]H. Douglas Price, "Careers and Committees in the American Congress," in *The History of Parliamentary Behavior,* ed. William O. Aydelotte (Princeton, N.J.: Princeton University Press, 1977), pp. 28–62. See also Bibby, Mann, and Ornstein, *Vital Statistics,* pp. 53–54.

Any interest they do have is most likely to be economic. If textiles, say, are an important element of the district's economy, special interest groups will be concerned about tariffs and the like. If the district includes firms with defense contracts, they will be interested in appropriations for defense. Usually the interest is not in strategy and such larger issues but in particular weapons. An example is the second congressional district of Connecticut. The largest industry in the district is Electric Boat, which builds submarines. In such cases—districts dependent on textiles, submarines, and so on—it really makes little difference that contributors will want the candidate to favor tariffs on textiles and large appropriations for submarines. No candidate who opposed them would have a chance of being elected in that district anyway.

Some single-issue groups, such as the nuclear freeze movement, are also interested in at least one aspect of foreign affairs, but their members are likely to be spread across the nation and not concentrated enough in any particular district to make a candidate tailor his or her views to gain their support. If the candidate supports their position, it is likely out of personal conviction.

In any case, once they are elected, members can escape the power of a group that was influential in putting them in, always provided that the policy is not one that concerns the majority of their constituents. All this is not to say that foreign policy and defense are not important but rather that members of Congress rarely incur obligations on such issues to particular individuals or organizations. The views on foreign affairs and defense they must consider are those of their entire constituency.

As for obligations they might incur to presidents because of the "coattail" effect, those presidents did not grant them that boon nor can they effectively take it away. Any president who uses his position and prestige to try to prevent a member from being reelected is doomed to disappointment. All members are familiar with the classic example of a president who tried. In 1938, a nonpresidential year, President Roosevelt, one of the most popular presidents in history, decided to purge his party of the conservative members who had obstructed his New Deal. He actively campaigned against them, equating their defeat with a victory for the New Deal itself. But Roosevelt's effort failed ignominiously. It seemed clear that many people who ardently supported Roosevelt himself thought it was good for the country to have some opposition to him in Congress, or at least they resented his interfering in what they regarded as local affairs. No president since then has forgotten the lesson, and few members of Congress have.

Likewise, members do not owe anything to the party leaders in Congress or to the governor and party leaders of their state.

THE POWER CENTERS WITHIN CONGRESS

The Committee System

Congress acting as a unit is a power center. But Congress is also a collection of power centers, many of which are rivals. The organization of both the House and the Senate is built around committees. "Congress," a member of the House once remarked, "is a collection of committees that come together in a Chamber periodically to approve one another's actions."[7]

The work load generated by the legislation proposed in Congress each year is staggering, far beyond the capacity of any individual member or of either body acting as a whole. The labor is therefore divided among committees. The Senate now has 17 standing committees with 84 subcommittees, and the House has 13 standing committees with 140 subcommittees. In addition, there are 4 joint committees with 6 subcommittees, as well as select committees, special committees, and task forces. Standing committees have continuing jurisdiction over particular subjects, such as appropriations, agriculture, armed services, foreign relations, and commerce.

Most of the work of the standing committees is actually done by subcommittees, which can be very powerful. They usually have the final word in their fields of jurisdiction and are only rarely overruled by the parent committee.[8]

The Leadership

The Speaker is the presiding officer of the House. Nominally elected by the whole House, the speaker is in fact elected by the caucus of the majority party. The majority floor leader and the majority whip are elected the same way. (The term "whip" was borrowed from the British Parliament, where it derived from the "whipper-in" of fox hunting who

---

[7]Clem Miller, *Member of the House* (New York: Scribners, 1962), p. 110.

[8]On the work, importance, and power of subcommittees, see George Goodwin, Jr., *The Little Legislatures: Committees of Congress* (Amherst: University of Massachusetts Press, 1970); Richard F. Fenno, Jr., *Congressmen in Committees* (Boston: Little, Brown, 1973); Norman J. Orstein, *Changing Congress: The Committee System* (Philadelphia: American Academy of Political and Social Science, 1974); Harvey C. Mansfield, Sr., "The Dispersion of Authority in Congress," in Mansfield, ed., *Congress Against the President* (New York: Praeger, 1974); Charles O. Jones, "The Role of the Congressional Subcommittee," *Midwest Journal of Political Science*, Vol. 6 (1962); Barbara Hinckley, *Stability and Change in Congress* (New York: Harper & Row, 1988); Matthew D. McCubbins and Terry Sullivan, *Congress: Structure and Policy* (Cambridge, Mass.: Harvard University Press, 1987); and the works on Congress cited throughout this chapter.

kept the hounds from straying from the pack.) The minority party caucus elects a minority leader and a minority whip. The leadership of the majority party includes the Speaker and the majority whip plus the chair of the party caucus and often the chairs of important committees or members whose personal prestige and seniority are great and whom the other leaders include in their sessions on planning and strategy.[9] The minority party leadership includes the minority leader, the minority whip, and the chair of the Party Caucus for the Democrats and of the Conference Committee for the Republicans. For Republicans it would also include the chair of the Republican Policy Committee. The minority leadership might also well include the senior minority members of key committees and other members to whom the leadership regularly turn.

The duties of the Speaker are to preside when the House is in session, to be the channel of communication with presidents when they are of the same party, and to be the formal head of the party in the House. As presiding officer, the Speaker performs all the duties associated with the post in any parliamentary body: recognizing members who want the floor, calling for the ayes and nays, announcing the results, and so on. With the help of a staff member who is a professional parliamentarian, the Speaker has the power to interpret the rules, to refer bills to committees, and to appoint members of select and conference committees. Although the House has the right to overrule a Speaker by a majority vote on any of these decisions, it rarely does so.

The Senate leadership is organized somewhat differently. The presiding officer is the vice president, who votes only in the event of a tie. In the vice president's absence, the president pro tempore of the Senate may preside. Presidents pro tempore are generally revered elders of the party in power. Although respected for their years and long service, they usually have little power and certainly none that derives from the title itself.

Because the Constitution thrusts the vice president on the Senate as its presiding officer, like it or not, the Senate, as mentioned, has taken care in its rules to make sure that the presiding officer, unlike the Speaker of the House, is without power (other than the incumbent's own personal influence). The rather thankless task of presiding can thus be

---

[9]On the increased importance of the party caucus and its chair as well as other members of the party leadership, see Larry Dodd, "Emergence of Party Government in the House of Representatives," *DEA News* (DEA stands for Division of Educational Affairs), American Political Science Association (Summer 1976); and William E. Sullivan, "Criteria for Selecting Party Leadership in Congress," *American Politics Quarterly* (January 1975). See also Garrison Nelson, "Partisan Patterns of House Leadership Change, 1789–1977," *American Political Science Review* (September 1977); and Barbara Sinclair, "Congressional Leadership: A Review Essay and Research Agenda," in *Leading Congress: New Styles, New Strategies* (Washington, D.C.: Congressional Quarterly, 1990).

passed around among juniors who would not be trusted if any policy were at stake.

The true leader of the Senate is the majority leader. Save that he does not preside, his duties are the same as those of the Speaker of the House. The majority leader's second in command is the majority whip. Both are elected by the party caucus. The minority party is generally led by a minority leader and a minority whip, also elected by the caucus.

The Seniority System

Until recently virtually the only way to become chair of a committee in either house was by seniority. Once members got on a committee, all they had to do to become chair was to outlast their fellow members. Consequently the chairs have usually been members from safe, one-party, often rural districts. When the Democrats controlled the Congress, Southerners held a disproportionately large share of committee chairs. When the Republicans were in control, committees were chaired principally by members from the Middle West and northern New England.

This system of selecting people who exercise so much power has probably been the single most criticized aspect of Congress. But it does have merits, principally that it is automatic and impersonal, which in Congress are precious considerations indeed. One member, following Lord Byron, remarked "It is not that Congress loves seniority more, but the alternatives less."[10]

Members of Congress believe that the alternatives to seniority so far proposed would lead to "politicking" in its worst sense, to logrolling of the most vicious kind, to personality clashes, to wheeling and dealing to benefit not the interests of constituents but the members' personal power, and to the most bitter and divisive kind of factionalism. After all, they argue, there are ways to get around the worst aspects of seniority. If a committee chair is senile or incompetent, those next in line can take care of things. If he or she is tyrannical, arbitrary, and on the wrong side of the ideological fence, time will resolve the matter. Many members of Congress (as opposed to outside critics of seniority) believe that the seniority system is the whipping boy for faults that have other causes. "Seniority," it is observed, "does no more than designate the chairman; his powers and duties depend on rules or procedures adopted by the committee on which he serves. Committee inertia may produce too strong a chairman, but the remedy is clear: reform rests with the committee itself."[11]

---

[10]Charles E. Clapp, *The Congressman: His Work as He Sees It* (Garden City, N.Y.: Doubleday, Anchor, 1964), p. 257.

[11]Ibid., p. 259.

By December 1975 both the Senate and the House had established procedures by which committee chairs had to stand for election in their party caucus or conference. Seventy-five new Democrats had been elected to the House, and they were mostly younger and more liberal than their seniors. They attempted to force out several of the older committee chairs who had reputations for arbitrariness, and they succeeded in ousting three of them. (A fourth, Wilbur Mills, chair of the Ways and Means Committee, whose problems of alcoholism and involvement with a strip-tease dancer had caused a scandal, withdrew rather than face the challenge.)

A number of observers saw in these developments the end of the seniority system. Others were more skeptical. In general the skeptics were right; seniority is still the determining factor most of the time. However, the possibility of being removed by an outraged caucus or conference and the threat of further reform are clearly making committee chairs more solicitous of the rank-and-file members and their views.[12]

THE LEGISLATIVE PROCESS

The process by which a bill becomes a law is enormously complicated and involves many stages.[13] If the law requires money to be spent, the whole process must be repeated in order for the money to be appropriated. For our purposes, however, only two of the many stages need be mentioned.

Once introduced, bills are assigned to committees. Various rules and traditions govern which committees get which bills, but a lot of work goes into drafting bills in such a way that they can be assigned to committees whose chairs are sympathetic. In 1963, for example, the civil rights bill was written to rest on the interstate commerce clause of the

---

[12]For a balanced discussion of the seniority system, see Barbara Hinckley, *The Seniority System in Congress* (Bloomington: Indiana University Press, 1971). See also her "Seniority 1975: Old Theories Confront New Facts," *British Journal of Political Science* (October 1976), in which she argues that the future of the seniority system depends mostly on whether the electorate returns "majority-party freshmen at a more than sluggish rate, or at a minimum do not defeat the present one and two term members." See also Maurice Tobin, *Hidden Power: The Seniority System and Other Customs of Congress* (Westport, Conn.: Greenwood Press, 1986).

[13]For descriptions see Lewis A. Froman, Jr., *The Congressional Process: Strategies, Rules, and Procedures* (Boston: Little, Brown, 1967); William J. Keefe and Morris S. Ogul, *The American Legislative Process: Congress and the States*, 2nd ed. (Englewood Cliffs, N.J.: Prentice Hall, 1968); Randall B. Ripley, *Congress, Process and Policy* (New York: W. W. Norton, 1975); Thomas P. Murphy, *The New Politics Congress* (Lexington, Mass.: D. C. Heath, 1974). idem, *How Congress Works*, 2nd ed. (Washington, D.C.: Congressional Quarterly Books, 1991) and Arnold R. Douglas, *The Logic of Congressional Action* (New Haven, Conn.: Yale University Press, 1990.)

Constitution. In the Senate this permitted it to be assigned to the Commerce Committee, chaired by the sympathetic Warren Magnuson of the state of Washington, rather than to the Judiciary Committee, chaired by the unsympathetic James Eastland of Mississippi. In the House the same language made the reverse possible; that is, the bill was assigned to the Judiciary Committee, chaired by the sympathetic Emmanuel Celler of New York, rather than to the Interstate and Foreign Commerce Committee, chaired by the unsympathetic Oren Harris of Arkansas.

Next the bill faces its most difficult hurdle—the committee's decision to consider it or simply to let it die. Both houses have rules to bring a bill to the floor if a committee fails to consider it, but these rules are rarely used and even more rarely successful. The fact is that 90 percent of all bills die in committee, and only 10 percent go on to become law. If the committee decides to go ahead with the bill, hearings, which are usually quite lengthy, are held.

Deciding How to Vote

At many stages of a bill's progress members have to vote, which is not a trivial matter. Almost all members try to inform themselves on pending legislation and certainly on the legislation that affects their districts directly or the country as a whole.[14] They often must turn to other sources for help in deciding how to vote, and this gives those sources power. Members acquire some information from other members, some from their staffs, some from their constituents, some from the press. Some of the more thorough and accurate information is actually supplied by lobbyists. Throughout this process members struggle to understand the legislation on which they must vote: what it really intends to accomplish, whether it will in fact accomplish this end, and what chance it has for passage—who supports it, who opposes it, and the parliamentary tricks and maneuvers available to both sides.

Inevitably the mass of material bearing on the issues overwhelms the members' capacities for absorption and understanding. Accordingly they look for shorthand cues to voting, which in a well-disciplined party

---

[14]On the sources of information that members use, see Donald R. Matthews and James A. Stimson, *Yeas and Nays: Normal Decision-Making in the U.S. House of Representatives* (New York: John Wiley, 1975); John W. Kingdon, *Congressmen's Voting Decisions* (New York: Harper & Row, 1973); Barbara Deckard, "Political Upheaval and Congressional Voting: The Effects of the 1960's on Voting Patterns in the House of Representatives," *Journal of Politics* (May 1976); idem, "Electoral Marginality and Party Loyalty in House Roll Call Voting," *American Journal of Political Science* (August 1976); Barbara Hinckley, "Issues, Information Costs, and Congressional Elections," *American Politics Quarterly* (April 1976); idem, "Policy Content, Committee Membership and Behavior," *American Journal of Political Science* (August 1975); and John W. Kingdon, *Congressman's Voting Decisions* (Ann Arbor: University of Michigan Press, 1989).

organization are supplied by the leadership. Members may also turn to a senior member in their state's delegation, to a member from an adjoining district, or to a congenial committee colleague for advice and comfort. They may consult external sources as well, such as trusted friends or advisers in their home districts or the results of polls. Ready answers from such quarters must take the place of detailed substantive knowledge of the many matters on which members must vote, a fact that was vividly illustrated late one evening in 1975. Russell Long was driving a Senate Finance Committee session through its revision of the 1975 tax reduction bill so as to be in time for floor action before the Easter recess. Some members complained that he was being too hasty, and Long responded by saying, "If all members insist on knowing what they are voting for before they vote, we're not going to get a bill reported before Monday."[15]

Of the many influences determining how members vote, constituency pressure seems to be the most important. This is obvious in the case of a district with a dominant industry affected by legislation. But constituency pressure also operates on other issues with a less direct impact on the district's economy.[16] One study shows a strong correlation between constituency opinion and the way members voted on civil rights, yet virtually no correlation on foreign policy issues.[17] Another study showed a high correlation between the demographic characteristics of constituencies and votes on social welfare, women's rights, racial, abortion, and law-and-order issues.[18]

---

[15]The late Harvey C. Mansfield, Sr., professor emeritus of Columbia University, personal communication.

[16]The following is based mainly on Kingdon's *Congressmen's Voting Decisions.* See also Matthews and Stimson, *Yeas and Nays;* John E. Jackson, *Constituencies and Leaders in Congress: Their Effects on Senate Voting Behavior* (Cambridge, Mass.: Harvard University Press, 1974); Morris P. Fiorina, *Representatives, Roll Calls, and Constituencies* (Lexington, Mass.: D. C. Heath, 1974); Aage Clausen, *How Congressmen Decide: A Policy Focus* (New York: St. Martins, 1973); Robert Erikson, "The Electoral Impact of Congressional Roll Call Voting," *American Political Science Review* (December 1971); John Jackson, "Some Indirect Evidences of Constituency Pressures on Senators," *Public Policy,* Vol. 16 (1967); Helmut Norpoth, "Explaining Party Cohesion in Congress," *American Political Science Review* (December 1976); John R. Johannes, *To Serve the People: Congress and Constituency Service* (Lincoln: University of Nebraska Press, 1984); and Bruce Cain, John Ferejohn, and Morris Fiorina, *The Personal Vote: Constituency Service and Electoral Independence* (Cambridge, Mass.: Harvard University Press, 1987).

[17]Warren E. Miller and Donald E. Stokes, "Constituency Influence in Congress," in *Elections and the Political Order,* eds. Angus Campbell, Phillip E. Converse, Warren E. Miller, and Donald E. Stokes (New York: John Wiley, 1966), p. 359. See also Jackson, *Constituencies and Leaders;* and Robert Bernstein *Elections, Representation and Congressional Voting Behavior* (Englewood Cliffs, N.J.: Prentice Hall, 1989).

[18]Benjamin I. Page et al., "Constituency, Party, and Representation in Congress," *Public Opinion Quarterly,* Vol. 48 (Winter 1984).

Fellow members of Congress are also particularly important influences, in part because members bargain for one another's votes on issues that are important to one but not the other. In this sense constituency influence is also at work. In part, however, the influence of fellow members is based on the need for expert advice. Members tend to become specialists, and others seek them out. Members also influence each other simply because they find colleagues with compatible views. When a member of Congress who is a friend and who has helped out with a vote in the past asks for another's vote, most members find it impossible to say no if the bill does not adversely affect their own districts.

As for pressures from the party, members are well aware that although the national, state, and congressional party organizations had little to do with their election, the party does exert influence. The process, however, is more psychological and ideological than the *realpolitik* of sticks and carrots. Because members identify with their party and its members, the psychological pressure to follow party policy is strong indeed.[19]

Pressures on members from the congressional leadership are subtle. The leadership itself tends to adopt the position of the ranking members of the committee that reported the bill under consideration.[20] The ranking members in turn exert some influence on members. In any case, the process is mutual and interactive. The party influences the leadership, the ranking members, and the ordinary members, but the leadership more often exercises its influence indirectly through the party than directly on the individual members. At the same time the ordinary members influence both ranking committee members and the leadership.

Most observers have mixed feelings about the influence of interest groups. Members pay careful attention to those groups that have a direct connection with their home districts as well as those that lobby on issues that attract wide attention inside and outside Congress, in the press, and throughout the nation. Members, however, do not necessarily vote according to the wishes of interest groups. (Chapter 14 discusses the function and power of interest groups in depth.)

The influence of the administration and the executive branch on the voting behavior of members does not appear to be great. As would be expected, members of the president's own party pay greater attention to the administration than do members of the opposition. The influence of their staff on how members vote seems to be small. Finally, what members read or hear in the mass media rarely seems to influence their

---

[19]Jerrold E. Schneider, *Ideological Coalitions in Congress* (Westport, Conn.: Greenwood Press, 1979), pp. 134, 195.

[20]Kingdon, *Congressmen's Voting Decisions.*

voting, although information on issues of high salience seems to be more influential than that on other matters. However, it seems probable that the indirect influence of the media is substantial.

Representation Versus Trusteeship

On issues that obviously and directly affect the well-being of their districts, members almost always vote the way their constituents want them to vote. If they did not do so, their constituents would almost certainly take revenge at the next election. On the more general issues affecting the nation as a whole, the question that has long troubled legislators in democracies is whether they should vote the way their constituents want them to vote when they believe their constituents are wrong. In other words, should legislators be representatives, who follow the instructions of constituents no matter what, or should they be trustees, who vote as their consciences tell them is best for their constituents and for society as a whole?

Perhaps the most famous proponent of the trustee theory was Edmund Burke, the eighteenth-century member of Parliament who defended the American colonies against some of the laws imposed by George III. Burke contended that the duty of the legislator was not to mirror the passing opinions of the voters but to exercise the legislator's own best judgment. He believed that the voters were likely to be uninformed, biased, and wedded to a narrow localism. For Burke a legislature was a place where deliberation, study, and debate could produce wiser and more mature views. (Although history does not reveal whether his views on representation were the reason, he was defeated at the first election after he stated them.) Studies indicate that members from marginal or "swing" districts tend to behave as representatives. It is the senior members from "safe" seats who can more often afford the luxury of voting as trustees.[21]

The worst quandary for members of Congress results from the fact that their constituents have short memories. Both the apathetic voters who do not care about a particular law and the voters who press for the law to pass but who turn out to be wrong about its benefits will not

---

[21]See Roger H. Davidson, *The Role of the Congressman* (Indianapolis: Bobbs-Merrill, Pegasus Books, 1969), p. 140; Heinz Eulau et al., "The Role of the Representative: Some Empirical Observations on the Theory of Edmund Burke," *American Political Science Review* (September 1959); Hanna Pitkin, *The Concept of Representation* (Berkeley: University of California Press, 1967); Charles E. Gilbert, "Operative Doctrine of Representation," *American Political Science Review* (September 1963) and R. Douglas Arnold, *The Logic of Congressional Action*, eds. Morris P. Fiorina & David W. Rhode, *Homestyle and Washington Work: Studies of Congressional Politics* (Ann Arbor: University of Michigan Press, 1989), Chap. 10.

hesitate to take vengeance at the next election. Thus members find themselves in a Catch-22 situation. Even if the opinion of their constituents turns out to be wrong in the long run, in the short run they will still make a member suffer for going against those opinions. On the other hand, if the member goes along with constituent opinion and that opinion in the long run turns out to be wrong, constituents will still not scruple to take vengeance. Thus members must not only predict both the results of the legislation and the voters' reaction to those results but also, if the results hurt the voters' interests, find ways to persuade them that they were wrong so they will not take vengeance in the short run. As one member of Congress stated, "You have to be as smart in prospect as they [the voters] are in retrospect"—the member's foresight has to be as good as the voters' hindsight.[22]

CONGRESS AND POWER

Congress is not monolithic; its power is exercised by the leadership, by the committee chairs, by the ordinary members, and by the Congress as a whole.

Leadership in the House

In 1910 Republicans and Democrats joined in a rebellion against the tyrannical power of Speaker Joseph Cannon. Since that time the Speaker's power has sometimes increased, sometimes decreased. Today, although the Speaker's power may seem rather modest, it can be fairly potent. With other members of the leadership, Speakers coordinate tactics in their party's floor fights, which makes them a center of communications not only with committee chairs and powerful individual members but also with the White House when the president is a member of their party. The source of their power, like the president's, is of course political brokering.

Speakers can do members many favors, large and small; they can also help keep members from getting something they want. Although the power to appoint members to desirable committees is no longer the exclusive right of Speakers, they still exert enormous influence on assignments. In a variety of ways Speakers can bank "due bills," or favors they have done for members that they expect to have returned some day. Members are both grateful for favors they have received in the past and anxious about those they might want in the future.

---

[22]Clapp, *The Congressman*, p. 178.

Reforms instituted in 1973–1974 actually increased the power of Speakers. In a sense, they now "own" the Rules Committee. Democratic Speakers in effect also "own" the Steering and Policy Committee, which has the power to assign Democratic members to standing committees. The Republicans have not held a majority in the House for many years, but if and when they do, they will likely make similar arrangements.

In recent years Speakers have recognized that if they go too far and flaunt their power, they can provoke revolt. "Vote your district first" was a catch phrase used for many years by both the Democratic Speaker Sam Rayburn and his Republican counterpart Joseph Martin. "Speaker Sam" used to say that he " 'never asked a man to cast a vote that would violate his conscience or wreck him politically.' "[23] As these quotations suggest, the hand of leadership in the House in the days of Rayburn and Martin was not very heavy, and it is undoubtedly even lighter today. But "Speaker Sam" used another saying even more frequently: "The way to get along is to go along." Recent Speakers have said that their only power is the power to persuade. This may be so, but the authority of Speakers, their legitimacy, and the carrots and sticks they control all ensure that if the Speaker has a mind to do some persuading, individual members will listen, and listen sympathetically.

Leadership in the Senate

Senate majority leaders, political scientist David B. Truman once remarked, must put together "fragments of power."[24] Although majority leaders do not preside in the Senate as the Speaker does in the House, they have the right to be recognized whenever they please. A more important fragment concerns the scheduling of legislation. Democratic majority leaders must consult the Policy Committee and Republican majority leaders the Chairman's Committee, but theirs is the largest voice in scheduling, which can be the source of much power.

Other fragments of their power are similar to those of Speakers. Being a center of communication for people who chair powerful committees, ordinary members, the House leadership, the White House, and power centers outside the government is in itself a source of power, as is the right to dispense certain minor amenities and the ability to ease the passage of members' favorite bills. "There is no patronage; no power to discipline; no authority to fire Senators like a President can fire members

---

[23]Alfred Steinberg, *Sam Rayburn: A Biography* (New York: Hawthorn, 1975), p. 351.

[24]David B. Truman, *The Congressional Party: A Case Study* (New York: John Wiley, 1959), p. 115.

of his Cabinet," Lyndon Johnson said when he was majority leader; "the only real power available to the leader is the power of persuasion."[25]

Here again, what these various fragments of power really constitute is what we have called political brokering, which is a source of power for presidents, Speakers, majority leaders, or any other person occupying a central political position.

The Power of Committee Chairs

In 1973 the Democratic party caucus in the House adopted a Subcommittee Bill of Rights that took away many of the powers of the committee chairs. Although seniority is still the basis by which a chair is chosen, the caucus must ratify the decision by a secret ballot. At the same time rules were laid down ensuring that subcommittees would be established, requiring that subcommittees act on legislation, and guaranteeing that staff time would be allocated fairly. Committee chairs and senior members of committees exercise most power over the narrow range of subject matter on which their committees have jurisdiction. This power comes not only from their jurisdiction but also from their expertise on the specialized issues. George Mahon of Texas, for example, chaired the House Subcommittee on Defense Appropriations for many years before he became chair of the main Appropriations Committee, and he held on to the subcommittee even after he headed the main committee. Year after year Mahon listened to the testimony of generals, admirals, and secretaries of defense. He questioned them and waited to see whether their recommendations finally succeeded or failed. He watched them come and go, but he stayed on. Probably no other person in Washington knew as much about military weaponry in its broadest aspects as George Mahon. Neither the leadership of the House nor its individual members would lightly go against his considered judgment on such matters. In fact, neither would generals or even presidents! Much the same is true for the chairs of many other committees.

Also great is the power of chairs to make trade-offs. Although a chair no longer has exclusive power, he or she has enough to influence legislation coming before the committee more than an ordinary member. This can also be translated into wider power. The most obvious example is seen in committees with jurisdiction over "pork-barrel" legislation, that is, legislation that puts a post office in one member's district, a dam in another's, and a federal building in still another's. The chair has influence over these decisions and one favor can generate another.

---

[25]Interview, *U.S. News and World Report,* June 7, 1960.

Chairs also command more staff than other members. When the Democrats lost control of the Senate in 1980, for example, Senator Edward M. Kennedy of Massachusetts lost the chair of a major standing committee, Judiciary, and two important subcommittees. With these chairs went the right to appoint seventy staff aides.[26] This had enabled Kennedy not only to exercise formidable influence over the work of the committee and the two subcommittees, but also to develop positions and to speak out nationwide on a host of other issues.

The Power of the Individual Member

The power of the individual member is the mirror image of the power of the leadership and the committee chairs. Senior members of the majority party are likely to be chairs of one or more subcommittees and thus will have some of the kind of power enjoyed by the chairs of standing committees. They are also likely to have accumulated some due bills with chairs and with the leadership. That they may themselves soon become chairs of standing committees will be taken into account by the leadership, by the present chairs, by interest groups, and by the bureaucracies in the executive branch.

New members of Congress, on the other hand, are low indeed in the power structure of Washington. What is particularly galling to them is not so much that their voice is so small on the great issues but that they have so little leverage with the bureaucracies. If the only way they can influence Congress and legislation is to accumulate seniority, then they must assure their reelection, which requires service to constituents and efforts that will give them publicity and name recognition. Yet much of what their constituents want and expect is dispensed by the bureaucracies. Members of Congress "perforce must become petitioners downtown, a role which often adds humiliation to frustration."[27]

Even new members of Congress, however, are not without power. Everyone understands that their chances of being reelected are good. If they are reelected, they will build up seniority, and when they do they are likely to remember both favors and slights. They also have their vote, which they are still free to cast as they choose. The knowledge that they have a home base beyond the reach of the leadership and the chairs gives them a sense of security. If they are pushed too far, they will balk; if too many are pushed too far, they will join in a rebellion against the leaders and the chairs. The leaders and the chairs understand all this and

---

[26]B. Drummond Ayres, Jr., "Kennedy Losing Forum in Senate as He Prepares to Yield Three Key Majority Posts," *The New York Times,* November 12, 1980, p. A25.

[27]Richard E. Neustadt, "Politicians and Bureaucrats," in *The Congress and America's Future,* ed. David B. Truman, 2nd ed. (Englewood Cliffs, N.J.: Prentice Hall, 1973), p. 121.

proceed accordingly. They apply a variety of pressures but at the same time recognize that persuasion is ultimately the only truly effective pressure.

CONGRESS VERSUS THE BUREAUCRACIES

So far we have been concerned with how power is distributed within Congress. But what about the power of Congress when it faces outward, toward the other power centers of government? Chapter 9 dealt with the relative power of the White House and Congress, but the power relations between Congress and the bureaucracies remain to be discussed.

Congress as a whole determines whether most programs—and therefore the bureaucracies that administer them—shall wax or wane. After the first Strategic Arms Limitation Talks (SALT I), for example, the top eleven people concerned with the negotiations were replaced, largely at the urging of conservative members of Congress who were unhappy with the terms of the agreement. It was apparently the threat of withholding funds as much as the threat of a fight against ratification of a second SALT agreement that caused the executive branch to acquiesce in the replacement of the officials.

Oversight

Another device by which Congress can influence or control the bureaucracies is the oversight responsibility. Congress has the responsibility to oversee the administration of its laws, which it does by monitoring the activities of the bureaucracies through its committee staffs, by hearings, and by testimony by agency officials. Oversight includes the formal power to investigate the bureaucracies not just through traditional hearings but also by hiring private investigators. Recent instances have included congressional investigations of the CIA and the FBI.[28]

The Legislative Veto

Another means that Congress used frequently in recent years to try to control the bureaucracies was the legislative veto. This was a requirement written into legislation that the executive or an agency of the executive must obtain permission from Congress before taking certain actions or, alternatively, the delegation of certain powers to an agency

---

[28]See Richard E. Cohen, "Will the 96th Become the 'Oversight Congress'?" *National Journal,* January 13, 1979; James P. Bowers, *Regulating the Regulators: An Introduction to the Legislative Oversight of Administrative Rulemaking* (New York: Praeger, 1990).

with the stipulation that Congress could nullify any such action it did not like.

Every president since Franklin D. Roosevelt has opposed the use of the legislative veto by Congress on the grounds that it is an unconstitutional interference with the power of the executive. But it was not until June 1983, in a historic but somewhat troublesome decision, that the Supreme Court upheld this view, sweeping aside over two hundred laws containing the provision that had been passed over a fifty-five-year period.[29]

It seems doubtful that the ruling will cause any permanent shift of power either to the Congress or the president. It will take several years to work out a new procedure, and during this period one or the other may enjoy a temporary gain, but in the end the power situation is unlikely to be changed radically. The major result will probably be that legislation will be written much more narrowly and that any delegation of power from Congress to the executive will be much more carefully considered before passage.

Subgovernments and Cozy Little Triangles

For the White House or an interest group to interpose itself between Congress and the bureaucracies is untypical. As a practical matter the White House cannot make more than a few bureaucratic programs its special concern. In truth, the White House does not really care about most of the great volume of what the bureaucracies administer. As for interest groups, what they want is likely to be what the congressional committee with jurisdiction wants. Members of Congress who are interested in a particular subject are probably interested because it affects their constituents, who in turn are probably members of the interest group. Indeed, what the bureaucrats want is often what both the congressional committee and the interest group want. It is only natural that bureaucrats come to identify with the people whose interests are their responsibility. Thus the civil servants of the Department of Agriculture come to identify with farmers, as do members of Congress whose districts include a large number of farmers. The result is often a little "subgovernment."[30]

For many years a classic example was the economy of sugar, until the legislation controlling it lapsed. Under this legislation sugar was managed by a government-sponsored cartel that determined how much

---

[29]*Jagdish Rai Chadha* v. *Immigration and Naturalization Service,* 103 S. Ct. 2764 (1983).

[30]Both this term and the example of the sugar lobby discussed following are drawn from Douglas Cater, *Power in Washington* (New York: Random House, 1964), pp. 17–18; also see Fiorina, *Congress: The Keystone of the Washington Establishment.*

should be grown in the United States, how much should be imported, and from what countries it should be imported. These decisions were made by the members of the subcommittee of the House Agriculture Committee, the representatives of the sugar lobby, and the director of the sugar division of the Department of Agriculture, all of whom pretty much agreed most of the time. The sugar subgovernment was thus dominated by the congressional subcommittee and the interest group, with the bureaucracy playing a decidedly subservient role, although the situation was somewhat complicated by the fact that the interest group was really two: the beet sugar industry and the cane sugar industry.

More often the situation is one that has been described as a "cozy little triangle" in which the subcommittee, the interest groups, and the bureaucracy all have enough power to avoid being completely dominated but not enough to ignore the desires of the others.[31] Consider the Forest Service bureaucracy. In its dealings with the Forest Service, Congress has all the powers just enumerated. It can write policy guidelines for the Service into legislation and can cut its appropriation. But the Forest Service is not without power of its own. It serves two well-organized constituencies: the lumber, cattle, and mining interests who want access to national forest lands, on the one hand, and conservationists, hunters, and fishermen, on the other. Even though there is frequent conflict of interest between these groups, the Forest Service identifies with both and tries to serve both. If Congress (or the White House) moves against the Service, it can count on the two interest groups to unite in its defense. At the same time the Forest Service can maintain its independence from the interest groups, if need be, by playing one off against the other and both off against the concerned committees of Congress.

Most of the time, then, Congress shares power with the bureaucracies, and both participate in the decision making. In their dealings with Congress, civil servants will always observe the tradition of deference and respect, even to the point of sycophancy. In fact, however, power is usually shared amicably among members of Congress, the bureaucracy, and outside interest groups in the kinds of subgovernments of cozy little triangles just described.

THE INTERPLAY OF POWER AND LEGISLATION

With power so divided—internally within each house, among the committees, among the chairs of the committees, between the chairs and the leadership, among individual members, between Congress and the bu-

---

[31]Both the phrase and the example that follows are drawn from Dorothy Buckton James, *The Contemporary Presidency* (New York: Pegasus, 1969), p. 126.

reaucracies, between Congress and the president, between Congress and the judiciary – it sometimes seems a wonder that any legislation is passed at all. The wonder increases when we recall the numerous stages through which a bill must go before becoming law and the many opportunities the different power centers have to block legislation or to twist its purpose. Especially favorable circumstances are needed to make into law a major legislative proposal that affects a substantial number of people, alters the principal rules under which we live, or accomplishes significant social change. Such major bills become law only under one of three sets of conditions: compromise, logrolling, or a national consensus.

Compromise

In the first set of conditions the people for and against the legislation compromise. The compromise is usually not completely satisfactory to either side, but both go along on the reasoning that "half a loaf is better than none." An example was the compromise on Medicare engineered by the chair of the Ways and Means Committee of the House. It adopted more generous provisions for payments, proposed by the Republicans mainly as a tactic to weaken the bill, and financed the more generous provisions by the payroll tax, proposed and ardently desired by the Democrats. Neither could vote against the compromise without appearing to abandon their own proposals.

Logrolling

In the second set of conditions concessions are made on one piece of legislation in exchange for acquiescence on another; this is logrolling. Consider the maneuvering that established the food stamp program as a permanent feature of the federal government.[32] Early in 1964, the House Agriculture Committee voted to table a bill to that effect sponsored by the administration. Northern Democrats needed a lever; they persuaded a California Democrat on the Rules Committee to hold up a bill granting funds for the study of tobacco and health that a number of Southern Democrats wanted. A deal was struck permitting the food stamp bill to be reported out of the Agriculture Committee in exchange for giving the tobacco bill a rule. In the meantime the Senate had added a wheat program to a bill setting up a cotton program that the House had passed. Again a deal was worked out by which Northern Democrats would vote for wheat-cotton and Southern Democrats would vote for food stamps. None of this legislation – tobacco, wheat, cotton, or food stamps – had enough support to pass alone. But logrolling got them all through.

---

[32]Ripley, *Congress, Process and Policy,* pp. 80–81.

A National Consensus

The third set of conditions under which a major piece of legislation can become law entails the formation of some sort of new national consensus. The process could be described as a matter of public education that creates a growing awareness of both a problem and a proposed solution until there is a general feeling that "its time has come." In the nineteenth century industrial workers began their struggle against poor pay and unsafe and unhealthy working conditions. Slowly they changed the attitudes of both the public and Congress until in 1935 the Wagner Act gave them the right to organize and bargain collectively. It was a hundred years, to cite another example, before blacks saw the civil rights legislation of the 1960s that marked the first real steps toward equality. President Truman proposed a national medical care program, but it was seventeen years before Medicare for the aged was passed, and a health program for all ages has yet to be established. However, health care was clearly moved much higher on the national agenda in November 1991, when the relatively unknown Harris Wofford used the health care issue so effectively to trounce Richard Thornburg, who had been Bush's attorney general and before that twice governor of Pennsylvania. Another issue that has risen to a higher place on the national agenda in the past few years is the problem of global warming and the universal need to reduce the risks of acid rain, ozone depletion, and climate change over the globe.[33]

As more and more of the general public and members of Congress come to recognize the existence of a problem or an injustice and then try to reach a consensus that a particular remedy is at least worth trying, resistance becomes weaker. In time legislation is passed, not all of a sudden but in a series of acts over several years. Racial justice is still far from complete, for example, and the struggle for health care for the entire population has only begun. But such is the way of building the national consensus for adopting major legislation, and it is usually the only way in which legislation accomplishes truly fundamental alterations in the authoritative rules governing society or truly fundamental social change.

Change in the Environment or Social Context

What might be termed a special case of the third set of conditions under which major bills become law is a sudden change in the situation or social context that makes urgent a measure that had been mired in controversy. The Marshall Plan to help the postwar recovery of Europe was making

---

[33]On global warming, see Francesca Lyman, *The Greenhouse Trap* (Boston: Beacon Press, 1990).

little progress in Congress when, in 1948, the Communists took over Czechoslovkia in a coup d'état – and the act whisked through. Legislation providing for the Alaska pipeline was bogged down in the marsh of Environmental Protection Act procedures. Then came the Arab oil boycott, and Congress passed a law that in effect exempted the pipeline from EPA procedures and any suit to block it.

SUMMARY

In sum, it is clear that the power of Congress is limited and that its own procedures and internal tensions limit its power even more. Yet many very serious observers believe that the American Congress is the most powerful legislative body in the world. The legislatures of the authoritarian countries are little more than rubber stamps. Even in the Western democracies, parliaments rarely have the power of the American Congress. In Great Britain, for example, the Parliament as a collegiate body can by a vote of "no confidence" force a general election. Parliamentary members of each party choose their party's leader, so the members of the majority party choose from among themselves who will actually be prime minister. Yet Parliament does not legislate in the way that the American Congress does. In Great Britain the detailed work of making the laws is done by the cabinet in close cooperation with the career bureaucracies. In the United States it is done in Congress in cooperation with the White House and the career bureaucracies, all of which share the power. In the United States, unlike most other countries, even the democracies, the legislative body does in fact legislate.

13

THE BUREAUCRATS

Bureaucracies are power centers. The major ones dealing with foreign affairs and defense are the Foreign Service of the Department of State, the Central Intelligence Agency, and the military. But before examining these three particular bureaucracies, a few points are necessary about bureaucracy in general.

THE STRUCTURE OF BUREAUCRACIES

The basis of all bureaucracy is a division of labor laid down by rules, that is, by laws or administrative regulations.[1] For example, the Department of Agriculture deals with agricultural problems, while the Department of Transportation deals with the problems of transportation. Private business bureaucracy—the "office"—is divided similarly. One part is concerned with manufacturing the product, another with personnel, and still another with sales.

In the American government the division of labor is sometimes based on clientele. The Department of Commerce serves business, and the Department of Labor serves workers. Sometimes the division of labor is based on "subject matters deemed to be related." Thus the Weather Bureau could be "related" to the Department of Agriculture when farmers were the principal customers or properly part of the Commerce Department when the airlines need more efficient weather service. Still

---

[1]The following is drawn from Max Weber, "Bureaucracy," in *From Max Weber,* ed. H. H. Gerth and C. Wright Mills (New York: Oxford University Press, 1946), pp. 196–244.

another division of labor is the nature of the work process, with an example being the Government Printing Office. Sometimes the division of labor is geographical, as in the Appalachian Regional Commission. Any large organization will embrace, at different levels, units based on all of these criteria: clientele, subject, process or occupational skills, and territory. Sometimes the division may even be based on time of day, as with a three-platoon police force.

A second principal characteristic of bureaucracy is hierarchical structure. A bureaucracy has a pyramidal structure divided into lower offices that are responsible to and supervised by higher ones. Decisions of a lower official can be appealed to a higher official.

A third characteristic is that bureaucratic jurisdiction and authority are carefully defined by strict rules that specify what the bureaus, offices, and individuals can deal with, how they must deal with it, and how they can ensure compliance with their decisions. Max Weber referred to this as the impersonal power of bureaucracies.

The management of the bureau is based on written documents or files. In both government and private enterprise bureaucracies, the files, the office equipment, and the money collected and paid out are all divorced from the private property of the people involved. This applies as well to the boss, whether the head of a government bureau or the president of a private business.

The work of the bureau follows general rules (laws or regulations or office policies) "which are more or less stable, more or less exhaustive, and which can be learned." Knowledge of these rules represents a special technical learning that the officials possess. Furthermore, the rules are supposed to be applied impartially, impersonally, fairly, and honestly— "without fear or favor."

Finally, bureaucrats are recruited on the basis of competence, special training, expertise, and experience. Although this principle may be violated more frequently than most people would like, bureaucrats in both government and business are supposed to be recruited and promoted not because they are the boss's brother-in-law or old friend, but because they are the best candidates available.

CRITICISMS OF BUREAUCRACY

The bureaucracies are often criticized for inefficiency, waste, duplication of effort, and similar outrages.[2] The trouble with these criticisms is that they forget that while efficiency, economy, and rationalization are impor-

---

[2]This section draws mainly on Harold Seidman, *Politics, Position, and Power: The Dynamics of Federal Organization,* 2nd ed. (New York: Oxford University Press, 1975). A debt is also owed to the following: Francis Rourke, *Bureaucracy, Politics, and Public Policy*
(footnote continues on page 207)

tant goals for most people much of the time, they are not always the most important goals. For the members of Congress who voted for the programs, for the president and other administration officials who supposedly provide overall policy guidance, and for the bureaucrats who run the organizations, the first-priority goals are contained in the programs themselves. It is getting the payments to retired people that most concerns those who set up and administer Social Security, not efficiency. It was getting the astronauts to the moon and bringing them back safely that the people involved in the National Aeronautics and Space Administration cared about most.

THE FUNCTIONS OF BUREAUCRACIES

What are the functions of the bureaucracies? What do bureaucrats actually do?

Many of the 3 million civilian employees of the government have jobs that are identical to other jobs in private industry and business. A great many federal employees, for example, spend their time responding to public requests for material on such matters as farm management or small business accounting. But the heart of bureaucratic work is the application of general laws, regulations, and policies to concrete cases. In the Social Security Administration this involves determining whether Jane Doe is entitled to Social Security payments and, if so, in what amount. In another part of the government it may mean deciding whether a particular school system is eligible for federal funds for a lunch program or whether the cold medicine manufactured by a particular drug company meets the government's food and drug standards. In the Department of Justice the job of applying general laws to concrete cases might involve deciding whether some arrangement recently made in the chemical industry is within the provisions of antitrust legislation, or whether

(Boston: Little, Brown, 1969); Norton Long, *Polity* (Skokie, Ill.: Rand McNally, 1962); Lewis C. Mainzer, *Political Bureaucracy* (Glenview, Ill.: Scott, Foresman, 1973); James Q. Wilson, "The Bureaucracy Problem," *The Public Interest*, Vol. 6 (Winter 1967); Emmette S. Redford, *Democracy in the Administrative State* (New York: Oxford University Press, 1969); Fred Mosher, *Governmental Reorganizations: Cases and Commentary* (Indianapolis: Bobbs-Merrill, 1967); Paul Van Riper, *History of the United States Civil Service* (New York: Harper & Row, 1958); David Rosenbloom, *Federal Service and the Constitution* (Ithaca, N.Y.: Cornell University Press, 1971); John Mach, *Public Servant: The Human Side of Government* (New York: Harper & Row, 1971); Joseph Harris, *Congressional Control of Administration* (Garden City, N.Y.: Doubleday, 1964), David Beetham, *Bureaucracy* (Milton Keynes, U.K.: Open University Press, 1987); John P. Burke, *Bureaucratic Responsibility* (Baltimore, Md.: The Johns Hopkins University Press, 1986); Eva Etzioni-Halevy, *Bureaucracy and Democracy* (London: Routledge and Kegan Paul, 1983); Richard Chackerian and Gilbert Abcarian, *Bureaucratic Power in Society* (Chicago: Nelson-Hall, 1984); and James Q. Wilson, *Bureaucracy: What Government Agencies Do and Why They Do It* (New York: Basic Books, 1989).

certain practices in labor unions are consistent with civil rights legislation.

Bureaucrats as Policymakers

Even at the lowest level of the work of applying general laws to specific cases, the individual bureaucrat obviously does a certain amount of policy making. Suppose an official of the Internal Revenue Service decides that the deductions a person has claimed for the cost of gasoline for a trip to Florida were allowable because the main reason for the trip was business, even though the person took a few days off to enjoy the beach. Such a decision interprets the law and thus makes policy, which is exactly what happens when a judge interprets the law.

If bureaucrats act like judges in making policy by interpreting the law in specific cases, they also act as judges in deciding disputes between individuals and between organizations. The regulatory agencies in particular hold hearings, listen to the arguments of rival sets of lawyers, take the testimony of witnesses, and hand down decisions that find for one side or the other. In 1946 complaints that certain bureaucracies exercised too much judicial power without the kind of appeals procedure that the court system provides led Congress to pass the Administrative Procedures Act, which made certain procedures, such as formal hearings, mandatory. More important, it gave the courts the power to reverse the decisions of the bureaucracies on points of fact as well as law. When an administrative agency acting as a judge rules against a person or an organization, that person or organization may appeal to the courts on the grounds that the agency not only did not correctly interpret the law but also that it did not give sufficient weight to or ignored certain facts.

Bureaucrats as Legislators

The policy-making functions of the bureaucracies go beyond interpreting the laws and acting as judges in disputes: The bureaucracies issue an enormous number of regulations, rules, and policy statements that have the effect of law in governing the activities of individual citizens, businesses, industries, labor unions, and even state and local governments. In this way they legislate. To be sure, they legislate under the same restrictions that apply when they make decisions of a judicial nature; that is, within the guidelines set down by law. But they still legislate. Congress frequently delegates to the bureaucracies the power to legislate because Congress itself does not have the time to pass laws in sufficient detail to govern many activities. Sometimes, if the truth be known, Congress delegates the power to legislate because it finds the political heat of making a decision too intense. It then passes the issue on to the bureaucracies as quickly as if it were a hot potato—as indeed it is, politically speaking!

This does not mean that the bureaucracies are free from the political pressures of competing interest groups, geographic regions, constituents, and all the other pressures that bear on Congress. Sometimes these pressures are just as effective with the bureaucracies as the threat of being defeated in the next election is with members of Congress, yet at other times the bureaucracies do not feel the pressure as intensely, which worries observers who are concerned that government be responsive to the people. The relative freedom of bureaucracies on certain issues is sometimes good, sometimes bad. It is good when it enables bureaucrats to assert and vindicate a larger public interest against a self-serving parochial claim. It is bad when it enables bureaucrats to be callously indifferent to hardships imposed on the helpless by some ironclad procedural rule.

Bureaucrats as Innovators

While bureaucracies legislate rules and regulations under guidelines established by Congress, they are also major instigators and shapers of the legislation that lays down those guidelines. Much of the legislation proposed in the president's program and introduced by individual members of Congress is actually originated and drafted in the bureaucracies. Finally, during congressional hearings, in informal conferences between congressional staff and bureaucrats, and in more formal presentations, the proposed modifications suggested by the bureaucracies change and shape legislation as it goes forward.

THE POWER OF THE BUREAUCRACIES

The bureaucracies, then, make policy, as do the president, the Congress, and the judiciary. In applying legislation to specific cases, they decide whether a law will or will not be implemented, and they interpret the legislation. They also make some of the rules under which we live and play a significant role in initiating, formulating, and shaping the legislation put forward by the president and actually issued by Congress. Thus the bureaucracies have power, lots of power.

Checks on Bureaucratic Power

There are, however, many checks on bureaucratic power. Some of these have already been suggested in the earlier chapters on the presidency, political appointees, and Congress. The president, as we saw, can exercise a certain amount of control over any of the bureaucracies, although some bureaucracies can be quite independent. On the other hand, some bureaucracies are totally dependent on the president and thus totally subservient. From a president's point of view, the trouble is that such bureaus are usually not those concerned with issues that are at the center of the political maelstrom. As one authority has written,

> a bureau has to be politically "orphaned" to be totally dependent on the man whom Americans hold responsible for the entire bureaucratic structure. An example of such a situation was the Children's Bureau in the Department of Health, Education, and Welfare. It had no political friends nor any particular organizational support, and it had traditionally experienced the anomaly of being headed by a spinster. The dependence of such a bureau on the President is hardly likely to be viewed by him as a political asset.[3]

The Children's Bureau was one extreme. At the other extreme most people think first of the FBI under J. Edgar Hoover, but there are probably hundreds of small and more obscure bureaus that may in fact be even more independent of the president's control precisely because they are obscure. The office responsible for sugar quotas was undoubtedly almost totally free from presidential control most of the time it existed, although not at all free from the control of either the sugar lobby or the subcommittee of the House Committee on Agriculture.

While presidents can exercise power across the board, a bureaucracy can exercise power only in the narrow range of policy over which it has jurisdiction. Ordinarily a bureaucracy centered between the two extremes can operate with considerable autonomy within this range. But if presidents are willing to work at it, if they play their cards well, if political appointees with jurisdiction are able and loyal to the president, and if political conditions surrounding the particular subject are not stacked too heavily against them, presidents can exercise considerable control over any particular bureaucracy.

Chapter 12 described the "cozy little triangles" composed of members of the congressional committees, the bureaucrats, and the interest and clientele groups associated with a particular issue. Viewed in one way, these triangles are a device for making a bureaucracy responsive to at least the segments of the population that are most directly affected by its work. Of course, the argument could be turned around: The triangles could be viewed as devices for excluding others from policy making in a particular area, including the White House and other bureaucracies as well as other parts of Congress. Would those excluded care even if they did know what was going on? The White House, the rest of Congress, and the general public are usually too busy with other problems to pay much

---

[3]Dorothy Buckton James, *The Contemporary Presidency* (New York: Pegasus, 1969), p. 127. The Children's Bureau has since been abolished and its functions transferred to other bureaus; See also Douglas Yates, *Bureaucratic Democracy: The Search for Democracy and Efficiency in American Government* (Cambridge, Mass.: Harvard University Press, 1982).

attention to the matters with which most of the triangles deal. None of them really cares who gets what in the way of sugar quotas, for example.

Thus the triangles can logically be viewed as devices by which power is shared and by which control is exercised over the bureaucracy by representatives at least of Congress and by the interested clientele group. They can also be seen as devices that create still another channel through which different segments of the citizenry can express their desires and needs to that part of government responsible for meeting those desires and needs.

THE NATIONAL SECURITY BUREAUCRACIES

The Foreign Service, the Central Intelligence Agency, and the armed services are the bureaucracies that deal with national security: foreign policy and military policy. If there are fears about the form and function of civilian bureaucracies, there are sometimes even greater fears about the form and function of the national security bureaucracies.

The Foreign Service

The Foreign Service, like the military, is a career service. Officers are recruited at the beginning of their careers and are expected to spend their lives in the service. They work their way up through the ranks and serve tours of duty in Washington and in foreign countries. Entry into the Foreign Service is by stiff written and oral examination, and a rather small number of vacancies occur in any one year.

Ambassadors are appointed by the president, with the advice and consent of the Senate. Traditionally people who supported the president in the preceding election through contributions or in other ways were rewarded with an ambassadorship. A defeated senator or House member of the president's party may also be given such a post. In recent years, however, ambassadors have increasingly been picked from among career Foreign Service officers. The Foreign Service itself is pressing for the proportion of ambassadors selected in this manner to be even higher.

One criticism of the Foreign Service that is met frequently among members of Congress is that its career officers are not typical Americans but "striped-pants cookie pushers"—socialites from effete, Eastern seaboard families of the highest socioeconomic levels. Critics say that, in addition to this background, the long years that Foreign Service officers spend abroad makes them out of touch with views at home. This fear was so pervasive that Congress included in legislation provisions requiring that these officers serve a certain proportion of their time in the United States and that they be brought back for home leave every two years.

The criticism that Foreign Service officers come mainly from privileged social and economic strata of society had considerable basis in fact before World War II. It was then a very small corps with few opportunities for training in language, and salaries and allowances were grossly inadequate. The people attracted to the service tended to be those who had already had special training or who had lived abroad in their childhood and had some private income to supplement the meager salaries.

Since World War II, however, the Foreign Service has changed fundamentally. A large number of officers with diverse background were brought in just after the war. The recruitment program now casts a much wider net than in the past. Pay and allowances have been made competitive with compensations in other professional careers, the Foreign Service Institute provides language and other kinds of training, and money is available for midcareer training of all kinds. Foreign Service officers must be better educated than the average American because of the nature of their jobs, but the Service is nevertheless as much a cross section of American society as any other profession.

It is true that a person who spends considerable time in a particular country develops a special understanding of its problems and frequently a fondness for its people. The Foreign Service itself jokingly refers to the tendency as a sickness: "localitis." But a special understanding of the problems of a country and a fondness for its people are not necessarily liabilities for a person representing the United States; more often each is an asset. In any event the provisions for periodic duty in the United States and home leave every two years undoubtedly overcome the worst symptoms that localitis may produce.

The power of the State Department.   One of the most persistent criticisms of the State Department and the Foreign Service is really a reflection of their power position, or more precisely their lack of power. The criticism, met frequently in the White House and the press, is that the State Department is a "fudge factory" that produces soft, "squidgy" recommendations and little leadership. It is slow in acting, requiring endless clearances from various bureaus and offices before making a move. It is indecisive in the actions it does take, and it rarely provides the other departments and agencies with the strong general leadership that is needed. In exasperation at all these faults, President Kennedy once called the State Department a "bowl of jelly."

Charges that the State Department is a fudge factory and a bowl of jelly are, unfortunately, not entirely unfair. The fault is not entirely that of the Foreign Service, however, for the problem is inherent in the nature of the work that the State Department and the Foreign Service are required to do and the position in which they find themselves. They have no natural constituencies in the general public and few natural allies in industry or other power centers. The military, by contrast, has natural allies in weapons industries, and it, like the CIA, has the patriotic appeal of being the instrument to smite our enemies. The task of the State Department is not to smite our enemies but to negotiate with them. Further, it deals with foreigners, and foreigners do not vote in American elections. While the military spends billions buying military hardware such as airplanes and tanks, the State Department budget goes almost entirely for salaries and expenses. Lacking the patriotic appeal of the military and lacking the allies in industry and among the electorate, the State Department has little power to stand up to the other bureaucracies, much less to exercise strong and effective leadership.

The Foreign Service is further weakened by the very nature of foreign affairs. It must deal with almost two hundred nations and a variety of international organizations, each of which has its own rivalries and interests that clash with those of others. Inevitably these clashing interests become reflected in the State Department itself. Men and women who deal with particular nations and problems naturally come to prefer that the United States adopt policies for improving relations with those states. The problem is that policies that help one nation may hurt relations with another. Look at how the State Department is torn over policy toward white South Africa. Offices that deal with South Africa directly or with matters in which South Africa is important because of trade, raw materials, or suitability for American bases are pressed to play down South Africa's segregationist apartheid policies. Offices responsible for relations with the nations of black Africa are pressed in exactly the other direction. Thus because of the very nature of foreign affairs, the State Department and Foreign Service bureaucracy can only rarely present a strong and unified front to the rest of the government.

The Central Intelligence Agency

The Central Intelligence Agency is only one part of the intelligence community of the U.S. government, which also includes the Defense Intelligence Agency of the Pentagon, G-2 of the Army, A-2 of the Air Force, the Office of Naval Intelligence of the Navy, the Office of Intelligence and Research of the State Department, and the National Security Agency (which deals with code breaking and electronic intelligence). The CIA has a legal monopoly on espionage and "covert political action" in foreign countries, such as supporting friendly political parties, encouraging a coup d'état, maintaining a "secret army" (as the CIA did in Laos), and sponsoring a supposed rebellion, as it did in 1961 in the Bay of Pigs debacle. The National Security Agency collects information by electronic means; all the other intelligence organizations (except the CIA) are consumers rather than gatherers of intelligence. That is, they research and analyze the information gathered by the CIA and the NSA and whatever else comes to the government through orthodox channels, such as the reports of Foreign Service officers and military attachés and foreign newspapers. Because it is the operating arm of American intelligence, the CIA has been the focus of much attention and concern.

The research and analysis side of the CIA is staffed with experts on particular countries. The pattern of recruitment and career is like that of other departments and agencies. In the "operating" side of the agency, the pattern is more like that of the Foreign Service. Officials are recruited young, and it is assumed that they will spend their lives in the Agency, rotating between posts abroad and tours of duty in Washington.

Created by the National Security Act of 1947, the CIA was directed to gather foreign intelligence. At the height of the cold war the CIA, like the FBI, enjoyed high public esteem and respect. It is generally conceded that the CIA and the military intelligence agencies "made important contributions to the nation's security and generally have performed their missions with dedication and distinction."[4]

The CIA, however, has come under heavy criticism for abuse of power, for carrying out operations that were illegal or morally questionable, and for doing things that had not been authorized by the president or other high authority. The particular activities that came under fire were such covert political operations as coups d'état, plots to assassinate foreign leaders, and "secret wars" involving foreign paramilitary units recruited and trained by CIA agents. An example often cited is the Bay of Pigs invasion of 1961, in which a brigade of CIA-trained Cuban exiles attempting to overthrow Castro landed in Cuba, only to be quickly defeated. Other CIA activities have included the secret army in Laos during the Vietnam war, the aid to the groups that overthrew President Salvador Allende in Chile in 1973, and alleged plots to assassinate foreign leaders.

Behind the disquiet over these incidents are some even more fundamental worries about the CIA. Putting aside the charges of waste and inefficiency, the serious allegations come to three. First, the pervasive secrecy of intelligence activities permits the CIA to pursue its own policies without regard for the rest of the government. Second, the atmosphere of plot and intrigue inevitably spills over into the domestic arena, threatening the very society that the CIA is supposed to protect. And third, the CIA represents a state within a state. Two journalists have

---

[4]*Foreign and Military Intelligence, Final Report of the Select Committee to Study Governmental Operations with Respect to Intelligence Activities* (Church Committee Report), United States Senate, 94th Cong., 2d sess, p. 424.

charged that there are "two governments in the United States today," one visible and the other invisible. They argued that "the Invisible Government has achieved a quasi-independent status and a power of its own," with the result that one cannot help suspecting "that the foreign policy of the United States often works publicly in one direction and secretly through the Invisible Government in just the opposite direction"—sometimes, the authors seem to suggest, even against the wishes of the president.[5]

The power of the CIA. For many people the peculiar problem of the CIA is that it has more power than other bureaucracies and that it is subject to less control and accountability. The CIA has a large staff; whereas the State Department at one time had three persons on its Laos desk, the CIA had six. This meant that the CIA could always afford to be represented at an interdepartmental meeting and that it could spare the people to prepare the papers that could, and sometimes would, dominate the meeting. The people of the CIA are outstandingly able, which in itself has been a source of power. The CIA also has money. The exact amount of its budget had been secret, but leaks as a result of congressional hearings have led to estimates that the total budget for all U.S. government intelligence activities is over $6 billion and for the CIA, $1 billion.[6]

The CIA's command of information has been another source of its power. In Washington the first people to have an item of information are the first to interpret its significance and the first on the scene for the discussion of its policy implications. Where information is an asset, command over information is the power to grant or withhold that asset—to a member of Congress, for example, or to the press.

In countries where intrigue is a way of life, the fact that a CIA agent represents the American secret intelligence service confers prestige that translates into power. The need to keep certain operations or sources of information secret gives those who have an official "need to know" a further dimension for making judgments and for understanding the reasons for what is happening. This too is power. For example, in the Eisenhower administration, those who knew of the peripheral reconnaissance flights that probed Soviet air defenses and of the U-2 flights over the Soviet Union itself were better able to understand some of what the Soviets were saying and doing than were people who did not know of these activities.

---

[5]David Wise and Thomas B. Ross, *The Invisible Government* (New York: Random House, 1964).

[6]*The New York Times,* April 1, 1977, p. A13; John D. Marks, *The CIA and the Cult of Intelligence* (New York: Alfred A. Knopf, 1974); and Philip Taubman, "Secrecy of U.S. Reconnaissance Office Is Challenged," *The New York Times,* March 1, 1981, p. A12.

The CIA also derives power from the fact that its function, like that of the FBI, is by nature politically appealing. The CIA was in the forefront of the cold war. Because its job, like that of the military, is to smite our enemies, it has the appeal of patriotism. In Congress the CIA's natural allies are the power centers of both houses: the members who are at the heart of the long-standing coalition of Southern Democrats and conservative Republicans. These facts are levers that a politically astute director of the CIA can use to great effect on Capitol Hill.

The zenith of CIA power probably came in the Eisenhower administration. The cold war was then at its height, and such an atmosphere of threat was bound to enhance the influence and power of both the military and the CIA. No public revelations of CIA abuses of power had yet been made, and its reputation was high.

Cutting the CIA down to size. Since the Eisenhower years the CIA's power has been reduced, although the revelations concerning its past activities have sometimes left the impression that it is riding as high as ever. President Kennedy was brought face to face with the problem of the CIA by the Bay of Pigs debacle. "It's a hell of a way to learn things," Kennedy said in the aftermath of the fiasco, "but I have learned one thing from this business—that is, that we will have to deal with the CIA."

Accordingly, during the rest of Kennedy's administration, the number and scope of the CIA's clandestine operations were greatly reduced.[7] During the Johnson administration this policy was continued. In the Nixon and Ford administrations, according to the available evidence, the CIA did not regain any of the power it had lost following the Eisenhower administration. Evidence presented in the Watergate hearings revealed that the CIA had been not so much a leader as a follower of the White House. It had, for example, merely gone along with White House requests for assistance in the illegal activities of the White House "plumbers" unit rather than instigating anything itself. This evidence reduced the CIA's reputation and credibility still further. The subsequent investigations of intelligence by the Church committee in the Senate and the Pike committee in the House undoubtedly had the same effect of cutting down the CIA's power by making public its past abuses.

Although the power of the CIA declined following the Eisenhower administration, the role of cloak-and-dagger operations in U.S. foreign policy may actually have been greater. During the Nixon administration, for example, the CIA became deeply involved in the coup against President Allende in Chile, and in the Ford administration it was just as

---

[7]For a more detailed account of Kennedy's policy toward the CIA, see Roger Hilsman, *To Move a Nation: The Politics of Foreign Policy in the Administration of John F. Kennedy* (Garden City, N.Y.: Doubleday, 1967), pp. 63–88.

deeply involved in the political struggle in Angola. Under the Reagan administration, however, many of the restrictions on the CIA were rescinded. This reduced the president's direct involvement in decisions about CIA activities and increased the CIA's autonomy.[8]

CIA accomplishments. Some things, however, ought to be said in defense of the CIA. In a world of sovereign nation-states, secret intelligence services are probably inevitably essential. And, as secret intelligence services go, the CIA has probably been better than most. Although the men and women of the CIA have made mistakes, they are dedicated officers with high standards of integrity and patriotism. Furthermore, they are more able than the staffs of most other agencies in Washington. Compared to many other parts of the government, the CIA, far from being a bastion of anti-Communist jingoism, has been a source of enlightened and sophisticated views on international affairs. Through its intelligence-gathering efforts, which have relied more on scholarly research and technical instruments (such as picture-taking satellites) than on cloak-and-dagger operations, the CIA has played a large part in making the U.S. government the best informed in the world.

Through its mechanisms of central coordination the CIA has prevented ridiculous and dangerous situations that might otherwise have occurred if the military services each had competing intelligence organizations stumbling over each other. In World War II, for example, none of the intelligence agencies had coordinating responsibilities. The Office of Strategic Services (OSS), the CIA's wartime predecessor, thought it was a brilliant idea to steal the Japanese military attaché's secret code from Japan's embassy in Portugal, which remained neutral during the war. The Japanese merely changed the code. The trouble was that the U.S. code-breaking agency had with great effort already broken the code, and now they had their work to do all over again! Without a central CIA such blunderings would still be everyday happenings.

In a patient (although sometimes painful) educational campaign waged through the tedious procedures by which national intelligence estimates are developed, the CIA has brought to the American government's analyses of events abroad an objectivity and sophistication that rise above the parochial views of the departmental intelligence organizations. The alternative to such a unifying view, especially on the major questions of Soviet missile and nuclear strength, the Sino-Soviet dispute, and Communist intentions and probable reactions, would have been a contest between competing estimates that would have torn policy asun-

---

[8]Charles D. Amesinger, *US Foreign Intelligence: The Secret Side of American History* (Boston: Lexington Books, 1990), p. 369.

der. General Curtis LeMay of the Air Force, for example, was a brave soldier and a great combat commander, but his understanding of the subtleties of international politics is suggested in his complaint that the United States was "swatting flies in South Vietnam when it ought to be going for the manure pile" in North Vietnam. What he wanted was to "bomb Vietnam back to the Stone Age." One can only imagine the consequences if the U.S. government had had to contend with competing intelligence estimates of this kind.

Remaining worries. Although the power of the CIA has been reduced from its cold war zenith, the problems of the CIA and the inherent tensions of conducting secret intelligence operations in a free society remain. One problem is that a secret intelligence service inevitably develops independent power to influence foreign policy and even to conduct foreign policy. Another is that secrecy and deception will always create problems in a free society. The Bay of Pigs illustrates one aspect of this; the insistence on secrecy prevented the participation of men and women who had knowledge that could have contributed to the making of sounder judgments.

A more subtle aspect of secrecy is that it tends to corrode confidence between the government on the one hand and the public and the press on the other, and even between one set of officials and another. In 1958 the Indonesian government charged that the United States was supporting a rebellion in Sumatra. *The New York Times* published a long and indignant editorial denouncing the Indonesians for what seemed such an obviously false charge. However, it turned out to be true. The *Times* was embarrassed, but the real damage lay in the press's growing cynicism and doubts about the truthfulness of the official statements of its own government.

The greatest tension is probably that between the conduct of covert political operations and our national reputation. Covert is usually taken to mean not completely secret but "plausibly deniable." For example, the soldiers who landed at the Bay of Pigs were not Americans but Cuban exiles who had been trained by the CIA. Everyone knew that the United States was behind the operation, but the theory was that since no Americans were actually in the landing, our responsibility was "plausibly deniable." The deviousness and intrigue of secret service techniques are inconsistent with a reputation for openness, respect for others, and idealism. In theory a country is justified in using every possible means to ensure its survival, especially in the face of a totally ruthless and evil enemy, such as Hitler's Germany. Allen Dulles, the director of the CIA during the Eisenhower administration, justified clandestine intelligence activities on just such grounds. The Communists, he argued, intended to "bury" us and had made extensive military preparations in secret. Dulles believed that this justified our taking whatever measures were needed to uncover their preparations. As long as Communist countries continued to use subversive means to bring down non-Communist regimes, he argued, those who oppose the Communists had to be prepared to meet the threat. This preparation might include the use of covert political actions of their own.[9]

As the United States relied more and more heavily on such means, its reputation suffered more and more. While one action may be "plausibly deniable," several hundred are not. Thus too heavy a reliance on the techniques of secret intelligence so corroded one of our major political assets – the belief in American intentions and integrity – that the possible gain from covert operations tended to be nullified.

Attempts at reform. In the mid-1970s both the Senate and the House appointed special committees to investigate the CIA and to recommend reforms. Through both legislation and presidential orders a number of such reforms were put into effect, including providing tighter procedures for approving covert operations, establishing congressional committees to oversee CIA activities, and putting limitations on what the CIA could do inside the United States and in watching American citizens abroad. When the Reagan administration came to power, it moved to loosen some of these restrictions on the grounds that they prevented the CIA from doing its job properly and thus jeopardized American security.

Many observers, however, believe the blame for many of the most disturbing CIA activities belongs not so much to the CIA as to the policymakers in the White House, the State Department, and the Department of Defense. Since the establishment of the CIA, they argue, the United States has come face to face with the perplexities of the postwar world and the Communist threat. It met the direct challenges by making alliances and building up its military strength. Yet again and again the United States has also encountered problems that did not yield to power alone, such as ineffectual governments, graft, politically apathetic populations, indifferent leaders, subversion, terrorism, and guerrilla warfare. If the United States had used its massive power to deal with these problems in ways that the world would have regarded as bullying, the result would have been political disaster. To many of the policymakers who faced these dilemmas of foreign policy, covert action seemed a reasonable way to fight the threat of Communist fire with fire. Since the action was covert, it promised to get around the obstacles: the moral problem of intervention and the political problem of appearing to be a bully.

---

[9]Allen W. Dulles, *The Craft of Intelligence* (New York: Harper & Row, 1963), pp. 48–51.

Covert action also had an aura of omnipotence, as if, like the movie character James Bond, Agent 007, it could accomplish miracles. The CIA lobbied for covert actions and used its independent power as leverage on presidents to obtain their approval. The policymakers were highly receptive to the CIA proposals and sometimes urged it to come up with proposals on occasions when it had not done so. The CIA's part in the rebellion in Indonesia during the Eisenhower administration, the Bay of Pigs invasion during the Kennedy administration, the secret army in Laos during the Johnson administration, the aid to those plotting to overthrow Allende in Chile during the Nixon administration, and many other activities were authorized by the president. Although in many of these instances the presidents were under heavy political pressure because of the independent power of the CIA, they still could have found ways to say no.

In other cases the initiative for covert action came not from the CIA but from the president, the White House, and the secretary of state. The evidence presented in congressional hearings indicating that it was President Nixon and Secretary of State Henry Kissinger who pushed the CIA into covert activities in Chile is only the most vivid example. The policymakers themselves were fundamentally responsible for making covert action a fad. Thus any proposal to curb covert action that does not impose restrictions on the president, the secretary of state, and the other policymakers as well as the CIA ignores one of the major parts of the problem.

The heart of the problem is power. It is the power of the president: Legislation that does not limit the president's power over the use of the CIA and covert action will accomplish little. It is the power of the CIA: The CIA has many of the attributes of a state within a state. In spite of the recent limitations the CIA still has the power in its operations department to create secret armies, navies, and air forces. In this the CIA has, on a small scale, some of the attributes of the Defense Department. In its research, analysis, and evaluation side, the CIA has the analytical and planning capabilities to formulate foreign policies. In this the CIA has some of the attributes of the State Department. As mentioned, in a world of sovereign nation-states, all nations will undoubtedly feel it necessary to maintain secret intelligence services to help ensure their survival, but it is possible to do so without permitting those services to become so powerful that they get out of hand. The British system might be a useful model. In Britain, the power to create armies, navies, and air forces—even very small armies, navies, and air forces—is confined to the military services. The British research and analysis functions are separated into an independent agency. The British espionage, counterespionage, and covert political action functions are assigned to a secret intelligence service, but the head of that service reports to the foreign minister and to a committee of other ministers chaired by the foreign minister, which in turn reports to the prime minister.

The Military

Military officers, like members of the Foreign Service, are recruited young and expected to spend their lives in the service. The only exceptions are during war, when a large number of civilians are recruited at all levels "for the duration," and in the period following a war, when some reserve officers have been given regular commissions. High school graduates are recruited for the U.S. Military Academy at West Point, the Naval Academy at Annapolis, and the Air Force Academy in Colorado; on graduation they enter the officer corps as second lieutenants and ensigns. Academy graduates make up much less than half the number of regular officers of the Army and the Air Force, but a somewhat higher percentage of naval officers. The rest are recruited from college Reserve Officers' Training Corps (ROTC) or from the ranks and attend Officer Candidate School.

As with the CIA, the special problem presented by the military bureaucracies is rooted in the fact of their power, which is broad and firmly based. The Pentagon has a general constituency of veterans' organizations, reserve and National Guard organizations, and patriotic societies like the Daughters of the American Revolution. Beyond this broad general constituency the Pentagon also has natural allies who are extremely powerful in their own right. The budget of the Pentagon for fiscal 1980, the year Reagan was elected, was $136 billion. For fiscal 1983, after Reagan's policies were in place, it was $205 billion. The last budget Reagan submitted, for fiscal 1990, was for $315.2 billion; for the Bush administration, the budget for 1991 was $306.9 billion.

Almost half of the military budget goes for the purchase of military hardware such as guns, ships, submarines, tanks, trucks, missiles, and electronic equipment. Consequently, the military has sympathetic friends and natural allies in the most powerful segments of industry and among the members of Congress who represent the states in which that industry is located. Because the military exercises control over the ultimate means of physical violence available to a society, its potential for power is theoretically unlimited. For this reason the military has regularly been the subject of suspicion and distrust, especially in democracies.

Every democracy faces the danger that its military forces will be used against the society that created them. One or the other party or political faction may gain control of the army and use it to seize political power or to prevent the transfer of power to rivals who have won it by constitutional means. A popular general–a "man on horseback"–may use the army to put himself in control of the state. The military as a group may set itself up as a state within a state that can veto or dictate a nation's policy. History is full of examples of all these situations. Caesar and Napoleon were both "men on horseback." The Bolsheviks subverted the loyalties of the naval garrison at Kronstad to help them seize power, and one faction or another of the Communist party has used the army against rivals within the party. The classic example of a state within a state was the Prussian army. Here was an officer corps that stood apart, almost disdaining direct political power yet regarding itself as the true repository of the national ethos. It did not hesitate to try to dictate policy whenever it believed it to be in the interest of the "higher" state the officer corps saw itself as representing.

A second criticism of the military is that it has too much power over military spending. The military appears to demand more weapons, and more sophisticated and expensive weapons, than critics think are needed. Because of its natural allies in industry and Congress and its broad appeal to the general public, the military gets, the critics feel, too large a share of the budget.

A third criticism—or fear—of the military is more subtle. Some critics see the military as playing too large a role in the making of our foreign policy. In a time of prolonged international tension such as the world has witnessed since World War II, the United States is involved in issues all over the world. It is engaged in military aid programs and has military bases in many countries, all of which affects its relations with almost every nation. Thus the military is not only powerful but also has a legitimate concern in nearly every aspect of U.S. foreign policy. At the same time these critics renew the charges against the military of being extremely conservative, nationalistic, aggressive, power-oriented, and simplistic, tending to meet the complex problems of diplomacy by a resort to crude force. Thus the criticism is a double one: The military has too large a role in the making of foreign policy, and the task of making foreign policy is too delicate for a military mind.

The principle of civilian supremacy. Fear that the military will produce a "man on horseback," that they will easily be subverted by a political faction, and that they will attempt to set themselves up as a state within a state are all traditionally countered by the principle of civilian supremacy, which means only that the use of a nation's armed might shall be determined by constitutional processes. If these processes are observed, a military leader cannot usurp power, no single political faction can subvert the military, and the military as a group will be unable to dictate policy from its essentially parochial viewpoint.

Whether a nation is successful in establishing and maintaining the principle of civilian supremacy depends on many factors. It depends first on the civilians. If there is to be civilian supremacy, the people must cherish their constitution and insist on rejecting any person or party who violates it, even in the name of a good cause. So far the United States has been relatively fortunate in the attitude of its civilians. During the Korean conflict, for example, General Douglas MacArthur disagreed with President Truman on the policy of keeping the war strictly limited, and he said so publicly on several occasions, in violation of Truman's instructions. Finally losing patience, Truman relieved MacArthur of his command. From the public opinion polls it seems clear that MacArthur was more popular than Truman and that the public shared the general's opinion on expanding the war. Yet no one seriously questioned President Truman's right to fire MacArthur or suggested that Congress should try to overrule Truman or oust him by impeachment.

Success in establishing the principle of civilian supremacy depends too on the military—on whether it is composed of loyal and conscientious public servants and, most important, whether it is woven into the fabric of national life or stands apart from it. That the American military is as deeply committed to the principle of civilian supremacy as any other segment of society seems beyond question. To anyone who knows the American military, books that raise the specter of a military coup d'état—like *Seven Days in May*—are simply not believable.[10] For every rather flamboyant, charismatic military leader like Curtis LeMay, George Patton, and Douglas MacArthur, whose images haunt civilian critics of the military, there are several generals like Matthew Ridgway, a West Pointer who helped keep us out of Vietnam in 1954; James Gavin, who led protest demonstrations against Vietnam in the 1960s; and George Catlett Marshall, who served as secretary of state as well as secretary of defense and whose far-seeing statesmanship not only gave us the Marshall Plan that helped rebuild Europe but also kept us out of the greatest quagmire of all, China. LeMay, Patton, and MacArthur were great military leaders, but their swashbuckling style and seemingly perfunctory commitment to civilian supremacy did not fit the ideal image that the American military cherishes of itself. If any such general tried to lead a coup, the military would be the first to blow the whistle.

One reason for the American officer corps' exemplary obedience to civilian control is that these officers have been drawn mainly from the middle and lower-middle strata of society. These are people who are themselves antimilitarist, opposed to any suggestion that war is an end in itself. Officer recruits do not acquire a new basic philosophy on joining their new profession; instead they carry over their old one. In this respect America's good fortune has been that it had no aristocracy that might

---

[10]Fletcher Knebel and Charles W. Bailey, *Seven Days in May* (New York: Harper & Row, 1962).

have sustained an effective effort to monopolize the officer corps.[11] Administrative practices in the armed forces have helped by avoiding ties to particular socioeconomic strata or regions. West Point cadets, Annapolis midshipmen, and Air Force Academy cadets are appointed by members of Congress and the president, which guarantees a geographic spread. Although many members of Congress choose their nominees from the results of a competitive examination prepared by the academies, the recruitment decision is largely *not* in the hands of the military, and only in the Navy have academy graduates ever constituted more than half of the officer corps.

Undoubtedly the most important reason for the professional officers' respect for the principle of civilian supremacy is the longstanding tradition in the services that the officer corps should not be "political." There is reason to believe, for example, that the first vote that General Dwight D. Eisenhower ever cast was in the election in which he ran for president. Officers' indoctrination in this tradition is both formal and informal. The point is made formally in the training of a young officer. But it is informally, from the endless expressions of approval and disapproval of the acts of fellow officers, superiors, and historical forerunners, that the young officer forms a set of criteria for the kinds of behavior that are appropriate in different circumstances. It is a tribute to the American military that these criteria are the same as those of the society as a whole.

The "military mind." People often talk about the "military mind." Civilians often assume that soldiers are trained to blind obedience and to use violence to solve every problem. On the second point, the fact is that historically most generals (except for general-politicians such as Napoleon) have been reluctant about entering war. One reason is probably that soldiers know better than most people the horrors that war brings. Another is that generals always feel that they are not quite ready. They always want another thousand tanks or airplanes or another million soldiers!

The first point, that soldiers are trained to blind obedience, comes from the fact that almost all armies have some version of boot camp or the plebe system in which recruits are ordered to do impossible tasks and worked to near exhaustion if not physically hazed. But here again anyone

---

[11]For a sociological and political study of the American officer corps, see Morris Janowitz, *The Professional Soldier: A Social and Political Portrait* (New York: The Free Press, 1960). See also Zeb B. Bradford, Jr., and James R. Murphy, "A New Look at the Military Profession," in *American Defense Policy*, ed. Richard G. Head and Ervin J. Rokke (Baltimore: The Johns Hopkins University Press, 1975); and Richard Halloran, "An Army for the 21st Century," in *The US Army: Challenges & Missions for the 1990s*, eds. Robert L. Pfaltz & Richard Schultz Jr. (Lexington, Mass.: Lexington Books, 1991).

who has actually experienced battle is familiar with what the military calls the "fog of war." By this the military means that once the bullets start flying, command and control by superior officers become extremely difficult. What is necessary on the field of battle is not blind obedience but intelligent initiative. Thus although almost all armies have adopted something similar to boot camp or the plebe system, the purpose is not to instill blind obedience, even though the soldiers themselves often think it is, but is to accustom the recruits to the feeling of panic—so that when panic comes to them on the battlefield, as it inevitably will, they know how to handle the emotion.

But the military does develop a mind-set that is in some ways different from that of ordinary people. No matter how hard the military tries to avoid the problem, life in the military will inevitably be more isolated and narrow than in the general population. Members of the profession of arms must work hard to maintain their competency, especially in an era of highly complicated weapons, and this preoccupation tends to isolate them. But other professions, such as scientists and doctors, are also isolated by the nature of their work. Consider the position taken by the American Medical Association (AMA) during the three or four decades when federal health legislation was a central issue. To say that the AMA's views during those years were Victorian is to be charitable (although it should be added that the organization has since undergone considerable change). The isolation of members of the military is greater than that of other professions simply because their work takes them to remote places. They occupy bases abroad, and their main posts at home are remote military reservations in the South and West that give them room for training maneuvers.

If the American military tends to be conservative, it is probably because the middle and lower-middle socioeconomic strata from which its members spring are conservative. Since these strata embrace the majority of Americans, one might well argue that the problem is not so much the military mind as it is the middle-strata American mind. When a narrow, specialized class (in the Marxist sense) and the profession of arms become one, as with the Junkers of Prussia, the goals of both will be reflected in child training. One then might be able to speak of the inevitable conservatism of the "military mind." But in a society in which the military is recruited in adulthood from a wide base, it seems doubtful that the act of putting on a uniform would make a person more sympathetic to one political philosophy than to another.

As for intellectual rigidity—an excessive emphasis on discipline and other personal qualities often attributed to the military—it seems reasonable that practicing the military art would encourage a person to develop the qualities such as decisiveness, energy, loyalty to the decisions of higher authority, and disciplined teamwork that are necessary to large organizations engaged in implementing rather than creating policies. By the nature of their concentration, soldiers would tend to neglect the virtues of thinkers and writers, including subtlety, qualifying judgments, and habits of probing the unspoken assumptions behind goals and ways of life. Military forces in peacetime must spend a much larger percentage of their time waiting for something to happen than do civilian bureaucracies (with the exception of firefighters). The waiting is filled with preparations of many sorts. Since anything orderly is better than sheer idleness, a great deal of time is devoted to maintaining records, paying meticulous attention to procedure and outward appearance, and–inevitably–making preparations that are really irrelevant, such as close-order drill. In an environment of isolation it is easy to move from this to the kind of preoccupation with form and procedure that would stifle mission-oriented people, that is, to a "bureaucratization" in the pejorative sense of the word.

In these respects, how different are soldiers from engineers or industrialists or business executives? Modern warfare calls for the orchestration of a wide range of specialized functions. Men and women must be trained and supplies, ammunition, and equipment provided for and transported great distances according to intricate schedules. War is a large-scale enterprise; like other large-scale enterprises, it has been bureaucratized. The skills of officers are those of executives and administrators in any large bureaucracy, public or private. They are the skills of planning and coordinating the efforts of teams of specialists. If officers have the skills of executives, they can be expected to have the bureaucratic rigidities of executives, and there is no question that business executives have such rigidities. It was, after all, a person from business and not a soldier who was the model for the "organization man."

It is perhaps useful to repeat that it was a soldier, General Matthew B. Ridgway, who in effect vetoed the proposal for an American intervention in Vietnam in 1954. And it was not the military who decided to make Vietnam an American war in 1965; the military was in general opposed to any limited land war on the mainland of Asia. Once the United States was in the war, the military pressed hard for a policy of victory, but it was the "militarists" in civilian clothes who got us into the war in the first place.[12]

The stereotype of the rigid, archconservative militarist thus has little validity when applied to the American military, and the concept of

---

[12]On this point see Arthur M. Schlesinger, Jr., *Robert F. Kennedy and His Times* (Boston: Houghton Mifflin, 1978); Hilsman, *To Move a Nation;* and idem, "Vietnam: The Decisions to Intervene," in *The Superpowers and Revolution,* ed. Jonathan Adleman (New York: Praeger, 1986).

the "military mind" is more confusing than helpful. Anyone, civilian or military, who is given responsibility for a nation's security would become preoccupied with the power aspects of policy problems. In this sense civilian secretaries of defense, if they do the job they are given to do, will quickly develop "military minds."

Military influence on resource allocation. Although the American military is no threat to our liberties, there remain two areas of concern on the nature of the power held by the military in American society. One is that the military has so much political leverage that it can obtain appropriations for quantities of weapons that it may not really need and thus take up too much of our national budget. The second is that the military has too much influence in the making of foreign policy and tends to be too oriented toward the use of force in its thinking about foreign affairs.

No gimmick will solve the problem of the military bureaucracy's influence on appropriations. The United States tried the "unification" of all the services under a single secretary of defense in 1947 to no avail. Since then secretaries of defense have used a number of managerial devices to centralize power in the hands of presidential appointees, but none of those gimmicks has worked either.

If the military is getting too big a slice of the federal tax dollar, it is because of its political leverage. But practically, there are only two ways of cutting down the size of that slice. One way is for those who feel neglected to organize as groups and to exercise their own political leverage to obtain a greater share for themselves. If too little is going to the elderly compared to what goes to defense, the best thing for the elderly to do is to organize themselves. The second way is for various groups–the press, academia, members of Congress, and pressure groups such as the League of Women Voters and Common Cause–to develop sufficient expertise in military and strategic matters to be able to mount credible counterarguments as well as political pressure. E. H. Carr, a British analyst of world politics who wrote between World War I and World War II, put this point well: "If every prospective writer on international affairs had been required to read an elementary text on military strategy, reams of nonsense would have remained unwritten."[13] Courageous presidents, backed by Congress, the press, public interest groups, and the general public *can* overcome military influence on the budget, but only if they are well informed as well as courageous.

Military influence on foreign policy. While it is inevitable that anyone, military or civilian, who is given responsibility for a nation's survival will become preoccupied with the power aspects of foreign affairs, it is

---

[13]E. H. Carr, *The Twenty Years' Crisis, 1919–1939* (London: Macmillan, 1946).

also clearly desirable that they do so. In a world of sovereign nation-states, we must look to our own security. Doing so requires that someone look carefully and continuously at the power aspects of international affairs, which is the job that the military has been given.

We do not want the military to be warmongers or to think that force is the only way to deal with international affairs. But if paying particular attention to the power aspects is what is meant by having a "military mind," most people would want the military to have exactly that kind of mind. The answer to the problem of excessive military influence on foreign policy cannot be to exclude the military from foreign policy deliberations. For most current foreign policy problems, some sort of military advice is absolutely vital. Although the tensions of the cold war have lessened, they have not ended. The world contains many dangers, actual and potential. What gives the task of meeting threats an almost exquisite complexity is that they are posed concurrently with a techno-logical revolution—in missiles, electronics, and nuclear warheads—so fundamental that it casts the entire structure of strategic doctrine into disarray. As this revolution in strategy continues, increasing in tempo, it creates new relationships among all the elements of international poli-tics. No president or secretary of state can develop effective foreign policies without continuous advice from military specialists.

A real danger does exist that the military's inevitable concern with the military aspects of foreign affairs will give national policy an exces-sive emphasis on force. But it is both sterile and dangerous to try to prevent this by confining the military to technical military problems and isolating it in a kind of military quarantine where it can have no effect on diplomatic and policy problems.

Reducing military influence.   Perhaps a better way to overcome the ten-dency of the military to put too much emphasis on force in foreign policy is to see that it has an understanding of political and economic matters as well as military ones. In part this need is being met at the undergraduate level in the service schools and in the postgraduate command and general staff colleges and the war colleges. The purpose is not to equip military officers to make the political and economic judgments that by right belong to civilians but to enable them to understand the context in which their advice on military matters must be judged. With this knowledge the military can be more effective in adapting military means to the political necessities laid down by higher authority.

Still another way of overcoming the tendency of the military to put too much emphasis on force is to make sure that it does not have the field to itself. If the military aspects of policy problems are to be considered only in their political context—as they should be—it is essential that the president, the Congress, the White House staff, the State Department, the press, and the interested publics outside government have an understanding of military and strategic matters. It is especially important that the White House and the State Department be peopled with strong and able persons, preferably those with some political leverage in their own right, who can serve as vigorous spokespersons for these political considerations.

SUMMARY

Indeed, this point can serve as a summary for the lessons of this whole chapter on bureaucracy. If government is to serve its ultimate purpose well and if democracy is to work, it is essential that the president, the Congress, the White House staff, political appointees, the press, and the interested public outside of government have an understanding of the specialized matters with which the bureaucracies deal and so be able to incorporate the broader interests of the people as a whole.

14

INTEREST GROUPS

Although interest groups are obviously power centers, it is difficult to assess just how much power they wield, partly because they exercise their power indirectly rather than directly. Another problem in assessing the power of interest groups is that there are so many of them. It has been estimated that Americans belong to over 100,000 associations, clubs, and private organizations. One book takes a thousand pages merely to list their names and addresses.[1] However, only a fraction of these organizations are interest groups in the sense that the term is used in government and politics. For those groups the list to which most people turn is that of organizations registered under the Federal Regulation of Lobbying Act of 1946. But even this list does not include some groups that clearly are interest groups in the political sense. Many groups, such as the National Association of Manufacturers, do not register on the grounds that lobbying is not their "principal purpose." Even more frustrating, the list does not include the interest groups that are not formally organized, yet some of these are the most powerful of all. One example is the highway lobby, the loose but very powerful alliance of construction firms, construction unions, the automobile, trucking, and oil industries, and the highway departments of the fifty states!

An interest group is any organization or coalition of organizations that attempts to influence public policy at any of the branches and levels of government—Congress, the courts, the executive, the bureaucracies, or

---

[1]*National Organizations of the U.S.* (Detroit: Gale Research, 1961).

state and local governments. Interest groups differ from political parties in several ways. Parties must have a policy for every issue before the government; interest groups have only one or a handful for the particular matters that concern them. Parties deal with elections; groups try to influence elections on occasion but mainly deal with legislation, executive decisions, judicial decisions, and the implementation of legislation and policy decisions. If the party loses an election, it is reduced to sniping away at those in power and their policies. If an interest group loses the legislative battle, it tries to influence the way the bureaucracy carries out the legislation.

The structure and division of powers of the American political system encourage the proliferation of interest groups. Great Britain's unitary government provides only a few places where influence can be applied, so there tend to be fewer interest groups. But they are still plentiful, and they are frequently larger than their American counterparts. Since both legislation and the implementation of policy are under one minister and since both Parliament and the executive are under the control of the prime minister, it is advantageous for groups interested in a particular policy to combine their forces. Thus Britain has one farm organization, one veterans' organization, one major business organization, and one medical society. The United States, in contrast, has the American Farm Bureau Federation, the National Farmers' Union, and the Grange; four active veterans' organizations; several major business organizations; and at least two major medical associations.

TYPES OF INTEREST GROUPS

The thousands of organized interest groups fall rather naturally into a relatively few types. The most common type is dedicated to furthering the economic position of its members. Most such groups are devoted to promoting a specific commodity, product, or type of business. Some random examples include the Walnut Growers' Association, the National Fertilizer Association, the National Association of Retail Druggists, and the Associated Milk Producers. Labor unions devoted to the interests of a single trade, such as plumbers, would be another example.

Another type of economic interest group includes those attempting to represent much larger economic interests. Among these are the American Farm Bureau Federation and the National Farmers Union, which try to represent something much wider than merely walnut or beet sugar growers; the Chamber of Commerce, which tries to represent business beyond ice cream manufacturers or retail druggists; and the National Association of Manufacturers, which tries to represent not just steel or automobile makers but manufacturers of all types. Here again, the AFL-CIO is an example of a labor union that tries to represent workers as a whole rather than a particular trade.

One variation of the economic interest group is the professional association. These include the American Medical Association, the American Bar Association, the American Association of University Professors, the Screen Actors Guild, the American Institute of Architects, and the Authors League of America.

Still another type of interest group strives for benefits for a special class of people. Veterans' associations like the Grand Army of the Republic, which represented Civil War veterans of the North, and the American Legion, which was founded after World War I, sought pensions and bonuses for veterans. The American Association of Retired Persons is another example of this type.

Another kind of interest group is one that seeks rights or privileges for a minority or another less privileged segment of the population. The National Association for the Advancement of Colored People, the Congress of Racial Equality, and the Southern Christian Leadership Conference all try to achieve racial equality and rights for blacks. Groups such as ACT UP (AIDS Coalition to Unleash Power) and the Gay Men's Health Crisis (GMHC) focus on AIDS education and prevention of discrimination against people with AIDS.

Certain interest groups began simply as associations of hobbyists. The National Rifle Association was started to bring together people interested in marksmanship, but it has become an interest group opposed to gun control legislation with an awesome passion. Another type of interest group pursues a goal that its members conceive to be moral or to contribute in some way to the public good. Examples are the American Society for the Prevention of Cruelty to Animals, the American Anti-Vivisection League, the American League to Abolish Capital Punishment, and the Anti-Saloon League. The Navy League, the Air Force Association, and the Association of the United States Army are dedicated to furthering the contribution of each of the services to national defense. Groups concerned with protecting the environment, wildlife, and wilderness areas, such as the Sierra Club, the Friends of the Earth, and the Environmental Defense Fund, also come under this category. So do the American Civil Liberties Union, which fights in the courts and in state and national legislatures for civil liberties, and the National Association for the Reform of Marijuana Laws, which tries to repeal laws against smoking or possessing small quantities of marijuana.

In the past decade or so, special interest groups concentrating on a single issue have grown enormously in both number and influence. The oldest and undoubtedly the most famous of these is the National Rifle Association. Others that have become particularly prominent are the antiabortion ("right to life") groups, the antinuclear energy groups, the environmentalist groups, and the Moral Majority, a coalition of fundamentalist Protestants with a strong following in the Bible Belt.

Some interest groups are dedicated to promoting a particular ideology. Americans for Democratic Action is devoted to liberal causes, whereas Americans for Constitutional Action is devoted to conservatism. The John Birch Society is an example from the radical right.

To the extent that they engage in activities that come under this category, churches and church federations are similar to the first type of interest group in that they pursue only one or two goals that their members believe to be moral or for the public good. Many church groups have on one or another occasion in our history lobbied for freedom of religion, tax-free status for themselves, legislation concerning divorce, birth control, abortion, aid to parochial schools, and legalization of bingo games.

Relatively few interest groups are active in foreign affairs and defense. However, the economic groups—industrial and business associations, farmers and other growers, and trade unions—are all active on issues such as tariffs and import quotas. Veterans' groups are involved in defense issues, but only intermittently, since their principal concern is the welfare of veterans. The various ideological groups, whether conservative or liberal, are also only intermittently involved, since their major concerns are domestic.

At first glance, one would expect the various ethnic associations, such as Irish-American, Polish-American, and Italian-American societies, to be active in foreign policy matters, but they are usually more concerned with preserving a cultural heritage than with current issues of U.S. policy toward their homeland. Those ethnic associations whose homeland was behind the "iron curtain" have usually supported the essentially bipartisan containment policy that the United States generally followed after World War II. Black American associations have been interested in U.S. policy toward South Africa and its segregationist apartheid policy, but they have not been as active as one might have expected. The reason of course is that their first priority has been to overcome injustice toward blacks here at home. The notable exception has been the various Jewish-American groups, which have generally been intensely interested and active in issues of U.S. policy toward Israel.

Political Action Committees

Under the legislation that reformed the financing of political campaigns (see Chapter 12), all these different types of interest groups are permitted to form political action committees (PACs) that can legally raise and spend money beyond the usual limits as long as they avoid coordinating their activities with a particular party or candidate—a rule that most critics believe has been almost totally ineffective. In any case, PAC contributions to congressional election campaigns totaled $55.3 million in 1980, $83.6 million in 1982, $105.3 million in 1984, $130 million in 1986, $150 million in 1988, and $149.8 million in 1990. These committees included environmentalists, educators, labor unions, and business and industry associations as well as strictly ideological groups from both the right and the left.[2]

THE INTERNAL GOVERNMENT OF INTEREST GROUPS

To understand the role that organized interest groups play in policy making, we need to know something of how they are themselves ruled. From whom do they derive their legitimacy and authority? Who decides what goals and tactics they shall pursue? At first it might seem impossible to generalize about how such a bewildering diversity of groups are ruled, but in fact some patterns are discernible.

Any discussion of the government of private, voluntary associations must begin with Robert Michels, a European sociologist whose work on the subject, first published in 1913, still troubles those who believe that human beings inherently and naturally prefer democratic government to other forms.[3] Michels focused his research on the social democratic parties of Western Europe since they had the deepest commitment to democracy, but his target was every voluntary organization with a substantial membership. His conclusion was that all such organizations live under the "iron law of oligarchy," or rule by the few. What happened, he found, was that the members were too busy with their own lives to devote much time or attention to the internal workings of the organization and the debate over its goals and tactics. Consequently, the active few became the leaders and made the policy decisions, which at best the membership only ratified. Differences invariably developed between the leaders and some members, but when members became dissatisfied, they usually did nothing more than grumble. Those who became really angry usually dropped

---

[2]See also, Philip M. Stern, *The Best Congress Money Can Buy* (New York: Pantheon Books, 1988); David Mayleby and Candice J. Nelson, *The Money Chase: Congressional Campaign Finance Reform* (Washington, D.C.: Brookings, 1990), and Harold W. Stanley and Richard G. Niemi, *Vital Statistics on American Politics*, 3rd ed. (Washington, D.C.: Congressional Quarterly Press, 1992).

[3]Robert Michels, *Political Parties* (New York: The Free Press, 1968). This is the most recent translation of the work that originally appeared in German.

out of the organization entirely. Only occasionally did a group of dissatisfied members attempt to reverse policy or to displace the leadership by organizing something like a rival political faction. Since the leaders had inside knowledge of the organization's affairs and control of its files, membership lists, treasury, and usually the paid bureaucracy, the rival faction rarely won. If they did, they usually became a new oligarchy—with different policies, perhaps, but no less oligarchic!

Michels's conclusion is overstated—no "law" in the social affairs of humankind is ever really "iron"—and exceptions to it can be found, but he obviously had a point.

Business Corporations

Congress and the state legislatures pass thousands of laws and the regulatory agencies issue thousands of rules and regulations designed to make business corporations conform to "democratic principles," except that instead of "one person, one vote," it is "one share, one vote." For instance, a public corporation must hold a meeting of shareholders at least once a year, which any shareholder may attend. By voting either in person at the meeting or by a proxy ballot, which may be mailed in, the shareholders elect a board of directors, which then chooses the officers of the corporation.

The law specifies that the boards of certain types of corporations, mainly those with fiduciary responsibilities, must include directors who are "unaffiliated," that is, who are not officers of the corporation and who have no connection with its management. The law further says that the decisions on certain kinds of broad policies can be made only by a majority vote of all the outstanding shares; that decisions on certain other, somewhat less broad policies can be made only by a vote of the board of directors; that certain other decisions can be made by management subject to ratification by the board or the shareholders; and that the remainder, including day-by-day operating decisions, can be made by management without reference to the board or the shareholders. Establishing the boards; holding the meetings; preparing, printing, and mailing the proxies; and fulfilling all the other requirements are costly and time-consuming tasks. Yet the entire procedure is virtually meaningless.

The reality is that the government of corporations is oligarchy. Most of the giant corporations have thousands of shareholders. For example, U.S. Steel has over 100 million outstanding shares, owned by about 250,000 shareholders, of which 35 percent are institutions such as pension funds, foundations, mutual funds, and various other corporate entities. The largest holding of shares, 16.71 percent of the total, is owned by the U.S. Steel employees' pension trust. No individual holds more than

0.26 percent of the common stock. The vast majority of shareholders are interested in only two things: the size and regularity of the dividends and the price of the stock on the New York Stock Exchange. Only a few care about who runs the corporation, the design of the products, the production rate, the pricing policy, the personnel, the promotion schedules, the retirement policies, or the policy of the corporation in relation to the government.

The few shareholders who do care about such matters can do almost nothing about them because there are so many shareholders and because most of them are preoccupied with their own lives. As private citizens they can join Ralph Nader's organization or a specific group that might be fighting some policy of the corporation; they can also go to their representative in Congress. Depending on the nature of the policy they dislike, they might go to the courts with a suit, file a protest with a regulatory commission, make themselves a nuisance at the annual meeting of shareholders, or try to get the press interested. But all this takes so much time and trouble for so little return that most dissatisfied shareholders do little more than sell their shares and put their money elsewhere. Only in an infinitesimal number of cases has it been possible to organize enough shareholders to challenge management by electing a rival slate of managers or outvoting them on a particular policy in a shareholders' meeting.

It is not just the small shareholder who displays this indifference to how the corporations are run. Generally the top managers of the giant corporations are not the grandchildren of the founders but career bureaucrats who have worked their way up the organizational ladder. Standard Oil is not run by a Rockefeller or Union Pacific by a Harriman. When a descendant of the founder does still hold a large proportion of the outstanding shares, that person is usually as uninterested in choosing management or determining policies as are most shareholders. Stewart Mott, for example, inherited a huge block of General Motors shares, but he has never been very interested in determining how the corporation was managed or in directing the power it could wield.

As a practical matter, top management chooses its own replacements, determines whom to nominate as directors, and decides on the policies to be recommended to the directors and the shareholders. Michels's "iron law of oligarchy" thus holds for the giant corporations even more solidly than for interest groups as such.

Labor Unions

Of all the organizations examined in this chapter, labor unions have had the deepest ideological commitment to democratic principles in their internal government. Yet, with few exceptions, they too conform to Michels's "law."[4] The reasons for this are the same. Because the members are too busy with other aspects of their lives, the activists become the leaders, who choose their own replacements and decide the policies. The leaders easily manipulate the membership, in conventions and in balloting, to ratify their choices and decisions. The leadership's knowledge of the internal affairs of the union and their control over the files, bureaucracy, and funds are such that it can almost always beat off an insurgent challenge. Therefore in the labor unions, as in the corporations, oligarchy is the rule.

THE TECHNIQUES OF INTEREST GROUP INFLUENCE

When we think of the techniques that interest groups use to influence government, the first word that comes to mind is "lobbying," a term that first came into use in the early nineteenth century in Albany, New York, where agents waited in the lobbies of the state legislature to buttonhole members.

In the field of foreign affairs and defense, lobbies trying to influence U.S. policy are maintained not only by Americans but also by a variety of foreign interests, including other governments. The embassies themselves perform lobbying functions, representing their countries' interests not only with the executive branch but also with the legislature, the press, and other interest groups. In addition many countries hire American lobbying firms to look after their interests. Sometimes a particular personality performs such a function. Madame Chiang Kai-shek, the wife of the leader of the Nationalist Chinese on Taiwan, was a most effective lobbyist for her government's interests in the United States. Occasionally, groups of Americans form a lobby to further the interests of some foreign government. A classic example is the Committee of One Million, an organization of Americans devoted to the Chinese Nationalists and in opposition to the Chinese Communists.

To many Americans the term "lobby" has sinister connotations that suggest all sorts of shady practices, including bribery. Certainly examples of bribery are not hard to find. Spiro Agnew, Nixon's vice president, resigned in the face of charges that he had accepted bribes and evaded his income tax. In the so-called Abscam scandals of 1980, an FBI agent posing as an Arab sheik offered bribes to a number of members of

---

[4]For the most notable exception, see Seymour Martin Lipset, Martin A. Trow, and James S. Coleman, *Union Democracy: The Internal Politics of the International Typographical Union* (New York: The Free Press, 1956).

Congress, seven of whom were convicted of accepting them. On the other hand, recent studies of lobbying in Washington maintain that bribery is rare—that it is risky, likely to backlash, and more often than not results in ruined careers, fines, and jail sentences.[5]

Certain payments and gifts may not be bribes in a technical sense but come very close. The Gulf Oil Company admitted making a number of illegal campaign contributions, although it should immediately be said that most of the members of Congress who had received these contributions did not know that they were illegal. Corporations have also tipped off government officials to upcoming business deals that would permit them to make a fortune. Another practice is to maintain corporate yachts, jets, or hunting lodges for the use of government officials. Or, if an official or a member of his or her family owns a company or is a member of a law firm, business can be directed his or her way. Enough members of Congress were sufficiently uneasy about these practices to pass legislation in 1977 setting new standards of ethics for themselves, and there is constant pressure to make the rules even stricter.

Another practice that has been growing is for an interest group to invite a member of Congress to address one of their meetings, for which the member is paid a handsome honorarium. A few senators have actually earned almost as much from these so-called lecture fees as from their salaries. Again, the practice has caused enough uneasiness in Congress to bring about restrictions. In 1982 the House voted to give its members a 15 percent pay raise—which even outsiders thought was overdue—but at the same time limited what members could earn from such sources as lecture fees to 30 percent of their salaries. The Senate finally followed the House lead in 1984.

But this move did not solve the problem. The practice of giving members of Congress lecture fees and "honorariums" for attending breakfast, luncheon, or dinner meetings with lobby groups has continued to grow. Members of Congress have been uneasy about this growth, but they have been fearful of the political backlash if they raised their own salaries, which most observers agree have fallen behind inflation and the salary that members of Congress could earn if they switched to business

---

[5]Lester W. Milbrath, *The Washington Lobbyists* (Skokie, Ill.: Rand McNally, 1963); L. Harmon Zeigler and C. Wayne Peak, *Interest Groups in American Society*, 2nd ed. (Englewood Cliffs, N.J.: Prentice Hall, 1972); Robert Prestus, *Elites in the Policy Process* (New York: Cambridge University Press, 1974); David B. Truman, *The Governmental Process: Political Interests and Public Opinion*, 2nd ed. (New York: Alfred A. Knopf, 1971); V. O. Key, Jr., *Politics, Parties, and Pressure Groups*, 5th ed. (New York: Crowell, 1964); Lewis A. Dexter, *How Organizations Are Represented in Washington* (New York: Bobbs-Merrill, 1969); Thomas P. Murphy, *Pressure upon Congress: Legislation by Lobby* (Woodbury, N.Y.: Baron, 1973); and Jeffrey Berry, *Lobbying for the People: The Political Behavior of Public Interest Groups* (Princeton, N.J.: Princeton University Press, 1977).

or industry careers. As a way around this political impasse, Congress set up an outside commission to study the problem and make recommendations. The commission duly recommended a 50 percent raise for Congress, but with the proviso that members could no longer accept honorariums. One of Reagan's last acts as president was to approve the recommendations. The Congress also provided that the commission's recommendations would go into effect automatically without a vote. But the idea of a raise as large as 50 percent caused a public outcry. The demand for a vote became overwhelming, and when it was taken, the pay raise was defeated – along with the restrictions on honorariums!

Influence Peddling

The foregoing are examples of the seamy side of lobbying that range from the outright illegal to ethically questionable. But what about the use of personal influence? Consider the following. The lobby group of a particular industry wanted an amendment added to tax legislation. They tried and failed to convince several members of the congressional committee having jurisdiction that without the amendment the legislation would cause their industry severe and, they believed, unfair damage. They then decided they needed another approach, and thus turned to a law firm headed by an ex-senator who was a close friend of the chairman of the committee. The firm also had on its staff a brilliant young expert on the kind of taxation and financial matters involved. The law firm set a fee of $5,000, win, lose, or draw. The ex-senator entertained the chair at dinner and persuaded him to give the lobbyist and the young tax expert half an hour to present their case. The tax expert did a first-rate job of convincing both the chairman and the committee staff of the damage that would result to the industry if the amendment were not added to the legislation. After the full committee had considered the matter, the amendment was included. The group's representative concluded that in view of the damage that their industry otherwise would have suffered, the legal fee was well worth it. In perfect sincerity he then added, " 'Of course, this was not lobbying, we were just honestly trying to do what we could to get good legislation.' "[6]

Campaign Contributions

As discussed, in an effort to eliminate the influence that wealthy contributors can have on government policy, presidential campaigns are today financed from the federal treasury. However, ways have been found to get around the contribution restrictions established by the reform. But even

---

[6]As quoted in Milbrath, *The Washington Lobbyists,* pp. 243–244.

the modest step of subsidizing campaigns has not yet been extended to House or Senate elections. Campaign contributions thus continue to come from both individuals and organizations, and they are an obvious way to get at least a sympathetic hearing from a member of Congress about legislation in which the contributor has an interest. A substantial amount of money is given by special interest groups through their PACs.

Massive Publicity Campaigns

Exerting pressure on the government through a mass advertising campaign is another lobbying technique, although it is available to only the most affluent groups. In 1968 and 1969 the American Automobile Association (AAA) fought a bill that would have permitted larger and heavier trucks on the highways with an expensive advertising campaign that featured a cartoon of a triple-trailer truck with the head of a voracious hog gobbling up the highways while the ordinary driver sat stalled in a hopeless traffic jam. The American Medical Association used mass advertising to fight Medicare legislation. In one year, 1962, the AMA is reported to have spent $1.3 million on public relations alone and a grand total of between $7 million and $12 million to fight the bill.[7]

Vengeance at the Polls

Still another means to exert influence is to retaliate at the polls. To do this effectively, however, the group must have a large membership, and the issue must be one that the membership feels affects them directly and is of overriding importance. The conservative member of the AAA who regards Senator Barry Goldwater as a hero and the liberal AAA member who regards George McGovern as a hero are not likely to vote against their heroes even if they had voted for the trucker bill. African-Americans, on the other hand, may well vote against someone whose general views they agree with if the person has voted against a civil rights bill. So too may labor union members vote against someone they agree with in general if the person has voted against labor legislation that workers regard as crucial.

Pressure by Publicity

Still another technique has been popularized by Ralph Nader. Nader started out by writing, speaking, testifying, and in other ways making himself a gadfly about automobile safety. More importantly, he wrote a book, *Unsafe at Any Speed,* that caused a sensation.[8] Aided by a group of young volunteers that included lawyers and college students, he set

---

[7]James Deakin, *The Lobbyists* (Washington, D.C.: Public Affairs Press, 1966), p. 222.

[8]Ralph Nader, *Unsafe at Any Speed* (New York: Grossman, 1965).

about to bring to public attention all kinds of abuses, unfair legislation, and special privileges. He and those who helped him are given credit for making important contributions to automobile safety and to various other pieces of legislation concerned with safety and consumer interests.

Protest Demonstrations and Violence

Protest demonstrations and physical violence have been used as a form of pressure by people who could be called interest groups since the very beginning of the republic. Shays's Rebellion in Massachusetts in 1786–1787 was one early instance. The labor troubles of the late nineteenth century saw both peaceful demonstrations and violence. The Anti-Saloon League used axes to break up the furniture in saloons. During the depression of the 1930s, veterans marched on Washington to demand a bonus. The struggle for civil rights in the 1950s and 1960s saw the use of the bus boycott by Martin Luther King, Jr., and his supporters, a number of peaceful sit-ins, and the famous and entirely peaceful march in Washington in 1963. It also saw violence, particularly in the riot in Watts in Los Angeles and in most other major cities following the assassination of King in 1968.

Everyday Interest Group Techniques

What of the more mundane techniques used by interest groups? Lobbyists, for example, watch the legislation that comes before Congress, the cases that come before the courts, and the rules and regulations under consideration in the regulatory commissions and the departments and agencies of the executive branch. Whenever they see an opportunity to propose something that will benefit their interest, they offer it. This can be done by submitting a formal paper to the appropriate committee of Congress or to the responsible agency, or by informally making the suggestion to a friendly member of Congress or staff member of the committee, department, or agency. Lobbyists also try to help sympathetic members of Congress all they can by supplying research, factual material, draft speeches, and the like. Much of the time, however, the lobbyists act defensively.[9] They watch proposed legislation and regulations and call attention to provisions that will be harmful to the people and organizations they represent. They remain alert to the scheduling of public hearings by Congress or the executive agency, prepare memoranda and briefs to present at those hearings, and either testify themselves or bring in representatives from their membership to do so.

They also watch what is happening in the courts and frequently file

---

[9]Truman, *Governmental Process,* pp. 353–362; and Dexter, *How Organizations Are Represented,* pp. 62–63.

amici curiae briefs. These briefs present the legal precedents and arguments favoring their position and frequently the results of an impressive amount of social, economic, political, and psychological research designed to show how the decision will affect the nation and various segments of the populace as well as their membership.

Interest groups will also watch for opportunities to file suit. The 1954 decision ordering school desegregation, *Brown* v. *Board of Education of Topeka,* is one example. Linda Carol Brown had to go to her school by a bus that arrived before the doors were opened, so she had to wait half an hour outdoors, often in cold weather. Going home, she had to walk past the railroad tracks and cross a dangerous intersection. Her parents tried to enroll her in a school only seven blocks from home, but that school was reserved for white children. The NAACP saw an opportunity and took the case all the way to the Supreme Court.[10]

As they follow legislation working its way through Congress or regulations being considered by an agency of the executive branch, interest groups may urge their membership to write, telephone, or telegraph their representatives in Congress or the appropriate agency. If the people respond out of genuine concern and in large numbers, such a grass-roots reaction can be very effective. If, however, the response obviously appears staged – if the letters are only form letters and if the telegrams all use the same language – the effort generally fails and may even have the opposite effect from that intended.

Lobbyists, then, follow the events related to matters with which their interest group is concerned. They present the group's case at hearings and on other occasions, file briefs and bring suit, keep the membership informed and alert as to what is happening and occasionally attempt to mount a grass-roots campaign of support, research matters of interest to the group, and make that research and similar materials available to those who hold official positions. In sum, lobbyists do whatever they can to mobilize sympathizers when the votes are finally taken.

THE FUNCTIONS OF INTEREST GROUPS

What functions do interest groups perform in the American governmental process? Some of their functions are useful but hardly earthshaking. Members of Congress point out that lobbyists and interest groups perform an important staff function for them: They provide thorough and

---

[10]For a dramatic account of the story of the struggle for civil rights culminating in the Court's decision, see Richard Klugar, *Simple Justice: The History of Brown* v. *Board of Education and Black America's Struggle for Equality* (New York: Alfred A. Knopf, 1976).

expert research. They gather information and develop the social, economic, political, and legal arguments that support their point of view. They frequently call attention to provisions in legislation that are based on ignorance or misinformation or that are simply hastily and badly considered. Members of Congress say that if they had to do this valuable and necessary work that interest groups do for nothing, they would have to have staffs several times as large as they have now and much more highly specialized. Officials in the executive branch are less dependent on this work of interest groups, but many of them find it useful.

Another useful role of interest groups is that of an ombudsman. Individual members turn to their Washington headquarters for help in redressing grievances, for aid in contacting the government agency having jurisdiction over their problem, and for advice on everything from filling out forms to obtaining benefits provided by existing law. Interest groups also needle the bureaucracies into action and protest when they are overly zealous.

The Aggregation of Interests

An even more important role of interest groups is representation and the "aggregation of interests." Perhaps the most accurate and useful definition of an interest group is a group of people with similar attitudes toward some area of human activity. Even though most interest groups have an oligarchic structure, they also have a communality of view and outlook. The Right to Life group, the women's liberation organizations, and the National Rifle Association are as much interest groups as are the Walnut Growers' Association, the sugar lobby, and the National Association of Manufacturers. Because they rest on shared attitudes, interest groups can and do serve the social and political function of aggregating interests. By various devices many groups build a consensus among conflicting views within their membership in order to develop common goals, priorities among those goals, and plans for attaining them.

Another aspect of the aggregation of interest is the bargaining, compromising, and consensus building that takes place between interest groups with conflicting interests. Business and labor groups, for example, frequently negotiate agreements that the legislature then gratefully passes as law.

Supplementing Representation

The entire interest group structure—including corporations and labor unions when they act as interest groups—provides an essential ingredient for the successful working of government in a large, complex, modern society. V. O. Key, Jr., points out that the explanation of the development of this "system of spokesmen for specialized segments of society probably rests in part on the shortcomings of geographical representation in a highly differentiated society." In a less complex society, the interests of a particular geographic district were more or less homogeneous, and whatever need there was for functional representation could easily be accommodated to geographical representation. But in a complex and interconnected society—one of continental dimensions—it is impossible for a legislator to look out regularly for interests that spread across many districts. "Organized groups supplement the system of geographical representation."[11]

Politics, Key argues, is not just elections (the politics for office). Elections are only the preliminary to the real stuff of politics, the politics of policy, the politics of decisions concerning what government and society shall do. "The decisions taken between elections constitute the basic stuff of politics, the pelf and glory for which men and groups battle." A working conception of the political process must take into account the interactions among groups, interests, and government institutions that produce such decisions. "Moreover, a working conception of the political system must make a place for organized interest groups: They not only seek to exert influence; they are a part of the political system."[12]

THE POWER OF INTEREST GROUPS

How effective are the techniques that interest groups use to influence policy? What power do they wield? The classical view was that interest groups were the principal proponents and opponents in the entire political process. Congress and the president accordingly served as political brokers and as the ratifiers of the results of the struggle among the interest groups. More recent studies have painted a quite different picture, however. Two major studies concluded that lobbyists try to activate and reinforce their supporters more often than they try to convert or pressure their opponents.[13] The findings indicated that when the legislation comes to a vote in Congress, about all the interest groups can do is to try to nudge their known sympathizers into making a special effort to be present when the vote is taken. Most of the time they do not even contact known opponents in Congress, being convinced that their minds are made up and that nothing the interest group can do or say will make a difference. Generally, interest groups work with their natural allies:

---

[11]Key, *Politics, Parties, and Pressure Groups*, pp. 158–159.

[12]Ibid., p. 158.

[13]Raymond Bauer, Ithiel DeSola Pool, and Lewis A. Dexter, *American Business and Public Policy* (New York: Atherton, 1963); and Milbrath, *The Washington Lobbyists.*

members of Congress who come from districts where important segments of the populace are sympathetic to the group and its cause. For these members interest groups provide all the help they can give. If they can manage contributions to their campaigns, they will make them. At the very least, they will buy tickets to one or two fund-raisers. But their principal effort is to provide information.

Members of Congress are short on staff. The interest group will research the issues with which they are concerned and make the material available to sympathetic members. They will also draft speeches on the subject for them. In the midst of a struggle over a piece of legislation in their field of interest, the member of Congress will call on the interest group for help more often than the interest group calls on the member.

The implication of these studies is that interest groups are little more than service organizations that members of Congress can use or ignore. However, both of these descriptions of the power of interest groups seem unpersuasive. With so many issues before government and the Congress, a more likely hypothesis is that the power of interest groups varies with the circumstances, the nature of the group, and the subject matter.

Various observations tend to support this notion. For example, one writer notes that members of Congress vote the way interest groups want them to not because the groups are strong and the members fear punishment but because the political parties are weak.[14] Since members are unsure about what power the interest groups have to punish them, they often go along. Others make the same point in more general terms: Where parties are strong, interest groups tend to be weak, and vice versa.[15]

Similarly, others point out that large interest groups are surprisingly ineffective. The reason lies in the workings of the so-called collective good. For example, if a consumer group succeeds in getting a price lowered, all consumers benefit, even those who did not join or contribute to the group. Unions call such people the "free riders." The larger the group, the less able it is to put pressure on free riders. Small groups have fewer free riders and, having both greater loss in the event of failure and greater gain in success, will tend to be more tightly organized and hence more effective.[16]

When a small, tightly organized group feels intensely about a very

[14]E. E. Schattschneider, *Party Government* (New York: Rinehart, 1942), p. 63.

[15]Edward C. Banfield and James Q. Wilson, *City Politics* (Cambridge, Mass.: Harvard University Press, 1963).

[16]Mancur Olson, *The Logic of Collective Action* (Cambridge, Mass.: Harvard University Press, 1965), p. 35.

narrow issue, it can sometimes be enormously powerful even against the majority view, if the majority is not organized and does not feel so intensely about the issue. Again, take the NRA as an example. Public opinion polls have included questions about gun control since the 1930s and never have less than 60 percent favored such legislation. An Associated Press–NBC poll in April 1981, for example, showed that 71 percent of the people favored laws requiring a police permit to buy a handgun, while only 25 percent opposed them and 4 percent were undecided. Yet the NRA, with only 1.8 million members, has successfully blocked gun control laws both nationally and in the states. It contributed more than $2 million to candidates favoring their stand in the 1980 election, picketed rallies of candidates opposed, and turned out very nearly 100 percent of their members (and relatives) to vote. "The real power of the rifle association," one newsman writes, "stems from the fervor of its members, their apparent devotion to a single, overriding issue and their determination to judge politicians on a 'for-us-or-against-us' basis."[17]

Some interest groups have added more militant tactics to their lobbying. "Operation Rescue," an antiabortion group, has attempted to block the entrance to clinics that perform abortions, courting arrest to publicize their views.

On the question of differences in power deriving from differences in subject matter, Theodore J. Lowi has distinguished three issue areas: distributive, regulative, and redistributive.[18] Distributive policies involve such issues as pork barrel legislation, tariffs, subsidies, and special tax breaks. Here the interest groups are very powerful. When they approach Congress on these issues, they can usually be satisfied without hurting anyone else very much, principally through logrolling. Potential conflict is most often resolved inside the committees of Congress, and only rarely does the matter come to a fight on the floor.

Regulatory policies are similarly specific and individual in their impact, but they cannot be so easily disaggregated, for here what benefits one group is more likely to hurt another. As a result, the conflict is resolved not by logrolling but by crude and vulgar bargaining and compromise. If it is not resolved in committee, it goes to the floor, where the roll call votes become very meaningful indeed.

Redistributive policies involve ideological conflict between social classes, such as the long struggle for workers' rights or racial equality. Here, Lowi says, the tendency is for conflict to be resolved and policy to be

---

[17]Steven V. Roberts, "Rifle Group Viewed as Key to Gun Law," *The New York Times,* April 15, 1981, p. A31.

[18]Theodore J. Lowi, *The End of Liberalism* (New York: W. W. Norton, 1969).

formulated in the executive branch, with Congress eventually ratifying the results. The interest groups as such wield little power.[19]

In any case, the evidence seems overwhelming that interest groups play a much less important role in foreign affairs than in domestic. To recapitulate, the ideological interest groups and those with similar interests, such as veterans, seem to be involved in foreign policy only episodically and never very intensely. The ethnic associations, with the exception of Jewish-American groups, are less concerned with policy than with preserving a cultural heritage. The loose association that President Eisenhower called the military-industrial complex is interested mainly in a high level of defense preparations rather than in specific foreign policy or defense issues in the sense of military strategy. Their interest is mainly in weapons and to some extent the various groups compete. For example, the Navy's desire for aircraft carriers competes with the Air Force's desire for strategic bombers, and all of the services compete for scarce dollars. The great array of economic interest groups concentrates mainly on tariffs, quotas, and other kinds of restrictive legislation. Occasionally, a particular corporation tries to influence general policy, as ITT attempted to influence policy toward Chile and President Allende during the Nixon administration. But even in that case, it is difficult to distinguish to what extent the policy resulted from pressure from ITT and to what extent Nixon and Kissinger were using the pressure from ITT to justify what they themselves wanted to do.

More typically corporations are timid, more likely to withdraw to safer fields for their investments and activities than to push the government into a more active role. Even companies whose business leaves no alternative but to be involved abroad, such as those dealing in sugar, rubber, oil, and the like, are more likely to be timid. A typical example was the behavior of the oil companies when Sukarno was president of Indonesia. Sukarno was nationalistic and belligerent, threatening confrontation with the great powers and all sorts of radical legislation against foreign corporations. On the face of it, the oil companies had a big stake in Indonesia. Their investment was over half a billion dollars, and the oil flow from Indonesia was large; Caltex alone took 230,000 barrels a day. The United States tried to bring about an accord between the oil companies and the Indonesian government, not because of pressure from the oil companies but to persuade the Sukarno regime to turn away from international adventuring and toward economic development. A meeting was arranged between the two sides in Tokyo, but to the astonishment of

---

[19]Michael T. Hayes, *Lobbyists and Legislators: A Theory of Political Markets* (New Brunswick, N.J.: Rutgers University Press, 1981).

the U.S. government, the oil companies refused to participate. They felt that even a favorable agreement was not worth it because the Sukarno regime was "erratic." They said that they had already written off the investments as a tax loss and that their real worry was that Indonesia's erratic behavior might interrupt the oil flow to their markets in the future, which was more important than either investments or highly favorable profits. The U.S. government had to bring enormous political pressure on the oil companies to get them to attend. As it happened, the final agreement was very favorable to the oil companies, and they ended up being delighted with the results.[20]

SUMMARY

It can be said that, in spite of their abuses, interest groups serve important functions in government. They are a channel for expressing the needs and interests of people to government. At the same time, they also serve as a channel for government to explain to people any special problems in supplying their needs. All successful political systems have some sort of institution that serves this function. In certain under-developed countries, for instance, it is fulfilled by the extended family system. In a democracy, this function is supposed to be served by the president and by members of the legislature, both of whom are elected by the people. But for some problems, elected representatives are less effective than is desirable. If the people concerned are relatively few in number and are not concentrated in one congressional district or state but in several, they may have difficulty finding an elected representative to champion their cause. The example of walnut growers illustrates the point. They were neither numerous nor concentrated, so their most effective course was to organize as an interest group which could go directly to the chair of the appropriate congressional committee. Thus even in a democracy, interest groups provide a useful alternative channel to elected representatives through which people can express their needs.

---

[20]The incident is recounted in my *To Move a Nation: The Politics of Foreign Policy in the Administration of John F. Kennedy* (Garden City, N.Y.: Doubleday, 1967). On interest groups, see also Graham Wootton, *Interest Groups: Policy and Politics in America* (Englewood Cliffs, N.J.: Prentice Hall, 1985); Peter Navarro, *The Policy Game* (New York: John Wiley, 1984); Jeffrey M. Berry, *The Interest Group Society* (Boston: Little, Brown, 1984); and Alan J. Cigler and Burdett A. Loomis, eds. *Interest Group Politics* (Washington, D.C.: Congressional Quarterly Press, 1986).

15

THE PRESS
AND TELEVISION

No one doubts that whoever controls the press wields power. The Constitution guaranteed freedom of the press precisely to counter the possibility that those who held political power could perpetuate their power by controlling public opinion through government propaganda. Today, however, the press has become a power center of its own. In fact, many people fear the reverse of what the framers of the Constitution had in mind: that the press itself might so shape public opinion as to control the government and dictate its policies. One senator, Jesse Helms of North Carolina, charged that CBS anchorman Dan Rather had a liberal bias and that he so influenced public opinion and hence government policy that he was a danger to the republic. Helms started a campaign among conservatives to buy enough shares of CBS so that they would become Rather's boss (the attempt failed).

Quite apart from the issue of power, throughout the history of the United States politicians at all levels have complained that the press was either putting them and their policies in an unfavorable light or failing to report their actions accurately. Every president since George Washington has made such charges. Woodrow Wilson said, "I am so accustomed to having everything reported erroneously that I have almost come to the point of believing nothing that I see in the newspapers." Franklin D. Roosevelt could see by their editorials that the owners, publishers, and editors of newspapers were opposed to him, and he was convinced that news stories reflected that hostility. He thus turned to radio and was tremendously effective with his "fireside chats." Harry S. Truman wrote to a reporter, "I wish you'd do a little soul searching and see if at great intervals, the President may be right." John F. Kennedy became so annoyed at the *New York Herald Tribune* that he canceled the White House subscription. Kennedy in fact was so worried that his policies would be filtered through an unsympathetic press that he followed Roosevelt's lead and tried to go over the heads of reporters and editors with the device of the live television press conference. Lyndon B. Johnson's relations with the press were so bad the administration had a "credibility gap." Johnson, less confident of his ability on radio and television than Roosevelt and Kennedy had been, fell back on seeing only a few reporters whom he regarded as friendly. Richard M. Nixon did this too, but he also counterattacked, using Vice President Spiro Agnew as his principal weapon. Agnew and Nixon accused the press of wielding inordinate power over public opinion and doing so irresponsibly, distorting the news to their own political biases. Carrying alliteration to its ultimate, Agnew accused the press of being "nattering nabobs of negativism!" President Carter charged that the press did not seek information in asking questions but sought only to trap him. President Reagan, who was so skilled in dealing with the public and the press that he was called the "Great Communicator," still voiced many of the same complaints and tried to control the circumstances in which members of his administration met with the press. In spite of his reputation of being the "Great Communicator," he actually had fewer press conferences than any president since the practice started. What usually happened was that the press shouted questions at him over the roar of the helicopter engines as he walked across the White House lawn at the start of a weekend visit to Camp David! Reagan held 53 press conferences in his eight years as president. Bush, on the other hand, by June 15, 1991, when he had been president only a year and a half, had already held 45.

The early fear that newspapers might control public opinion was magnified with the advent of television. Now that words could be combined with pictures, the impact on the public seemed likely to be irresistible. This fear led to the rule that equal time must be given to candidates of the major parties, and it meant that the Federal Communications Commission had the power to refuse to renew a station's license if its reporting failed to meet standards of objectivity and fairness.

Similar fears are reflected in the suspicions of Congress about public relations organizations in the Pentagon and other executive departments and agencies. Their worry is that the bureaucracies might evade congressional control or even come to dictate to Congress by manipulating public opinion through propaganda. The fear that political advertising might buy elections has agitated both parties at one time or another. It has also disturbed groups such as Common Cause that seek limits on campaign spending. Numerous books and articles, among them *The Selling of the President, 1968,* have charged that presidential candidates (in this instance Nixon) have been packaged by Madison Avenue advertising firms in new, slick "images" and sold to the public like soap.[1]

GOVERNING THE PRESS: WHO DECIDES?

In the nineteenth and early twentieth centuries, the biases of news stories in some newspapers were unbelievable. Today the political preferences and ideological commitments of owners, publishers, and managers have less to do with what public affairs events are covered, how the stories are written, and where they are placed in the paper than one might think. Large newspapers are usually owned by corporations, which frequently control a chain of papers, and they have a duty to make a profit for their stockholders. Costs are high and competition is stiff. In the words of one study:

> In order to show a profit, papers must have a substantial circulation and a good deal of advertising. . . . Reader attention is gained by emphasizing stories with high human interest appeal – sports, crime, local personalities, and the high-jinks of movie stars. Political news, though it does have a place, is subordinate because most readers are not terribly interested in politics. An excessive emphasis on public affairs, therefore, is unlikely so long as appeal to readers is a prime consideration.[2]

Little space is accordingly given to public affairs; sports, crime, murder, and sex scandals dominate the news. Since a large circulation is essential to make the business pay, the owners, publishers, and managers are reluctant to alienate any particular group of readers, so the space they do allot to public affairs is usually very bland. The exceptions are stories of corruption and sex scandals among public officials. Both get thorough treatment.

Advertisers too seem to be more interested in circulation than in the content of public affairs stories. Business leaders are reluctant to use their advertising to influence the way in which newspapers handle the

---

[1]Joe McGinnis, *The Selling of the President, 1968* (New York: Trident, 1969). See also Gary D. Orren and Nelson W. Polsby, *Media and Momentum: The New Hampshire Primary and Nomination Politics* (Chatham, N.J.: Chatham House, 1987); Richard Armstrong, *The Next Hurrah: The Communications Revolution in American Politics* (New York: Peach Tree Books, 1988); Doris A. Graber, ed., *Media Power in Politics*, Section Three (Washington, D.C.: Congressional Quarterly Press, 1984); Christopher F. Arterton, *Media Politics: The News Strategies of Presidential Campaigns* (Lexington, Mass.: D.C. Heath, 1984); and Richard Joslyn, *Mass Media and Elections* (Reading, Mass.: Addison-Wesley, 1984).

[2]Nelson W. Polsby and Aaron B. Wildavsky, *Presidential Elections: Strategies of American Electoral Politics*, 3rd ed. (New York: Scribners, 1971), p. 74.

news precisely because it might be bad for their business. They are more likely to take their advertising away if a newspaper has alienated a large group of readers, even if they are opposed to the ideology of those readers.

The conclusions seem inescapable: With few exceptions the owners, publishers, managers, and advertisers do not attempt vigorously to influence which or how news stories are written. If the newspaper sells well or the television station's ratings are high, these people will be inclined to overlook differences between the treatment of the news and their own opinions. Readers and listeners, for their part, generally seem to be more interested in stories that are exciting or entertaining: those that deal with sex, crime, and violence.

Of the news on public affairs that is reported, it is not so much the newspaper and television people who determine what is reported and how it is reported, but the highest-level policymakers—presidents and their appointees. They may hold background briefings for the press, leak stories to their favorite reporters, or interpret the news in an attempt to get one policy adopted or another defeated. But this too is only a partial answer, for it is these same people who constantly complain that the press has "irresponsibly" or prematurely reported a story.

In still another sense it is not people at all who make the decisions about reporting but the mechanics of the process of getting out the news, or what James Reston of *The New York Times* calls the "tyranny of technique."[3] What Reston means is that many of the decisions are made by the tradition that stories should answer the questions of "who-what-when-where-and-why," meet the deadline of the afternoon dailies, fulfill the need for a new lead, and satisfy other purely journalistic imperatives.

Some of these traditions derive from the history and mechanics of the wire services, the Associated Press (AP) and the United Press International (UPI). The wire services in most countries were established by the government or, in a few cases, by press entrepreneurs for profit. In America, the AP was founded in 1848 not by the government or an individual but by a number of newspapers as a nonprofit cooperative association that would save them money because one correspondent in a major city or a foreign country could serve them all. Newspapers then were unabashedly partisan; since the AP had to serve everyone it had to avoid offending the extreme right, the extreme left, the people in between, and all sorts of religious and regional biases. Accordingly, the tradition grew that AP stories would stick to the "facts" without bias, partisanship, or "interpretation." In turn, the wire services set the tone

---

[3]James Reston, *The Artillery of the Press: Its Influence on American Foreign Policy* (New York: Harper & Row for the Council on Foreign Relations, 1967). The phrase is the title of Reston's second chapter.

for nearly all newspapers in the country. They defined what was "normal" and shaped what was taught in journalism schools.

The wire services had a profound effect on American journalism. Reston explains that the wire services must serve

> a vast continental country covering four different time zones, with some parts facing on the Pacific and some on the Atlantic, some looking north and some south, some living in the Arctic and some in tropical climes. Accordingly, news has to be written so that a news story on, say, international trade has to be filed at length for maritime cities interested in international commerce and in brief for agricultural towns concerned primarily with the price of corn.[4]

The wire services therefore invented the "headline" or all-purpose story that could be published at length in big city papers, cut in half for papers in the middle-sized cities, and reduced to a paragraph in small towns:

> It created a tradition of putting the most dramatic fact in the story first—the hot angle—and then following it with paragraphs of decreasing importance. Thus it encouraged not a balanced but a startling, even a breathless, presentation of the news, featuring the flaming lead and the big headline.[5]

Television, with its inexorable time pressure that forces reporters to boil down even the most momentous policy decisions to 45 seconds, has made what was once a tendency an iron law. This technique not only distorts the news and omits interpretation and analysis but also tends to downplay or even ignore why something happened in the first place. Reporters trained in the who-what-when-where-and-why wire service technique must often leave out the why.

The Tendency to Simplify and Dramatize

Stories on public affairs are bland and uninformative when it comes to providing interpretation, analysis, or an explanation of why something happened. At the same time they simplify and highlight any fact that has an element of drama. Drama is conflict. Drama is winning and losing. When the Senate in 1981 voted to support President Reagan's deal to sell Saudi Arabia five AWACS airplanes and associated arms worth $8.5 billion, the stories drew blazing headlines that Reagan had won an enormous victory. Careful and thorough readers could learn that the planes had something to do with radar and warning of air attack, that

---

[4]Ibid.
[5]Ibid., p. 15.

they were related to the defense of the Saudi oil fields, that Israel objected strongly to the deal, that the Reagan administration defended the deal on the grounds that it would further the "peace process" between Israel and the Arab states, and that the president's prestige would suffer if the Senate rejected the deal. But there were few clues in the stories as to the military strategy that made the AWACS so important, just why the deal would further the "peace process," and, if so, why Israel objected so strongly—or even what the acronym AWACS stood for (Air-borne Warning and Control System).

If the print press is bad in these respects, TV is even worse. In January 1984, for example, the eight Democratic candidates for president held a three-hour debate in New Hampshire in preparation for the primary. Next morning NBC news reported the clash between John Glenn and Walter F. Mondale, in which Glenn criticized Mondale for the cost of the programs he advocated and for his call for legislation to protect the American automobile industry from foreign competition and Mondale called Glenn's figures "baloney." NBC also reported the criticism several of the candidates had of one of the moderators, Phil Donahue, "who prodded and challenged the candidates as if they were guests on his syndicated television show." The commentaries centered on whether Mondale was hurt or Glenn was helped by the debates, but not a word was said about anything that any of the candidates said on the issues.

When Congress overrides or fails to override a president's veto, to give another example, the press plays it up even when the bill is not very important. This is because someone "won" and someone "lost." Americans like sports; in sports people win or lose.

In the 1988 Bush-Dukakis campaign, the effect of TV was even more baleful. TV's demand for stories that were dramatic but still no more than 30 seconds long led to the "sound bite." The speech writers for the candidates strove to provide one punchy, dramatic, quote: the sound bite. The one that is best remembered from the 1988 campaign was George Bush's "No more taxes! Read my lips!" Most sound bites are also delivered against some appropriately dramatic background. Thus Bush demanded that school children be required to recite the pledge of allegiance during a visit to a factory that manufactured American flags.

Drama, finally, is corruption and sex. When a young woman who had worked as a typist on a committee chaired by Representative Wayne Hayes revealed that she could not type and that her real job was to be Hayes's mistress, the story was at the top of the news in every newspaper and on every television and radio program. Gary Hart was knocked out of the 1988 Democratic primaries by the revelation that he had spent a weekend with an attractive model who was not his wife.

If anyone in high office takes a bribe or is involved in an activity that suggests a conflict of interest, the same thing happens. It is right and proper that the full glare of publicity be turned on such doings. The point is that in cases of corruption and sex, we can be sure it will be, but when it comes to a new proposal for a national health care bill or for a new source of energy, we cannot be sure at all that the story will get more than a one-paragraph mention on page 33.

These factors influence all editors in the same way. They choose which stories to print and decide how to cut them and where to place them in the paper or on television or radio for the same reason: not to alienate readers and advertisers. This makes them deemphasize analysis and interpretation and emphasize the dramatic and sensational.

These criticisms of the press are not completely fair, however. Owners, editors, columnists, and reporters have pride in their profession and a commitment to public service. This pride and commitment are both demonstrated by the fact that the foregoing criticisms are drawn from their own books and articles. In truth the people of the news world find themselves caught on the horns of a dilemma. The mass public is interested in drama, conflict, violence, and sex. A newspaper or a television or radio station that fails to report such matters fully and concentrates instead on reporting and interpreting the more serious aspects of public affairs may find that their audience and advertisers will go elsewhere.

The News Magazines

The weekly news magazines are different from newspapers, TV, and radio in a number of ways. They have a national rather than a local audience. Since they must cover national events, they cannot avoid covering public affairs as well as sports, medicine, science, the arts, education, and business. Newspapers have other subjects with which to titillate their readers and thus can afford to be neutral on public affairs to the point of dullness. The news magazines, however, must find ways of making public affairs exciting and interesting without alienating significant groups of readers, which is no mean trick.

Some news magazines have made their reporting interesting by developing a jazzy writing style full of interest-piquing detail, even though the detail is usually totally irrelevant to the issue. "United States Ambassador to Transylvania, J. Thomas Jones, turned off his alarm clock last Friday morning, opened the drawer of his bedside table, took out his Magnum .38 pistol, and checked to see that it was full of ammunition." The story then goes on to describe the ambassador's meeting with the prime minister of the country. The ambassador certainly did not take his pistol to that meeting, but the reader is left with an impression that diplomacy in Transylvania is really a James Bond, Agent 007, affair.

Some weeklies maintain reader interest by slanting their stories. In part the slant is ideological. The bulk of their readers tend to be white

Anglo-Saxon Protestants (WASPs) who are upper-income, business and professional suburbanites. Such people tend to be conservative, so the weeklies tend to slant the news in that direction. Moreover, the slant is also likely to point up and exaggerate the qualities of the story that make it entertaining. As a reporter for one of the top news magazines remarked in disgust after the main office had refused to correct a story that he had discovered was grossly inaccurate, "My editors prefer drama to truth."[6]

The Need to Manufacture News

The mechanics of publishing may also force reporters to manufacture news that deemphasizes interpretation and analysis and emphasizes simplification and drama. Douglass Cater tells a story of a treaty before the Senate for ratification. The Senate voted to approve the treaty at 3:30 P.M., in time for the headlines of the late afternoon papers in the big cities but not in time for the smaller papers. The latter would demand a new "top" for the story when they printed it the next day. The AP reporter looked over the transcript and found that one senator had been particularly critical of the treaty. He then started trying to find a senator who would attack the first senator's remarks on the ground that they weakened the president's authority, for such a comment would give the story a new lead. He telephoned seven senators before he was able to find one who was willing to make the criticism. But the story was hardly spontaneous or even really true; the reporter had thought it up and gone to considerable effort to find a senator to make it happen.[7]

But creating stories is not new in the news world. In his autobiography Lincoln Steffens tells how he and another reporter around the turn of the century almost ruined the budding career of Theodore Roosevelt, who was then police commissioner of New York City, by creating a "crime wave" simply by reporting stories that were usually ignored as too minor to publish.

GOVERNMENT AND THE PRESS

The relation between the press and the government is complex. In the first place, government officials have as much to do with what makes the headlines as reporters do. After all, their decisions and actions are what the news people are reporting. Officials also shape the news by what they

---

[6]Personal communication.

[7]Douglass Cater, *The Fourth Branch of Government* (Boston: Houghton Mifflin, 1959), pp. 108–110.

say to reporters, what they emphasize, and what they omit. It is thus not only reporters who omit analysis and interpretation, simplify, play on the dramatic, and even manufacture stories. In the spring of 1976, just before the Defense Department budget was to be considered by Congress, stories coming out of the Pentagon said that the Soviet Union had "vastly" increased its defense spending and that if Congress cut the defense budget, the United States would become a "second-rate power." A good example of simplification and dramatization!

It is also not just the press that creates a crisis by reporting something that is normally ignored. It is no accident that during the cold war Soviet submarines were invariably sighted off the Atlantic coast of the United States shortly before the hearings on the budget for the Navy. As for manufacturing stories, the example of Senator Joseph McCarthy and his Communist witch hunt is still the best. That set of lies created one of the longest-lasting domestic crises since World War II.

Less important stories are rather frequently manufactured by people in the first ring of policy making. Critics of Secretary of State Henry Kissinger accused him of giving the press background briefings that led them to report that war in the Middle East could be expected momentarily, so that when peace rather than war broke out, he would get the credit. This particular accusation may go too far, but similar things happen often enough. Each year the House Appropriations Committee cuts the budget for items on which contracts have already been let in accord with previous legislation. The press reports their noble action, and a little while later the cuts are quietly restored in supplemental appropriations.

The Press as an Arm of the Government

One of the great fears of the media is that they might be used by the government to carry out its decisions. The media want to be the critics of government and would go to great lengths to avoid becoming an instrument of government, but they know they are being used by the White House, the cabinet, Congress, and bureaucrats. And there is little they can do about it. Officials are their source for news, and officials use them to transmit what the officials see as news in the form they want to be made public.

What government officials tell reporters *is* news, although it may not be all the story, and it may be colored. The best the press can do is to try to learn what may have been left out and to find and report opposing views. When the secretary of agriculture releases an optimistic review of administration farm policy, the press prints it. But then reporters ask whether he left something out and look for farmers or other officials who think the farm policy is a disaster.

The only time the press willingly becomes an arm of the government is when they do not publish information in the area of foreign and defense policy that might be dangerous to national security. Even here, however, government officials have accused the press of being reckless by defining national security too narrowly. This particular charge is open to debate. The Nixon administration was very angry with *The New York Times* for printing the Pentagon Papers, a collection of documents on the history of U.S. involvement in Vietnam. It even attempted to get the Supreme Court to block publication. But the Court refused and was undoubtedly right. It may be that the Pentagon Papers were embarrassing to the government and that they damaged the good opinion of the United States in a number of countries. But since the papers dealt with past actions, it is doubtful that their publication actually harmed the nation's security.

The same issue was involved when President Reagan ordered a clamp down on dealings with the press in January 1982. Thereafter no member of the Reagan administration dealing with national security matters could meet with the press without permission, and afterward a full report of what was said had to be submitted to the president. The White House said that disclosure of classified documents had become a "problem of major proportions," but when pressed for an example cited only the leak to the press of the decision not to sell advanced military aircraft to Taiwan.[8] The example illustrates the true nature of the problem. The leak had occurred while a high American official was actually en route to Peking to explain the decision to the Communist leaders of China, who had objected to the possibility of such arms sales. It was undoubtedly embarrassing to the administration to be scooped, but clearly the leak had not endangered U.S. security.

President Bush successfully limited press coverage of the Persian Gulf War by establishing military press censorship pools that carefully controlled the information made available to television networks and newspapers. Because of these restrictions on the media, the press played a much less significant role in the Gulf War than it had in the war in Vietnam.

Presidents continue to try to stop leaks despite the failures of all modern presidents, including Nixon, who actually created a small organization in the White House specifically instructed to stop leaks (accordingly nicknamed the "plumbers"). One of the first statements Bush made after the election was that he would tolerate no leaking in *his* administration. *New York Times* columnist William Safire, a Republican, like Bush, who had served as a speech writer for President Nixon was apparently one of Bush's targets, since he had revealed many of Bush's staffing plans

---

[8]*The New York Times,* January 13, 1982, p. B22.

in a column three weeks before the election. Safire found Bush's statement that he would tolerate no leaks extraordinarily naive for a man who had served so many years in Washington, and Safire devoted a whole article on the subject of leaks, ending by naming his source:

> The leaker, Mr. President-elect, is my left thumb. I suck on it, stare at the wall, put myself in your shoes, bounce the ideas sucked out of my thumb off a few detail-savants, read the papers, listen up at dinner parties, calibrate the horror all this stimulates among your aides, and—springo!—a massive leak, and it's hell to pay for weeks around the Oval Office.[9]

Media Self-restraint

On matters dealing with planned actions, the press has usually been rather careful. James Reston writes that he and *The New York Times* knew that the United States was flying the U-2, the high-altitude reconnaissance plane that took pictures of Soviet missile development during the Eisenhower years. In fact, Reston says, they knew about it a full year before a U-2 was shot down in 1960, but they did not publish the fact. The *Times* also learned that President Kennedy planned to blockade Cuba to prevent the Soviets from completing a nuclear missile base there in 1962 and, a year earlier, that Kennedy had approved the plan to land a CIA-trained force of exiled Cubans at the Bay of Pigs. In each case the president asked the *Times* not to publish the information on the grounds that it would ruin the operation, and the *Times* did what he asked. Later Kennedy said he was glad they had agreed to his request in the case of the Cuban missile crisis but sorry they had in the case of the Bay of Pigs, for the United States achieved a brilliant success in the former and suffered a miserable fiasco at the latter. Advance publicity would have turned the former into a defeat and forced cancellation of the latter.

As a practical matter the press will always be extremely careful about publishing information concerning U.S. plans for future moves in defense and foreign affairs. Whether presidents are right or wrong, it is they who are elected to make such decisions, not the *Times*. If the *Times* had published the missile story, it would have been usurping the power of the elected president. If the Soviets had succeeded in establishing a missile base and then used it to blackmail the United States on some vital issue of foreign policy, many people would have demanded that the *Times'* publisher and editors be brought to trial for treason. And if the *Times* had revealed the plans for the Bay of Pigs operation, thus forcing

---

[9]William Safire, "Bush's Secret Leaker," *The New York Times*, December 19, 1988, p. A17. For a series of articles on how the press influences public policies, see Doris A. Graber, ed., *Media Power in Politics*, Section Five; and James Deakin, *Straight Shots: The Reporters, the White House, and the Truth* (New York: William A. Morrow, 1989).

its cancellation, the paper would not have been credited for preventing a disaster but would have been blamed for ruining a victory! And how could anyone prove or disprove either charge?

FREEDOM OF THE PRESS

Freedom of the press has traditionally meant the freedom to express opinions contrary to those of the government. In America this battle has long since been won. One study of the press in ninety-four countries found that the American press was one of the sixteen that enjoyed the most freedom.[10] In fact, some observers believe that the American press enjoys a bit too much freedom. In Great Britain the libel laws are very strict, and the press is restrained in what they say and write about public figures. Public officials often sue. In addition, Great Britain has an Official Secrets Act that is much stricter than such legislation in the United States. By contrast, in the United States the press can write a false story about a public official without fear of being sued successfully unless the libeled official can show beyond doubt that the press printed the story with "reckless disregard" for its truth or falsity, which is very difficult to substantiate.[11]

Accordingly, in the United States today the heart of the controversy is the freedom of the press to obtain information from the government and freedom of reporters to keep secret the identities of their sources. In 1966 Congress passed the Freedom of Information Act, which required government agencies to make available information that did not concern national security, personnel files, investigatory records, an agency's "internal" documents used in arriving at a decision, and certain other materials. Shortly afterward the Supreme Court held that the courts had no right to determine whether the president or other executive branch official's act of classifying a document "secret" was valid or done merely to cover up errors or misjudgments.[12] In 1974 Congress overrode President Ford's veto of a measure that gave the courts the right to make their own judgment of whether information in fact involved national security. Other measures were passed that were designed to make it easier to obtain information that did not involve national security. But the tendency in the past few years has been in the opposite direction, toward tightening controls over information.

---

[10]R. L. Lowenstein, *World Press Freedom*, publication no. 11 (Columbia, Mo.: Freedom of Information Center, 1967).

[11]*The New York Times* v. *Sullivan*, 376 U.S. 254 (1964).

[12]*EPV* v. *Mink*, 410 U.S. 73 (1973).

The problem will undoubtedly continue. Periodically the executive tries to stop leaks. The attempts by Reagan and Bush are the most recent. Every president has tried. But the press will continue to have a strong incentive to dig out what the government would like to keep secret. People inside the government will also continue to have strong convictions on policy, and when policy decisions go against them, they will continue to try to appeal to the general public—by leaking to the press.

THE POWER OF THE PRESS

Research on the effect of the press on how people vote or on how Congress, the courts, and the executive make policy decisions has not been very revealing.[13] One reason is probably that there are so many influences at work. It is thus extraordinarily difficult to separate out the exact effect of the press alone, since its influence is indirect rather than direct. However, even though the press and television may not change beliefs, they do seem to reinforce them.[14] Also, one study indicates that a newspaper endorsement of a candidate in some circumstances might add as much as five percentage points to what the candidate would otherwise have received.[15] At the same time, there is simply no question that press coverage and especially TV coverage enormously increase a candidate's name recognition—and that all candidates behave accordingly.

In assessing the power of the press, the press itself would stress its limitations and restraints. Many thoughtful journalists and scholars have written extensively about both.[16] Members of the press would also point out that power within the press is diffused. Publishers, owners, editors, reporters, advertisers, readers and viewers, and the policymakers themselves all have a voice in what is reported and how it is reported. The press is far from being monolithic. During the Vietnam war, for example, it had its full share of both hawks and doves.

---

[13]See, for example, Thomas E. Patterson and Robert D. McClure, *The Unseeing Eye: The Myth of Television Power in National Elections* (New York: G. P. Putnam, 1976).

[14]David O. Sears and Richard E. Whitney, "Political Persuasion," in *Handbook of Communication,* eds. Ithiel de Sola Pool et al. (Chicago: Rand McNally, 1973).

[15]Robert S. Erikson, "The Influence of Newspaper Endorsements in Presidential Elections: The Case of 1964," *American Journal of Political Science,* Vol. 20 (May 1976).

[16]Reston, *Artillery of the Press;* Cater, *Fourth Branch of Government;* Bernard C. Cohen, *The Press and Foreign Policy* (Princeton, N.J.: Princeton University Press, 1963); and George F. Will et al., *Press, Politics, and Popular Government* (Washington, D.C.: American Enterprise Institute, 1972). Also see J. Herbert Altschull, *Agents of Power: The News Media in Human Affairs* (New York: Longmans, 1984); and Austin Ranney, *The Channels of Power: The Impact of Television on American Politics,* (New York: Basic Books, 1983).

Yet the press obviously does have great power. In some areas it has much the same kind of power as ordinary interest groups. It also has two additional powers that are particularly potent. One might at first think that one of these is the power to editorialize, or to persuade by voicing opinions. But most interest groups have this kind of power. Most can raise money to advertise; if not, they can attempt to persuade in person. Furthermore, editorials seem to have only a modest effect in changing people's minds, as will be illustrated when voting behavior is considered.

Focusing Attention

The first of the two particularly potent powers of the press is the power to turn the spotlight on a certain problem or issue, as Lincoln Steffens did when he created his crime wave. When the press shares a measure of agreement, it has the power to move an issue to a position near the top of the national agenda for government action. Even if the crisis has been created by the press, the government must deal with it. The reporters and editors of an important newspaper such as *The New York Times* or the *Washington Post* (which are read by everyone in Washington) could undoubtedly force changes in, say, welfare legislation by diligently searching out and reporting every abuse of the laws they could find. The few studies that have looked at the correlation between what people thought were the important issues and what the newspapers and television had been saying were the important issues show that correlation to be high.[17]

Playing the News

The second of the two significant powers of the press is the way the press can "play" the news. Consider what happened in Vietnam at the time of the Tet offensive in 1968. During the Vietnamese New Year, called Tet, the Communists launched an offensive on some of the major cities and also put a few guerrillas inside the compound of the American embassy. Most of the press played this news very dramatically, implying that the Viet Cong were 10 feet tall and could strike anywhere in Vietnam almost at will. The stories also suggested that the optimism that had been coming from the American embassy and military in Saigon and from the Pentagon, the State Department, and the White House in Washington had been exposed as false. The Johnson administration, on the other hand, interpreted the offensive as a "desperate last gasp" of a defeated enemy, comparing it to the German attack at the Battle of the Bulge in

---

[17]Maxwell E. McCombs and Donald R. Shaw, *The Emergence of American Political Issues: The Agenda Setting Function of the Press* (St. Paul, Minn.: West, 1977).

World War II, and as a total failure resulting in prohibitive casualties for the Communists.

Which of these interpretations was to win the struggle for general acceptance was vitally important to the Johnson administration. If the enemy was virtually defeated and victory only a few months away, public and congressional support could undoubtedly be sustained. But if the Viet Cong were stronger than ever, which meant that the war would have to go on for a long time at even higher levels of sacrifice, then public and congressional support would almost immediately collapse.

With the benefit of hindsight it can be argued that both interpretations were gross oversimplifications. But in the end it was the press interpretation that prevailed. As a result even more members of Congress, leaders outside of government, and the attentive public joined the opposition to the war and so helped create the situation that caused President Johnson to initiate negotiations in Paris and to withdraw from the presidential race of 1968.

Thus the conclusion seems inescapable that how the press plays the news, or the interpretation of events implied in the story itself, can be a decisive influence on policy. It shares this power with the first ring of policymakers, but this very fact is a measure of just how much power the press wields. In fact, its power to influence events in the way it plays the news is sometimes deplored by the press itself. An editorial in *The New York Times* went so far as to say that it was press play rather than votes that made Jimmy Carter a front-runner for the Democratic nomination in 1976:

> New Hampshire is one of the smallest states in the Union. Fewer than one-third of its voting-age population participated in this year's primary. Former Gov. Jimmy Carter of Georgia polled less than one-third of the Democratic votes. Yet that showing—based on no more votes than would be cast in a few Assembly districts in Brooklyn—was appraised with the utmost gravity and sufficed to get Mr. Carter on the cover of both national newsmagazines.[18]

The Tension Between Reporters and Policymakers

Policymakers are impelled to portray their decisions and actions in a favorable light; they would be less than human if they did not. Their incentive is especially high to conceal the disagreements that occurred in developing a policy and to emphasize the final agreement. For the press, however, it is the conflict inherent in the political process that is dramatic and worthy of attention. Thus the incentive for the press is to

---

[18]*The New York Times,* "The Week in Review," March 7, 1976, p. 14.

report, emphasize, and even exaggerate the disagreements as they happen.

The fact that reporters and policymakers have different goals yet are both impelled to simplify and dramatize inevitably leads to tension between them. Woodrow Wilson's complaint that everything was reported erroneously and Kennedy's canceling a White House subscription can be matched with examples from most of the other presidents. Not only do presidents and other policymakers complain of inaccuracy, they often come to believe that the press is interested only in drama and that press questions are often designed to trick them into some silly error that will get a headline.

The Deeper Dilemma

But this kind of tension is only at the surface. Below lies a deeper tension that poses a dilemma in any free society. Those who are directly engaged in making policy, as we have said, must try to build a coalition among various power centers. Through compromise, logrolling, and other processes they try to achieve consensus on a particular policy. Presidents, members of Congress, the bureaucracy, and interest groups must bargain, find allies, make compromises, and do many other things to build a consensus strong enough to pass legislation or adopt policies. All this takes time. A certain amount of secrecy is also essential to allow for the necessary negotiating, bargaining, and pulling and hauling. Participants in the policy-making process know that if their constituents learn too soon how far they have to back down and what compromises they have to make, there may be no agreement at all and hence no policy decision.

In foreign affairs at certain times some measure of secrecy simply *must* be maintained, and not just on matters involving military security. Henry Kissinger, for example, defended the extraordinary secrecy surrounding the negotiations that led to Nixon's visit to China and subsequent measures to "normalize" relations on the grounds that premature exposure would have permitted the China lobby, which was sympathetic to the regime in Taiwan and which opposed the policy, to mount a campaign that might well have made the trip impossible.

But similar pleas for a certain amount of secrecy are heard not only in the realm of foreign affairs. Members of Congress frequently argue that premature exposure of the negotiating, bargaining, and compromising they must use to get a health care bill or a tax reform bill passed would give narrow interest groups the ammunition they need to kill the measure entirely.

The press, on the other hand, is driven to learn and reveal developments as they occur. But this is done not only to create a blazing headline or sell papers. It is true that presidents and not *The New York Times* are elected to make foreign policy, but no one argues that making foreign policy should be the monopoly of presidents. If we are to be a democracy, we want as wide participation as possible in the making of all kinds of policy. Kissinger may have been right in saying that premature disclosure would have given the China lobby an opportunity to prevent a warming toward Communist China. But in a democracy doesn't the China lobby too have a right to participate? But if secrecy is maintained, how can they take part? The same is true of the Bay of Pigs incident, the Cuban missile crisis, and the war in the Persian Gulf.

As for the argument by members of Congress that premature disclosure by the press permits "narrow interest groups" to sabotage legislation, this position too has another side. It is frequently the "premature exposure" by an alert press that prevents "narrow interest groups" from slipping through some measure that gives them special benefits at the expense of everyone else. If anyone other than the top officials is to have a say in the decision, the public must be informed of what is going on before the decision is final. How can the general public, interest groups, affected citizens—or for that matter members of Congress—have any input if the decision is made in total secrecy?

The dilemma, then, is real. There is a persuasive argument that the political process of policy making requires a certain amount of secrecy, as the framers of the Constitution realized from the opening moment of the convention, when they passed a resolution that the proceedings should be "entirely secret." Yet there is an equally persuasive argument that without publicity at a certain stage, people with a stake in the policy who are not in the innermost circles will have no voice at all, and the fundamental purpose of democracy will be denied. What gives this dilemma its almost exquisite irony is that no one has yet found a solution.

16

PUBLIC OPINION

Although public opinion is not a power center as such, the opinion of the public seems likely to influence policy decisions. At the very least the power centers involved in making policy decisions will take public opinion into account. But what precisely do people mean by the expression "public opinion"? Obviously the "public" has opinions about many things, including basketball players, rock stars, soap, and candy bars. But it is not the public's opinion about these things that elected officials, journalists, and scholars have in mind when they speak of public opinion. They are concerned rather with the opinion of the mass of the population on public policies and problems and the people who deal with them. V. O. Key, Jr., put it simply: Public opinion is nothing more than "those opinions by private persons which governments find it prudent to heed."[1]

---

[1]V. O. Key, Jr., *Public Opinion and American Democracy* (New York: Alfred A. Knopf, 1961), p. 14. In addition to the works cited, this chapter draws on the following: Edward Dreyes, *Political Opinion and Behavior* (Belmont, Calif.: Wadsworth, 1970); Robert Chandler, *Public Opinion—Changing Attitudes on Contemporary Political and Social Issues* (New York: Bowker, 1972); Bernard Hennessy, *Public Opinion* (Duxbury, Mass.: Duxbury Press, 1975); and Dennis Ippolito, *Public Opinion and Responsible Democracy* (Englewood Cliffs, N.J.: Prentice Hall, 1976). On the methods to gauge public opinion, see also H. L. Nieburg, *Public Opinion: Tracking and Targeting* (New York: Praeger, 1984). On how the beliefs of workers affect their voting behavior, see Craig Reinarmas, *American States of Mind: Political Beliefs among Private and Public Workers* (New Haven, Conn.: Yale University Press, 1987). See also, Barry Sussman, *What Americans Really Think and Why Our Politicians Pay No Attention* (New York: Pantheon Books, 1988); Paul R. Abramson, *Political Attitudes in America: Formation and Change* (San Francisco: W. H. Freeman, 1983); Daniel Yankelovich and Sidney Harman, *Starting with the People* (Boston: Houghton Mifflin, 1988) and Albert Cartril, *The Opinion Connection: Polling, Policy and the Press*

(footnote continues on page 267)

POLITICAL SOCIALIZATION

What affects the way people think about issues of public policy and politics? The process begins on the day of birth. From that time they are surrounded by people and institutions that influence the way they will think about such things: parents, brothers and sisters, friends, neighbors, school, church, and a bewildering variety of other institutions and groups, from the Boy Scouts to the gang that hangs out at the drugstore or local beer parlor. Ethnic background, geographic region, and socioeconomic level also have influence. Social scientists have called the process by which these groups, organizations, and institutions mold the way people think "political socialization," and a great deal of research has been done on the subject. However, here we can only list the major influences.[2]

Family

The foremost institution through which the individual becomes politically socialized is the family. As the infant grows into the child, the child into the adolescent, and the adolescent into the adult, it is the family that is the first link to the outside world. The family attempts to instill values, is the first to interpret public events, and passes on the culture as a whole. The family also attempts to inculcate in the individual its own view of both the society and the political system by which the society is governed.

Peer Group Pressure

People talk about the "generation gap," and there is a general assumption that children tend to rebel against both parents and authority. During the anti-Vietnam student riots in 1968–1969, many people assumed that the students were rebelling against authority, both parental and govern-

---

(Washington, D.C.: Congressional Quarterly, 1991). On the attitudes of women, see Keith T. Poole and L. Harmon Ziegler, *Women, Public Opinion, and Politics: The Changing Political Attitudes of American Women* (New York: Longman, 1985).

[2]See, for example, Robert W. Connell, *The Child's Construction of Politics* (Forest Grove, Ore.: International Scholarly Book Services, 1975); Richard Dawson, *Political Socialization, An Analytical Study* (Boston: Little, Brown, 1969); David Easton and Jack Dennis, *Children in the Political System* (New York: McGraw-Hill, 1969); Mary Ellen Goodman, *Race Awareness in Young Children* (New York: Macmillan, 1964); Edward Greenberg, *Political Socialization* (New York: Atherton, 1970); Herbert Hyman, *Political Socialization* (New York: The Free Press, 1959); Lawrence Kohlber, "Moral and Religious Education and the Public Schools: A Developmental View," in *Religion and Public Education* ed. Theodore Sizer (Boston: Houghton Mifflin, 1967); Kenneth Langton, *Political Socialization* (New York: Oxford University Press, 1969); Seymour Lipset, *Political Man: The Social Bases of Politics* (Baltimore: The Johns Hopkins University Press, 1981); and Orit Ichilor, ed., *Political Socialization, Citizenship and Democracy* (New York: Teacher's College Press, 1990).

mental. But a surprisingly large number of the leaders of the student revolt were the sons and daughters of politically radical parents. The mother of one of the leaders of the upheaval at Columbia University, for example, referred to him proudly as "my son, the revolutionary." Bettina Aptheker, a leader of the riots at the University of California at Berkeley, was the daughter of a longtime member of the Communist party and a famous radical in his own right, Herbert Aptheker. Referring to the way they were brought up as radicals, student leaders of the period used to say that when they were babies their parents had put them in "red diapers." In general, the "generation gap" seems to be another example of "journalistic hype."[3]

Religion

Whether it is the church or the family that instills religious values, those values also have their effect on political attitudes. The Jewish community tends to be liberal on most issues, both economic and those concerned with liberties and rights. Catholics tend to be liberal on economic issues but less so on the others. Protestants tend to be more conservative on the full range of issues. Jews are overwhelmingly Democrats. Catholics also tend to be Democrats, while white Protestants in the North tend to be Republicans.[4]

Schools

Schools, as one would expect, play a major role in political socialization. No society would tolerate having its schools used to teach its children that some other form of culture or social and political system was better. The spectrum of teaching ranges from deliberate indoctrination on specific issues to a rather general inculcation of positive attitudes toward the particular country, its government, and its general culture and attitude system.[5]

---

[3]On "red diapers," see Kenneth Kenniston, *Young Radicals: Notes on Committed Youth* (New York: Harcourt, Brace, 1968); on "journalistic hype," see Robert S. Erikson and Norman R. Luttbeg, *American Public Opinion: Its Origins, Content, and Impact* (New York: John Wiley, 1973), pp. 135–136.

[4]Robert S. Erikson and Norman R. Luttbeg, *American Public Opinion: Its Origins, Content, and Impact,* 2nd ed. (New York: John Wiley, 1979), and Garret Ward Sheldon, *Religion and Politics: Major Thinkers on the Relation of Church and State* (New York: P. Lang, 1990).

[5]Robert D. Hess and Judith V. Torney, *Development of Basic Attitudes and Values Toward Government and Citizenship During the Elementary School Years,* pt. 1 (Washington, D.C.: U.S. Office of Education, 1965); Roberta S. Siegel, "Image of a President: Some Insights into the Political Views of School Children," *American Political Science Review* (March 1968): 216–226; and Christopher F. Arterton, "The Impact of Watergate on Children's Attitudes Toward Political Authority," *Political Science Quarterly* (June 1974): 269–288. The generally accepted view that socialization processes foster the status quo has been
(footnote continues on page 269)

Culture and Nation

A particular person may end up as a right-wing extremist, a left-wing extremist, or anywhere in between. But it is rare indeed that a person can escape his or her culture and national value system and attitudes. If one has grown up in an Asian culture, one inevitably acquires ways of looking at the world that are different from those of someone raised in a Western European culture. In earlier times, it was the tribe, the village, or the region that was the cultural unit. Today it is the nation-state. Within one nation-state people usually (but not always) speak one language, share a common history, and go through the same educational system; they often also belong to the same church. Karl W. Deutsch, in a pioneering work, argued that the nation-state and nationalism arose from a marked increase in social communication over a wider area than in former times and that it resulted in a shared process of social learning and habit forming.[6] This is why some nation-states, such as Switzerland, that do not share a single language may still have a single nationalism. Even though the Swiss speak four languages, they are still one nation, Deutsch argues, because

> each of them has enough learned habits, preferences, symbols, memories, pattern of landholding and social stratification, events in history, and personal associations, all of which together permit him to communicate more effectively with other Swiss than with the speakers of his own language who belong to other peoples.

To illustrate this point Deutsch quotes the editor of a prominent German-Swiss newspaper:

> "I found that my German was more closely akin to the French of my [French-Swiss] friend than to the likewise German [Ebenfallsdeutsch] of the foreigner. The French-Swiss and I were using different words for the same concepts, but we understood each other. The man from Vienna and I were using the same words for different concepts, and thus we did not understand each other in the least."[7]

One further role of the nation in political socialization needs to be discussed. As one authority writes,

---

challenged by Robert Coles. See his "What Children Know About Politics," *New York Review of Books,* February 20, March 6, and March 20, 1975. See also Coles's five-volume study, *Children in Crisis* (Boston: Little, Brown, 1968–1978).

[6] Karl W. Deutsch, *Nationalism and Social Communication: An Inquiry into the Foundations of Nationality* (New York: John Wiley, 1953).

[7] Ibid., p. 75.

The nation is today the largest community which, when the chips are down, effectively commands men's loyalties, overriding the claims both of the lesser communities within it and those which cut across it or potentially enfold it within a still greater society, reaching ultimately to mankind as a whole. In this sense the nation can be called a "terminal community" with the implication that it is for present purposes the end point of working solidarity between men.[8]

All those who write on nationalism speak in much the same way of the emotion that it puts into people's loyalties and note that people die in the name of nationalism and that they seem to do so in modern times more willingly than for church, ideology, class, or any other claimant to their loyalty. What remains to be explained, then, is the emotion, for that is obviously a key to the process of political socialization.

People speak of their love of country. Every school child has heard the line: "Breathes there a man with soul so dead, who never to himself has said, 'This is my own, my native land'?" There is beauty in the plains, rivers, and mountains of every country, but all humanity can love the Grand Canyon, Yosemite, the Alps, the Himalayas, or the Andes. The poet's words were referring to more than just the land. They were referring to the people of the land as well, the feeling of identity with others of the same tribe or village or—in modern times—the same nation.

What seems to be happening is that the emotional content of nationalism, which is really political socialization under another name, is related to the reference points around which personality is integrated. The integration of personality, or the development of "identity," which is in fact a major element of political socialization, is a complex process of interaction among the individual and his or her parents, family, peer group, school, and community. Many of the reference points—the values, attitudes, and ways of looking at the world—come from a very broad culture. Some of the values and attitudes around which both the French and the American personalities are integrated, for example, may be the same, deriving from Western culture broadly conceived. But beginning with the latter part of the eighteenth century, the principal value and attitudinal framework for personality integration has been increasingly supplied by the nation-state. Hence the emergence of the emotion.

Nationality becomes part of the self, part of the individual identity. It is the larger identity that permits a person to relate to other human beings effectively. In this sense what social scientists call political socialization is not just political socialization but also cultural socialization. Even more than that, it is part of the integration of personality and

---

[8]Rupert Emerson, *From Empire to Nation: The Rise and Self-assertion of Asian and African People* (Cambridge, Mass.: Harvard University Press, 1960), p. 96.

identity. A Welsh nationalist (it is typical that he was a secondary school teacher of Welsh literature and language), commenting on the steady submersion of things Welsh into the larger British culture and nation, put it most poignantly: "Soon," he said, "there will be no fellow human left who loves the things I love or even hears sounds the way I hear them or sees the earth and sky the way I see them. As a Welshman, death will be more final for me."[9]

Political Culture

Political culture is the set of attitudes and beliefs that makes a person distinctively American, British, French, Japanese, or Chinese. Beginning with Alexis de Tocqueville, a young French aristocrat who wrote an insightful analysis of America and American democracy after a long visit in 1830–1831, both casual observers and social scientists have written about the set of beliefs and attitudes that are peculiarly American. Different observers have given them different names—the "American character," the "American creed," the "American psychocultural syndrome," and so on—but they all refer to what we have called political culture. Considering how difficult it is to be "scientific" about such matters, these commentaries agree on a remarkably large number of characteristics.[10]

First, as Tocqueville noted, Americans have a commitment in their ideals, laws, and customs to what he called "equality of condition"—egalitarianism. Americans as a people aspire to the ideal of equality, or at least equality of opportunity. For long periods, they try to ignore their

---

[9]Personal communication.

[10]Alexis de Tocqueville, *Democracy in America* (New York: Random House, Vintage Books, 1945); Francis J. Grund, *The Americans* (Boston: Marsh, Capen, and Lyon, 1837); Charles Dickens, *American Notes for General Circulation* (New York: Harper, 1842), James Bryce, *American Commonwealth* (New York: Commonwealth, 1908); M. Y. Ostrogorski, *Democracy and the Party System in the United States* (New York: Macmillan, 1910); Andre Siegfried, *America Comes of Age* (New York: Harcourt, Brace, 1927); D. W. Brogan, *Government of the People* (New York: Harper, 1933); Margaret Mead, *And Keep Your Powder Dry* (New York: William A. Morrow, 1943); Geoffrey Gorer, *The American People* (New York: Norton, 1948); Clyde Kluckhohn and Florence R. Kluckhohn, "American Culture: Generalized Orientation and Class Patterns," in *Conflicts of Power in Modern Culture,* ed. Clyde Kluckhohn and Florence R. Kluckhohn, Seventh Symposium of Conference on Science, Philosophy and Religion (New York: Harper, 1947); Gabriel A. Almond, *The American People and Foreign Policy* (New York: Harcourt, Brace, 1950); and Gunnar Mydral, *An American Dilemma: The Negro Problem and Modern Democracy* (New York: Harper, 1944). See also Herbert McClosky and John Zaller, *The American Ethos: Public Attitudes Toward Capitalism and Democracy* (Cambridge, Mass.: Harvard University Press, 1984); W. Russell Neuman, *The Paradox of Mass Politics: Knowledge and Opinion in the American Electorate* (Cambridge, Mass.: Harvard University Press, 1986); and Calvin F. Exoo, ed., *Democracy Upside Down: Public Opinion and Cultural Hegemony in the United States* (New York: Praeger, 1987).

violations of the ideal—slavery, racial prejudice, ethnic prejudice, and all the rest—but their consciences are troubled. Individualism is a second characteristic; that is, Americans tend to value people for what they themselves have accomplished rather than for their family or class. Another American trait is an emphasis on worldly and private values at the expense of public and spiritual values (in spite of periodic outbursts of evangelism) combined with an extraordinary competitiveness. Americans also tend toward a moral dualism. They prefer policies that are both morally "good" and "good for business." The Marshall Plan to help Europe recover from the devastation of World War II, for example, was presented as humanitarian in the short run and good for American trade in the long run. Optimism, a faith in the American dream of success and prosperity for everyone, is another characteristic. Finally, Americans tend to be committed to a rule of law, resenting arbitrariness in government, and to feel the obligations of civic duty.

PUBLIC OPINION

This system of values and attitudes resulting from political (or cultural) socialization is the base from which public opinion is built. But it is only the base. People's opinions on public issues are subject to many additional influences, and the result is not one public opinion but many.

Not One Public but Many

One of the early experiments in public opinion research was conducted in Cincinnati in 1947. The United Nations had just been formed and had been very much in the headlines. Yet a poll showed that about a third of the people in Cincinnati were not familiar with the UN. Then, with the cooperation of a variety of public service organizations like the League of Women Voters, for three months Cincinnati was blanketed with information that gave the answers to the questions in the poll. The poll was then repeated—and the results were exactly the same! About a third of the people remained as ignorant of the United Nations as they had been before. Those who had gone to the lectures, read the articles, and listened to the special radio programs were those who had already been interested and informed.

What the researchers discovered was that there is not one public but many. The third of the people who know little or nothing about the United Nations is not the same third who know little or nothing about, say, agricultural policy. People specialize. For example, a university professor with an international reputation in world politics listened to the 8 A.M. CBS world news on his car radio five days a week from 1965 to

1975. Every morning 4 of the 15 minutes were devoted to sports—baseball, basketball, football, or whatever sport was in season. Yet when asked to name famous sports stars in any field, he could name only one, Joe Namath, then quarterback for the New York Jets. What had happened? During those 4 minutes he let his mind wander to other things. He simply was not interested in sports.[11] In sum, for each set of issues there is what Gabriel A. Almond has called an attentive public: a group of people who are concerned about the particular subject, frequently because it affects them directly, sometimes because it merely interests them.[12]

Intensity of Opinion

Opinions vary in intensity. A small minority who feel intensely about an issue can often exercise more influence than a rather large majority who feel the opposite way less strongly. The classic example has already been mentioned: Polls show that something like 60 percent of the population have favored gun control legislation for several decades, but the tiny minority who are opposed to it feel so intensely that they have so far had their way.

Saliency of Opinion

A characteristic of public opinion closely related to intensity is known as impact, relevancy, or saliency: How directly does the issue affect me? For example, many people might disapprove of inflation in general terms yet not feel intensely about it because their own incomes are increasing at about the rate of inflation. However, retired people living on fixed pensions might find the impact, or saliency, of inflation very high because it impinges directly on their lives.

Volatility of Opinion

Another characteristic of public opinion is whether it is volatile and temporary or stable and permanent. The 1975–1976 revelations that the FBI had engaged in illegal surveillance and electronic bugging of American citizens sparked public outrage. Then feelings died down rather quickly, and no major reforms were actually instituted. Opinion on the Vietnam war changed from rather strong support in 1965–1966 to rather widespread opposition in 1967–1968. A much more stable set of opinions

---

[11]National Opinion Research Center, Chicago, IL, *Cincinnati Looks at the United Nations, 1948*. The experience of the university professor is based on personal communication.

[12]Almond, *The American People and Foreign Policy*.

has been that concerning the place and rights of women in society. The movement to give women the vote took decades to succeed, and it was opposed by a large percentage of women as well as men.

Clustering of Opinion

Public opinion must also be examined to see whether it clusters. Does opinion cluster in a geographical region such as the South or the Middle West, or is it concentrated in urban, rural, or suburban areas? Do opinions on a particular subject cluster among the young, the middle-aged, or the elderly? Do they cluster according to religion, national origin, or ethnic background? Do blue-collar workers have opinions different from those of the higher income, better educated strata? Do opinions on different subjects tend to cluster? If a person favors government programs that provide jobs for everyone, is that person also likely to favor compulsory medical insurance, day care centers, welfare programs, and the food stamp program? If individuals favor most of these domestic programs, are they likely to favor a large defense budget? Or will they want just the opposite? Or is there no relation at all between the two sets of opinions?

Sources of Information on Public Opinion

At one time the major sources of information on public opinion for both elected officials and candidates were the political party organization and friends and acquaintances. Ward heelers, local party activists, and party committee members and chairs received complaints and solicited opinions and then reported them up the ladder of the organization. Officials and candidates asked friends and acquaintances what people were thinking. The most common phrase among professional politicians was, "What have you been hearing lately?"

Interest groups were another major source of information on public opinion. As the government bureaucracy grew and more people served "in the field," it too became a channel of information for officials if not for candidates. The county extension agents of the Department of Agriculture, for example, listened to what farmers were saying. They reported what they heard to Washington, and eventually the more important information reached the secretary of agriculture and the president. Newspapers served as still another channel. Members of Congress have always subscribed to all the newspapers published in their district. For most of our history presidents have made arrangements to be kept informed about what the large papers of the country were saying about the mood and opinions of the public. All these sources are still used, but in recent years the major source of information about public opinion has been the systematic and increasingly "scientific" public opinion polls, of which the Gallup and Louis Harris polls are probably the best known.

Newspapers and other media may subscribe to them and publish their results. In addition, many private polling organizations will conduct a survey on a particular subject for anyone willing and able to pay the fee. There are also academic polling organizations, such as the Survey Research Center of the University of Michigan.

Public opinion polls. It would be physically impossible to ask all of the 183 million Americans eligible to vote what they think. To ask even one out of every twenty would be prohibitively expensive. As a consequence, polls usually question about two thousand people, which is about 1/100,000 (0.00001) of the total number, or 1/1,000 of 1 percent (0.001 percent). Is the thinking of 1/1,000 of 1 percent of the population an accurate reflection of what so many million people think? Within certain fairly small margins of error, it is. The reasons for this lie in the mathematical principles of statistics.

Consider the election of 1988. Let us assume that two weeks before the election, 48 percent of the 183 million people eligible to vote supported Bush, 45 percent supported Dukakis, and the remaining 7 percent were either undecided or supported someone else. According to the mathematics of statistics, if you had randomly asked 100 people whom they were voting for, their answers would have indicated a 95 percent chance that between 38.2 percent and 57.8 percent of the total voting population supported Bush. If you had questioned 1000 people randomly, you could have said there was a 95 percent chance that between 44.9 percent and 51.1 percent supported Bush. If 1 million voters had been randomly sampled, you could have said there was a 95 percent chance that between 47.9 and 48.1 percent were for Bush. When the total number of possible voters is as large as 183 million, a randomly selected sample of moderate size (say, 1000 or 2000) can give a good idea of opinion within the entire 183 million. Increasing the sample beyond this moderate size has only marginal effect. Thus if your sample had included 2000 voters, you could have said there was a 95 percent chance that between 45.8 percent and 50.2 percent of the voters were for Bush (48 percent plus or minus 2.2 percent). In other words, questioning 2000 people randomly gives a 95 percent chance of being within 2.2 percent (either way) of reflecting what all the 183 million think at that time. On election day, 54 percent actually voted for Bush, and 46 percent voted for Dukakis.[13]

Random samples. Accuracy is possible, however, only if the sample is entirely random. If the total number of people to be sampled (what statisticians call the universe or the population) is 200 million and the

---

[13]"Unofficial 1988 Presidential Election Results," *Congressional Quarterly*, November 12, 1988, p. 3245.

sample is to be 2000, one way to obtain a truly random sample is to put all 200 million names in a hat and interview the first 2000 that are picked out blindly. Obviously, locating and interviewing these 2000 would be prohibitively expensive. Therefore, polling firms have devised a number of ways to approximate a random sample. One way is to pick a certain number of geographical units at random. The pollster could pick a number of precincts at random, for example, and then in each precinct pick a certain number of people to interview at random.

Quota samples. However, even this approximation of a truly random sample is expensive, so the polling organizations frequently fall back on a quota sample. From experience and the findings of scholarly research the pollsters try to determine the kinds of backgrounds and situations that are likely to be related to the question to be asked. If the question has to do with taxes, for example, they will probably establish different categories of income (upper, middle, lower) and occupation (business, worker, farmer). If experience shows that the question is related to religious or ethnic background, these categories will be used. Then, using census data, the polling organization chooses a sample that will contain the same percentage of each category that is contained in the population as a whole. If the category is religion, the sample will contain 72 percent Protestant, 21 percent Catholic, 3 percent Jewish, and 4 percent "other"— the same percentages that are found in the population as a whole. Although the quota sample is not as accurate as a purely random sample, it is so much easier and cheaper to use that the pollsters are willing to accept the rather small loss in accuracy. With most of today's polls of the American electorate, there is a 95 percent certainty that the margin of error due to chance alone is plus or minus 2.2 percent.

Reasons for error. Polls can err for reasons other than the nature of the sample. Questions must be carefully phrased to avoid influencing the person being interviewed. Suppose that in the spring of 1992, when everyone assumed that President Bush would be running for a second term, this question were asked in a poll: "If the election were held today, would you vote for President Bush or Governor Mario Cuomo?" The wording of that question would lead some voters to answer "President Bush" simply because of the prestige attached to the title. Other factors that may influence answers include whether the interviewer appears to be a "prying outsider" or "one of us" and whether the person being interviewed has just had a quarrel with a spouse.

The greatest possibility for error today probably lies in how the "undecided" vote is allocated. In presidential election polls usually as many as 5 to 7 percent of the people interviewed will say that they are still undecided even as late as four or five days before the election (some of these may actually have made up their minds but do not want to tell the interviewer). Pollsters try to allocate the undecided vote in the light of experience and other information. But the task is tricky, and in a close election pollsters can be wrong because of this factor alone.

Polls and predictions. The polls do not predict the outcome of an election. They do nothing more than try to measure opinion at the moment the sample is taken. The undecided must finally make up their minds, and people can and do shift their opinions in numbers that may throw a close election one way or another. The results of the 1968 election show the hazards of polling. With Nixon winning 43.4 percent of the vote and Humphrey taking 42.7 percent, a shift of only 0.4 percent, which was well within the margin of error, would have swung the election the other way. Moreover, a study of all the polls taken during the last few weeks before the election shows that opinion was shifting significantly from Nixon to Humphrey. Many analysts are convinced that if the election had been held two or three days later, Humphrey would have won. Thus in 1968 the most that polls could tell you was that the election would be close. In 1984, however, with Reagan running 12 points ahead of Mondale only two weeks before the election and with the percentage of "undecideds" being very small, the total potential error was well below the 12-point difference. Pollsters felt confident that Reagan would in fact win, since it seemed very unlikely that such a large number of voters would switch in just the two weeks remaining. The same thing happened in 1988. Two weeks before the election Bush was running 12 to 13 percentage points ahead of Dukakis, and most political analysts felt that such a big lead could not be overcome in so short a time.

Some political observers worry that the polls might actually influence an election through the "bandwagon" effect. In other words, if the polls show one candidate to be winning, some voters might decide to switch so they could say they voted for the winner or to stay home on the ground that their vote would not make any difference. The possibility is real, but not enough research has been done to determine how important this effect may be.

Ideology and the Clustering of Opinion

In trying to assess the effect of public opinion on government policy, analysts look for how opinions cluster around factors such as ideology, socioeconomic strata, region, age, race, ethnic background, and religion. Under the category of ideology, most analysts talk about "liberals" and "conservatives," concepts they concede are fuzzy but, they argue, still useful. Even so, Americans are at best ambivalent when it comes to being "liberal" or "conservative." One study concluded that Americans were "ideologically conservative" but "operationally liberal."[14] Thus when Americans are asked about their general ideas about the role of government, they tend to be conservative, agreeing with the statement, for example, that "the government has gone too far in regulating business and interfering with the private enterprise system." Yet when asked about specific programs in education, unemployment, poverty, urban renewal, public housing, or medical care that in fact call for more government regulation and interference, a much higher percentage are in favor.

In considering how opinion clusters around liberal and conservative positions, analysts in general look at four categories of issues: the economy, civil liberties, civil rights and race relations, and foreign policy. On economic issues, liberals tend to favor government policy designed to create high levels of employment, higher taxes for the rich, and higher government spending on education, medical care, housing, and the like. Conservatives take the opposite position. On policy about civil liberties, conservatives want the sort of laws that are tougher on criminals, limit provocative speech, and crackdown on drug abuse. Liberals, on the other hand, want to protect the rights of the accused; eliminate penalties on "victimless" crimes such as possessing a small quantity of marijuana; and protect free speech, even if it means letting Nazis, Communists, and Ku Klux Klanners make statements that most Americans find outrageous. On the category of civil rights and race relations, liberals support such policies as strong federal measures for desegregation, equal job opportunities, and compensation to minorities for past injustice. Conservatives want to go more slowly on such matters. On the fourth issue, foreign policy, conservatives favor a tough stance toward potential threats, strong support for governments in Central America and other places under pressure from leftist insurgency movements, and high expenditures on defense. Liberals favor negotiating with our enemies; trying to lead governments under pressure from the left to pay more attention to winning the support of their peoples; and placing somewhat less emphasis on defense spending and more on arms control agreements.

However, research indicates that most people are not consistently liberal or conservative across all four of these categories or even within a single category! However, certain groups do tend to hold a particular combination of views. For example, people who are liberal on economic policy but conservative on policies concerned with cultural tolerance are frequently female manual workers with no more than a high school

---

[14]Lloyd A. Free and Hadley Cantril, *The Political Beliefs of Americans* (New Brunswick, N.J.: Rutgers University Press, 1967), p. 3. For more on presidential election predictors see Paul J. Laurakas and Jack Hadley, eds., *Polling and Presidential Coverage* (Newbury Park, Calif.: Sage, 1991).

education.[15] People who are the reverse—liberal on policies about cultural tolerance and conservative about economic policy—are frequently college-educated business executives. People who are conservative on both issues are frequently rural Protestant Southerners; people who are liberal on both issues are frequently college-educated professionals. From merely reading the newspapers, anyone can find other examples of both groups and individuals who are liberal on one set of issues and conservative on another. The late Senator Henry M. ("Scoop") Jackson of Washington, for example, had an almost perfect liberal voting record on domestic issues, but he was strongly conservative on foreign policy and defense. Ardent members of labor unions tend to be liberal on economic policy and conservative on both law-and-order and civil rights issues. African-Americans tend to be liberal on both economic policy and civil rights but conservative on law-and-order issues.

Opinion clusters also change with time and circumstances. At one time it could be safely assumed that people with a high income, such as business executives, lawyers, doctors, and other professionals, would be conservative. Recent research indicates, however, that some kinds of high-income business executives and professionals—whites under age 30 with a college education—have become more liberal.[16] This particular change has been so dramatic that a number of analysts have talked about the rise of a "new class" of people who hold prominent positions in the society not because of their wealth or their jobs but because of their education and technical expertise. One study of the attitudes of Democrats toward divorce, abortion, homosexuality, marriage between blacks and whites, pornography, the right of a homeowner to refuse to sell to blacks, and protecting the environment, showed "new class" Democrats to be more liberal than "old class" Democrats by anywhere from 38 to 62 percentage points![17]

On foreign affairs and defense, the attitude of the general public also tends to be more tentative and to defer more to the judgment of government leaders than in domestic fields. Because both foreign and defense policies are highly technical and esoteric and because both concern our survival as individuals and as a nation, most people are reluctant to go against the judgment of the country's leaders. They also tend to

---

[15]Seymour Martin Lipset and Earl Raab, *The Politics of Unreason* (New York: Harper & Row, 1970), Chap. 11 passim. See also James A. Stimson, "Belief Systems: Constraint, Complexity, and the 1972 Election," *American Journal of Political Science*, Vol. 19 (1975).

[16]Everett Carl Ladd, Jr., "The Unmaking of the Republican Party," *Fortune*, September 1977.

[17]Everett Carl Ladd, Jr., "The Democrats Have Their Own Two-Party System," *Fortune*, October 1977; and idem, *Where Have All the Votes Gone?: The Fracturing of America's Political Parties* (New York: W. W. Norton, 1982).

err on the side of caution and to change their views slowly. But they do change. The majority, for example, eventually turned against American involvement in the Vietnam war, and there is increasing evidence that many people are questioning traditional defense policies and more willing to consider such alternatives as arms control agreements—especially as they watch the turmoil of change in the Soviet Union.

The American people clearly shared a consensus on foreign and defense policies for almost two decades following World War II that centered on "containing" the Soviet Union through such alliances as NATO, heading off Communism through foreign aid, intervening in "limited wars" against the Communists such as Korea and Vietnam, and maintaining a high level of defense preparedness. It is often remarked that this consensus has broken down and that the American public, like its leaders, are increasingly divided on questions of foreign policy and defense. The usual explanation is that the breakdown began with the Vietnam war. But it may well be that the beginning was not the war but the Cuban missile crisis, for it was then that the United States first came face to face with the realities of the nuclear age. In its aftermath many people began to wonder whether nuclear weapons had so fundamentally changed international politics that traditional policies for dealing with international threats had become obsolete and to begin to speculate about alternatives. If so, the Vietnam war only dramatized one aspect of a reassessment by the American public that had already begun. The events inside the former Soviet Union will probably accelerate this reassessment.

17

THE ELECTORATE

Individual men and women have a variety of ways in which they can influence the decisions of government, such as by belonging to an interest group (see Chapter 14). But it has always been assumed that the primary way that ordinary people can affect governmental policy is by voting. Is this true? Even if the electorate can influence domestic policy, does it really have power to influence decisions in foreign affairs and defense?[1]

WHY PEOPLE VOTE THE WAY THEY DO

No aspect of political science has been the focus of more research than the question of why people vote the way they do. But all this research seems to have generated more controversy than agreement. Roughly speaking,

---

[1]John H. Kessel assembled a rather complete bibliography on the question of the influence of the electorate on policy up to 1972. See his "Comment: The Issues in Issue Voting," *American Political Science Review* (June 1972). For valuable works since then, see James N. Rosenau, *Citizenship Between Elections: An Inquiry into the Mobilizable American* (New York: The Free Press, 1974); Jack DeSario and Stuart Langdon, eds., *Citizen Participation in Public Decision Making* (Westport, Conn.: Greenwood Press, 1987); Kim Ezra Shienbaum, *Beyond the Electoral Connection: A Reassessment of the Role of Voting in Contemporary American Politics* (Philadelphia: University of Pennsylvania Press, 1984); Denise L. Baer and David A. Bositis, *Elite Cadres and Party Coalitions: Representing the Public in Party Politics* (Westport, Conn.: Greenwood Press, 1988); and Richard Flacks, *Making History: The Radical Tradition in American Life* (New York: Columbia University Press, 1988). Other works on the electorate and voting behavior include A. James Reichley, ed., *Elections American Style* (Washington, D.C.: Brookings, 1987); Gerald M. Pomper,
(footnote continues on page 282)

there are two major schools of thought. One school says that people vote the way they do because of social determinants and the personalities of the candidates. The other says that people vote because of their policy preferences on issues, at least when they can learn enough about the issues and the stands of the candidates to make rational decisions.

Social Determinants

Angus Campbell and his associates at the University of Michigan Survey Research Center are among those who have been impressed with the influence of social determinants on voting. They devised a fourfold test of whether policy preferences were the determining factor:

1. Voters must have opinions about a given issue.
2. They must have some idea of the government policy on that issue.
3. They must perceive some difference between the political parties on the issue.
4. They must care enough about the issue to make the first three prerequisites influence their decisions on how to vote.[2]

On the very broad question of the New Deal, for example, a very high percentage of voters met the first three tests. A majority also voted for the candidate and party who shared their opinion: They voted for Roosevelt, Truman, and other Democrats if they favored the New Deal and for the various Republican candidates if they opposed it. Thus the majority of voters met the fourfold test.

On other issues, however, the Michigan group found that the voters did not meet their test.[3] On some questions the majority voted according to their party identification (74 percent of those whose parents were

Voters, Elections, and Parties: The Practice of Democratic Theory (New Brunswick, N.J.: Transaction Books, 1988); Gary C. Jacobson and Samuel Kernell, *Strategy and Choice in Congressional Elections,* 2nd ed. (New Haven, Conn.: Yale University Press, 1982); Peter B. Natchez, *Images of Voting/Visions of Democracy* (New York: Basic Books, 1985). See also, William Flanigan and Nancy H. Zinyale, *Political Behavior of the American Electorate* (Dubuque, Iowa: William C. Brown, 1988).

[2]Angus Campbell et al., *The American Voter* (New York: John Wiley, 1960). See also Sidney Verba and Norman H. Nie, *Participation in America* (New York: Harper & Row, 1972); Warren Miller, "The Political Behavior of Electorate," *American Government Annual 1960–1961* (New York: Holt, Rinehart and Winston, 1960); *Report of the President's Commission on Registration and Voting Participation* (Washington, D.C.: U.S. Government Printing Office, 1963); V. O. Key, Jr., *Politics, Parties and Pressure Groups,* 5th ed. (New York: Crowell, 1964); Lester M. Milbrath, *Political Participation* (Skokie, Ill.: Rand McNally, 1965) and Michael Avey, *The Demobilization of American Voters: A Comprehensive Theory* (New York: Greenwood Press, 1989).

[3]Campbell et al., *American Voter,* pp. 183–187.

identified as belonging to a party regarded themselves as belonging to the same party).[4] They also voted according to their socioeconomic status, their educational background, their interest group affiliation (such as a labor union), their age group, their sex, and their race. They were influenced by the personality of the candidates as well. Eisenhower's infectious grin and winning personality were more important for a lot of voters than their party affiliation, and the Republicans showed they understood this when they adopted the slogan, "I like Ike."

The fact that party affiliation was so important in voting behavior might indicate that the voters were divided ideologically. The Michigan study, however, came to the opposite conclusion. The researchers found that only 2.5 percent of the public at large and 3.5 percent of the voters could be classified as thinking about political matters in such ideological terms as liberal or conservative. Another 9 percent were classified as "near ideologues," which meant that their ideology influenced but did not determine their conclusions. A larger group thought about candidates and parties in terms of being favorable or unfavorable to particular social groups. Another segment identified candidates and parties with "good times" or "bad times." The largest group expressed nothing at all related to issues in their evaluations of candidates and parties; they were loyal to a party, and they talked about the personalities of the candidates.

Coherency of Attitudes

The Michigan survey failed to find any coherency of beliefs. Looking at the different issues—welfare legislation, foreign policy, federal economic programs, minority rights, and civil liberties—they did not find consistently liberal or conservative clusters of attitudes.

Independents

The Michigan survey also shattered the long-cherished belief that independents were particularly intelligent, issue-oriented voters who carefully studied what the candidates and parties said about the issues and voted accordingly:

> Far from being more attentive, interested, and informed, Independents tend as a group to be somewhat less involved in politics. They have somewhat poorer knowledge of the issues, their image of the candidate is fainter, their interest in the campaign is less, their concern over the outcome is relatively slight, and their choice between competing candidates, although it is indeed

---

[4]Ibid., p. 147.

made later in the campaign, seems much less to spring from discoverable evaluations of the elements of national politics.[5]

Implications of the Research

The findings and conclusions of this research and similar research that followed suggested "sociological and psychological models which conceived of voting almost as a 'deterministic' act."[6] The personality of the candidates is equally important, and on occasion, such as with the New Deal legislation, issues play a role. But even so, these conclusions were terribly discouraging to those who believe that in a democracy voters determine what is best for themselves as individuals and for the nation as a whole. It is discouraging even to those who have more modest hopes concerning the role of the people in determining policy and believe that the people at least become aware of the issues, make judgments about the policies and actions of the competing parties, evaluate the qualifications and personalities of the candidates, and then cast a reasoned, rational vote.

The usual interpretation of the findings is that voters vote the party of their parents, grandparents, and even more remote ancestors. They vote according to social determinants: economic status, education, religion, ethnic and racial background, geographic region, and urban, suburban, or rural location, and they are impressed with the personality of the candidates. But they devote no thought (or as little thought as possible) to how they are going to vote. The implication is that the voters behave as unintelligently as a bunch of sheep.

The Rival View: Issue-oriented Voters

Among those who were particularly disturbed by these findings and their implications was the late V. O. Key, Jr. He set out to challenge the "deterministic" interpretation of the behavior of voters in what was to be his last book, *The Responsible Electorate*. Key examined the survey data available on the Roosevelt elections of 1932, 1936, 1940, and 1944; the

---

[5]Ibid., p. 43.

[6]Mark A. Schulman and Gerald M. Pomper, "Variability in Electoral Behavior: Longitudinal Perspectives from Casual Modeling," *American Journal of Political Science*, Vol. 19 (February 1975). Schulman and Pomper were referring specifically to Paul Lazarsfel, Bernard Berelson, and Helen Gaudet, *The People's Choice*, 2nd ed. (New York: Columbia University Press, 1948); Bernard Berelson, Paul Lazarsfeld, and William McPhee, *Voting* (Chicago: University of Chicago Press, 1954); Eugene Burdick and Benjamin Page, "Comment: The Assessment of Policy Voting," *American Political Science Review* (June 1972); Campbell et al., *The American Voter*, and Jeffrey Smith, *American Presidential Elections: Trust and the Rational Voter* (New York: Praeger, 1980).

Truman election of 1948; the Eisenhower elections of 1952 and 1956; and the Kennedy election of 1960 to determine whether policy issues had affected voting.

On the basis of his research, Key concluded that most voters base their choices on policy preferences. They do so, he argued, about as rationally and intelligently as could be expected, given the information available and the frequent ambiguity and confusion about issues as they are presented in campaign debate:

> The perverse and unorthodox argument of this little book is that voters are not fools. To be sure, many individual voters act in odd ways indeed; yet in the large the electorate behaves about as rationally and responsibly as we should expect, given the clarity of the alternatives presented to it and the character of the information available to it.

Key concluded that the electorate is not "straitjacketed by social determinants or moved by subconscious urges triggered by devilishly skillful propagandists." On the contrary, he argued, the electorate is "moved by concern about central and relevant questions of public policy, of governmental performance, and of executive personality."[7]

This "manful effort" on Key's part to show that voters are issue oriented after all met with a reaction that was at best ambivalent. Many political scientists wanted to believe his conclusions, but they were troubled by some of his methods and by the fact that the evidence on which he was forced to rely was inadequate. In subsequent years an impressive number of scholars have interested themselves in the same question.[8] The question is obviously important. The implications if the voters are issue oriented are quite different from those if the voters are not. The question is also an extremely interesting intellectual puzzle.

Key was essentially correct in saying that the voters are issue oriented, at least some of the time, but, issues have undoubtedly been more important recently than they were in the 1950s. The times have become more issue oriented. The parties have become more conscious of issues and are more polarized, and the public is more aware of this polarization. Some researchers concluded that the platforms of the two parties do in fact differ significantly and that voters are generally aware

---

[7]V. O. Key, Jr., *The Responsible Electorate.* (Cambridge, Mass.: Harvard University Press, 1966), p. 7.

[8]A partial listing would include the works of Gerald M. Pomper, Richard W. Boyd, Norman H. Nie, Walter Dean Burnham, Richard A. Brody, Benjamin I. Page, John H. Kessel, Mark A. Schulman, John L. Sullivan, Robert E. O'Connor, Arthur H. Miller, Warren E. Miller, Alden S. Raine, Kristi Andersen, Thad A. Brown, David Repass, Robert Y. Shapiro, John C. Pierce, John Field, and Ronald Anderson.

of the differences.[9] Another study found that rival candidates usually differ sharply on issues and that the elected candidate usually votes in line with his campaign promises.[10] Although it often takes years, the parties do in fact turn most of their platform promises into legislation and policy.[11]

However, the views of the voters on issues are not detailed, and as a result their influence on policy is indirect. The candidates and the parties must anticipate the voters' reaction to their actions. Legislators may become aware that their constituents want something and introduce a bill to achieve it. When this occurs, voters have influenced policy. At the same time there is an interaction between members and their constituents. A member may persuade voters that a particular measure is to their benefit, and the voters' reaction may persuade the member to modify the bill in different ways.

Other findings make similar points. For example, people who move to the suburbs do not automatically become Republicans.[12] There is also evidence that candidates and their parties frequently do offer alternative policies to the voters and that if they are elected they vote in accordance with their proposals. It may thus well be rational for voters to vote the party when they are not too well informed on certain issues or on the views of the particular candidates but have a liberal or conservative preference.[13] At the same time a study of Vietnam as an election issue in 1968 showed that even though the public was intensely interested in the subject, the candidates (Nixon and Humphrey) succeeded in making the war a "nonissue" by taking equally fuzzy stands on it.[14]

One group of researchers believe they have found weakening commitment to party in other evidence. A growing number of people, mainly the young, not only register as independents but act as independents even when they register with a major party. These same researchers also found that issues are increasing in importance.[15] On the other hand,

---

[9]Gerald M. Pomper, *Elections in America: Control and Influence in Democratic Politics* (New York: Dodd, Mead, 1968).

[10]John L. Sullivan and Robert E. O'Connor, "Electoral Choice and Popular Control of Public Policy: The Case of the 1966 House Elections," *American Political Science Review* (December 1972), p. 1264.

[11]Benjamin Ginsberg, "Elections and Public Policy," *American Political Science Review* (March 1976), p. 41.

[12]Richard L. Rubin, *Party Dynamics: The Democratic Coalition and the Politics of Change* (New York: Oxford University Press, 1976), p. 18.

[13]Sullivan and O'Connor, "Electoral Choice," p. 1264.

[14]Benjamin I. Page and Richard A. Brody, "Policy Voting and the Electoral Process: The Vietnam War Issue," *American Political Science Review* (September 1972).

[15]Norman H. Nie, Sidney Verba, and John R. Petrocik, *The Changing American Voter* (Cambridge, Mass.: Harvard University Press, 1976), p. 1.

many have raised questions about the methods and evidence this group of scholars used, and the debate has raged hot and heavy.[16] The fact is that careful research produces evidence to support all of the following propositions:

1. Many voters are indeed influenced by issues, depending on events and circumstances.
2. Party affiliation continues to be a very reliable guide to the way people will vote.
3. Incumbents have a formidable advantage in elections.

Issues. In certain circumstances there can simply be no doubt that people vote on issues. When civil rights is a major topic, blacks overwhelmingly vote for the candidate advocating civil rights. The same is true of labor union questions, farm concerns, and many others when the issue is specific, when it clearly helps or hurts a particular group, when it is debated by the candidates, and when the candidates have clear-cut and obviously different stands. Issues also clearly determine votes on much grander questions if all the circumstances are right. This was certainly the case when voters ratified Roosevelt's New Deal in the presidential election of 1936. But when analysts try to answer the question of just what issues affect just what votes any more precisely, the going becomes very rough indeed.

Party affiliation. Statistics alone show that party affiliation continues to be a reliable indicator most of the time, but why this is so is more difficult to determine. The best answer seems to be the one already given: There are differences between the parties that voters are aware of, and when the issues are not dominating or when the candidates' views on the issues are fuzzy, voters feel—correctly—that voting the party is the most rational way of influencing government decisions in the direction they desire.

Incumbency. Here again statistics alone show that incumbency is important, although it is much more important for members of the House than the Senate. Incumbent members of the House are almost invariably reelected if they choose to run. With few exceptions the only members who are defeated are those who have become senile, have been involved in a sex or bribery scandal, have been redistricted, or are first-termers who rode the coattails of a popular presidential candidate into a seat that is normally safe for the other party.

The advantages of incumbency hold for both liberals and conserva-

---

[16]See, for example, Michael Margolis, "From Confusion to Confusion: Issues and the American Voter (1956–1972)," *American Political Science Review,* Vol. 71 (March 1977).

tives, even when the incumbents are clearly of the opposite ideology from the majority of their constituents. For example, for many years a large majority of Arizona's second congressional district voted into the House the very liberal Stewart Udall and later his equally liberal brother, Morris Udall. Yet when the very conservative Barry Goldwater was running for the Senate, the same voters gave equally large majorities to him in the same district!

Once more the difficult question is why? The evidence is meager, but enough exists to justify at least some speculations. One theory is that some of those who voted for Udall did not vote at all for senator and that some of those who voted for Goldwater did not vote at all for representative. Another is that voters do not believe that Congress is as important as the presidency, the courts, and the executive in making decisions they care about and thus are not as issue oriented in congressional elections. Stewart Udall himself speculated that many voted for both Goldwater and him because they felt that both men were "sincere and hard working."[17] A third possibility is that since there are 435 members of the House and 100 members of the Senate, the vote of any one member is not going to be decisive on any one issue. The voters can therefore safely ignore a member's stand on a certain issue either because they like his position on other issues or because they are grateful for constituent services the member has performed.

It seems obvious that the reasons people vote as they do are similar to their reasons for forming opinions. The major difference is that voting usually involves a choice between only two candidates of the two major parties, a fact with important consequences. Suppose a person has strong opinions about (1) lower unemployment even at the cost of additional inflation; (2) reduced defense expenditures; (3) additional measures to ensure equal rights for blacks, including busing to integrate the schools; (4) decentralization of federal programs to give more power to state and local governments; (5) abortion; (6) extension of Medicare to the entire population through compulsory health insurance; (7) welfare programs, including food stamps, day care centers for the children of working mothers, and aid to dependent children; (8) tougher measures for dealing with drugs and crime in the streets; and (9) the personalities and capabilities of the Democratic and Republican candidates. The voter may like what the Democrat has to say on four of the issues and what the Republican says on another four—and end up deciding on the basis of his or her own estimate of the personalities and capabilities of the candidates. Or the voter may detest everything the Democrat says on all of the issues but the one of unemployment versus inflation, and yet give so much

---

[17]Personal communication.

importance to that issue as to end up voting for the Democrat. In a poll taken a few weeks before the 1984 presidential election, 53 percent felt that they would be better off financially with Reagan rather than Mondale as president. They were then asked how they felt about thirteen other issues such as Reagan's handling of the economy, his dealings in foreign affairs, the risk of nuclear war under Reagan, and whether Reagan was more for special interests and Mondale more for the average man. On ten of these thirteen issues, 63 to 86 percent disapproved of Reagan's stand but they were still going to vote for him.[18]

A superficial look at this poll leads one to conclude that the American voters are venal—that they vote their pocketbook and are indifferent to everything else. But buried in the data are two very suggestive hints. One is that the electorate perceived the overall situation, both international and domestic, as not very dangerous. They saw no looming war, economic depression, or high unemployment. If this was in fact their perception, they could afford to vote on personality rather than issues. They liked Reagan even though they did not like his policies. The second hint is that so many Reagan voters split their votes in 1984 that both the Senate and the House were controlled by the Democrats. If voters liked Reagan as a person but did not like his policies very much, then it would be entirely rational to vote for Reagan as president and at the same time give control of both the Senate and the House to the Democrats, who opposed the Reagan policies these voters did not like. Something very similar seems to have happened in the 1956 election, when the voters gave Eisenhower a second term but gave control of both the Senate and the House to the Democrats.

Balancing Out Competing Views

No matter how issue oriented they are, when voters must choose between only two candidates, each associated with a particular party, they must somehow assign weights and priorities to their opinions on the issues in order to boil them down to this single choice. Voters who perceive little difference between the stands of the two candidates may choose on the basis of past party loyalties. Others may put so much weight on a single issue that their choice hinges on that alone. They may see their choice as lying between two rascals who advocate equally unacceptable policies and decide to flip a coin or to stay home. Given these and other possibilities, it is no surprise that trying to learn how voters reach their decisions has puzzled everyone who has made the attempt. "What I want," President Lincoln once observed, "is to get done what the people

---

[18]*Washington Post Weekly Edition,* October 1, 1984, p. 37.

desire to have done, and the question for me is how to find that out exactly." Occasionally people will vote for reasons that are little short of frivolous. But if some people vote some of the time for reasons that are frivolous, most people vote most of the time for reasons that are, like the workings of other aspects of the governing of America, both complicated and subtle.

THE INFLUENCE OF THE ELECTORATE

Presidential elections have been categorized as either maintaining elections, deviating elections, or realigning elections.[19] Most elections maintain the existing pattern of support. This trend is occasionally interrupted by a deviating election, in which the minority party is in power for a time because of an unusually attractive candidate or special circumstances. A realigning election occurs when there is a fundamental shift in the coalition of support for each of the parties.

Consider an occasion in which (1) a single issue that is perceived as affecting the lives of the mass of the people dominates a campaign; (2) the issue is debated by the candidates; (3) the two candidates and parties are perceived as offering quite different policies for dealing with the issue, and (4) the candidate who is elected carries out the policy offered in the campaign. In these circumstances the electorate has clearly voted for the candidate and party whose policy they prefer and the elected official has carried out his or her promises. It can thus truly be said that the electorate has decided on the policy.

Such an election might also bring a realignment of support for the parties. This is what happened in 1936, when the dominant issue was Roosevelt's New Deal. Roosevelt's program was pragmatic and eclectic rather than starkly ideological, but it was clearly headed in the direction of a welfare state, which the Republicans vehemently opposed. Circumstances such as these, however, probably occur not more than once in a generation, if that often.

Could the election of 1980 be similarly classified as the electorate's ratification of a radical shift in policy? In the campaign Reagan did propose a very drastic change in the economic policy of the federal government, and he won. On the other hand, the evidence is that the majority of the voters did not like either of the candidates or their programs very much (only 27.38 percent of the registered voters actually

---

[19]Angus Campbell et al., *Elections and the Political Order* (New York: John Wiley, 1966). See also Walter Dean Burnham, *Critical Elections and the Mainsprings of American Politics* (New York: W. W. Norton, 1970).

voted for Reagan, and many of these were apparently voting against Carter rather than for Reagan).[20] There is evidence that the voters were disenchanted with the policies that the federal government had been pursuing for several years, but there is very little evidence that they understood just what it was that Reagan was proposing, partly because he failed to make it clear and partly because they did not take the trouble to find out. In fact, the 1980 election probably should not be classified as one in which the voters approved a radical shift as they did in 1936, when they had had time to understand fully the New Deal.

As it turned out the 1984 election could not be said to have ratified Reagan's economic program, as the 1936 election had ratified the New Deal. Although Reagan's program had been a radical shift in policy, for the election to have ratified the change, three conditions would have to have been met. First, the consequences of Reagan's economic policies would have to have been well understood by the electorate. Second, the election would have to have been perceived as being fought principally on this issue and not on the personalities of Reagan and Mondale. In other words, both candidates would have to have been perceived as being equally appealing in terms of personality, and Mondale would have to have been perceived as having run on a platform condemning Reagan's policies, rather than merely promising to modify them or to be more "efficient." Third, no other major issue could have been perceived as overshadowing the economic issue, neither personality nor future tax increases, nor terrorist bombings in the Middle East. As it happened none of these conditions was fully met.

The Moving Center

The fact is that societies rarely make radical shifts. When they do occur, the shift is more likely to come about not in a single election but gradually, with the center of opinion moving in the direction of the revolutionary change and with both parties moving with the center. That the two parties tend to move with the moving center is the source of the familiar complaint that their policies do not differ significantly and that they seem to function as Tweedledum and Tweedledee. Yet this is exactly what one would want if the majority view is to prevail on a certain issue. If a graph of mass opinion takes the form of a bell curve and if the majority view is to prevail, both parties should and almost always will take positions only slightly to the right or left of center. They would do the same if the curve took the form of three bells, as some researchers believe it did in 1973 (see Figure 17.1). A party that does not move toward

---

[20]See *Time Magazine,* November 7, 1980, pp. 31, 35.

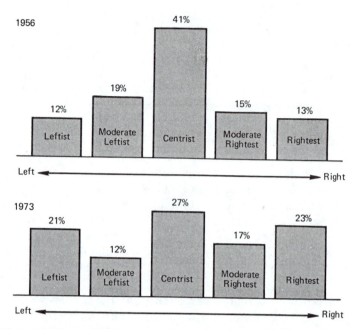

FIGURE 17.1. Distribution of Population on Political Beliefs, 1956 and 1973. From Norman H. Nie, Sidney Verba, and John R. Petrocik, *The Changing American Voter* (Cambridge, Mass.: Harvard University Press, 1966), p. 143. Copyright © by The Twentieth Century Fund.

the center when the center is known is a party of fools—or one with a death wish. When both parties tend toward the center of what is the known desire of the majority, the policy preferences of the mass of the people are being followed.

Qualifications of the Candidates

When there are no dominant issues the voters may still make a judgment about the qualifications and personalities of the candidates, but it is unlikely that one party will put up a highly qualified, likable candidate and the other will put up a person with few qualifications and a repulsive personality. When there is no dominant issue and the candidates are fairly evenly balanced in terms of qualifications and personality, the voters may influence policy by voting their party preferences, but again only if three conditions obtain: (1) There is a genuine ideological difference between the parties (such as liberal versus conservative); (2) the voters perceive these differences clearly; and (3) the victorious candidate and party are committed to the ideology and carry out those commitments in the policies they adopt. The various works cited in this chapter suggest that this situation may occur more often than most of us had realized.

Reward and Punishment

The electorate clearly rewards good past performance and punishes bad. Here the influence of the electorate is quite indirect. The polls showed that the majority of the electorate approved of President Johnson's 1965 decision to bomb North Vietnam and to send American combat troops to South Vietnam. Yet when the policy failed and the war merely dragged on, the polls showed that the majority turned against both the policy and Johnson. It was in fact the evidence of the changed attitude of the electorate that led Johnson to his decision not to run for reelection in 1968.

As mentioned, although the majority of the electorate had strong opinions about the Vietnam war, their opinions did not affect voting significantly in 1968 because the two candidates were perceived as offering essentially the same policy of gradual reduction in the American role in the war provided the Communist side met certain conditions.[21] However, by disapproving past policy and threatening (through the polls) to vote against anyone who wanted to continue that policy, the electorate indirectly forced both candidates to advocate at least a gradual reduction in American involvement. As Johnson's vice president, Humphrey had supported past policy, and there is plenty of evidence that Nixon wanted a military victory in Vietnam just as badly as Johnson did. It thus seems clear that the electorate forced both candidates to change their policy positions. Nixon and his administration dragged out the war for four more years but they ended up without a victory. For many years, presidents will hesitate a long time before they intervene in a situation that has any resemblance, no matter how superficial, to Vietnam. Many observers, for example, believe that President Ford and his secretary of state, Henry Kissinger, wanted to intervene with U.S. troops in Angola but decided against that move because of their fear of a reaction in both Congress and the general public stimulated by the experience in Vietnam. Many of the same observers believe that the Reagan administration would have sent U.S. troops to El Salvador and Nicaragua except for the same fear and that the only reason they did send troops to Grenada was that the island was so tiny (133 square miles) and the population so small (slightly more than 100,000) that an invasion could not possibly take more than a couple of weeks, too short a time to generate any significant political opposition. The Gulf War, on the other hand, was perceived as

---

[21]Page and Brody, "Policy Voting," p. 985.

something entirely different—an international aggression involving oil rather than a Communist-led insurrection. If these observers are correct, the electorate indeed influenced policy.

The electorate is also likely to punish the "ins" for what it does not like even when the government's policies were not really responsible for the condition. For example, Hoover and the Republicans did not cause the Great Depression, but many people certainly voted against Hoover in 1932 because it had occurred or because he was not seen to be dealing with it with sufficient vigor.

Mixed-issue Elections

In most elections there is no dominant issue, no overwhelming difference in candidate personality, and no great failure for which the "ins" should be punished. And the electorate does not always perceive major ideological differences between the candidates of their parties. In most elections the issues are instead a mixture of unrelated, individual questions, and no one can be certain whether those who voted for a winning candidate and party did so because of or in spite of their policy stand on a particular issue.

In 1948 President Truman tried to make the election a referendum on the antiunion section 14B of the Taft-Hartley Act, which outlawed closed shop union agreements. The press portrayed the campaign as though the election were such a referendum. Yet polls showed that most voters had never heard of 14B. Furthermore, because 14B was labeled the "right to work" law, some prounion voters became confused and voted for Thomas Dewey, who favored 14B, rather than Truman, who opposed it.[22] Nevertheless, when Truman won he claimed that he had a mandate to change the law on the grounds that a majority had had an opportunity to reject him if it opposed his stand on that law. He had made the law an issue in the campaign, had promised to change the law if elected, and was therefore honor bound, he argued, to carry out his promise. As long as presidents consider themselves in some way compelled to carry out the policy they advocate in a campaign, the electorate influences policy, even if the majority view on that policy remains obscure.

Summary

The public, then, does influence public policy in the way it votes, although the influence is often indirect, subtle, and extraordinarily complicated. The influence of the public must therefore be added to the other

---

[22]Kevin V. Mulcahy and Richard S. Katz, *America Votes: What You Should Know About Elections Today* (Englewood Cliffs, N.J.: Prentice Hall, 1976).

influences on public policy—those of interest groups, political parties, and the institutions and organizations of what has been called the intermediate structure. The conclusions of this chapter can be expressed as four rather simple questions and answers:

1. Do people vote on issues? Sometimes.
2. Do the people vote rationally and in their best interests on issues? Occasionally but not always, and perhaps not even most of the time.
3. Is the vote of the people the decisive voice on issues? Very rarely, but every few decades, on vital questions, yes.
4. Do the voters influence government decisions on issues as opposed to deciding them? Yes, and more often than most people might think. But the influence is exercised indirectly by the way that politicians calculate both what the people want and how effective a particular policy will be in achieving that goal.

HOW POLICYMAKERS ESTIMATE VOTER PREFERENCES

This final statement, that the influence of voters is filtered through the calculations of politicians, brings up one further complication. Because policymakers in the executive branch and in Congress assume that people's votes are influenced by their policy preferences, and because they fully understand that voters take revenge for the results of past performance and policies (whether or not they had approved the policy initially), presidents and other policymakers continually make judgments about the policy preferences of the electorate and shape policy in accordance with those judgments. Although hundreds of examples in both domestic and foreign affairs could be cited, we shall consider just one from foreign affairs.

In the campaign of 1960 John F. Kennedy made considerable political hay of the fact that a Communist, Fidel Castro, had come to power in Cuba during the Eisenhower administration. Yet Kennedy was convinced that, while the electorate did not like this development, it was unwilling to use American troops to remove Castro, and he promised that he would not permit such a move. During the Bay of Pigs he allowed the brigade of exiles to invade Cuba, but he stuck to his refusal to permit the use of American troops in spite of considerable pressure from both inside and outside the government. He apparently reasoned that a significant proportion of the electorate had voted for him because of his promise not to use American troops and thus felt obligated to keep the promise. What is more, the public reaction to the Bay of Pigs reinforced Kennedy's belief that the electorate did not want American troops to intervene in other, similar situations. During the Laos crisis of 1962 and on several occasions in the continuing crisis in Vietnam, he said, "If the American people don't want me to use troops to remove a Communist government only ninety miles off our coast, how can I ask them to send troops to prevent a Communist takeover nine thousand miles away?"[23] Even though the electorate had not been asked to express itself formally on this issue, it did influence policy. Kennedy had looked for evidence of the public opinion on this issue. Whether the evidence he found was conclusive or entirely accurate, he did find evidence, and he made a judgment about the policy preferences of the electorate in accordance with that evidence. The electorate's policy preferences, or at least Kennedy's *perception* of their policy preferences, did in fact influence his decision—profoundly.

---

[23]Kennedy made this statement in at least two meetings of the National Security Council; see Notes on NSC Meetings, Hilsman Papers, Kennedy Library. He made a similar statement to Nixon: " 'In any event, I don't see how we can make any move in Laos, which is 5000 miles away, if we don't make a move in Cuba, which is only 90 miles away.' " (Richard M. Nixon, "Cuba, Castro and John F. Kennedy," *Reader's Digest,* (November 1964).

18

FOREIGN AFFAIRS

This chapter gives a brief history of U.S. foreign relations and then describes the major current foreign policy issues facing the United States. Finally, the chapter summarizes and elaborates on the role and influence of the different power centers on foreign policy, drawing on the earlier chapters on the presidency, Congress, the bureaucracy, the press, public opinion, and the electorate.

In the early days of the republic, the role of the federal government in most policy areas was small or nonexistent and grew to giant proportions only over time. However, in foreign affairs—and in defense—the federal government began with the predominant role. Indeed the Constitution provided that foreign relations should be the monopoly of the federal government. In his farewell address George Washington advised the country to avoid becoming entangled in Europe's quarrels, which in effect was saying to make the most of the protection afforded by the geographic isolation created by the Pacific and Atlantic oceans. For many decades the country did what Washington suggested. The War of 1812 and its surrounding diplomacy were really the concluding chapter of the Revolution, a matter of convincing Britain and the world that the United States was determined to follow an independent course. The Mexican War and its surrounding diplomacy were part of the westward expansion, which was also behind other landmarks in early foreign policy, including the Louisiana Purchase, the purchase of Alaska, and the occasional troubles with Britain over the Canadian border.

These matters aside, foreign affairs throughout the middle of the nineteenth century consisted mainly of trying to prevent further incursions into the western hemisphere by the European powers and using diplomacy to promote trade. The Monroe Doctrine, which was the major policy statement of the former goal, announced that the United States would regard European intervention in the hemisphere as "the manifestation of an unfriendly disposition toward the United States." Trade, of course, was vital to the United States, and the country was a trading nation from the beginning. Europe, China, Latin America, and Africa were all trading partners, and diplomatic relations inevitably followed.

THE UNITED STATES BECOMES A WORLD POWER

The first overseas war came in 1896. When the Cubans rebelled against an oppressive Spanish governor in 1894, the economic and strategic interests pulling the United States into Latin American affairs were reinforced by ideology: New World democracy against Old World autocracy. The Spanish-American War cost little in lives or treasure, but in the aftermath some segments of American opinion became giddy with dreams of empire, while others were bitterly opposed. In the end the United States did not stand in the way of Cuban independence, but it did make a colony of the Philippines.

When World War I swept over Europe, the United States was slowly but surely drawn in. Following the war the United States, after bitter debate, rejected membership in the League of Nations and retreated into a new isolationism. But the rise of Hitler and Nazism in the 1930s posed a frightening menace. At first isolationist sentiment was so strong that President Franklin D. Roosevelt gave only material aid to the allies.[1] The implications of Hitler's philosophy and the dynamism of events would undoubtedly have led the United States into World War II sooner or later, but the matter was settled when the Japanese attacked Pearl Harbor on December 7, 1941.

THE COLD WAR

The Bolshevik revolution in Russia during World War I and the rise of Communist ideology that called for violent revolution throughout the world frightened many Americans. Accordingly, the United States did not recognize the Soviet Union until the Roosevelt administration in 1933. Then, during World War II, the American people watched the heroic Soviet resistance to the Nazi onslaught with admiration. Roosevelt

---

[1]See Robert E. Sherwood, *Roosevelt and Hopkins, An Intimate History* (New York: Harper & Row, 1948), p. 229.

and other Americans believed that the wartime alliance between the United States and the Soviet Union could be the foundation of a new world peace and that the United Nations could be successful where the League of Nations had failed. The United Nations was formed in 1945. It has served as the umbrella for a host of international activities that have been a great boon to humankind, among them the World Health Organization and the Food and Agricultural Organization. The UN has also served as a forum for debate and interchange among nations and especially as a place where the smaller and the underdeveloped countries could make their voices heard. But it has not been the keeper of the peace and the world government in embryo that some had wanted it to be. Recently, it served as a forum for legitimizing the U.S. decision to use force to drive Iraq out of Kuwait.

The Cold War Chronology

Hope was high that the wartime American-Soviet alliance would usher in a period of friendship that would be the cornerstone of world peace. But the hope was quickly dashed, and instead came the cold war.

At the end of World War II, Soviet occupation troops in Poland and the other Eastern European countries took steps to strengthen local Communist parties and to eliminate non-Communist parties. Communist forces in Greece waged a guerrilla war against the government from sanctuaries in Communist Yugoslavia and Bulgaria. To Western nations these actions seemed direct violations of agreements reached at the Yalta conference and at the later Potsdam conference. Winston Churchill, in a speech at Fulton, Missouri, in March 1946, exercised his talent for phrase making by saying that the Soviets had rung down an "iron curtain" across the continent of Europe.

The Truman Doctrine and the Marshall Plan

The European winter of 1946–1947 was unusually severe, a heartbreaking burden piled on top of the destruction and starvation of the war. In February 1947 the British informed Washington that they could no longer continue their aid to Greece and Turkey. President Truman recommended and Congress promptly passed a $400 million economic and military aid program for the two countries. Truman's justification for the American decision, which was quickly dubbed the Truman Doctrine, was that "it must be the policy of the United States to support free peoples who are resisting attempted subjugation by armed minorities or by outside pressures."

A few weeks later the United States proposed a massive program to help Europe recover from the war. Known as the Marshall Plan (named for Secretary of State George C. Marshall), the offer was extended to all victims of the war, including Communist countries, although many American officials hoped that the Communists would not accept. At first the Soviet Union seemed interested, but in the end it rejected the offer on the grounds that a joint plan and a collective undertaking would be an infringement of sovereignty. The other Communist countries followed suit.[2]

The North Atlantic Treaty

In the period following World War II, West Berlin was an island occupied by a token force of Americans, British, and French in the sea of East Germany occupied by Soviet forces. In June 1948 the Soviets blockaded the city, and the Allies responded with an airlift of food, coal, and other supplies. By this time many Americans were thoroughly alarmed. They pressed for concrete steps to deter the Soviet Union from any direct move, which they feared might soon follow. Arguing that both World War I and World War II could have been prevented if Germany had known that the United States would eventually enter the wars, proponents of deterrence insisted that the American determination to stand by its Western European allies must be made completely clear. The results were the North Atlantic Treaty, proposed in 1948 and ratified in 1949, and a military aid program to supplement the Marshall Plan.

Events in Asia

Events in Asia reinforced the conclusions that the proponents of deterrence had drawn from what had been happening in Europe. The Soviets were extending substantial aid to the Chinese Communists in their civil war with Chiang Kai-shek and the Chinese Nationalists. The United States sponsored negotiations between the two sides to establish a coalition government, but neither really wanted it. In 1949 the Nationalists fled to the island of Taiwan, 90 miles off the Chinese Coast, and the Communists took over the mainland.

The Korean War

In June 1950 a North Korean force of both armored and infantry divisions attacked South Korea at several points across the thirty-eighth parallel. The Security Council of the United Nations met in the absence of the Soviet Union, which was boycotting the meetings at the time, and

---

[2]Andre Fontaine, *History of the Cold War from the October Revolution to the Korean War, 1917–1950*, trans. D. D. Paige (New York: Random House, 1968), pp. 328–329; and John L. Gaddis, *The United States and the Origins of the Cold War, 1941–1947* (New York: Columbia University Press, 1972).

voted to call upon UN member states to help South Korea with troops. The United States dispatched air forces initially and then substantial ground forces. A number of other countries sent smaller contingents.

Many people in Europe and America feared that the attack on South Korea was a prelude for an attack on West Germany by East Germany or even for an attack on Western Europe by the Soviet Union itself. These fears led to the formation of the North Atlantic Treaty Organization (NATO) and a unified multinational military command, Supreme Headquarters, Allied Powers Europe (SHAPE), under the command of General Dwight D. Eisenhower.

By 1952 the Korean conflict had reached a stalemate. Neither side was willing to escalate the level of fighting or was able to win without escalating. After President Eisenhower took office in 1953, negotiations finally reached an uneasy settlement along the existing fighting line.

Indochina

Prior to World War II, Indochina was a French colony consisting of what is now Vietnam, Laos, and Cambodia. When the war ended, the French were defeated in their attempt to reestablish their colonial rule and in 1954 began to withdraw their troops. The United States decided to stay out of the conflict, largely as the result of opposition to intervention by General Matthew B. Ridgway, as described in Chapter 1.

The Cuban Missile Crisis

In the summer and fall of 1962, as described in Chapter 1, the Soviets deployed nuclear missiles to Cuba, the United States responded with a blockade, and the Soviets eventually agreed to withdraw the missiles. Following the crisis Kennedy delivered a speech at American University asking both the American people and the Soviet Union to be more tolerant of each other and calling for concrete steps toward peace. He called specifically for a ban on nuclear testing. The Soviet Union responded, and a limited treaty was signed shortly thereafter.

Détente and Its Deterioration

The Johnson administration's intervention in Vietnam with American combat troops in 1965 slowed the move toward reducing tensions between the United States and the Soviet Union, although some progress was made. Following the withdrawal of American troops from Vietnam during the Nixon and Ford administrations and the fall of South Vietnam to the Communists in 1975, relations between the Soviet Union and the United States improved, resulting in a period of so-called détente. Very soon, however, relations deteriorated again, partly because of the Soviet invasion of Afghanistan and the imposition of martial law in Poland; partly because of the Carter administration's policy on human rights, which entailed public criticism of Soviet treatment of dissidents; and partly because of the Reagan administration's hard-line policy toward the Soviets.

The People's Republic of China

After American and South Korean forces had initially defeated the North Koreans, they proceeded to occupy North Korea. Communist China then sent troops into Korea, pushing the American and South Korean forces back to what was essentially the original border between North and South Korea. Both sides suffered heavy casualties. A truce was finally negotiated, but it was followed by many years of hostility between the United States and China.

Shortly after the Cuban missile crisis and the signing of the limited nuclear test ban treaty, President Kennedy authorized an attempt to open the door to a normalization of relations with China. After Kennedy's death, President Johnson also endorsed the attempt. However, the effort failed partly because Communist China was apparently not ready for normalization but mainly because of the U.S. intervention in the war in Vietnam.[3] The beginnings of normal relations were finally arranged in 1972, after the American withdrawal from Vietnam, when President Nixon visited Peking. During the Carter administration the process was completed, when the two countries exchanged ambassadors. A prolonged period of good relations with the West followed, in part as a consequence of Deng's introduction of market reforms. However, in 1989 the Chinese government put down student "prodemocracy" demonstrations in Tiananmen Square with troops and tanks. Several students were killed, and a large number arrested. As a result, relations with the West were once more strained.

THE UNITED STATES AND THE DEVELOPING WORLD

Most U.S. foreign policy following World War II, even the relations with the developed countries of Western Europe and Japan was dominated by the tension with the Soviet Union and the People's Republic of China. In the meantime, however, there was turmoil in the developing world of Latin America, Asia, and Africa.

---

[3]For a detailed description of the attempt, see Roger Hilsman, *To Move a Nation: The Politics of Foreign Policy in the Administration of John F. Kennedy* (Garden City, N.Y.: Doubleday, 1967), pp. 275–357.

The relationship between Latin America and the United States has always been special, beginning with the Monroe Doctrine. The relationship has also been marked by tension. American business interest in Latin America has led to charges of economic exploitation. Kennedy's authorization of an invasion of Cuba at the Bay of Pigs by a CIA-trained brigade of Cubans, Johnson's intervention with American troops in the Dominican Republic, Nixon's use of the CIA to support a right-wing military coup in Chile, the Reagan administration's invasion of Grenada and its support for the Contras, and the Bush administration's invasion of Panama—all aroused Latin American fears of the "Colossus of the North."

In Africa in the postwar period most of the former colonies gained their independence. One extremely difficult and dangerous problem was white South Africa's continued policy of apartheid, or racial segregation.

The Middle East has been a special case in international relations because of its huge oil supplies, its strategic position, and the continued dispute between Israel and the Arab countries. Since the establishment of the Israeli state in 1948, U.S. policy during both Republican and Democratic administrations has been to try to keep on friendly terms with both the Arabs and the Israelis while working to keep Soviet influence at a minimum and making sure that Israel's armed forces remained strong enough to prevent an Arab victory in any of the recurrent wars. This general policy has enjoyed wide support, but its particulars have frequently been disputed.

The harsh Israeli response to the rebellion of the late 1980s—the *intifada,* or uprising—by the Palestinians living in areas occupied by Israel evoked much criticism in the United States from American Jews as well as others. On the other hand, the decision announced near the very end of the Reagan administration by Secretary of State Shultz that the United States would enter into direct negotiations with the Palestine Liberation Organization (PLO) evoked a corresponding criticism in Israel.

The Gulf War

The Gulf War was described in some detail as one of the case studies. By way of summary and conclusion, three points should be made. The first is that the military operation was a resounding success. The second is that it is so far impossible to tell whether or not the negotiations that the war set in motion will bring about an overall peace that will end the hostility between Israel and the Arab states. The third is that the political consequences of making the war primarily an American operation were at best unfortunate and may well turn out to be disastrous.

Only the third point requires discussion. In the Korean conflict, President Truman forbade any bombing of the Chinese supply lines north of the Yalu, in spite of the Chinese intervention. In the Vietnam war, President Johnson went over the list of targets selected for bombing each day, approving some and scratching out others. Many in the military, especially in the Air Force, resented Truman's decision as forcing the military to fight with one hand tied behind its back and Johnson's as unwarranted nitpicking. Others, however—recalling Clauswitz's dictum that war is politics by other means and Georges Clemenceau's remark that war is too important to be left to generals—thought that both Truman's and Johnson's interventions were proper exercises of political responsibility. George Bush, on the other hand, gave the military carte blanche.

Understandably, when there is any doubt about whether or not to bomb a particular target the military usually opt to bomb. If there is any possibility at all that the target contributes to the enemy's war effort, the military feel an obligation to knock it out if possible—for the perfectly understandable reason that they are anxious to keep casualties among their own people to an absolute minimum. The long-term political consequences of a decision to bomb particular targets is not the responsibility of the military; neither is the military equipped to make such judgments by either training or experience.

However, many among the American military question whether demolishing Iraq's electrical generating capacity, its water purification systems, and its sewage systems made any useful contribution to winning the war. On the other hand, the civilian deaths due to bombing these particular installations were large—especially among children—and continued long after the war was over. Not just the Iraqi people but almost all Arabs and many among Third World peoples regard hitting these particular targets as one more illustration of the West's wanton disregard for Arab and Third World life. In any case, there is little question that Bush's failure to exercise the kind of oversight that Truman did in Korea and Johnson did in Vietnam brought political consequences that will haunt the United States for a long, long time.

Mikhail Gorbachev and the Breakup of the Soviet Union

After Mikhail S. Gorbachev came to power in the Soviet Union, it became clear that he was feeling his way toward a major shift in the very nature of the Soviet society and that this would be followed by equally profound shifts in both foreign and defense policy.

One of his first moves was to announce that the Soviets would withdraw their forces from Afghanistan.

On the domestic scene Gorbachev launched on two parallel policies. One was *perestroika*—"restructuring"—that is, reorganizing the institutions of the Soviet government. Although he did not explain exactly what he meant by this, people in the West came to believe that it meant lessening the power of such instruments of government control as the KGB and increasing the power of institutions more responsive to the people, such as the legislature and the presidency (which office Gorbachev himself assumed). The other was *glasnost*–"openness"–by which Gorbachev seemed to mean not only less censorship and more freedom of speech and the press but also more participation by the mass of the people.

Then in October 1986, President Reagan and Gorbachev held a summit meeting in Reykjavik, Iceland.

In the words of an editorial in *The New York Times,* the meeting produced "a roller coaster, first of hope, then disappointment and now confusion."[4] Apparently Reagan went to Iceland expecting that the talk on arms control would be specific and narrow. Somehow, however, he found himself talking with Gorbachev about banning *all* nuclear weapons within ten years. After the talks, Moscow said that Reagan and Gorbachev had indeed discussed banning all nuclear weapons. At first Washington stated that the talk had been about banning only *ballistic missiles,* yet later admitted that banning all nuclear weapons had been discussed but only as a "long-term goal." The rest of the world sensed that someone was not telling the whole truth, for neither the Soviet Union nor the United States would seriously contemplate leaving China, Britain, and France with unopposed nuclear forces, not to mention the countries that were suspected of having developed some sort of nuclear weapons, such as India, Pakistan, Israel, and South Africa.

Summit meeting in Washington. Reagan and Gorbachev met again in Washington in December 1987 to sign the Intermediate Nuclear Forces (INF) treaty and to agree on the goals for future negotiations on long-range missiles (the Strategic Arms Reduction Talks, or START).

Increasingly it became clear that Gorbachev was determined to carry out fundamental changes in the Soviet Union–in its political ideology, in its economic philosophy, and in its foreign and military policies. In a speech to the United Nations General Assembly on December 7, 1988, he praised democracy and human liberty, rejected class warfare and ideological conformity (which had always been the keystones of Marxism-Leninism), called for tolerance of diversity throughout the world, and rejected economic and cultural isolation. He promised to respect human rights and pledged that the Soviet Union would not interfere in the internal affairs of other countries. He also rejected the use of force in

---

[4]*The New York Times,* October 13, 1986, p. A18.

international affairs. To drive his point home, Gorbachev then announced that the Soviet Union would reduce its armed forces by 500,000 men and 10,000 tanks and that it would begin to withdraw its forces from all of Eastern Europe, including East Germany—signaling to the world that he had concluded that the gigantic effort to bind the Eastern Europe countries to the Soviet Union in a military alliance and to supply them with military equipment was no longer worth the effort.

For its part, the newly elected Bush administration was clearly surprised by Gorbachev's initiative, and its response was hesitant.

But events in Eastern Europe and the Soviet Union moved like a whirlwind. Soviet troops were withdrawn from Germany and Eastern Europe, and in 1991 the Warsaw Pact was dissolved.

At the same time Gorbachev's withdrawal from Eastern Europe and his domestic policies of *perestroika* and *glasnost* had opened a Pandora's box. In the summer of 1991, a number of high party officials and members of the military high command attempted a coup d'état and put Gorbachev under house arrest at his vacation home. Troops also surrounded the government buildings in Moscow. However, other troops came to the rescue, and the coup failed.

The next step was that Boris N. Yeltsin, president of the Russian Republic (which was one of fifteen republics that made up the Soviet Union) led a move to break up the highly centralized Soviet Union and form something more like a confederation. Latvia, Estonia, and Lithuania declared their independence. Eleven of the other republics formed the so-called Commonwealth of Independent States—Russia, Belarus, Ukraine, Kazakhstan, Armenia, Azerbaijan, Uzbekistan, Kyrgyzstan, Moldova, Tajikstan, and Turkmenistan.[5] The fifteenth Soviet republic, Georgia, was wracked by what amounted to a civil war, and its application for membership was denied—at least for the time being.

The Commonwealth of Independent States was formed on December 21, 1991. On December 25, 1991, Gorbachev resigned as president of the Union of Soviet Socialist Republics. The next day the Supreme Soviet, the country's highest legislative body, declared the Soviet Union dissolved.

Continuing and Future Problems

For over four decades the central problem of foreign affairs for the United States was its relations with the Soviet Union. Many observers in the West hailed the Soviet withdrawal from Eastern Europe and the breakup

---

[5]Five of the former Soviet republics adopted new English language versions of their names: Byelorussia became Belarus; Kirghizia became Kyrgyzstan; Moldavia, Moldova; Tadzhikistan, Tajikstan; and Turkmenia, Turkmenistan. And what was formerly called *the* Ukraine became simply Ukraine.

of the Soviet Union as the end of the cold war and the beginning of an era free at last from the threat of a superpower war fought with intercontinental missiles and nuclear warheads. But the truth is that the future remains fluid and uncertain.

First, the Commonwealth of Independent States is still far from being a democracy. At the local level, at least, members of the former Communist party apparatus are still very strong. Even if the Communist party as such is truly dead, a Communist-like dictatorship remains a possibility. As related earlier, a number of high party officials and members of the military high command attempted a coup d'état in the summer of 1991. It failed, but worsening economic conditions, shortages of food and fuel, and discontent among the military and the KGB, whose roles no longer seem essential, may well bring another, better organized attempt.

Other unwelcome scenarios are also possible. In the political upheaval in late 1991 Gorbachev faded as a dominant figure and Yeltsin emerged. But Gorbachev might be tempted into forming an alliance with the hard-line military and the KGB to return to power. If he did so and was successful, a return to a more centralized, even dictatorial system would hardly be surprising.

Another unwelcome scenario might involve Yeltsin. In early 1992, he was being hailed as an advocate of democratic reform both inside and outside the Soviet Union. But when he was head of the Moscow apparatus, he had a reputation for heavy-handedness that is hardly consistent with a unshakably deep commitment to democracy. He, too, might make an alliance with the hardliners and return to a centralized, even dictatorial system.

Even if none of these worst case scenarios comes to pass, the portentous problem of the former Soviet Union's stockpile of nuclear warheads and missiles remains. The military aspects of the breakup of the Soviet Union will be discussed in Chapter 19.

Even if these more frightening possibilities do not materialize, the political instability in Eastern Europe will still present formidable problems. The rival nationalisms held in check the past forty years can bring unbelievable bloodshed—as the fighting between rival factions in the Republic of Georgia suggested and the virtual civil war between Serbs and Croats accompanying the breakup of Yugoslavia demonstrated with sickening clarity.

And all this is over and beyond the wrenching economic problems that will face both Eastern Europe and the former Soviet Union as they attempt—as they most surely will—the transition from tightly controlled, centralized economies toward something more nearly resembling economies dominated by the market. And there is the further problem of just how the economies of Eastern and Western Europe will be connected—which could range anywhere from full integration to mutual exclusion.

Economic Problems

Economic problems, in fact, are likely to move to the center of attention in other parts of the world as well. Over the past two decades, the United States has lost its dominant position in several economic fields. Its loss of preeminence in the manufacture of automobiles to Japan is only the most dramatic example.

Japan, in fact, has obviously become America's premier economic rival. In recent years, Japan has enjoyed a gigantic trade surplus with the United States, and resolving the problem is extraordinarily difficult. The structure of Japanese businesses and their system of distribution are exclusionary. Japanese firms maintain unique relationships with each other and between themselves and the Japanese government that are hard for foreign businesses to penetrate. In one effort to resolve their differences, the Structural Impediments Initiative was launched in 1989, indirectly emerging from the Super 301 amendment to the Omnibus Trade and Competitiveness Act of 1988. These talks were based on the notion that difficulties in trade relations were not a result of inherent political problems between the two countries, but rather that the structure of their economies do not lend themselves well to optimal trade relations. At this point, however, the talks have been ineffective because neither side is willing to restructure its economy – a wrenching process that would be enormously costly.[6]

In January 1992, in a somewhat desperate attempt to shore up both the sagging American economy and his own sagging popularity in the public opinion polls, President Bush went on a trip focused mainly on Japan. The trip was billed as aimed directly at the economic problems between the two countries and the steady loss of American jobs. Bush was accompanied by a group of top American industrialists, especially from the automobile industry. The president succeeded in persuading the Japanese to promise to try to increase their imports of American cars and to buy $10 billion more in American-made automobile parts. But the carmakers that accompanied Bush on the trip denounced the Japanese pledges as "woefully inadequate."

The problems facing the United States in the economic aspects of foreign affairs is, of course, related to its domestic economic problems. During the Reagan administration the United States accumulated a deficit that was greater than the *total* of all the deficits since 1789. During the first two years of the Bush administration this unprecedented

---

[6]Stephen D. Cohen, "The United States–Japanese Trade Relations," *Current History,* April 1991, pp. 152–155.

deficit doubled. Many observers believe that unless drastic measures are taken to reduce the deficit, disaster is inevitable.

The recession gripping the country in 1991–1992 also created an equally formidable problem of debt for businesses as well as the government. On December 17, 1991, Alan Greenspan, chairman of the Federal Reserve Board, said that he doubted that the "utterly unprecedented" debt burden of consumers and businesses would be resolved in some "standard, easily measurable way."[7] Huge layoffs by companies like General Motors and IBM weakened public confidence in future wage earnings and led to lowered consumer spending and corporate investment. Consequently, despite the efforts of the Federal Reserve to stimulate the economy by lowering interest rates, the economic outlook remained bleak.

THE POWER LINEUP

The earlier chapters on the president, the president's staff, the political appointees, the national security bureaucracies, the Congress, the interest groups, the press and TV, public opinion, and the electorate looked at a wide variety of power centers. Not all of these involve themselves in foreign affairs, however, and those that do rarely participate equally in all aspects of such policy.

In foreign affairs, presidents have more power than in any other sphere, as Chapter 9 discussed. To recap the earlier argument, the president was given more power in foreign affairs because the framers of the Constitution recognized that in such matters the survival of the nation might require quicker and more decisive action than could be expected from the legislature. These constitutional powers are reinforced by present-day political considerations that stem from the same argument. The most frequent example is the Cuban missile crisis of 1962. President Kennedy had about a week to decide on a course of action, and the deliberations had to be secret to prevent the Soviets from taking counteraction. Most members of Congress doubt that there is a practical way for Congress to participate in such decisions.

Even technical and procedural considerations tend to strengthen the president's hand. Congress has great power over any policy that requires spending significant amounts of money. In a great many areas, including health policy, Social Security, welfare, and agricultural policy,

---

[7]Louis Uchitelle, "Pessimism at the Fed: For the First Time Greenspan is Suggesting Rate Cuts Alone May Not Revive Economy," *The New York Times,* December 17, 1991.

spending money is a major issue. Because defense policy is largely concerned with buying weapons or establishing the size of the armed services, it is no accident that Congress has great power in this area. But most of the State Department's budget is for the "salaries and expenses" of the career foreign service and the Washington staff, which is a very small amount of money compared to what is required for defense. Most foreign policies are questions of diplomacy, negotiations, declarations of national intentions, support for this or that country in the United Nations, and the like. Such policies do not require spending significant amounts of money. The only exception is foreign aid, and the total aid in recent years has been very small—less than 5 percent, for example, of the military budget.

Thus presidents can effect an extremely important change in foreign policy without involving Congress to any great extent. President Truman took the United States to war in Korea without a vote of Congress. President Johnson also took it to war in Vietnam without a congressional vote. Reagan invaded Grenada, and Bush invaded Panama—both without congressional votes. But perhaps the best example of the power of the president to take the country to war is President Bush's decision to go to war against Iraq. Bush *did* put the question to Congress for a vote, and although the vote was very close, it *did* support his decision to go to war. But probably the single most important reason that the vote went the way it did was because Bush had taken the country so far down the road to war that to reverse his action at that late stage would have had very serious international consequences.

Congress

Congress does, however, exercise power in foreign policy, even though that power is indirect and eludes precise description. In domestic policy Congress can occasionally take the initiative and force a new policy, but this is rarely so in foreign affairs. In foreign policy the executive calls the tune, for the reasons outlined. Although members of Congress are a focal point for the flow of information on public policy, they cannot handle large volumes of it. In foreign affairs especially, it is only on crises that they can focus for any length of time.

On day-to-day matters, and to an important extent even on crisis matters, it is the executive who controls the detailed flow of information from overseas. There need be no conscious intention to suppress one kind of information and emphasize another to accomplish much the same result as deliberate suppression and emphasis. Few people with an intimate knowledge of government believe that U.S. officials deliberately and consciously lied about how the war was going in Vietnam, for example, but everyone acknowledges that wishful thinking, self-delusion, and defensiveness in fact did lead to the distortion of information. Members of Congress did become the focus for information pointing in the opposite direction, but they could not be certain about the reliability of their data, and they were hesitant to pit themselves against the authority of the executive and reluctant to join those who did. Even when passions run less deep than they did over Vietnam, the policy position of the executive will affect how information is presented. In such a massive flow of information, merely winnowing the raw data down to what one person could conceivably absorb would of itself present a distorted and one-sided picture of the situation.

The increasing technicality of foreign affairs also robs the Congress of its power. Understanding the nature of Third World nationalism, the subtleties of the Soviet incursion into Afghanistan, or the anarchical power struggle in Iran after the fall of the shah and the subtle influence that the militants exercised by holding American hostages requires expert knowledge, and it is the executive who has the greater command over experts. As a consequence, it is the executive who sets the framework in which policies are discussed and who defines the problems the United States will address as a government and the alternatives from which the courses of action will be chosen.

This command of both information and expertise gives the executive the intellectual initiative in making foreign policy. The Congress as a whole can criticize; it can add to, amend, or block an action by the executive. But Congress can only occasionally force executive attention on the need for a change in policy and only rarely develop and secure public approval for its own policy.

The executive also has an "instrumental" initiative in foreign affairs. It is the executive who carries out a policy and who deals with problems face to face. In doing so the executive must inevitably make a host of secondary decisions that can and do set new lines of policy. It is also the executive who conducts negotiations with other powers and in these negotiations can make promises and commitments that Congress cannot fail to honor without doing the country as a whole much harm—as happened when Bush asked Congress to approve his decision to go to war against Iraq. Frequently, indeed, the executive may proceed without any formal reference to Congress at all, as Reagan did when he ordered the invasion of Grenada and as Carter did in setting a policy toward the Soviet incursion into Afghanistan. Nor did Johnson formally refer to Congress in the series of decisions that led to making Vietnam an American war, save the Tonkin Gulf Resolution, which was really passed after the fact and in circumstances in which the Congress felt it had little choice but to go along. There are hundreds of other examples as well, dating back to the beginnings of the republic.

This weakness of the Congress in exercising direct control or in taking initiatives in foreign affairs and the power of the executive to proceed in so many matters without reference to Congress or even to evade the expressed desires of Congress are only part of the story. Congress participates only fitfully in the actual formulation of foreign policy and takes formal action only in approving or rejecting appropriations, treaties, and resolutions and in confirming the appointments of ambassadors and other high officials. Yet it is equally clear that Congress plays a decisive role in setting the tone of many policies and the limits on many others. Even though this role is subtle and indirect, it is nevertheless effective. The most dramatic example is seen in the case of China policy in the twenty-five years following World War II, during which Congress took the lead in solidifying a rigid policy toward Communist China culminating in the viciousness of the McCarthy witch hunts.

Once such a broad consensus is fixed, inertia rules. It then takes almost heroic action to overcome even the mildest congressional resistance. President Kennedy wished to bring about a change in China policy, but progress was painfully slow. At first he sought to recognize Communist Mongolia, but the Nationalist government on Taiwan objected, and that government's friends in Congress quickly shot the proposal down. Nothing dramatic or specific would have been accomplished by recognizing Mongolia; the effects would have been symbolic and psychological, foreshadowing a coming change in China policy. But herein lies the difficulty, for when the purpose is to change policy in the face of massive inertia, it is essential to be able to point to the immediate results of such a change to help beat off counterattacks.

Legally and constitutionally, Kennedy could have recognized Mongolia and followed with other steps leading to a basic change in China policy. But he would have had to be willing to accept the consequences, not just angry speeches and threats of impeachment but retaliatory action on a whole range of other matters over which Congress has more direct legal and constitutional power. To be specific, if Kennedy had recognized Mongolia, appropriations for both his Alliance for Progress in Latin America and his aid program for the newly independent nations of Africa would have been heavily cut. Kennedy chose to wait for another and better day.

It is here that the peculiar and somewhat elusive power of Congress lies. In one sense the role of Congress in foreign affairs is negative and limit setting; it is the power of deterrence and the threat of retaliation. On some specific detail of foreign policy, presidents may frequently ignore the Congress with complete impunity, but on the fundamental issues that persist over time, they must have the cooperation and acquiescence of Congress, even if they are not required to have their formal and legal consent. Although presidents may ignore individual members of Congress and even powerful heads of committees, they must bring the

Congress and its leaders along in any basic policy. Here again, the president is the "president-in-sneakers" trying to induce the members of Congress to "climb aboard."

The Foreign Affairs Bureaucracies

The foreign affairs bureaucracies are the State Department and the foreign service stationed in embassies abroad, the CIA, and the military. The military presents a special case that will be discussed in Chapter 19. In one sense the nonmilitary bureaucracies have unusually large power in foreign affairs, yet at the same time they are more dependent on the president and the White House than most bureaucracies for two reasons. First, the subject of foreign affairs, as mentioned, is esoteric. Expertise is needed, and the foreign affairs bureaucracies have a very large share of this expert knowledge. Second, there are few organized constituencies for foreign policy in the American population and certainly nothing like the constituencies for farm policy, business policy, and the like. When the Department of Agriculture is under pressure from the president to do something the department's bureaucracy does not like, it has various ways to mobilize counterpressure on the president from the farm constituencies and from members of Congress representing those constituencies. But foreigners do not vote in American elections, and the State Department and the CIA are consequently more at the mercy of the president and the White House than most bureaucracies.

NONGOVERNMENTAL POWER CENTERS

Special Economic Interests

Special economic interests can be expected to try to influence the government for their benefit. One notorious example was the attempt by International Telephone & Telegraph (ITT) to persuade the U.S. government to intervene on its behalf against the pro-Marxist Allende government of Chile, and ITT's apparent involvement with the CIA in the overthrow of the Allende government.[8] Companies that are dependent on imported raw materials (for example, oil, rubber, bauxite, and chromium) can also

---

[8]For the story of the early activities of ITT in Chile during the Allende regime see Anthony Sampson, *The Sovereign State of ITT* (New York: Stein & Day, 1973). The involvement of ITT with CIA is described in the Church Committee hearings: *Foreign and Military Intelligence, Final Report of the Select Committee to Study Governmental Operations with Respect to Intelligence Activities* (Church Committee Report), U.S. Senate, 94th Cong., 2nd sess.

be expected to press for foreign economic and political policies that they think will further their business.

Sometimes the different economic interests cancel each other out. Textile manufacturers and associated unions, for example, want to exclude foreign imports. American television and electronics firms have also been exclusionist in the face of foreign competition (from the Japanese Sony Corporation, for example). The American manufacturers of jet aircraft and other products that require complex technology tend to be on the other side of the debate, and some industries manage to be on both sides at the same time! Automobile manufacturers, for example, want the government to help them sell American cars abroad yet simultaneously to exclude foreign cars from the American market.

Frequently American corporations and foreign governments find that they have common interests that go against the U.S. government's policies. This has been true on several occasions in the Middle East, when U.S. support of Israel was opposed by American oil companies closely connected to some of the Arab governments. American corporations also sometimes find themselves being pushed by the American government. When the Indonesian government under Sukarno was engaged in a confrontation with Malaysia and Great Britain, the United States, in an attempt to prevent war, persuaded Sukarno to consider a plan by which the United States and a number of other countries would give Indonesia economic aid. Part of the deal was a new agreement with the oil companies to increase Indonesia's foreign exchange earnings. Although the deal also promised to be profitable for the oil companies, they balked. In their eyes the risk that their customers' supplies might be disrupted because of the political instability of Indonesia outweighed the benefits of greater profits. In the end the U.S. government had to put pressure on the oil companies to force them to continue the negotiations.[9]

Looking at the full range of both foreign affairs and economic interest groups, three general conclusions seem justified. First, when the considerations of economic interest groups point in one direction and political, strategic, or ideological considerations point in the other, the latter almost always dominate. When the Carter administration imposed a grain embargo on the Soviet Union in retaliation for the incursion into Afghanistan, for example, it was clear that the American farmers, shippers, and other businesses concerned with grain would be hurt much more severely than the Soviets, who obtained almost all of the grain denied by the United States from Argentina and other countries. Yet the protests from the farmers and their allies were mild. Perhaps a more dramatic example was the Vietnam war. The American business commu-

---

[9]The story is related in greater detail in my *To Move a Nation*, pp. 387–390.

nity had almost no investments or other economic interests of any kind in Vietnam. A few engineering companies that built American military bases in Vietnam profited from the war, as did the manufacturers of helicopters. But the overall effect of the war on American business and industry was disastrous: increased taxes and nearly runaway inflation, which bankrupted many businesses and brought many others very close to bankruptcy. Yet the business and industrial community generally supported the war, principally for ideological reasons.

Second, economic interest groups rarely attempt to influence foreign policy decisions directly, except for such very specific economic matters as tariff policy. The ITT-Chile case is the exception, not the rule. The rule is more often the behavior of the oil companies in the Indonesian situation. This suggests that the flag does not follow economic interests, at least in modern times, but rather that economic interests follow the flag. Put another way, economic interests tend to be not adventuresome and bold but timid and sometimes even cowardly!

Third, economic interest groups are so rarely aggressive in their attempts to influence foreign policy because the government as a whole — the president, the White House, and the State Department — is deeply concerned with American economic interests abroad and will generally pursue those interests without much prodding from the businesses and industries concerned. Government officials are just as aware of economic interests and just as interested in pursuing them as the most sophisticated and involved American companies doing business abroad. The government, furthermore, is considerably more aware and interested than many companies who actually do depend on foreign trade but conduct it through third and fourth parties rather than directly. A member of Congress from an agricultural district does not need to be told by the local farmers where their economic interests lie in some particular, seemingly unrelated piece of legislation. On the contrary, the member is more likely to be aware of the situation before the farmers and to be the one to alert them so as to build support for the member's efforts in their behalf. More often than not, the same is also true of the U.S. government and American economic interests abroad.

Ethnic and Nationality Groups

Of the ethnic and nationality interest groups, the most active and by far the most effective in influencing foreign and defense policy are Jewish organizations advocating support for Israel. Some Irish organizations support the Irish Catholics in Northern Ireland, but there is little in the issue that directly engages U.S. foreign policy. During the cold war Eastern European minority groups generally supported a rather firm anti-Communist position. During most of the postwar period this stand was in line with the basic position of the U.S. government, most members of Congress, and most of the public. Although in general these groups opposed liberalizing relations with their Communist-controlled homelands, they never mounted particularly heavy pressure on the government.

The Press and Television

Probably the most important influence the press and TV exert in foreign policy is the way they play the news, as was described in Chapter 15. The way a story is reported does help set the political agenda, although officials do have as much influence on whether a story makes the front page as does the press. In the early months of the Reagan administration, for example, the guerrilla warfare in El Salvador received a great deal of attention in the media, as described earlier, but this was as much due to the public statements of Secretary of State Alexander M. Haig, Jr., as to the press.

In any case, the action of the government is affected by how the press plays a story, whether the story is given more or less prominence or portrayed in a way that makes the events seem vital to U.S. interests. How the press reports a story affects the reaction of the attentive publics, and an official is better able to predict that reaction by studying the press play. In effect the press is interpreting information in terms of the values and interests of its readers, just as an interest group interprets information for its membership. The difference is that with the interest group the emphasis is on the upward function of expressing values and interests to the central decision makers, while with the press the emphasis is on the downward interpretation of how decisions will affect the values and interests of the general public. But the press performs the upward function as well by the kinds of stories it reports and the kinds of questions it asks.

The Mass Public

Public opinion as a mass phenomenon influences foreign affairs only on very broad questions that persist over time, such as the distrust of the Soviet Union arising out of disagreements following World War II combined with a more deeply rooted fear of Communism. Another example is the gradual disenchantment of the general public with the Vietnam war.

The Attentive Publics

Except for such very broad, long-lasting issues, it is the attentive publics rather than the mass public that affect foreign affairs. Other than special economic interest groups, ethnic and nationality groups, and the like, there is a small but rather vocal set of attentive publics on different segments of foreign affairs. Their influence is subtle, but it is undoubtedly a factor.

Ideological Differences

In all the immediate U.S. foreign policy problems, ideological attitudes shaped by the long series of rather traumatic events since World War II seem likely to be as influential as any of the particular interests just discussed. The long history of the cold war, the tensions with China, the Berlin blockade, the Korean conflict, the Cuban missile crisis, and the Vietnam war have left indelible impressions in the minds of the nation's political leaders, members of Congress, the bureaucracies, the newspaper and academic worlds, the attentive publics, and the mass public. Almost everyone favors preserving the nation's security, protecting its vital interests, enhancing its prosperity, and maintaining its position in the eyes of the world. Yet there is room for vast disagreement about what precisely will accomplish these general goals. Some see the answer in an aggressive foreign policy in which the United States intervenes actively abroad, backed up by defense forces that are second to none. Others see the answer in an internationalist policy that tries to maintain friendly relations with everyone of whatever ideological persuasion and depends heavily on the United Nations and other international bodies. Throughout the cold war some saw the Soviet Union and China as implacable enemies, others viewed them as pursuing goals different from those of the United States without inevitably being aggressive. Still others were emotionally and intellectually committed to a policy of isolationism. All these essentially ideological attitudes are no less powerful than those that are shaped by economic and other considerations.

As described in Chapter 16, the American people shared a consensus on foreign and defense policies for almost two decades following World War II that centered on containing the Soviet Union through such alliances as NATO, heading off Communism through foreign aid, intervening in limited wars against the Communists, and maintaining a high level of defense preparedness. During the Cuban missile crisis, however, the United States first came face to face with the realities of the nuclear age. In its aftermath many people began to wonder whether nuclear weapons had so fundamentally changed international politics that traditional policies for dealing with international threats had become obsolete and started to speculate about alternatives. Others continued to see the Soviet Union as a completely uncompromising enemy with whom no real accommodation could be made. The Vietnam war dramatized and exacerbated this division among both American leaders and the public at large. The next major influence on American attitudes about foreign affairs will, of course, be the course of events in the former Soviet Union.

19

DEFENSE POLICY

Defense or national security policy is really an aspect of foreign policy. This point is illustrated by a story about General Omar Bradley, who was chairman of the Joint Chiefs of Staff, and Dean Acheson, who was undersecretary of state at the time. They had supposedly agreed that if Bradley ever said, "This is a purely military problem," or if Acheson ever said, "This is a purely political problem," the speaker had to get up and leave the room. National security policy, broadly defined, includes such matters as the Truman Doctrine and the North Atlantic Treaty. However, the aspects of defense policy that concern us here are strategy, arms control, and weapons.

This chapter first outlines the history of the strategic debate since World War II. It then briefly recounts the history of arms control negotiations. Next the chapter takes up weapons policy. Rather than recounting the history of the struggle over weapons, it describes the pattern usually followed in deciding policy by using the MX (Missile Experimental) as an example. The chapter then summarizes and elaborates on the role and influence of the different power centers on defense policy. Next, it analyzes the military and strategic factors that led to the Soviet Union's withdrawal from Eastern Europe, and, finally, it speculates on the consequences of the breakup of the Soviet Union for military and strategic questions.

THE DEBATE ON NUCLEAR STRATEGY

The fundamental debate lying behind the struggles in the headlines over weapons and budgets is about nuclear strategy.[1] It began with Winston Churchill's notion of a "balance of terror." In a nuclear age, his argument went, the United States and the Soviet Union are like two scorpions in a bottle. If either strikes, the other will still have enough strength to strike back, and both will die. Thus peace will come, he argued, through mutual terror. What is more, he said, this peace born of terror will paradoxically be rather stable, simply because both sides know the consequences and will act with the utmost caution. During the Cuban missile crisis this point was made succinctly by a piece of graffiti scrawled on the blackboard in a State Department briefing room: "In a nuclear age," it read, "nations make war as porcupines make love—carefully."

This strategic situation came to be known as "mutual assured destruction," and with gallows humor it was quickly dubbed MAD, suggesting that we live in a mad, mad world. The point of MAD is that defense is simply impossible. So the only protection is through deterrence, arms control, or a combination of the two.

In the early years of the nuclear age, stockpiles of nuclear bombs were small. Ballistic missiles were still in their infancy, so the delivery vehicles were manned bombers. Consequently, nuclear strategy seemed straight-forward, at least for the United States. On the military side of the equation, a stockpile of nuclear bombs and a strategic air force to deliver them were the starting points. On the political side, events in Eastern Europe and in Greece escalated into the cold war and were interpreted in the West as evidence of Soviet aggressiveness. Arguing that Hitler could have been deterred and World War II prevented had it been clear that the United States would eventually enter the war, the allies responded with the North Atlantic Treaty. They believed that this statement of intentions, added to the stockpile of nuclear bombs and the strategic air forces, would make a fully adequate deterrent.

The first complication came with the realization that apart from

---

[1]See the various works by Bernard Brodie, Thomas Schelling, George Kennan, Henry Kissinger, William Kaufmann, Warner Schilling, Herman Kahn, George Quester, Glenn Snyder, Robert Jervis, James King, Colin Grey, Patrick Morgan, Hans Morgenthau, Michael Howard, McGeorge Bundy, Alexander George, Richard Smoke, Theodore Greenwood, and Robert McNamara, among others. For an overview see the collection of articles from *Foreign Affairs* edited by William P. Bundy, *The Nuclear Controversy: A Foreign Affairs Reader* (New York: New American Library/Meridan for the Council on Foreign Relations, 1985).

being destroyers of population centers, nuclear weapons would be most economically effective in opening up gaps in a defensive line and against very large concentrations of troops that were massing for an attack or had just landed on a hostile shore, as in the Allied invasion of Normandy. The debate was whether this meant a line of defense in Europe was needed even in peacetime, before actual war was threatened. But none of the allies was willing to finance the large standing armies that a peacetime defense line would require.

Then in 1950 North Korea attacked South Korea. Rightly or wrongly, the conclusion accepted quickly throughout the West was that the attack indicated that the Communist world was willing to take extremely high risks. The response in the West was to end the debate, to form Supreme Headquarters Allied Powers Europe (SHAPE), to station troops in peacetime along a defensive line facing the border between East and West, and to ease the financial burden by rearming Germany.

The strategic argument for these measures is illustrated by the briefing given to officers arriving for duty at SHAPE. On one wall of the briefing room was a two-story enlargement of a photograph of Normandy taken on a very clear day from an altitude of about 10,000 feet shortly before the breakout from the beachhead. Every foxhole was clearly visible. The briefing officer then dropped down an overlay of the Hiroshima bomb. Every single foxhole was obliterated. "Gentlemen," the briefer would say, "a Normandy landing is no longer possible. If we are pushed off the European continent, we will never, ever get back."

Massive Retaliation

A stockpile of nuclear weapons, strategic air forces, and NATO seemed adequate deterrents until early in the Eisenhower administration, when it was clear that the allies were not willing to finance conventional forces sufficient to match the Russians man for man and division for division. Thus the decision was made to rely on battlefield nuclear weapons to make up the difference.

Deterrence seemed assured at the level of either nuclear war or a global war pitting the Soviet armies against the American, but complications arose about lesser levels of aggression. The problem came to be called the "stability/instability" paradox. Nuclear war was so unthinkably destructive and mutual annihilation so certain that both the United States and the Soviet Union seemed to be deterred from pursuing any policies or actions that would increase the risk of confrontations between the two superpowers. But this very stability at the top of the strategic spectrum seemed to be a temptation for lesser aggressions. The Communist world, the argument ran, could encourage limited wars by proxy, such as the attack by North Korea on South Korea, with a high level of confidence that the risks would be small. The stability at the level of nuclear war and war between the superpowers made for instability at the level of lesser wars.

It was to deal with these smaller wars that in January 1954, just one year after President Eisenhower was inaugurated, his secretary of state, John Foster Dulles, announced what came to be known as the doctrine of massive retaliation. This doctrine held that the United States would no longer meet aggression in the same terms that the aggression had been made. The United States, for example, had responded to the attack by North Korea with exactly the same weapons with which the attack had been made: infantry, armored divisions, and aircraft using conventional (nonnuclear) bombs. Henceforth, Dulles declared, the United States would depend "primarily upon a great capacity to retaliate instantly by means and at places of our own choosing." The implication was that any attack made with conventional forces, such as that in Korea, would be met with air power armed with nuclear weapons and that the response might be on Moscow or Peking rather than at the point of attack.

The military policy that accompanied the doctrine of massive retaliation was nicknamed the "new look." In practical terms it meant that the budgets of both the Army and the Navy, but especially the Army, were to be cut severely and their forces reduced, while the budget of the Air Force would be greatly increased.

Criticism of Massive Retaliation and the "New Look"

Opponents of massive retaliation and the "new look" argued that such a policy limited the United States to only one response: nuclear war. An accidental outbreak of violence, for example, could be met only with nuclear weapons, which would obviously increase the risk of World War III, and a nuclear World War III at that. What is more, the critics argued, such a policy lacked credibility. It was simply not believable that the United States would have launched a nuclear war in response to the attack on South Korea by North Korea. If a threat is to be an effective deterrent, it has to threaten something that the potential aggressor believes will actually be done.

Flexible Response

By the election of 1960 the Democrats, their supporters in the Army and Navy, and academic specialists in defense policy had developed a rival doctrine known as flexible response. The theory here was that the United States should have balanced military forces consisting of missile forces, missile-carrying submarines, land-based bombers, carrier-based bombers, conventional nonnuclear ground forces, and conventional naval forces. In this way the United States could respond to threats of any kind and at any level in precisely the same terms in which they were made. Pointing to the Korean conflict, the advocates of flexible response argued that the United States should be able to meet any level of threat without raising the level of the fighting and that this was the only way to ensure that a small and limited war would remain small and limited. In addition, potential aggressors would be more effectively deterred because the threat of a response by the United States would be more credible.

The Kennedy and subsequent administrations followed the policy of flexible response by providing for sizable ground and naval forces as well as air and missile forces. After much debate, NATO gradually adopted the policy informally with formal adoption finally coming in 1967.

Soviet Strategy

As described in Chapter 2, the Soviets had hoped to build their ICBM force around a behemoth of a missile that proved to be just too large and unwieldy to serve as an operational ICBM. It was this failure that led them to deploy IRBMs and MRBMs to Cuba in 1962. Following the Cuban missile crisis the Soviets embarked on a long-term buildup of not only their strategic missile forces but all other forces as well, including battlefield nuclear forces, missile-launching submarines, and conventional forces for both land and sea.

Although the Soviets did not seem to have engaged in the kind of long and tortured debate on strategy that took place in the West, changes in Soviet strategy did occur, usually driven by technological developments. During the Stalin period, Soviet strategy was to deter the United States by threatening to retaliate by conquering and occupying Western Europe with Soviet ground forces. But at the same time the Soviets were building a huge stockpile of medium-range ballistic missiles (MRBMs with a range of 1000 miles) and intermediate-range ballistic missiles (IRBMs with a range of 2000 miles). Soviet strategy was thus changed to deter the United States by adding to the conventional threat to Europe a nuclear threat as well.

From Khrushchev to Brezhnev, 1964–1985

In 1964, when Khrushchev was ousted and Brezhnev took over as leader of the Soviet Union, Soviet policy became that of "ensuring" that the military would be given "all it needed to defend the homeland." For the next decade, the Soviet Union modernized and increased its armed forces of all sorts: missile, air, ground, and sea. Soviet military writings from this first decade of the Brezhnev years saw war as consisting of two phases. The first would be a nuclear exchange, and destruction would be widespread. The second phase would be an attempt by both sides to achieve victory "in the ruins" with conventional forces. There was also speculation that wars might occur in which only conventional weapons were used and even that limited nuclear warfare might be possible. In any case, Soviet strategists believed that nuclear war was not only possible but also that it could be won if the Soviet Union continued to build toward nuclear as well as conventional superiority.

Some time in the early 1970s, the Soviet Union perceived that it had achieved "nuclear parity." Shortly thereafter, around 1977, Soviet economic growth slowed down, and a decision was made to cut the growth in defense spending by pegging it to the growth in the economy itself. At about the same time, in the mid-1970s Brezhnev began to challenge the view that a nuclear war could be won. In a famous speech at Tula in January 1977, he said that no one could win a nuclear war and denied that the Soviet Union was trying to achieve nuclear superiority. He followed this speech with an announcement to the United Nations in 1982 that the Soviet Union was willing to sign with the West a pledge of "no first use." His offer was not accepted, however, since the Western leaders believed that the result would be Soviet dominance because of their huge superiority in ground forces.

The Soviet Buildup and Countervailing Strategy

As the Soviet buildup proceeded following the Cuban missile crisis, the debate on strategy in the West focused on just what constitutes an adequate deterrent. MAD was a strategic situation, not a strategy. From time to time one administration or the other studied the possibility of adopting a counterforce strategy that could prevent the destruction of American cities by destroying the attacking missiles first. But Churchill's balance of terror held, and mutual destruction continued to be assured. A counterforce strategy would have to provide at least two very accurate missiles to attack each of the enemy's missiles, but then the enemy could just build more missiles. The enemy would also have to build only one additional missile for each two that the United States would have to build.

Under Robert S. McNamara, the Defense Department made a stalwart effort at a compromise on a counterforce strategy, one that could destroy at least enough enemy weapons to limit the damage. But even a damage-limiting strategy seemed out of reach.

As the American stockpile of bombs and missile warheads grew and as missiles of all kinds were developed and deployed, the Pentagon's planning for nuclear war, should it come, was essentially eclectic. The basic assumption was that deterrence would be more effective if the targets were chosen to make economic recovery difficult rather than to destroy population centers as such. But this actually made little difference, for hitting the targets that would make economic recovery difficult would inevitably also destroy most Soviet population centers. Warheads were also earmarked for feasible military targets, and whenever a capability was developed for hitting a smaller military target, such as a missile complex, the target was added to the list. The list itself was eventually integrated into the Single Integrated Operational Plan (SIOP).

At some stage at least one group within the Pentagon argued that targeting military installations was actually a more effective deterrent than targeting population centers. The Soviet population is not as urban as the American, and destroying Soviet cities might kill no more than 30 percent of the population. The Soviets suffered 20 million casualities in World War II, yet they continued to function as a society. Thus they might not be deterred by just the loss of population, even one as high as 30 percent. The loss of their fighting capacity, however, would ensure that they could not profit from war, hence targeting their fighting capacity should be a more effective deterrent than just attacking population centers.

Progressively during the Nixon, Ford, Carter, and Reagan administrations, U.S. doctrine and force procurement moved toward a posture that strove for deterrence through giving the president a range of counterforce options as well as countercity options. Eventually, during the Carter administration this eclectic strategy was given a name: the countervailing strategy. However, in spite of its name this strategy was still composed largely of MAD. In effect, it was one of providing a second-strike force but at several different levels and with a certain number of counterforce options. For example, in certain circumstances it might be wise to avoid hitting the enemy's command, control, communications, and intelligence capabilities (in military jargon, C^3I) so that he would be able to order his forces to cease fire. The countervailing strategy did not aspire to destroy the Soviet capacity to retaliate, which seemed impossible, nor even to limit the damage of a Soviet retaliation, which seemed equally elusive. Its goal was rather to enhance deterrence across the full range of conceivable scenarios.

One school of thought argued that developing a range of counterforce options would be stabilizing and deter the adversary at all levels more effectively. An opposing school argued against developing this range of options. First, the opponents maintained a countervailing strategy requires huge missile forces, and the cost is astronomical. It also could spur the adversary on to even greater efforts, thereby fueling the arms race. What is worse, they claim, is that a countervailing strategy is bound to be *not* stabilizing but *destabilizing*. As one state develops more options with more accurate weapons, it conveys to the adversary a growing potentiality of being able to strike first. Faced with even a rather remote possibility that its capacity to retaliate would be destroyed, the adversary would be forced to consider a policy of launching on warning—and the warning might be false. If the United States and the Soviet Union followed this countervailing strategy, they would be like two old-time Western gunfighters in a saloon—each eying the other suspiciously and tensed to draw the instant the other showed any sign of making a move, even to scratch his nose.

Technological improvements can change a weapon from one that is second strike and therefore stabilizing into one that is first strike and therefore *destabilizing.* For example, as long as one missile could carry only one warhead and as long as missiles were not very accurate, deterrence was easy to maintain, and the peace was rather stable. But two developments made the problem of deterrence much more difficult.

The first enabled one missile to carry up to ten warheads. Not only that, these so-called multiple, independently targeted reentry vehicles (MIRVs) could be directed to targets at locations hundreds of miles apart. Before the invention of MIRVs, if one country launched a preemptive, counterforce strike and missed one or two of the enemy's missiles, those missiles would probably be able to destroy one or two of the preempting country's cities. But with MIRVed missiles, if the preempting country missed one or two of the enemy's missiles, it could lose ten to twenty of its own cities.

At the same time the accuracy of the U.S. MX missile and the Soviet equivalent was improved so awesomely that their warheads were able to strike within less than 750 feet of a target at a range of 6000 to 7000 miles. This development meant that no missile, regardless of how much it had been hardened, could survive a first strike, and a hardened missile was no longer a second-strike missile.

With these developments, the world began to enter a period in which one missile launched in a surprise first strike could aim two warheads at each of five land-based missiles in fixed silos of the victim's retaliatory, second-strike force so accurately that the chances would be extremely small that any of the missiles being attacked would survive. In this situation, to have the kind of secure, second-strike force necessary for an effective deterrent, both sides will have to concentrate on submarine-based missiles, mobile land-based missiles, or a force of bombers large enough to keep a high proportion of them constantly airborne.

The "Star Wars" Strategy

Some time after President Reagan took office, he was appalled that the choice for defense was limited to deterrence, arms control, or a combination of the two and proposed a massive research effort to restore the possibility of defense. The idea was to develop a defense system based in space that would prevent missiles from reaching the U.S. homeland. Soviet launching sites would be monitored by spy satellites and attacked the minute they started a launch by lasers from other satellites or by other space-based weapons. A second line of defense would attack in midflight any missiles that broke through the first defense. Satellites would carry nonnuclear weapons such as chemical lasers or neutral particle beams. To this defense would be added such weapons as X-ray lasers triggered by nuclear explosions in space and launched from submarines or bases on the ground. A final defense would be ground-based lasers or interceptors to attack incoming missiles during the last stages of their flight, as they descended to their targets.

The objections to Reagan's "star wars" strategy were several. One was of course that the systems to implement such a defense have yet to be invented and may not be even possible. A second is that the expense is almost incomprehensible, with a figure of over a trillion dollars mentioned only as a starter. A third objection is that even if the weapons can be invented, it still leaves open a wide variety of countermeasures. Satellites are very vulnerable, and once they were eliminated the system would no longer work. Unless a way can be found to permit the satellites to survive a first strike, the "star wars" defense system would be destabilizing rather than stabilizing.

"Star wars" opponents also argued that even if a reasonably reliable and effective system could be invented, the world would still be MAD. For the world to stop being MAD, a system would have to be 100 percent effective, for if only 1 percent of the attacking missiles reached their targets, the casualities would still be in the millions.

Another objection was that the "star wars" defense would not protect against either manned bombers or cruise missiles, the air-breathing, low-flying, robot-piloted drones that can deliver nuclear warheads with great accuracy. Protection against cruise missiles or bombers with a low radar profile, such as the Stealth bomber, would require an entirely different system, more like the old air-defense systems.

Response in NATO Strategy

In any case, the official NATO strategy continued to be flexible response. But the elimination of intermediate-range nuclear weapons and the reductions in troops and conventional weapons as a result of the lessened threat from what had been the Soviet empire weakened the effectiveness of a flexible-response strategy. Flexible response requires a large number of troops and a great deal of military hardware. The most obvious result of the several cuts was that NATO no longer had the range of options that it once had to meet a military emergency. Consequently, at the NATO summit meeting of November 7–8, 1991, in Rome, the NATO members agreed to a new strategy calling for smaller and more mobile forces, structured in such a way that capabilities could be mobilized when necessary rather than kept permanently in being. Political developments and arms control agreements promise—if all goes well—the beginning of a post–cold war era of greatly reduced military tension.

ARMS CONTROL AND DISARMAMENT, 1945–1991

During the cold war era, the United States and the Soviet Union intermittently engaged in negotiations on the subject of arms control and disarmament.[2] The Soviet position in the 1940s and 1950s was that negotiations must begin with the elimination of weapons of all kinds, that is, general and complete disarmament. The United States considered it unfair to be asked to give up its advantage in nuclear weapons without some concrete concession from the Soviet Union, and it therefore regarded the Soviet proposal as nothing more than propaganda. The United States, for its part, insisted that any agreement must include procedures for on-site inspection within each country. But the Soviets felt that inspection by foreigners, even UN observers from neutral countries, would inevitably introduce outside influences into their political system. Consequently they were suspicious that the American proposals had ulterior motives designed to undermine their government.

There was some movement in arms control, notably, the Antarctica Treaty, but essentially matters rested until the Cuban missile crisis of 1962, when both sides looked down the gun barrel of nuclear war and shrank back from the holocaust they saw there. Kennedy realized that the crisis had been a sobering experience for both parties and thus within a few months offered his proposal for a limited nuclear test ban treaty, which was signed in August 1963. In 1967 another treaty banned the use of space satellites as platforms for nuclear weapons. In 1968 a draft treaty to prevent the spread of nuclear weapons to states that did not already have them (the nonproliferation treaty) was approved by the UN General Assembly. Within a short time sixty countries had signed the treaty, with

---

[2]See John Newhouse, *Cold Dawn: The Story of SALT* (New York: Holt, Rinehart and Winston, 1973); Ralph E. Lapp, *Arms Beyond Doubt: The Tyranny of Weapons Technology* (Chicago: Cowles, 1970); Thomas W. Wolfe, *The SALT Experience* (Cambridge, Mass.: Ballinger for the RAND Corporation, 1979); Strobe Talbot, *Endgame* (New York: Harper & Row, 1979); idem, *Deadly Gambits* (New York: Alfred A. Knopf, 1984); Alan Platt, *The U.S. Senate and Strategic Arms Policy, 1969–1977* (Boulder, Colo.: Westview, 1978); Michael Krepon, *Strategic Stalemate: Nuclear Weapons and Arms Control in American Politics* (New York: St. Martin's, 1984); Paul Huth and Bruce Russett, "What Makes Deterrence Work? Cases from 1900 to 1980," *World Politics* (July 1984); Chihiro Hosoya, "Miscalculations in Deterrence Policy: Japanese-U.S. Relations, 1938–41," *Journal of Peace Research*, Vol. 2 (1968); and Alexander George, Philip J. Farley, and Alexander Dallin, eds., *U.S.–Soviet Security Corporation: Achievements, Failures, Lessons* (New York, Oxford University Press, 1988).

the United States and the Soviet Union being among the first. However, France, China, India, Israel, Egypt, Argentina, Brazil, South Africa, and Japan refused to sign, although Japan later did. France, China, and India subsequently constructed and tested nuclear weapons. Also, it has been generally believed for some years (and confirmed by CIA documents released to the newspapers on January 27, 1978) that Israel had long since completed all the component parts for a nuclear weapon.

Treaties followed forbidding the use of the ocean floor as a site for nuclear weapons and the development, production, or stockpiling of biological and toxic weapons. These were helpful steps, but none of them struck at the central problem of the huge stockpile of nuclear warheads and missiles that remained in the arsenals of the Soviet Union and the United States.

The SALT I Agreements

In late 1969 the Strategic Arms Limitation Talks (SALT) were begun in Helsinki, Finland. Almost two and a half years later the so-called SALT I agreements were signed in Moscow by Nixon and Leonid Brezhnev. The first agreement, the "interim agreement," placed ceilings on the number of ICBMs and submarine-launched ballistic missiles each side would be permitted. A separate agreement on antiballistic missiles (ABMs) specified that the Soviet Union and the United States would each limit their antiballistic missile sites to two with one hundred missiles at each.

Although the SALT I agreements were widely welcomed, they left both sides with significant worries and dissatisfaction. The Soviets had been allowed 1608 ICBMs and 950 submarine-launched missiles, while the United States had been allowed 1054 ICBMs and 710 submarine-launched missiles. The disparity reflected the existing situation and was also intended to compensate the Soviets for the technological lead that the United States enjoyed as well as certain disadvantages the Soviets suffered because of geography, principally their two-front problem with a newly hostile Communist China on one border and capitalist Western Europe on the other. However, the difference in ceilings bothered many Americans both inside and outside government, and Senator Henry M. ("Scoop") Jackson successfully sponsored an amendment that ensured that both sides would have equal numbers in any future agreements. Another sore point for the American side was the fact that the treaties did not do much to keep the Soviets from continuing to develop their very heavy missiles, which had at least the potential of launching a first strike against American retaliatory forces.

For their part, the Soviets were not happy with the failure of the agreements to do much about the American lead in technology, although they correctly foresaw that they would be the long-term beneficiaries of unrestricted MIRV technological development. Another problem for the Soviets was the so-called forward-based systems. The Soviets contended that American tactical aircraft based in Europe or on aircraft carriers were capable of delivering nuclear weapons to the Soviet homeland and therefore should be counted among the strategic forces of bombers and missiles.

The SALT II Agreements

On November 24, 1974, President Gerald Ford and Secretary Leonid Brezhnev met in the Soviet city of Vladivostock, where they agreed on an outline or framework for further negotiations that took another four and a half years.

An agreement was finally reached which Ford's successor, President Carter and Brezhnev signed in Vienna in 1979, but the opposition, especially in Congress, was substantial, since both liberals and conservatives had their own particular objections. Although the Joint Chiefs of Staff endorsed the treaty as a modest but useful step, the Pentagon representative in the SALT II negotiations, General Edward L. Rowny, resigned in protest shortly before the signing, saying that SALT II left the United States with a "window of vulnerability," a phrase later adopted by Ronald Reagan in the presidential campaign of 1980. Rowny then went to work for Senator Jesse Helms to try to prevent ratification of the treaty.

However, it seems clear that the greatest liability the treaty suffered was that even though it had been crafted over three separate administrations, the name on the bottom line was Jimmy Carter. His handling of foreign affairs had earned hostility from Democrats as well as Republicans, and it seems doubtful that SALT II would win enough votes in Congress to be ratified. When the Soviets invaded Afghanistan all doubt was removed, and Carter withdrew the treaty from consideration.

Intermediate-range Nuclear Forces

Separate negotiations on what were first called theater nuclear forces (TNF) and later intermediate-range nuclear forces (INF), IRBMs, and MRBMs with ranges below 5000 miles, had begun in October 1980. Following the adoption of SALT I, the Soviets developed the SS-20. Because its fuel was solid rather than liquid, it was a more reliable weapon. It was also MIRVed with three warheads, highly accurate, and transportable by truck. But since its range was just under 5000 miles, it was not classified as an ICBM, which would have made it subject to the SALT I limitations on mobility. Thus Soviet deployment of the SS-20 reawakened the old fear in Europe about "decoupling," the fear that the Americans might not be willing to use ICBMs against the Soviet Union in retaliation for an attack that was confined to Europe. Chancellor

Helmut Schmidt of West Germany was particularly concerned, arguing that if SALT did not constrain the Soviets from deploying powerful weapons below the strategic level, such as the SS-20, then NATO must deploy theater nuclear weapons to offset them. The answers were the intermediate-range Pershing IIs and the cruise missile.

However, feelings in Europe were ambivalent. Most Europeans wanted an arms control agreement, specifically SALT II. The dilemma was that delay in developing and deploying the Pershings and the cruise missiles might mean that Europe would have neither a meaningful arms control agreement nor theater nuclear forces to offset the SS-20.

After many months of negotiating moves and countermoves, the military on both sides came to the conclusion that the SS-20 and Pershing II had very little real military value. Accordingly, the INF treaty was signed in December 1987 specifying that both weapons be withdrawn from the European theater. It was the first time that both sides agreed to eliminate a whole class of weapons. It was also the first time that the Soviets accepted the idea of on-site inspection to verify that the missiles had in fact been removed. These innovations paved the way for the next steps—the Treaty on Conventional Armed Forces in Europe (CFE I) and the Strategic Arms Reduction Talks (START) and the resulting treaty.

CFE I, which provided for more substantial reduction in weapons than any previous agreement, was signed in November 1990. Under it, the Soviet Union and its Warsaw Pact allies agreed to reduce their 41,000 battle tanks to 13,000 and their 57,000 armed combat vehicles to 20,000. The U.S. reductions were smaller, since it had fewer to begin with, but they were also substantial.[3]

The CFE I treaty was perhaps the most important step in arms reduction yet achieved. Since the end of World War II, the Soviet Union and its Eastern European allies had a huge advantage in conventional arms and armies. This gave them the capacity to launch a surprise attack that might be able to overwhelm the NATO defenses before the West could be mobilized. Second, conventional forces are more costly to produce and maintain than nuclear forces, and the Western allies were constantly disputing what the balance between nuclear and conventional forces should be and how the costs should be shared.

Strategic Arms Reduction Talks Treaty

On July 31, 1991, Mikhail Gorbachev and George Bush signed the Strategic Arms Reduction Talks treaty. The agreement had been under discussion for the better part of a decade, and its signing marked a new era of

---

[3]Thomas Graham, Jr., "The CFE Story: Tales from the Negotiating Table," *Arms Control Today,* Vol. 21, no. 1 (January/February 1991), p. 9.

cooperation between the superpowers. As in INF and CFE I, Gorbachev made concessions that none of his predecessors would have even imagined. This was especially true of the verification procedures, which were more liberal than any the Soviet Union had ever agreed to before.[4]

On June 17, 1992, Presidents Bush and Yeltsin agreed to reduce each side's long-range missile warheads from 11,500 to between 3,000 and 3,500. This seemed impressive at first, but skeptics pointed out that 50 percent of the American population living in 70 metropolitan areas could be destroyed by only 200 warheads, while 50 percent of the Russian population living in a larger number of metropolitan areas could be destroyed by only 300 warheads.

WEAPONS POLICY DISPUTES

Ever since the end of World War II controversy has been fierce over weapons policy, over proposals for an antiballistic missile (ABM) system, the B-1 supersonic bomber, the B-2 Stealth bomber designed to be invisible to radar, the Trident nuclear missile submarine, the cruise missile, the neutron bomb, the MX missile system, and the so-called "star wars" proposal.

The development of various weapons policies follows a remarkably similar pattern. First, either the military present what they would like to see developed to the scientists and engineers or the scientists and engineers present the concept of a new weapon to the military. When the weapon is a new tank or airplane with unusual specifications, it is usually the military who present their "wish list" to the scientists and engineers. When it is something really esoteric, like the original atomic bomb, the hydrogen bomb, or the neutron bomb, it is the other way around. A compromise is then hammered out in debates within the executive branch, among the different services if necessary, among the various concerned offices in the Pentagon, the State Department, and with the White House. The proposal for the new weapon is then presented to Congress and eventually to the public. Debate takes place within the various congressional committees and in the press and among outside specialists in the attentive publics of industry, academia, and the like. Typically Congress does not reject a new weapon but frequently stretches out its procurement and in the process changes or limits it. Occasionally, this takes so long that the weapon is superseded by an even newer concept and so abandoned.

---

[4]Jack Mendelsohn, "Why START," *Arms Control Today,* Vol. 21, no. 3 (April 1991), p. 4.

The MX as a Case Study

The MX is a good example of this process. It started life as an item on the military "wish list." The military wanted a missile that could carry a number of warheads that could be independently directed to different targets (a multiple, independently targeted reentry vehicle, or MIRV), that was extremely accurate, and that was land based but also mobile. Steady improvements in missile accuracy, in ways of making weapons smaller but with greater throwweight (the total weight that could be hurled into a ballistic orbit), and in the technology of MIRVs were beginning to make it possible to fulfill the wish. By the spring of 1973, during the Nixon administration, the MX proposal began to be debated within the Pentagon. The debate then widened to include the State Department, the CIA, and the White House. Funds were requested from Congress for research and development. Each year thereafter Congress debated the new requests for funds, made some changes, and reduced the funds but always provided a portion of what was wanted.

The press, outside specialists, and the attentive publics for defense policy also joined the debate. As the weapon came close to production, the debate shifted to the larger strategic issues that it raised, as described. The most acrimonious question was how the MX should be based. Dozens of so-called basing modes were proposed, debated within the Pentagon and within the administration, and many were discarded. President Ford actually decided on basing the MX missiles in long tunnels. The opposition in Congress was strong, and when Carter became president he abandoned the idea. Instead, he proposed putting two hundred MXs on railroad cars that would shuttle them around a 4500-mile "racecourse" dotted with protected launching pads. The opposition in Congress to this proposal was also strong, and when Reagan became president he killed the idea. The notion of putting the MX missiles close together in a "dense pack" on a single site was suggested on the theory that in an attack the incoming Soviet missiles would actually damage other incoming Soviet missiles, and that a substantial number of the MX missiles would survive and could be launched. This, too, was killed by opposition in Congress and outside the government.

As the debate on basing went on, opponents to the whole MX program in Congress and elsewhere kept chipping away, trying to cut down the number of missiles to be produced or to kill the program entirely. President Carter asked for funding for two hundred MX missiles, and Congress finally appropriated funds to build twenty-one. President Reagan requested funds to build one hundred MXs, and Congress authorized money for another twenty-one but with the condition that the money could not be spent until Congress had another chance to vote on the question in the spring of 1985. At that time Congress cut the program once again, authorizing only fifty missiles as the final goal—of which funds for forty-two had been voted.

Although no one thought it a very good idea because it made these fifty MXs so vulnerable, the Reagan administration decided to put them in the old Minuteman silos. The Reagan administration as it was leaving office recommended another 50 MXs to be based on a racecourse. But the Bush-Yeltsin agreement described above called for dismantling all MX missiles.

THE POWER LINEUP ON DEFENSE POLICY

The earlier chapters on the president, the president's staff, the political appointees, the national security bureaucracies, the Congress, the interest groups, the press and TV, public opinion, and the electorate looked at a wide variety of power centers. Not all involve themselves in defense questions, however, and those that do rarely participate equally in all three aspects of defense: strategy, arms control, and weapons policy. The military, of course, are always involved in all three, but usually they act not as one power center but at least three—Army, Navy, and Air Force— and sometimes more, as when the Navy splits between the advocates of aircraft carriers and the advocates of missile-carrying submarines!

Presidents and presidential advisers cannot avoid being involved in all three aspects of defense policy, but their participation in questions of strategy is intermittent at best. President Eisenhower, his staff, Secretary of State John Foster Dulles, and the State Department did involve themselves in strategy when they established the policy of massive retaliation. Their motivation was budget worries rather than an interest in strategy, but the effect was much the same. Inevitably, strategy became an issue in the 1960 campaign. The Democrats developed the alternative strategy of flexible response, which guaranteed that Kennedy and his staff would be involved in issues of strategy following his election. McNamara tried desperately throughout his tenure as secretary of defense under both Kennedy and Johnson to get control of strategy through target selection and SIOP, but he had only partial success. Succeeding presidents have not been very deeply involved in questions of strategy, with the exception of Reagan's "star wars" proposals, which are regarded as a highly unorthodox, if not bizarre, kind of participation.

Of the other departments and agencies only the CIA is involved in the full range of defense issues. The State Department is next most likely to be involved in defense matters across the board, since all three aspects have political implications involving relations with either a potential enemy or our allies. The Arms Control and Disarmament Agency also becomes involved in all three aspects, but less in strategy than in the others. Treasury and Commerce participate in a rather small way in both weapons policy and arms control, but not in strategy.

Among the committees of Congress, some, especially those dealing with foreign affairs, defense, and intelligence, are involved in all three aspects of defense, although here too the participation in debates on strategy is intermittent. Of the others, the appropriations committees are the most involved, but again the involvement with weapons policy is by far the greatest.

In the second and third rings of power, academics are the most likely to be continuously involved across the whole range of defense policy. Before World War II, few academics were interested in defense. But following the invention of nuclear weapons and missiles, academic centers devoted to research on defense sprang up in every major university. A handful of the press also interests itself in the full range of defense policy, as does an equally small "attentive public." Beyond this, a few organizations that could be called interest groups have been organized, with the most prominent being the nuclear freeze movement.

The Military-Industrial Complex

Most of the power centers involved with foreign affairs are also concerned with defense. In addition there is what President Eisenhower warned against in his farewell address: the military-industrial complex. There is, however, nothing sinister in this alliance. The military has been given responsibility for the nation's security, and its duty is to fight hard for strong defenses, large armies, navies, and air forces, and the latest, most powerful, and most sophisticated weapons.[5] The military will thus naturally be skeptical about arms control agreements and diligent in examining such agreements for loopholes and hidden advantages for the other side. Indeed, if it were not, most people would ask whether it was doing its job. The individual services will also fight hard for their particular weapons. The Air Force will fight for manned bombers like the B-1; the Navy will fight for missile-carrying submarines like the Trident and for aircraft carriers; and the Army will fight for ground forces, tanks, and battlefield nuclear weapons. On such questions the military will be able to wield great power. The subject is the security of the nation, and the military forces are the experts on the subject. To oppose them on the narrow subject of weapons is difficult and politically dangerous.

---

[5]In addition to the works cited in earlier chapters, see Adam Yarmolinsky, *The Military Establishment: Its Impact on American Society* (New York: Harper & Row, 1971); Henry L. Trewitt, *McNamara: His Ordeal in the Pentagon* (New York: Harper & Row, 1971); and Bruce M. Russett, *What Price Vigilance? The Burden of National Defense* (New Haven, Conn.: Yale University Press, 1970).

The industrial side of the complex is equally predictable. Inevitably aircraft and missile manufacturers will favor large air forces and missile arsenals, the people who make submarines and aircraft carriers will favor strong navies, and those who make tanks and artillery will favor large armies. These industries in turn quarrel among themselves about the relative merits of the weapons they produce.

The military industries also exercise great power. They command all the national security and patriotic arguments that the military offers, and they also have economic arguments. A large military budget means not only high industrial profits but also jobs. The unions associated with these industries will be powerful allies, as will the merchants and operators of business in regions in which the factories are located. The members of Congress from those districts will be diligent lobbyists for the cause and powerful allies.

The point was made in down-to-earth terms by Representative Joseph P. Addabbo, a Democrat from Queens and head of the appropriations subcommittee on defense. On a visit to the headquarters of the Rockwell International Corporation, he noticed a map of the United States with strings radiating from the plant to every subcontractor building a part of the B-1 bomber. The strings covered the entire map. Later, when he was leading a fight to kill the B-1 bomber program, the consequences of all those strings came home to him. "One by one I was losing members," he recalled. "They said to me, 'Joe, they've built a plant in my district. I need the jobs.' "[6]

Both the military and the associated industries are likely to have strong views on foreign policy issues related to defense, and their positions are likely to be on the hawkish side. However, two final observations must be made. First, the leverage the military-industrial complex is able to exercise depends on how directly a particular issue relates to defense. On a question that concerns bases or troops overseas, the military and their industrial allies will have great influence. For years a number of powerful people favored drastically reducing American troops stationed in Germany and Korea; returning to Japan sovereignty over Okinawa, where the United States had a huge base; and cutting down on the use of bases in the Philippines, the Portuguese Azores, and elsewhere. Among the advocates of this policy were Mike Mansfield, for many years majority leader of the Senate; J. William Fulbright, chairman of the Senate Foreign Relations Committee; other leaders in both the Senate and the House; presidents and others in the White House; top officials in the State Department; and prominent persons in the newspaper and academic worlds and among the attentive publics. But the military and

---

[6]*The New York Times,* May 17, 1985, p. 1.

their allies in industry and Congress fought the reductions and succeeded in preventing many of them and delaying the rest. On the other hand, on foreign policy and national security issues less directly related to military defense, such as détente, the leverage of the military-industrial complex is not so great.

Second, it is a mistake to assume that the military will always be hawkish on all foreign policy issues. As described, it was a general, Matthew B. Ridgway, who prevented the U.S. government from intervening in Vietnam in 1954. In 1965, when President Johnson decided to bomb North Vietnam and send in American ground combat forces, the military was also decidedly unenthusiastic. But once the United States was committed to the war in Vietnam, the military pressed hard for whatever measures were needed to win a victory. In late 1984 and early 1985, Secretary of Defense Caspar W. "Cap" Weinberger and Secretary of State George P. Shultz engaged in a rather sharp public debate on the use of force, but it was the secretary of state who took the more hawkish position. In general the military-industrial complex favors a high level of preparedness and "tough" foreign policies, but they shy away from entering wars, especially limited wars. Once committed to fighting, however, the military will usually oppose any settlement short of victory.

Changes Under Gorbachev and the Future of Defense Policy

Gorbachev came to power in 1985. Along with many of the civilian party leaders, he had apparently not liked the way that Brezhnev had kowtowed to the military. Soviet discontent with the military was highlighted by the war in Afghanistan, the deployment of the intermediate-range SS-20 aimed at Western Europe without full consideration of its political implications, the shooting down of a Korean airliner, and the ability of a young West German to fly his light plane through Soviet air defenses to land in Red Square in Moscow. Gorbachev apparently seized these opportunities to force the retirement of some senior Soviet generals and to make fundamental changes in both the high command and defense policy.

On defense spending, Gorbachev changed the formulation from promising the military "all it needed to defend the homeland," as in Brezhnev's time, to ensuring that the military would "remain at a level that rules out the strategic superiority of the forces of imperialism." Soviet spokesmen also began to distinguish between "parity," implying absolute equality with the West in every aspect of defense, and "reasonable sufficiency," defined, to repeat, as a force level that "rules out superiority by the forces of imperialism." At the same time, Soviet spokesmen stressed the "defensive nature" of Soviet military posture and argued that its goal is to prevent or deter war.

In the early years of Gorbachev's rule, Soviet military doctrine apparently anticipated a long war conducted mainly with conventional weapons. This policy conceded that nuclear weapons might be used, especially battlefield nuclear weapons deployed by the NATO forces. But the argument was that such use would be limited because of fear of escalation. Essentially, the position was that Churchill's balance of terror, or MAD, still held. Since both sides had forces that could survive an attack and strike back at the other's homeland, the NATO forces would be careful, the Soviets reasoned, to limit their use of nuclear weapons, even if they did use some of them on the battlefield.

Effect of the Gorbachev Revolution on Defense

The Soviet preoccupation with defense in the decades following World War II was understandable. Twenty million Soviet soldiers had been killed in the war. Another five to fifteen million men, women, and children had died of hunger or disease in the German-occupied territories or in places under siege such as Leningrad. Germany was the focus of Soviet fears, but the fear of Germany inevitably broadened to include the whole of the West and particularly the United States.

These fears led Stalin and his successors to give extremely high priority to defense. But the fact was that the Soviet economy simply could not compete with that of the United States. The U.S. gross national product (GNP) was about $4.5 trillion. During the cold war years, the United States spent about 6 to 7 percent of this on defense–between $270 billion and $315 billion a year.

Western economists during this period estimated that the Soviet GNP was about $2 trillion. On the other hand, Soviet economists writing after *glasnost* thought it was much lower, perhaps only about $1.5 trillion or even as low as $1 trillion. Many Western economists have since come to believe that these lower figures were nearer the mark. On Soviet defense spending, exact figures are impossible. But estimates range from 15 percent to 25 and even 30 percent. So the Soviet defense budget cost the Soviet people somewhere between a low of $150 billion and a high that could have been as much as $400 billion out of a much, much lower GNP.

But as time went on, developments in military technology were turning Germany, even a united Germany, into a third-rate power in military terms–a power that was stronger than Sweden, Switzerland, and the Netherlands but far, far less powerful than the United States or the Soviet Union. It seemed increasingly clear that Germany, sitting as it does in the middle of Europe within 10 to 15 minutes of Soviet missiles armed with nuclear warheads, was no longer a threat. No nation with territory that is less than continental size can play the nuclear game. Japan and England came to understand this, and so did Germany.

In spite of the death and destruction the Soviet people suffered at German hands, even the Soviet leaders began to understand the realities of nuclear weapons and missiles. As described earlier, Brezhnev recognized that no one could win a nuclear war in his speech at Tula in 1977.

After Gorbachev came to power, he gradually came to the conclusion that the gigantic effort to bind the Eastern Europe countries to the Soviet Union in a military alliance and to supply them with military equipment was no longer worth the effort. Soviet troops were withdrawn to the Soviet Union and the Warsaw Pact was dissolved.

Many observers felt that without the burden of keeping the Eastern European countries as satellites, the Soviet Union would be stronger both economically and militarily. However, as we saw in the preceding chapter, with his withdrawal from Eastern Europe and his domestic policies of *perestroika* (restructuring) and *glasnost* (openness), Gorbachev had opened a Pandora's box, and the old Soviet Union quickly broke up. The question then became: What will happen to the armed forces of the former Soviet Union? Not only did these forces consist of the full panoply of conventional forces—tanks, artillery, infantry, and so on—it also included a stockpile of twenty-seven thousand nuclear warheads of all types and somewhere in the neighborhood of fifteen thousand missiles capable of delivering nuclear warheads to almost any country in the world, including the United States.

Of the eleven members of the Commonwealth of Independent States, five agreed on having unified armed forces—Russia, Kazakhstan, Armenia, Tajikistan, and Kyrgyzstan. The other six insisted on having their own independent armies—Azerbaijan, Belarus, Moldova, Turkmenistan, Ukraine, and Uzbekistan.

In early January 1992, Ukraine asked Soviet troops in its territory to take oaths of loyalty to Ukraine or to serve elsewhere in the Commonwealth. It also laid claim to the entire Black Sea fleet of the former Soviet Union. The Ukrainian defense minister, Konstantin Morozov, speaking to a press conference in Kiev said, "Our strategic line is that Ukraine is a sea-going power and should have its own fleet. And it will have one." However, a compromise was reached giving part of the fleet to Russia and part to Ukraine.

The most ominous problem, however, was obviously nuclear weapons and missiles. Long-range missiles armed with nuclear warheads had been stationed in Russia, Ukraine, Belarus, and Kazakhstan. Various news media reported that some nuclear weapons and missiles were being moved from the other republics to Russia, and on December 16,

1991, Yeltsin said that eventually all the members of the Commonwealth would eliminate nuclear weapons except Russia. However, the president of Kazakhstan declared that Kazakhstan would keep nuclear weapons as long as Russia did. However, he also said that it would be willing to put the weapons on its territory under a central command if Russia did the same.

The United States pledged $400 million to help the new Commonwealth of Independent States dismantle its short-range nuclear weapons. In December 1991, Secretary of State Baker made a special visit to Russia and other members of the Commonwealth to determine, among other things, just what kind of controls would be placed on nuclear weapons during the transition to whatever political arrangement eventually comes out of the turmoil.

These two efforts were welcome, but many observers were disappointed that the United States had not come forward with more imaginative and far-reaching proposals. They believed that the tumultuous events in the former Soviet Union present humankind with an unparalleled opportunity for a true end to the Soviet-American rivalry and the first steps toward some sort of international mechanism, perhaps through the UN, for accomplishing political and social change by peaceful procedures and so abolishing war forever.

President Bush has said that he is uncomfortable with what he calls "the vision thing." But many believe that if humankind is to survive its diabolical military inventions, "the vision thing" is our only hope.

20

CAN THE AMERICAN
SYSTEM COPE?

THE LOCUS OF POWER

Will the American political system we have described be able to cope with
the problems that lie ahead? This system is one in which power is
dispersed among a wide variety of organizations and individuals. The
president and his staff in the White House constitute the most powerful of
these power centers, but the presidency is far from being all powerful.
The Congress has enormous power and is one of the few legislatures in
the world that does in fact legislate. Political appointees have power, as
do the bureaucrats in the great departments, the press, the interest
groups, a wide variety of organizations in what David Truman called the
"intermediate structure,"[1] and the mass electorate. On any given issue a
relatively small coalition among this welter of power centers can exercise
a veto. It is extraordinarily difficult for the American society to embark
on any really new enterprise of any size. Only two presidents in modern
times have succeeded in getting a major program adopted: President
Roosevelt and his New Deal and President Reagan and his economic
program.

The problems that lie ahead in foreign affairs and defense are
formidable. The awesome power of nuclear weapons and the incredible
range, speed, and accuracy of missiles have made war unthinkable. The

---

[1]"The American System in Crisis," *Political Science Quarterly* (December 1959); and
The Governmental Process: Political Interest and Public Opinion, 2nd ed. (New York: Alfred
A. Knopf, 1971).

turmoil in the former Soviet Union has been hailed as marking the end of the cold war. In response, the United States reduced its short-range, tactical nuclear weapons and other forces stationed in Europe, and the former Soviet Union did the same. Even after the 1992 Bush-Yeltsin agreements, both sides retained an awesome stockpile of nuclear weapons and the intercontinental ballistic missiles to deliver them. Humankind remains at enormouse risk. The turmoil in the former Soviet Union could produce a new, aggressive dictator. An American decision to intervene in some new Middle Eastern crisis might start a spiral of violence that gets out of control. Or one side or the other may do something that leads to a missile crisis like that in Cuba but which the two sides handle with less skill than Kennedy and Khrushchev handled the one in 1962.

And if only modest progress has been made in arms control, not even a beginning has been made in creating the international political structures that are even more important to lasting peace than banishing the actual weapons.[2] Humankind must find a way to limit its numbers so that future generations will not press so heavily upon the resources of what is, after all, a rather limited "spaceship earth." Humankind must find new sources of energy and new raw materials of all kinds. If life is to continue on the planet, humankind must discover ways of ending the pollution of air and water. This agenda will require a new technology and international economic institutions to ensure its spread and to regulate the world's economic efforts and trade so that all of humanity can share its fruits.

Reflecting on the complexity and difficulty of these problems and the untidy, frequently stalemated American political system, one wonders whether the system can cope. What is discouraging is how difficult it will be to get such disparate myriad power centers to agree on policies for meeting these complex problems. The past certainly contains some notable failures. An example is one that sociologist Daniel Bell used to illustrate the need for more wide-spread and systematic efforts to look at very long-range problems that might emerge in the future.[3] Sometime in the late 1920s or early 1930s the American people made a decision that fundamentally shaped the world in which we live today. It determined the style and rhythm of our lives, the pattern of the cities and the suburbs, the landscape of the countryside, and even the air we breathe. Yet so momentous a decision made no headlines, was not the subject of

---

[2]For a discussion of these issues and those mentioned below see Roger Hilsman, *The Crouching Future: International Politics and U.S. Foreign Policy, a Forecast* (Garden City, N.Y.: Doubleday, 1975).

[3]Daniel Bell, "Introduction," in *The Year 2000: A Framework for Speculation on the Next Thirty-three Years,* Herman Kahn and Anthony J. Wiener (New York: Macmillan, 1967).

debate in Congress, was not agonized over by the president, and was never an issue in an election. What happened was that tens of millions of American families almost subconsciously came to accept that the arrangement that would assure them of the "good life" was a single-family dwelling on an individual plot of land. If a plot of land and a house could not be had near the job or convenient to public transportation, cheaper land was available within commuting distance, and mass-produced automobiles made this dream feasible. At every income level the American family set about to acquire its own dwelling on its own plot of land and its own automobile.

Everyone who lived at the time understood in some subliminal way that this mass decision had been made. But no government planner, no journalist, no academic expert set about to examine systematically its implications for succeeding generations. No one asked what kind of world this decision would create (although a few did speculate in a rather idle way). Yet it would have been no great trick to forecast the consequences; no crystal ball or towering genius was needed. A simple extrapolation of trends in population and per capita income would have indicated the number of houses required, the amount of land they would take up, and the number of automobiles there would be. Further calculations would have indicated the miles of roads required and the additional land they would take up. The emissions of an internal-combustion engine were known, so straightforward multiplication would have suggested the amount of air pollution involved. After these estimates had been made, further predictions would have sketched in the shape of the future world: urban sprawl, decline of the inner cities, traffic congestion, and the pollution of water and air.

Had society and government faced head on the issue of building our society around separate dwellings and private automobiles, the decision might still have been the same. But clearly measures could have been taken to lessen the worst of the consequences. However, while the job of forecasting the consequences would have been rather easy, no organized group or government agency took it up and forced the government and society as a whole to face the issue. It can be argued that in a pluralistic process of government decision making, an individual will rarely be heard and will almost always be disheartened by the difficulty of organizing a group with enough power to force the government and society to face an issue of this kind. Therefore only those problems that directly and immediately affect a segment of the population in which the people can fairly easily identify with each other are likely to provoke individuals into forming interest groups. Farmers, industrialists, and workers can be so provoked, but consumers are not easy to arouse. Furthermore, few people will discern the kind of long-range problems resulting from the absent-minded or mindless mass decision to build a world of individual houses on separate plots of land from which people commute to work and do their shopping by automobile. Thus such latent issues are likely to be ignored or overlooked in a society in which power is diffused among a large number of power centers. (Latent issues are those that might be central to broad segments of society if they were publicly articulated but remain latent precisely because they are not widely discussed.)

As we have seen, a political system composed of multiple power centers gives a veto to a relatively small coalition of those power centers who oppose some new initiative, even though that initiative protects certain segments of society from harmful action by the rest. The question here, however, is this: Is a society in which independent power centers can block positive action by the society as a whole really capable of rapid and fundamental change to meet the kind of problems that in fact lie ahead of us today?

Power: Concentrated or Dispersed?

It is sometimes argued that the trend is in exactly the opposite direction and that far from fearing the consequences of a dispersion of power, we should fear the consequences of a concentration of power. Some who have tried to discern the future pattern of the distribution of power foresee a "principate" of power consisting of the president and his immediate cohorts.[4] Yet the situation that has developed since World War II could hardly be described as a further concentration of power in the hands of the executive. On the contrary, it has been a diffusion of power or, more accurately, a proliferation of additional power centers. Some sociologists and political scientists have seen the American system as being controlled by a "power elite."[5] Robert A. Dahl has been a foremost critic of the power-elite theories, subscribing instead to a pluralist view of American society.[6]

---

[4]Bell, *The Coming of the Post-Industrial Society.* For a discussion of how various analysts have treated the problem of the locus of power in a superindustrial society, see Roger Hilsman's *The Crouching Future,* pp. 126–166.

[5]C. Wright Mills was the first of the modern "power elitists." See his *The Power Elite* (New York: Oxford University Press, 1956). Others include G. William Domhoff, Floyd Hunter, Gabriel Kolko, and Kenneth Prewitt and Alan Stone. See also Thomas R. Dye and L. Harmon Ziegler. Authors who have taken an opposing view include Robert A. Dahl, Henry S. Kariel, T. B. Bottomore, and Peter Bachrach.

[6]In addition to the works by Dahl cited in earlier chapters, see his *Polyarchy* (New Haven, Conn.: Yale University Press, 1956); *A Preface to Democratic Theory* (Chicago: University of Chicago Press, 1956); *After the Revolution? Authority in a Good Society* (New Haven, Conn.: Yale University Press, 1970); *Who Governs? Democracy and Power in an American City* (New Haven, Conn.: Yale University Press, 1961); and *Democracy in the United States: Promise and Performance* (Skokie, Ill.: Rand McNally, 1972).

But this debate still left many observers uneasy about the special position large corporations seem to occupy in American society. A possible explanation has been offered by Charles E. Lindblom.[7] Lindblom points out that the United States and all the other democracies have economic systems based on private enterprise and the market. So most of the property, including factories and industry, is not owned by the government, and most of the decisions on the production of goods and services are made as a result of the push and pull of market demand and supply. However, Lindblom's argument runs, government officials cannot be indifferent to how well business performs its functions. "Depression, inflation, or other economic distress can bring down a government. A major function of governments, therefore, is to see to it that businessmen perform their tasks." But because of constitutional restraints in the democratic societies, and especially the law of private property, government cannot command business to perform. Government can forbid certain kinds of business activity, and it can regulate business activity, but it cannot make business do things. Government therefore "must induce rather than command. They must therefore offer benefits to businessmen in order to stimulate the required performance." Lindblom's argument is summarized in the following words:

> In the eyes of government officials, therefore, businessmen do not appear simply as the representatives of a special interest, as representatives of interest groups do. They appear as functionaries performing functions that government officials regard as indispensable. When a government official asks himself whether business needs a tax reduction, he knows he is asking a question about the welfare of the whole society and not simply about a favor to a segment of the population, . . .
>
> Any government official who understands the requirements of his position and the responsibilities that market-oriented systems throw on businessmen will therefore grant them a privileged position. He does not have to be bribed, duped, or pressured to do so. Nor does he have to be an uncritical admirer of businessmen to do so. He simply understands, as is plain to see, that public affairs in market-oriented systems are in the hands of two groups of leaders, government and business, who must collaborate and that to make the system work government leadership must often defer to business leadership. . . .
>
> Thus politics in market-oriented systems takes a peculiar turn, one largely ignored in conventional political science. To understand the peculiar character of politics in market-oriented systems requires, however, no conspiracy theory of politics, no theory of common social origins uniting government and business officials, no crude allegation of a power elite

---

[7]Charles E. Lindblom, *Politics and Markets: The World's Political-Economic Systems* (New York: Basic Books, 1977); and *Democracy and the Market System* (New York: Oxford University Press, 1988). See also Michael Schwartz, *The Structure of Power in America: The Corporate Elite as a Ruling Class* (New York: Holmes and Meier, 1987).

established by clandestine forces. Business simply needs inducements, hence a privileged position in government and politics, if it is to do its job.[8]

In the struggle with the Executive branch, Congress has lost some power, but that power has gone not so much to the executive as to a variety of groups and subgroups within the intermediate structure. This pattern ranges across domestic affairs. African-Americans, Spanish-Americans, and Native Americans are all organizing and demanding a voice in their own affairs. Teachers, the police, sanitation workers, and welfare recipients are better organized and determined to be heard. Local communities are demanding a larger voice in school policies. Even the federal government's poverty program failed on the issue of lack of local participation and control. In domestic affairs presidents may still be first among the power centers, but they are first among many. They are hardly principates.

Only in foreign affairs have presidents resembled principates since World War II, and here presidents have indeed reigned supreme. For example, President Truman had to have congressional approval for the Marshall Plan and the North Atlantic Treaty, but it is doubtful that anyone could have successfully opposed him. As for the Truman Doctrine and Truman's decision to enter the war in Korea, he needed no formal approval whatsoever. Neither did Eisenhower need formal approval to land American troops in Lebanon. Kennedy did not need it for his Bay of Pigs decision, his decision to neutralize Laos, or his action in the Cuban missile crisis. Johnson did not need it to intervene in the Dominican Republic, to bomb Vietnam, and to send American combat troops to South Vietnam. Nixon did not need it to mine Haiphong harbor, to invade Cambodia, and to launch a massive bombing campaign on North Vietnam in December 1972. Ford did not need it when he ordered American forces into combat in the Mayaguez incident. Reagan did not need it to order American troops to invade Grenada. President Bush did not need it to invade Panama—but in the case of the war against Iraq, he realized what valuable insurance congressional approval would be if the war went badly, and he was shrewd enough to get it, even though the vote was narrow.

However, the very fact of these decisions, especially those involving Vietnam, has led to attempts to curb the power of the president in foreign affairs. That these presidents should have such awesome power has troubled people at every level of American society, and Johnson's stubborn and insistent Vietnam policy turned doubts into determination for a number of people who were in a position to do something. Nixon's contin-

---

[8]Lindblom, *Politics and Markets,* op. cit., p. 175.

uation of the Vietnam war for four years and his imperious decisions to mine Haiphong harbor, to invade Cambodia, and to launch the massive bombing campaign on North Vietnam reinforced this determination. Furthermore, this mood is not confined to liberals. Senator John Stennis, a ranking conservative in the Senate, said that the most important lesson of the Vietnam war was that no president should be allowed to send American troops abroad without a declaration of war by Congress.[9]

Effect of the War Powers Act

The result of the congressional attempt to limit the power of the president, the War Powers Act, was not impressive, but the effort alone had some effect. Since Vietnam presidents have been reluctant to take the kind of action that appeared likely to involve the United States in another such bloody, drawn-out struggle. What is more, Congress and the press have been extraordinarily vigilant and aggressive in watching for signs of any such action. Finally, a long-run increase in the number of power centers seems inevitably to work to lessen the power of presidents in foreign affairs. Relatively few power centers today have a stake in an aggressive foreign policy, and as the overall number of power centers grows, the percentage with such a stake will become smaller still. Presidents inclined to go adventuring in foreign fields will find it more and more difficult to enlist the support they need. Iraq's invasion of Kuwait and the importance of Middle Eastern oil provided an extremely unusual set of circumstances and an excuse, whether or not it was really valid, that President Bush manipulated with exceptional skill to enlist the support of public opinion and the Congress. But even so, the vote authorizing him to wage war on Iraq was very, very narrow.

Power Diffused

Thus power in the future superindustrial society seems, if anything, likely to be even more diffused than it is today, spread among a larger number of power centers of more nearly equal strength. A number of patterns have established themselves: egalitarianism, higher education for more people, affluence and the time and freedom it brings, fuller and more rapid communications, and greater interdependence of the economy. These will combine into an overall political trend toward bringing more participants into the policy-making process and giving them more nearly equal power.

However, it is clear that individuals will have difficulty exercising influence as *individuals*. Only people with expertise, prestige, and gifts of

---

[9]*Washington Post*, January 12, 1972, p. A2.

persuasion in speaking and writing will be able to exercise individual influence. Others will exercise their power through organizations. There will be more of these groups, however, and they will wield greater yet more nearly equal power. Thus the political arena will be marked by further diffusion of power among a greater number of power centers, and the intermediate structure will contain more power centers with greater voices.

The most obvious worry is the difficulty of adopting sufficiently bold measures when power is so diffused. But some observers have a deeper, more subtle concern. David B. Truman, for example, worries about the fact that so many of the top people in the intermediate structure are not aware that they are really part of the governing apparatus.[10] He believes that this may make society peculiarly vulnerable to crises, both domestic and foreign. In time of crisis the top officials of each particular institution may be prone to look after their own group's interests and fail to make the sacrifices necessary for the survival of the society as a whole. When the society is under threat, a diffused power and leadership structure leaves it unclear just who should take the initiative. The implication is that a superindustrial society in which power is even more diffused than it is today would not be able to cope well with the kinds of problems just discussed.

Even with the present diffusion of power among multiple power centers, latent concerns or consequences often go unnoticed, as several observers have remarked. This is because only groups, not individuals, will be listened to, and it is difficult and time consuming to form effective groups. Any system that relies on groups to identify and define issues will inevitably be concerned with questions that the leadership thinks will arouse the membership (conceding even the iron law of oligarchy) rather than with those they ought to recognize for their own merits. The plight of the elderly for much of our history is one such issue, and a more recent example is the need for adequate health care for all segments of the population.

This fragmentation of power suggests a poignant irony. It is usually assumed that the injustices in American society come from a concentration of power and that those who wield power are blind to these injustices. But many of the injustices may arise from the opposite situation: the scattering of power among a bewildering array of rather small groups that makes building a consensus for positive action a formidable task. Change on many matters would be more easily accomplished if power were concentrated. The National Rifle Association, to return to an exam-

---

[10]David B. Truman, "The American System in Crisis," *Political Science Quarterly* (December 1959), pp. 481–498.

ple used several times in this book, with a membership of less than 1 percent of the population, has successfully blocked gun control legislation, while in an absolute monarchy or a dictatorship a gun control law could be instituted by the decision of just one person.

If this is so, it seems likely that it would be even more difficult to change matters in which attitudes are deep and widely held. An example of such an issue is the place of women in society, and an illustration of how difficult it is to change attitudes on such a basic issue was the treatment of Anita Hill, a professor at the University of Oklahoma Law School, in the hearings on her charges that Clarence Thomas, whom President Bush had nominated for a place on the Supreme Court, had sexually harassed her. Several senators suggested that she was mentally unbalanced, and many women, even those who had been sexually harassed themselves, criticized her for making her charges public. The point that it is difficult to change attitudes that are deep and widely held was the one that Tocqueville made when he predicted that racial prejudice in the United States would actually increase following the abolition of slavery, in part because the United States is a democracy: An "isolated individual may surmount the prejudices of religion, of his country, or of his race; and if this individual is a king, he may effect surprising changes in society; but a whole people cannot rise, as it were, above itself."[11]

Consequences of Power Diffused

The diffusion of power among a welter of small groups also seems to explain the society's failure to take steps to protect the environment, conserve resources, take bold initiatives toward peace, and in other ways provide for the future. Each small group, because it is small, feels it must look only to its own welfare rather than to the good of the society as a whole. Because of this fragmentation a small coalition of power centers can often veto or block an action that the majority really wants. Thus many of the evils of American society seem to flow from the dispersion of power, from the proliferation of many power centers exercising their power over different segments of public policy. The long oppression of blacks, the persistence of poverty amid affluence, the failure to provide truly equal rights for women, the decline of the cities, and the pollution of air and water seem to stem from the fact that the power to do something about the problems is difficult to muster. The very profusion of so many centers of power makes building the kind of consensus necessary for positive action a formidable task. Often any one of dozens of power

---

[11]Alexes de Tocqueville, *Democracy in America*, The Henry Reeve Text, Vol. 1 (New York: Vintage Books, 1957), p. 389.

centers can veto a measure, but it takes agreement among a very large number of them to force through a positive change. Power is so diffused among so many centers of power that the American society moves only slowly and ineffectively to right injustice or provide for the future.

Policy is made through a political process. Power is an element in politics. But power diffused can lead to evil as surely as power concentrated. Herein lies the irony.

INDEX